A Tutorial on the Dispensation of Bahá'u'lláh

Exploring the Fundamental Verities of the Bahá'í Faith

Fazel Naghdy

This book was approved by the review committee of the
National Spiritual Assembly of the Bahá'ís of Australia on 26 July 2010.
Cover design by Zohreh and Naysan Faizi, Designers Inc.

ISBN-13: 978-0909991166

DEDICATION

To Golshah, children and grandchildren

CONTENTS

ACKNOWLEDGMENTS

This book would not have come into existence without the encouragement and support I received from many of my friends during its development. I am grateful to all of them. I also wish to express my appreciation to Michael Thomas, Yvonne Woźniak, Phillip Hinton and Dr Michael Ward who assisted me in editing this work.

PREFACE

Striving to acquire a more adequate understanding of the Revelation of Bahá'u'lláh is identified by Shoghi Effendi as the first duty and the focus of sustained efforts of every faithful follower of the Bahá'í Faith. Although a full comprehension of such a Revelation is beyond the limits of our understanding, a clearer understanding of its basic truths will empower us to derive a fresh inspiration and take further nourishment that in turn will support and maintain our services to the Cause.[1]

Towards assisting us to fulfil this obligation, Shoghi Effendi wrote "The Dispensation of Bahá'u'lláh" letter in 1934 to the Bahá'ís of the West, which was published in 1938 with a selection of his other letters in a book entitled *The World Order of Bahá'u'lláh.*[2] "The Dispensation of Bahá'u'lláh" provides an accurate and clear description of the fundamental verities of the Bahá'í Faith concerning the station of its Central Figures as well as the twin crowning institutions of the Guardianship and the Universal House of Justice. Grasping and upholding these verities will enrich the spiritual life of the individual.

This tutorial is designed to assist you in the study of "The Dispensation of Bahá'u'lláh" and to assimilate its content. It is called a tutorial to emphasize the concept underlying its development. In a tutorial, a tutor facilitates learning for an individual or a small group. The content and structure of the tutorial have been designed and developed to simulate, as much as possible, the tutor-tutored relationship in a self-paced personal study.

The tutorial identifies the main themes covered in the Guardian's letter, and maps the related paragraphs into chapters. Hence, the 130 paragraphs of "The Dispensation of Bahá'u'lláh" are apportioned for study across 27 chapters. The size and complexity of each chapter reflects the content and intricacy of

---

1 Shoghi Effendi, *The World Order of Bahá'u'lláh*, Bahá'í Publishing Trust, Wilmette, Illinois, USA, first pub. 1938, p. 100.

2 Shoghi Effendi, *The World Order of Bahá'u'lláh*, Bahá'í Publishing Trust, Wilmette, Illinois, USA, first pub. 1938.

the issues addressed in the paragraphs included therein. The title chosen for each chapter reflects the main theme covered in the selected paragraphs.

In addition, two extra chapters address those questions that arose following the sudden passing of Shoghi Effendi and the lack of any lineal descendant to succeed him as the next Guardian. The first chapter explores the possible reasons that Shoghi Effendi did not leave a will nor appoint a successor. The second chapter examines the defection of Charles Mason Remey after the passing of Shoghi Effendi, and his unsubstantiated claim to the Guardianship.

Each chapter starts with an introduction that highlights the key concepts addressed. The paragraphs covered in the chapter are then listed. This is followed by a description of the background information on the terminologies, references and mystical concepts contained in each paragraph. Near the end of each chapter is a series of activities to consolidate your learning and to assist you to develop a deeper understanding of the content. Most chapters conclude with a Glossary of relevant difficult words and terminologies.

To derive the most benefit from your study, please follow the procedure explained below:

1. Read carefully the paragraphs covered in each chapter and reflect on them.
2. Identify the concepts and issues that you do not fully understand. Formulate them as a set of questions.
3. Read the content of the chapter and look for answers to your questions.
4. Reflect on the answers to obtain a deeper meaning.
5. Complete the activities given in the chapter. Sometimes you may need to refer to other sources to answer a question.

Fazel Naghdy
November 2012

1. FIRST CHAPTER OF HISTORY

1.1 Introduction

This lesson covers paragraphs 1–3. Read these paragraphs and reflect on the contents before starting the lesson. In this section of his letter, Shoghi Effendi highlights the significance of the first ninety years of the Bahá'í era and identifies distinctive stages in the evolution of the Faith towards its Golden Age.

In this chapter, you need to look for and understand the following **key points**:

a) In the opening paragraph of the letter, Shoghi Effendi reflects on the evidences that convince every impartial observer of those eternal truths that motivate the life of the Faith of Bahá'u'lláh and must continue to drive it towards its destined sovereignty.
b) The "eternal truths" are those aspects of a revelation that do not change from one Dispensation to another.
c) Shoghi Effendi outlines the station of the Central Figures of the Bahá'í Faith and highlights their distinction.
d) The Heroic Age started with the Declaration of the Báb on 23 May 1844 and ended with the passing of 'Abdu'l-Bahá on 28 November 1921.
e) The Formative Age is the period of evolution of the Faith towards the unfoldment of its potential and the emergence of the World Order envisaged by Bahá'u'lláh.
f) The Formative Age consists of a number of epochs that would gradually emerge.
g) The Golden Age is the stage of perfection and realisation of the goals of the Dispensation of Bahá'u'lláh.

1.2 Paragraphs under study

To the beloved of God and the handmaids of the Merciful throughout the West. Fellow-labourers in the Divine Vineyard:

1. On the 23rd of May of this auspicious year the Bahá'í world will celebrate the 90th anniversary of the founding of the Faith of Bahá'u'lláh. We, who at this hour find ourselves standing on the

threshold of the last decade of the first century of the Bahá'í era, might well pause to reflect upon the mysterious dispensations of so august, so momentous a Revelation. How vast, how entrancing the panorama, which the revolution of four score years and ten unrolls before our eyes! Its towering grandeur well-nigh overwhelms us. To merely contemplate this unique spectacle, to visualise, however dimly, the circumstances attending the birth and gradual unfoldment of this supreme Theophany, to recall even in their barest outline the woeful struggles that proclaimed its rise and accelerated its march, will suffice to convince every unbiased observer of those eternal truths that motivate its life and which must continue to impel it forward until it achieves its destined ascendancy.

2. Dominating the entire range of this fascinating spectacle towers the incomparable figure of Bahá'u'lláh, transcendental in His majesty, serene, awe-inspiring, unapproachably glorious. Allied, though subordinate in rank, and invested with the authority of presiding with Him over the destinies of this supreme Dispensation, there shines upon this mental picture the youthful glory of the Báb, infinite in His tenderness, irresistible in His charm, unsurpassed in His heroism, matchless in the dramatic circumstances of His short yet eventful life. And finally there emerges, though on a plane of its own and in a category entirely apart from the one occupied by the twin Figures that preceded Him, the vibrant, the magnetic personality of 'Abdu'l-Bahá, reflecting to a degree that no man, however exalted his station, can hope to rival, the glory and power with which They who are the Manifestations of God are alone endowed.

3. With 'Abdu'l-Bahá's ascension, and more particularly with the passing of His well-beloved and illustrious sister the Most Exalted Leaf—the last survivor of a glorious and heroic age—there draws to a close the first and most moving chapter of Bahá'í history, marking the conclusion of the Primitive, the Apostolic Age of the Faith of Bahá'u'lláh. It was 'Abdu'l-Bahá Who, through the provisions of His weighty Will and Testament, has forged the vital link which must for ever connect the age that has just expired with the one we now live in—the Transitional and Formative period of the Faith—a stage that must in the fullness of time reach its blossom and yield its fruit in the exploits and triumphs that are to herald the Golden Age of the Revelation of Bahá'u'lláh.

1.3 Eternal truths

In the opening paragraph of his letter, Shoghi Effendi reflects on the evidences that convince every impartial observer of those eternal truths that motivate the life of the Faith of Bahá'u'lláh and must continue to drive it towards its destined sovereignty.

In order to discern those evidences, Shoghi Effendi encourages the observer to:

- Ponder on the unique and striking spectacle that has emerged as the result of development of the Faith over this period.

- Envisage the conditions surrounding the birth and emergence of the Revelations of the Báb and Bahá'u'lláh.
- Look back at the sorrowful struggles that signalised the emergence of the Revelation of the Báb and accelerated its progress.

The "eternal truths" are those aspects of a revelation that do not change from one Dispensation to another. According to 'Abdu'l-Bahá, the content of every Divine Revelation can be divided into two parts. "*The first part is essential and belongs to the eternal world. It is the expression of the love of God, the knowledge of God. This is one in all the religions, unchangeable and immutable.*"[1] These are the "eternal truths" of a revelation. "*The second part is not eternal; it deals with practical life, transactions and business and changes according to the evolution of man and the requirements of the time of each prophet.*"[2]

In the introduction to *The Kitáb-i-Aqdas*, the Universal House of Justice provides further clarification on the meaning of the term "eternal truths". It explains: "*The Kitáb-i-Aqdas* reiterates those eternal truths enunciated by all the Divine Messengers." The eternal truths consist of "the unity of God, love of one's neighbour, and the moral purpose of earthly life".[3]

There are references to "eternal truths" in other Sacred Writings of the world religions. For example Gautama, the Buddha counsels His followers, "*I am not the first Buddha Who came upon earth, nor shall I be the last. In due time another Buddha will arise in the world, a Holy One, a supremely enlightened One ... an incomparable Leader of men ... He will reveal to you the same eternal truths which I have taught you.*"[4]

1.4 Brief comparison

In paragraph 2, Shoghi Effendi outlines the station of the Central Figures of the Bahá'í Faith and underlines the differences in their rank.

a) Bahá'u'lláh is the incomparable personage of this Revelation who dominates the entire Bahá'í Dispensation with His unique glory, serenity and majesty.

b) United with Bahá'u'lláh in the power and authority which shapes the destiny of this Dispensation, though subordinate to Him in rank, is the Báb. Bahá'u'lláh and the Báb are the twin Figures of this Dispensation.

c) Finally, there is 'Abdu'l-Bahá, who occupies a station entirely different from that of the twin Figures, though possessing a glory and power that only Manifestations of God are given. His is a station that no individual, however exalted, can ever attain

---

1 'Abdu'l-Bahá, *Divine Philosophy*, p. 150.

2 'Abdu'l-Bahá, *Divine Philosophy*, p. 150.

3 The Universal House of Justice, in the preface of *The Kitáb-i-Aqdas*, p. 2.

4 See Abu'l-Qásim Faizi, *An explanation of the Greatest Name*, p. 4.

In the later parts of the letter, Shoghi Effendi provides a more detailed explanation on the station of the Central Figures.

1.5 Heroic, Formative and Golden Ages

The entire history of the Revelation of Bahá'u'lláh can be divided into three ages or stages known as the Heroic, Formative and Golden. Each age on its own consists of a number of epochs or periods.

1.5.1 Heroic Age

The first stage is the Heroic Age, otherwise referred to by Shoghi Effendi as the Primitive Age or the Apostolic Age. This stage began with the Declaration of the Báb on 23 May 1844 and ended with the passing of 'Abdu'l-Bahá on 28 November 1921, or "more particularly", as the Guardian states, with the passing of the Greatest Holy Leaf, the sister of 'Abdu'l-Bahá, in July 1932.

The Heroic Age of the Bahá'í Era is unique in its impact and spiritual power. The Guardian describes it thus: "This Primitive Age of the Bahá'í Era, unapproached in spiritual fecundity by any period associated with the mission of the Founder of any previous Dispensation, was impregnated, from its inception to its termination, with the creative energies generated through the advent of two independent Manifestations and the establishment of a Covenant unique in the spiritual annals of mankind."[1]

The Guardian has identified "three distinct epochs, of nine, of thirty-nine and of twenty-nine years duration" in the Heroic Age which are "associated respectively with the Bábí Dispensation and the Ministries of Bahá'u'lláh and of 'Abdu'l-Bahá."[2]

1.5.2 Formative Age

The Transitional or Formative Age is the period of evolution of the Faith towards the unfoldment of its potentials and the emergence of the world order envisaged by Bahá'u'lláh. In the Bahá'í Writings there is no indication of the duration of the Formative Age. However, Shoghi Effendi indicates that the Formative Age consists of a number of epochs[3] that will gradually emerge.

In one of his letters, Shoghi Effendi describes the major events to occur during the Formative Age. He foresees that during the succeeding epochs:[4]

a) The "last and crowning stage in the erection of the framework of the Administrative Order of the Faith of Bahá'u'lláh—the election of the Universal House of Justice—will have been completed,
b) *The Kitáb-i-Aqdas*, the Mother-Book of His Revelation, will have been codified and its laws promulgated,
c) the Lesser Peace will have been established,

---

1 Shoghi Effendi, in *Lights of Guidance*, p. 488.
2 Shoghi Effendi, in *Lights of Guidance*, p. 488.
3 Shoghi Effendi, in *Lights of Guidance*, p. 488.
4 List form is added for emphasis and further reference.

d) the unity of mankind will have been achieved and its maturity attained,
e) the Plan conceived by 'Abdu'l-Bahá will have been executed,
f) the emancipation of the Faith from the fetters of religious orthodoxy will have been effected,
g) and its independent religious status will have been universally recognized."[1]

A number of these developments including (a) and (b) have been fully accomplished and significant progress is made towards fulfilling (c) and (e).

Thus far the Bahá'í Faith has passed through the following epochs of the Formative Age:

a) The first epoch began with the ministry of Shoghi Effendi as the Guardian of the Bahá'í Faith in 1921 and ended in 1944–46, the closing of the first century after the Declaration of the Báb. This epoch witnessed "the birth and the primary stages in the erection of the framework of the Administrative Order of the Faith."[2]
b) The Second Epoch that began in 1946 and ended in 1963 with the election of the first Universal House of Justice. "This epoch extended the developments of the first epoch by calling for the Consummation of a laboriously constructed Administrative Order, and was to witness the formulation of a succession of teaching plans designed to facilitate the development of the Faith beyond the confines of the Western Hemisphere and the continent of Europe .... The Second Epoch thus clearly demonstrated the further maturation of the institutions of the Administrative Order."[3]
c) The third epoch began in 1963 and ended in 1986. "The period of the third epoch encompassed three world plans, involving all the National Spiritual Assemblies, under the direction of the Universal House of Justice, namely, the Nine Year Plan (1964–1973), the Five Year Plan (1974–1979), and the Seven Year Plan (1979–1986). The third epoch witnessed the emergence of the Faith from obscurity and the initiation of activities designed to foster the social and economic development of communities."[4]
d) The fourth epoch began in 1986. The Universal House of Justice announced the inception of this new epoch of the Formative Age in a letter dated 2 January 1986 to the Bahá'ís of the World.[5] The fourth epoch highlighted the significant developments that had occurred in the "organic

---

1 Shoghi Effendi, *Citadel of Faith*, p. 6.

2 Shoghi Effendi, *Citadel of Faith*, p. 5.

3 The Universal House of Justice, *Messages from the Universal House of Justice*, 1963–1986, p. 713.

4 The Universal House of Justice, *Messages from the Universal House of Justice, 1963–1986*, p. 715.

5 The Universal House of Justice, *Messages from the Universal House of Justice, 1963–1986*, pp. 715–716.

growth of the Cause of God" during the third epoch. In the previous epochs, the national plans were largely derived from the Bahá'í World Centre. In the New epoch the specific goals for each national community were formulated within the framework of the overall objectives of the Plan through consultation between National Spiritual Assemblies and the Continental Board of Counsellors.

e) The fifth epoch started in 2001. The Universal House of Justice announced the inception of this epoch of the Formative Age in a letter dated 16 January 2001 to the Bahá'ís of the World: "... as the construction projects on Mount Carmel approached their completion, and as the internal processes of institutional consolidation and the external processes towards world unity became more fully synchronized. ... the extraordinary dynamics at work throughout the Conference [of the Continental Boards of Counsellors in January 2001] crystallized these indications into a recognizable reality."[1]

Additional epochs can be anticipated in the Formative Age, as the tasks to be completed in this Age are many and challenging. *The Will and Testament of 'Abdu'l-Bahá* provides the link between the Heroic Age and the Formative Age.

1.5.3 Golden Age

The Golden Age is the stage of perfection and realisation of the goals of the Dispensation of Bahá'u'lláh. The initial stages of the Golden Age will be synchronized with the "emergence of a world community", "the consciousness of world citizenship", and "the founding of a world civilization and culture."[2] Shoghi Effendi regards such developments as "the furthermost limits in the organization of human society" on this planet. Although "man, as an individual, will, nay must indeed as a result of such a consummation, continue indefinitely to progress and develop."[3]

In the course of the Golden Age, humanity will witness that "the banner of the Most Great Peace, promised by its Author, will have been unfurled, the World Bahá'í Commonwealth will have emerged in the plenitude of its power and splendour, and the birth and efflorescence of a world civilization, the child of that Peace, will have conferred its inestimable blessings upon all mankind".[4] Such outcomes will be unfolded through "successive epochs" of the Golden Age.[5]

---

1 The Universal House of Justice, Message to the Bahá'ís of the world, Announcement of the fifth epoch, dated 16 January 2001.

2 Shoghi Effendi, *The World Order of Bahá'u'lláh*, p. 163.

3 Shoghi Effendi, *The World Order of Bahá'u'lláh*, p. 163.

4 Shoghi Effendi, *Citadel of Faith*, p. 6.

5 The Universal House of Justice, *A Wider Horizon, Selected Letters from the Universal House of Justice 1983–1992*, p. 179.

1.6 Activities

1. Consider the following statement from paragraph 1:

   "On the 23rd of May of this auspicious year the Bahá'í world will celebrate the 90th anniversary of the founding of the Faith of Bahá'u'lláh. We, who at this hour find ourselves standing on the threshold of the last decade of the first century of the Bahá'í era, might well pause to reflect upon the mysterious dispensations of so august, so momentous a Revelation."

   a) What are the dispensations referred to in this statement?

   ____

   ____

   ____

   b) Why are these dispensations referred to as "*mysterious*"?

   ____

   ____

   ____

2. In paragraph 1, Shoghi Effendi refers to the emergence and development of the Faith as the "gradual unfoldment of this supreme Theophany". What does he mean by the term "supreme Theophany"?

   ____

   ____

   ____

   ____

   ____

   ____

3. In paragraph 1, Shoghi Effendi mentions three evidences that convince any unbiased observer of the 'eternal truths' enshrined in the Faith. Reflect on these evidences and share your understanding.

   ____

   ____

   ____

   ____

   ____

   ____

4. Consider the following statement from paragraph 2:

   "Dominating the entire range of this fascinating spectacle towers the incomparable figure of Bahá'u'lláh, transcendental in His majesty, serene, awe-inspiring, unapproachably glorious."

   Describe your understanding of the attributes used by Shoghi Effendi in reference to Bahá'u'lláh:

   a) Transcendental in His Majesty

   ____

b) Serene

c) Awe-inspiring

d) Unapproachably glorious

5. Consider the following statement from paragraph 2:

   "Allied, though subordinate in rank, and invested with the authority of presiding with Him over the destinies of this supreme Dispensation, there shines upon this mental picture the youthful glory of the Báb, infinite in His tenderness, irresistible in His charm, unsurpassed in His heroism, matchless in the dramatic circumstances of His short yet eventful life."

   Describe your understanding of the attributes used by Shoghi Effendi in reference to the Báb:

   a) Infinite in His tenderness

   b) Irresistible in His charm

   c) Unsurpassed in His heroism

   d) Matchless in the dramatic circumstances of His short yet eventful life

6. Consider the following statement from paragraph 2:

   "And finally there emerges, though on a plane of its own and in a category entirely apart from the one occupied by the twin Figures that preceded Him, the vibrant, the magnetic personality of 'Abdu'l-Bahá, reflecting to a degree that no man, however exalted his station, can hope to rival, the glory and power with which They who are the Manifestations of God are alone endowed."

   a) Who are the Twin Figures preceding 'Abdu'l-Bahá?

   b) How was the personality of 'Abdu'l-Bahá "*magnetic*"?

   c) What is the overall meaning of this statement?

7. Why is it possible to take the passing of the Greatest Holy Leaf as the end of the Apostolic Age of the Bahá'í Faith?

8. Reflect on the current state of the fifth epoch of the Formative Age. How is it different from the fourth epoch?

1.7 Glossary

Term	Meaning
Allied	United, joined
Ascendancy	Supremacy, power, domination
Auspicious	Having signs of success
Awe	Fear mixed with admiration or reverence
Awe-inspiring	Filling one with awe; overwhelming, breathtaking
Dimly	Not brightly or clearly
Entrancing	Captivating, fascinating
Exploit	An act, remarkable for its brilliance or daring; a bold deed
Efflorescence	Blossoming
Forge	Make by any means, to invent
Four score years and ten	Ninety years
Grandeur	Glory, splendour
Herald	Proclaim, foretell
Impel	Push, drive
Momentous	Significant
Motivate	Force, drive
Outline	Summary of the main points with no detail. Drawing of scene shown only by lines
Panorama	Scene, picture, view of a wide area
Revolution	Turning, passing
Score	Twenty
Serene	Calm, tranquil
Spectacle	Vision, image, scene, impressive or remarkable sight
Sub-ordinate	Placed in a lower order
Theophany	Visible manifestation of God to man
Threshold	Beginning, entrance
Tower	To soar, to rise above surrounding objects
Towering	Lofty, overwhelming
Transcendental	Beyond the reach of ordinary, everyday, or common thought and experience
Unroll	Unfold, uncover
Unsurpassed	Not exceeded, Not excelled
Well-nigh	Almost, nearly
Woeful	Sad, unhappy

2. SHOGHI EFFENDI'S PURPOSE IN WRITING THE LETTER

2.1 Introduction

This chapter covers paragraphs 4–5. Read these paragraphs and reflect on the contents before starting the lesson. In this section of his letter, Shoghi Effendi describes how the spiritual forces released through the Revelations of the Báb and Bahá'u'lláh have been crystallising into the institutions of the World Order of Bahá'u'lláh under the care of the "chosen stewards" of the Faith. The main purpose of writing this letter, the Guardian states, was to clarify some important fundamental verities of the Faith to those who are building the Bahá'í Administrative Order, in order to assist them in effectively undertaking their important task.

In this chapter, you need to look for and understand the following **key points**:

a) The effectiveness of the institutions of the Faith developed during the Formative Age is determined by the degree of our efforts and the extent to which we model our lives on the exemplary bravery and sacrifices of the early believers.
b) Shoghi Effendi refers to the Bahá'í institutions as instruments channelling the spiritual forces released through the Revelations of the Báb and Bahá'u'lláh towards erecting the structure of the Bahá'í Commonwealth.
c) Shoghi Effendi describes his purpose in writing "The Dispensation of Bahá'u'lláh" as being to explain certain fundamental verities concerned with the station of the Central Figures of the Bahá'í Faith and the twin institutions of the Guardianship and the Universal House of Justice.
d) The fundamental verities of the Faith are many and include truths and realities that form the core of the Revelation of Bahá'u'lláh.

2.2 Paragraphs under study

4. Dearly beloved friends! The onrushing forces so miraculously released

through the agency of two independent and swiftly successive Manifestations are now under our very eyes and through the care of the chosen stewards of a far-flung Faith being gradually mustered and disciplined. They are slowly crystallising into institutions that will come to be regarded as the hallmark and glory of the age we are called upon to establish and by our deeds immortalise. For upon our present-day efforts, and above all upon the extent to which we strive to remodel our lives after the pattern of sublime heroism associated with those gone before us, must depend the efficacy of the instruments we now fashion—instruments that must erect the structure of that blissful Commonwealth which must signalise the Golden Age of our Faith.

5. It is not my purpose, as I look back upon these crowded years of heroic deeds, to attempt even a cursory review of the mighty events that have transpired since 1844 until the present day. Nor have I any intention to undertake an analysis of the forces that have precipitated them, or to evaluate their influence upon peoples and institutions in almost every continent of the globe. The authentic record of the lives of the first believers of the primitive period of our Faith, together with the assiduous research which competent Bahá'í historians will in the future undertake, will combine to transmit to posterity such masterly exposition of the history of that age as my own efforts can never hope to accomplish. My chief concern at this challenging period of Bahá'í history is rather to call the attention of those who are destined to be the champion-builders of the Administrative Order of Bahá'u'lláh to certain fundamental verities the elucidation of which must tremendously assist them in the effective prosecution of their mighty enterprise.

2.3 Forces of the Twin Revelations

In paragraph 4, Shoghi Effendi describes the process through which the Bahá'í Administrative Order is emerging. The mighty spiritual forces released through the Revelations of the Báb and Bahá'u'lláh are the original substance of these institutions. During the Formative Age, the energies latent in these forces are crystallising into the institutions of the Bahá'í Faith through the care of the chosen followers of Bahá'u'lláh. Such institutions will become the "glory and hallmark" of the Dispensation of Bahá'u'lláh.

In many of his letters, Shoghi Effendi has described the nature and impact of the creative spiritual forces released through the Twin Revelations of the Báb and Bahá'u'lláh. He describes "That God-born Force," as "irresistible in its sweeping power, incalculable in its potency, unpredictable in its course, mysterious in its workings, and awe-inspiring in its manifestations—a Force which, as the Báb has written, *'vibrates within the innermost being of all created things,'* and which, according to Bahá'u'lláh, has through its *'vibrating influence,' 'upset the equilibrium of the world and revolutionized its ordered life'*."[1] Shoghi Effendi also refers to this Force "as limitless in its range and incalculable in its potency."[2]

Regarding the influence of this Force, Shoghi Effendi states, "such a Force, acting even as a two-edged sword, is, under our very eyes, sundering, on the one hand, the age-old ties which for centuries have held together the fabric of civilized society, and is unloosing, on the other, the bonds that still fetter the infant and as yet unemancipated Faith of Bahá'u'lláh."[3]

In another letter, Shoghi Effendi points out that the Revelation of Bahá'u'lláh inaugurates the stage of maturity in the development of humanity. Hence, "His [Bahá'u'lláh's] appearance has released such spiritual forces which will continue to animate, for many long years to come, the world in its development."[4] Although there will be many Manifestations of God after Bahá'u'lláh, "they will be all under His shadow. Although they may abrogate the laws of the Dispensation, in accordance with the needs and requirements of the age in which they appear, they nevertheless draw their spiritual force from this mighty Revelation."[5]

Shoghi Effendi further explains in this letter, "Whatever progress may be achieved, in the later ages, after the unification of the whole human race is achieved will be but improvement in the machinery of the world. For the machinery itself has already been created by Bahá'u'lláh. The task of continually improving and perfecting this machinery is one that later Prophets will be called upon to achieve. They will move and work within the orbit of the Bahá'í cycle."[6]

2.4 Effectiveness of the institutions

In paragraph 4, Shoghi Effendi expounds on the elements that will ensure the effectiveness of the institutions of the Faith developed during the Formative Age. He identifies two factors:

a) The degree of the efforts that we make.
b) The extent to which we attempt to model our lives on the exemplary bravery and sacrifices exercised by the early believers.

Shoghi Effendi refers to the Bahá'í institutions as an instrument channelling the spiritual forces released through the Twin Revelations towards erecting the structure of the Bahá'í Commonwealth that will signal the advent of the Golden Age of the Bahá'í Faith.

As an instrument, the Bahá'í Administration is not a replacement for the Faith, but "a channel through which His [Bahá'u'lláh's] promised blessings

---

1 Shoghi Effendi, *The Advent of Divine Justice*, p. 46.
2 Shoghi Effendi, *The Advent of Divine Justice*, p. 15.
3 Shoghi Effendi, *The Advent of Divine Justice*, p. 47.
4 Shoghi Effendi, from a letter written on behalf of the Guardian to an individual believer, 14 November 1935, *Lights of Guidance*, p. 473.
5 Shoghi Effendi, *Directives from the Guardian*, p. 61.
6 Shoghi Effendi, *Directives from the Guardian*, p. 62.

may flow."[1] He warns the believers against any rigidity in the Bahá'í Administration as it "would clog and fetter the liberating forces released by His Revelation."[2]

In another letter, Shoghi Effendi states: "... the Bahá'í administration is only the first shaping of what in future will come to be the social life and laws of community living."[3]

2.5 Fundamental verities

In paragraph 5, Shoghi Effendi describes his purpose in writing his letter. Firstly, he stresses that his intention was not to:

a) Review the great events that had occurred from the inception of the Cause in 1844 up to the time of writing.[4]
b) Analyse the spiritual forces originating those events or the impact of those forces on peoples and institutions of nearly every continent of the world.

At that particular stage in the history of the Bahá'í Faith, Shoghi Effendi rather intended to explain certain fundamental verities of the Faith, the understanding of which would greatly assist the endeavour of those who are building the Bahá'í Administrative Order.

The fundamental verities of the Bahá'í Faith are many and include truths and realities that form the core of the Revelation of Bahá'u'lláh. In a letter written on his behalf to an individual, Shoghi Effendi explains that by "'verities of the Faith' he means the great teachings and fundamentals enshrined in our Bahá'í literature; these we can find by reading the books, studying under Bahá'í scholars at summer schools and in classes, and through the aid of study outlines."[5]

The Universal House of Justice explains: "Consolidation must comprise not only the establishment of the Bahá'í administrative institutions, but a true deepening in the fundamental verities of the Cause and in its spiritual principles."[6] The Universal House of Justice then identifies the concepts upon which the believers should strive to consolidate:

> "Understanding of its [the Faith's] prime purpose in the establishment of the unity of mankind, instruction in its standards of behaviour in all aspects of private and public life, in the particular practice of Bahá'í life in such things as daily prayer, education of children, observance of the laws of Bahá'í marriage, abstention from politics, the obligation to contribute to the Fund, the importance of

---

1 Shoghi Effendi, *The World Order of Bahá'u'lláh*, p. 9.
2 Shoghi Effendi, *The World Order of Bahá'u'lláh*, p. 9.
3 Shoghi Effendi, in *Lights of Guidance*, p. 79.
4 8 February 1934
5 Shoghi Effendi, a letter written on his behalf to an individual believer, 19 April 1947, Lights of Guidance, p. 484.
6 The Universal House of Justice, in *Lights of Guidance* (2nd edition), p. 594.

> the Nineteen Day Feast, and opportunity to acquire a sound knowledge of the present-day practice of Bahá'í administration."[1]

In "The Dispensation of Bahá'u'lláh", the Guardian addresses only those fundamental verities that are concerned with the station of the Central Figures of the Faith, and the twin institutions of the Guardianship and the Universal House of Justice.

---

1 The Universal House of Justice, in *Lights of Guidance* (2nd edition), p. 594.

2.6 Activities

1. Identify the major instruments that the Bahá'í community has developed in building the Bahá'í Administration up to the present time.

2. Describe your understanding of the nature of the spiritual forces released through the twin Revelations of the Báb and Bahá'u'lláh.

3. What is the exact meaning of the statement that the institutions of the Faith will be the "hallmark and glory" of the Golden Age of the Bahá'í Dispensation (paragraph 4)?

4. Why does the effectiveness of the institutions of the Bahá'í Faith depend on the degree of our efforts and the sacrifices we make in building them?

5. Why did Shoghi Effendi not intend to analyse in his letter the events that occurred during the heroic age?

6. What are the "fundamental verities" of the Faith?

7. Why is it important for the individual to learn about the fundamental verities of the Faith?

8. What are the concepts identified by the Universal House of Justice on which the believers should strive to consolidate?

2.7 Glossary

Term	Meaning
Assiduous	Diligent
Blissful	Happy in the highest degree
Efficacy	Power to produce effects
Elucidation	Explanation
Enterprise	Endeavour, project
Hall-mark	Any evidence of true worth
Muster	Collect, gather
Onrushing	Violently rushing
Posterity	Future generations
Precipitate	Hasten
Prosecution	Undertaking
Steward	Someone who is trusted with the management of estate of another
Sublime	Something lofty or of grand style
Swiftly	Rapidly

3. INTERNATIONAL STATUS OF THE BAHÁ'Í FAITH

3.1 Introduction

This chapter covers paragraphs 6–8. Read these paragraphs and reflect on the contents before starting the lesson. In this section of his letter, Shoghi Effendi briefly reviews the international status that the Faith had achieved by the time of writing the letter. In light of such status, Shoghi Effendi feels responsible as the Guardian of the Bahá'í Faith to place emphasis "upon certain truths which lie at the basis of our Faith" and to clarify its root principles. He also states that developing an adequate understanding of the breathtaking Revelation of Bahá'u'lláh is the first duty and goal of every individual believer.

In this chapter, you need to look for and understand the following **key points**:

a) Shoghi Effendi provides some brief statistics to illustrate the rise and steady consolidation of the Bahá'í institutions.

b) At the time of writing the letter, various components of the Bahá'í Administrative Order including the Local and National Spiritual Assemblies had begun to emerge and function according to a unified form and spirit in forty countries.

c) In the annual report of the National Spiritual Assembly of the Bahá'ís of the United States of America presented to their National Convention of April 1935,[1] there were glimpses of unprecedented victories achieved by the American Bahá'í Community.

d) Despite all the restrictions imposed on them, the Persian Bahá'í community finally succeeded in developing and implementing a comprehensive plan to elect their first National Spiritual Assembly in 1934.

e) Shoghi Effendi refers in paragraph 6 to important testimonies on the significance and greatness of the Bahá'í Faith from prominent people

---

1 *The Bahá'í World*, vol. VI, 1934–1936, p. 198.

around the world at the time of writing the letter.

f) The persecution of the Bahá'ís in Muslim countries, such as Írán, 'Iráq and Egypt had been a source of proclamation for the Faith.

g) Striving to attain an adequate understanding of the Revelation of Bahá'u'lláh should be the first duty of every faithful believer.

3.2 Paragraphs under study

6. The international status, which the Religion of God has thus far achieved, moreover, imperatively demands that its root principles be now definitely clarified. The unprecedented impetus which the illustrious deeds of the American believers have lent to the onward march of the Faith; the intense interest which the first Mas͟hriqu'l-Ad͟hkár of the West is fast awakening among divers races and nations; the rise and steady consolidation of Bahá'í institutions in no less than forty of the most advanced countries of the world; the dissemination of Bahá'í literature in no fewer than twenty-five of the most widely-spoken languages; the success that has recently attended the nation-wide efforts of the Persian believers in the preliminary steps they have taken for the establishment, in the outskirts of the capital-city of their native land, of the third Mas͟hriqu'l-Ad͟hkár of the Bahá'í world; the measures that are being taken for the immediate formation of their first National Spiritual Assembly representing the interests of the overwhelming majority of Bahá'í adherents; the projected erection of yet another pillar of the Universal House of Justice, the first of its kind, in the Southern Hemisphere; the testimonies, both verbal and written, that a struggling Faith has obtained from Royalty, from governmental institutions, international tribunals, and ecclesiastical dignitaries; the publicity it has received from the charges which unrelenting enemies, both new and old, have hurled against it; the formal enfranchisement of a section of its followers from the fetters of Muslim orthodoxy in a country that may be regarded as the most enlightened among Islamic nations—these afford ample proof of the growing momentum with which the invincible community of the Most Great Name is marching forward to ultimate victory.

7. Dearly beloved friends! I feel it incumbent upon me, by virtue of the obligations and responsibilities which as Guardian of the Faith of Bahá'u'lláh I am called upon to discharge, to lay special stress, at a time when the light of publicity is being increasingly focussed upon us, upon certain truths which lie at the basis of our Faith and the integrity of which it is our first duty to safeguard. These verities, if valiantly upheld and properly assimilated, will, I am convinced, powerfully reinforce the vigour of our spiritual life and greatly assist in counteracting the machinations of an implacable and vigilant enemy.

8. To strive to obtain a more adequate understanding of the significance of Bahá'u'lláh's stupendous Revelation must, it is my unalterable

conviction, remain the first obligation and the object of the constant endeavour of each one of its loyal adherents. An exact and thorough comprehension of so vast a system, so sublime a revelation, so sacred a trust, is for obvious reasons beyond the reach and ken of our finite minds. We can, however, and it is our bounden duty to seek to derive fresh inspiration and added sustenance as we labour for the propagation of His Faith through a clearer apprehension of the truths it enshrines and the principles on which it is based.

3.3 Progress made by American believers

In paragraph 6, Shoghi Effendi refers to two important developments in the American Bahá'í Community at that time; the extraordinary momentum generated as the result of the contribution made by the American believers to the progress of the Faith and the interest raised throughout many different nations by the first Mashriqu'l-Adhkár in the West (in Wilmette, near Chicago, Illinois).

In the annual report of the National Spiritual Assembly of the Bahá'ís of the United States of America presented to the National Convention, April 1935,[1] there were glimpses of unprecedented victories achieved by the American Bahá'í Community. It reads: "In no previous year of which there is record were there so many enrolments of new believers as in this Bahá'í year. Both in the number of new members added to the existing communities, and in the number of groups prepared for election of a spiritual Assembly for the first time, this period was one of remarkable growth. The teaching of the Cause, reinforced by the mysterious power of the Mashriqu'l-Adhkár made more effective by the knowledge of the nature of the Bahá'í community, received a vast stimulus, inaugurating a movement forward surely destined to acquire greater emphasis with every successive year."

Another evidence of the impact of the Mashriqu'l-Adhkár in Wilmette was the results produced by the exhibition of the model of the temple in the Century of Progress Exposition in Chicago in 1933. According to a report published in the Bahá'í World,[2] the model was located in a prominent position in the hall where all the visitors would pass in front of it.

The organiser of the exhibition has estimated that 10,000 people from different parts of the world passed daily through the hall and listened to the attendants' description of the temple. Around 50,000 pamphlets titled "What is the Bahá'í Faith?" were distributed among the visitors. The exhibition produced immediate outcomes. Many of those who saw the model visited the temple and attended public meetings there. There was also an increased demand for Bahá'í literature.

---

1 *The Bahá'í World*, vol. VI, 1934–1936, p. 198.

2 *The Bahá'í World*, vol. V, 1932–1934, p. 318.

3.4 Evolution of institutions

In paragraph 6, Shoghi Effendi provides some brief statistics to illustrate the rise and steady consolidation of the Bahá'í institutions.

At the time of the passing of 'Abdu'l-Bahá, the Bahá'í institutions were fully defined but not established.[1] Although 35 countries where open to the Faith,[2] the Bahá'í Administration was not yet realized. During his ministry, Shoghi Effendi channelled the efforts of the Bahá'í community into fully establishing the institutions of the Bahá'í Administration.

At the time of writing "The Dispensation of Bahá'u'lláh", various components of the Bahá'í Administrative Order including the Local and National Spiritual Assemblies had started to emerge and function according to a unified form and spirit in forty countries. In 1934, eight National Spiritual Assemblies had been established in the following regions:[3] the British Isles, Germany and Austria, India and Burma, Egypt and Sudan, the United States and Canada, 'Iráq, Persia, and Australia and New Zealand.

3.5 Developments in Persia

In paragraph 6, Shoghi Effendi also refers to the achievements of the Persian Bahá'í Community. Despite all the restrictions imposed on them, the Persian Bahá'í community finally succeeded in developing and implementing a comprehensive plan to elect their first National Spiritual Assembly in 1934. More than five hundred local communities participated in the election of delegates to attend the first National Convention held over 8 days at the end of April 1934. In the Convention, 84 of the 95 elected delegates were present.

During this period a large piece of land on the slopes of Mount Alburz, northeast of Ṭihrán, was purchased for the eventual construction of the first Mashriqu'l-Adhkár in Írán. The land measured more than 125 hectares. The Iranian authorities confiscated this land during the recent persecution of the Bahá'ís in Írán.

3.6 Testimonies

In paragraph 6, Shoghi Effendi refers to important testimonies to the significance and greatness of the Bahá'í Faith from prominent people around the world at the time of writing the letter. The most important perhaps is the

---

1 Horace Holley, "The World Order of Bahá'u'lláh—Present Day Administration of the Bahá'í Faith", *The Bahá'í World*, vol. v, 1932–1934, pp. 181–187.

2 Hands of the Cause residing in the Holy Land: *The Bahá'í Faith: 1844–1963: Information Statistical and Comparative, Including the Achievements of the Ten Year International Bahá'í Teaching & Consolidation Plan 1953–1963*, cited at http://bahai-library.com/handscause_statistics_1953–63.

3 Owen Battrick: *Achievements and Victories of the Guardianship: Statistics, chronology, and bibliography* cited at http://bahai-library.com/achievements_victories_guardianship.

statement made by the Queen Marie of Rumania[1] in which she mentions the writings of the Bahá'í Faith as "a great cry toward peace, reaching beyond all limits of frontiers, above all dissension about rites and dogmas." She then commends to her readers that: "If ever the name of Bahá'u'lláh or 'Abdu'l-Bahá comes to your attention, do not put their writings from you. Search out their books, and let their glorious, peace bringing, love-creating words and lessons sink into your ears as they have into mine."[2]

A list of prominent people with their statements on the Faith is given in volume V of *The Bahá'í World,*[3] which includes:

Professor E.G. Browne (1862–1926)

Professor Browne was a British orientalist from Cambridge University who has published many books and articles on the Bábí and Bahá'í religions. As the only Westerner to meet Bahá'u'lláh (at Bahjí in 1890), he has described the details of this meeting thus:[4]

> "Though I dimly suspected whither I was going and whom I was to behold (for no distinct intimation had been given to me), a second or two elapsed ere, with a throb of wonder and awe, I became definitely conscious that the room was not untenanted. In the corner where the divan met the wall sat a wondrous and venerable figure ... The face of him on whom I gazed I can never forget, though I cannot describe it. Those piercing eyes seemed to read one's very soul; power and authority sat on that ample brow ... No need to ask in whose presence I stood, as I bowed myself before one who is the object of a devotion and love which kings might envy and emperors sigh for in vain!
>
> A mild dignified voice bade me be seated, and then continued: "Praise be to God that thou hast attained! ... Thou hast come to see a prisoner and an exile ... We desire but the good of the world and the happiness of the nations; yet they deem us a stirrer up of strife and sedition worthy of bondage and banishment ... That all nations should become one in faith and all men as brothers; that the bonds of affection and unity between the sons of men should be strengthened; that diversity of religion should cease, and differences of race be annulled—what harm is there in this? ... Yet so it shall be; these fruitless strifes, these ruinous wars shall pass away, and the 'Most great Peace' shall come ... Do not you in Europe need this also? Is this not what Christ foretold? ... Yet do we see your kings and rulers

---

1. *The Bahá'í World*, vol. V, 1932–1934, pp. 322–232.
2. *Toronto Daily Star*, 4 May 1926. "In Appreciations of the Bahá'í Faith", p. 10.
3. *The Bahá'í World*, vol. V, pp. 322–350.
4. Edward G. Browne, *A Traveller's Narrative* (New York: Bahá'í Publishing Committee, 1930), pp. xxxix-xi

> lavishing their treasures more freely on means for the destruction of the human race than on that which would conduce to the happiness of mankind … These strifes and this bloodshed and discord must cease, and all men be as one kindred and one family … Let not a man glory in this, that he loves his country; let him rather glory in this, that he loves his kind ….”

Dr Auguste Forel (1848–1931)

Forel was a psychiatrist, researcher of the brain and of ants, the director of the clinic Burghölzli, and a professor at the University of Zurich. In 1902 he made this testimony on the Faith: “I learned at Karlsruhe of the supraconfessional world religion of the Bahá'ís, founded in the Orient seventy years ago by a Persian, Bahá'u'lláh. This is the real religion of ‘Social Welfare’ without dogmas or priests, binding together all men of this small terrestrial globe of ours. I have become a Bahá'í. May this religion live and prosper for the good of humanity! This is my most ardent desire.”[1] He has also stated, “The Bahá'í Movement for the oneness of mankind is, in my estimation, the greatest movement today working for universal peace and brotherhood.”[2]

Helen Adams Keller (1880–1968)

Helen Keller was an American lecturer, author, and activist. Although she was deaf and blind since early childhood, she overcame her disabilities and became well known internationally for her efforts to educate others about the blind and raising funds for related charities. She was deeply committed to social change.

In a personal letter Helen wrote to an American Bahá'í after reading the Braille edition of *Bahá'u'lláh and the New Era,* she comments:

> “The philosophy of Bahá'u'lláh deserves the best thought we can give it. I am returning the book so that other blind people who have more leisure than myself may be ‘shown a ray of Divinity’ and their hearts be ‘bathed in an inundation of eternal love’”.
>
> “I take this opportunity to thank you for your kind thought of me, and for the inspiration which even the most cursory reading of Bahá'u'lláh's life cannot fail to impart. What nobler theme than the ‘good of the world and the happiness of the nations’ can occupy our lives? The message of universal peace will surely prevail. It is useless to combine or conspire against an idea which has in it potency to create a new earth and a new heaven and to quicken human beings with a holy passion of service.”[3]

---

1 Shoghi Effendi, *God Passes By*, p. 375.
2 Shoghi Effendi, *God Passes By*, p. 375.
3 “References to the Bahá'í Faith”, in *The Bahá'í World*, vol. VIII, pp. 621–622.

President Masaryk of Czechoslovakia (1850–1937)

Thomas Masaryk was an Austro-Hungarian Czechoslovak politician as well as a sociologist and philosopher. He was the founder and the first president of Czechoslovakia. In an audience with an American Bahá'í journalist in Prague in 1928, he comments in reference to the Bahá'í Faith:

> "Continue to do what you are doing, spread these principles of humanity and do not wait for the diplomats. Diplomats alone cannot bring the peace, but it is a great thing that official people begin to speak about these universal peace principles. Take these principles to the diplomats, to the universities and colleges and other schools, and also write about them. It is the people who will bring the universal peace."[1]

Ernest Renan (1823–1892)

A French philosopher and writer, Renan is best known for his influential historical works on early Christianity, and for his political theories. He made moving comments testifying to the events surrounding the declaration of the Báb and His martyrdom as recorded in *The Bahá'í World.*[2]

Leo Tolstoy (1828–1910)

The Russian writer, considered by many as the world's greatest novelist commented in a letter written to Madame Isabel Grinevskaya, dated 22 October 1903:

> "I have known about the Bábís for a long time, and have always been interested in their teachings. It seems to me that these teachings, as well as all the rationalistic social religious teachings that have arisen lately out of the original teachings of Brahmanism, Buddhism, Judaism, Christianity and Islám distorted by the priests, have a great future for this very reason that these teachings, discarding all these distorting incrustations that cause division, aspire to unite into one common religion of all mankind ... The teachings of the Bábís which come to us out of Islám have through Bahá'u'lláh's teachings been gradually developed and now present us with the highest and purest form of religious teaching."[3]

3.7 Independence of the Faith

The persecution of the Bahá'ís in Muslim countries, such as Persia, 'Iráq and Egypt has been a source of proclamation for the Bahá'í Faith. In paragraph 6, the Guardian refers to an incident that occurred in Egypt resulting in the Islamic court confirming the independence of the Bahá'í Faith from Islám.

---

1 "References to the Bahá'í Faith" in *The Bahá'í World*, vol. VIII, p. 622.

2 "References to the Bahá'í Faith" in *The Bahá'í World*, vol. VIII, pp. 617–618 (in French).

3 "References to the Bahá'í Faith" in *The Bahá'í World*, vol. VIII, pp. 610–611.

There was no civil law in Egypt in 1925 and hence all Egyptian subjects were under the control of Islamic law regarding matters such as marriage, divorce, etc. Some Muslim women, whose husbands had become Bahá'ís, appealed for divorce on the basis that their husbands had abandoned Islám. In considering the appeal, the Islamic court, after detailed consideration of the fundamentals of the Bahá'í Faith, ruled on the 10 May 1925:

> "All these prove definitely that the Bahá'í religion is a new religion, with an independent platform and laws and institutions peculiar to it, and shows a different and contradictory belief to the beliefs and laws and commandments of Islám. Nor can we state a Bahá'í to be a Muslim, or the reverse; as we cannot say of a Buddhist or a Brahman or a Christian that he is Muslim or reverse ..."[1]

3.8 Assimilating the basic verities

In paragraphs 7 and 8, Shoghi Effendi once more stresses the importance of the basic verities of the Faith. Grasping and upholding these verities will enrich our spiritual lives and will help us to counteract the mischievous plans of a stubborn and watchful enemy.

Shoghi Effendi states that striving to acquire a more adequate understanding of the Revelation of Bahá'u'lláh is the first duty and focus of the sustained efforts of every faithful follower of the Bahá'í Faith. Although a full comprehension of such a Revelation is beyond the limits of our understanding, a clearer understanding of its basic truths will empower us to derive a fresh inspiration and take further nourishment that in turn will support and maintain our services to the Cause.[2]

---

1 *The Bahá'í World*, vol. III, 1928–1930, p. 51.

2 Shoghi Effendi, *The World Order of Bahá'u'lláh*, p. 100.

3.9 Activities

1. In paragraph 6, Shoghi Effendi refers to some cases through which the international status of the Faith was elevated. Provide a specific example for each case.

2. Describe your understanding of the following statement from paragraph 7:

   "These verities, if valiantly upheld and properly assimilated, will, I am convinced, powerfully reinforce the vigour of our spiritual life and greatly assist in counteracting the machinations of an implacable and vigilant enemy."

3. How can grasping and upholding the basic verities of the Bahá'í Faith assist in counteracting the machinations of those hostile to the Faith?

4. Describe your understanding of the following statement from paragraph 8:

   "An exact and thorough comprehension of so vast a system, so sublime a revelation, so sacred a trust, is for obvious reasons beyond the reach and ken of our finite minds. We can, however, and it is our bounden duty to seek to derive fresh inspiration and added sustenance as we labour for the propagation of His Faith through a clearer apprehension of the truths it enshrines and the principles on which it is based."

5. Why is a full comprehension of the Revelation of Bahá'u'lláh beyond the limits of our understanding?

6. How is the current Bahá'í Administration different from that which existed at the time of writing the letter?

7. How can a better understanding of the basic truths of the Faith give us fresh inspiration and further nourishment for our services to the Cause?

3.10 Glossary

Term	Meaning
Apprehension	An understanding, or a grasp of the meaning of
Assimilate	To understand completely and be able to use properly
Beyond one's ken	Outside the limits of one's knowledge
Bounden	Archaic form of past participle of bind; bound (to do something) Morally or legally obligated (to do something)
By virtue of	As a result of
Charge	Accusation
Counteract	To reduce or oppose the effect of (something) by opposite action
Discharge	To perform (a duty or promise) properly
Dissemination	Spreading (news, ideas, etc.) widely
Ecclesiastical	Connected with the Christian church
Enfranchisement	Setting free
Fetters	Chains, shackles or restraints that prevent freedom of movement or action
Hurl	To throw with force
Illustrious	Famous; widely known and admired for ones great works
Imperatively	Urgently
Impetus	Momentum
Implacable	Impossible to satisfy, change, or make less angry
Incumbent	Necessary as a duty or obligation
Invincible	Too strong to be defeated
Machination	A clever plan for doing harm, evil plot or scheme
Orthodoxy	Canonically accepted doctrines or practices
Reinforce	To add strength or support to
Stupendous	Astonishingly impressive
Sustenance	Nourishment
Testimony	A formal statement that something is true
Unprecedented	Never happened before
Unrelenting	Continuous, without decreasing in power or effort
Valiantly	Very bravely
Vigilant	Continually watchful or on guard
Vigour	Active strength or force of mind or body

4. TESTIMONY OF THE BÁB

4.1 Introduction

This chapter covers paragraphs 9–12. Read these paragraphs and reflect on the contents before starting the lesson. In this section of his letter, Shoghi Effendi illustrates the greatness of the Revelation of Bahá'u'lláh through the testimonies given by the Báb in His Writings. He initially highlights the station of the Báb as the promised Qá'im. He then cites a number of statements from hadiths, *the Persian Bayán*, and the Qayyúmu'l-Asmá' in reference to Bahá'u'lláh and the eminence of His Revelation.

In this chapter, you need to look for and understand the following **key points**:

a) Bahá'u'lláh has testified to the greatness of the Revelation of the Báb in *The Kitáb-i-Íqán*.
b) In the *Bayán*, the Báb evaluates His Revelation and His book (The Bayán) against the Revelation and Writings of *Him whom God shall make manifest* (Bahá'u'lláh).
c) In an address to Vaḥíd, the Báb points out the importance of believing in Bahá'u'lláh.
d) In a prayer, the Báb contrasts His Revelation with the Revelation of Bahá'u'lláh.
e) In the Qayyúmu'l-Asmá', the Báb prophesies the hardships He would endure and His eventual martyrdom in the path of Bahá'u'lláh.

4.2 Paragraphs under study

9. In a communication addressed to the American believers I have in the course of my explanation of the station of the Báb made a passing reference to the incomparable greatness of the Revelation of which He considered Himself to be the humble Precursor. He Whom Bahá'u'lláh has acclaimed in *The Kitáb-i-Íqán* as that promised Qá'im Who has manifested no less than twenty-five out of the twenty-seven letters which all the Prophets were destined to reveal—so great a Revealer has

Himself testified to the pre-eminence of that superior Revelation that was soon to supersede His own. "*The germ,*" the Báb asserts in the Persian Bayán, "*that holds within itself the potentialities of the Revelation that is to come is endowed with a potency superior to the combined forces of all those who follow me.*"[1] "*Of all the tributes,*" He again affirms, "*I have paid to Him Who is to come after Me, the greatest is this, My written confession, that no words of Mine can adequately describe Him, nor can any reference to Him in My Book, the Bayán, do justice to His Cause.*"[2] "*The Bayán*", He in that same Book categorically declares, "*and whosoever is therein revolve round the saying of 'Him Whom God shall make manifest,' even as the Alif* (the Gospel) *and whosoever was therein revolved round the saying of Muḥammad, the Apostle of God.*"[3] "*A thousand perusals of the Bayán,*" He further remarks, "*cannot equal the perusal of a single verse to be revealed by 'Him Whom God shall make manifest.' ... Today the Bayán is in the stage of seed; at the beginning of the manifestation of 'Him Whom God shall make manifest' its ultimate perfection will become apparent .... The Bayán and such as are believers therein yearn more ardently after Him than the yearning of any lover after his beloved .... The Bayán deriveth all its glory from 'Him Whom God shall make manifest.' All blessing be upon him who believeth in Him and woe betide him that rejecteth His truth.*"[4]

10. Addressing Siyyid Yaḥyáy-i-Dárábí surnamed Vaḥíd, the most learned, the most eloquent and influential among His followers, the Báb utters this warning: "*By the righteousness of Him Whose power causeth the seed to germinate and Who breatheth the spirit of life into all things, were I to be assured that in the day of His manifestation thou wilt deny Him, I would unhesitatingly disown thee and repudiate thy faith .... If, on the other hand, I be told that a Christian, who beareth no allegiance to My Faith, will believe in Him, the same will I regard as the apple of Mine Eye.*"[5]

11. In one of His prayers He thus communes with Bahá'u'lláh: "*Exalted art Thou, O my Lord the Omnipotent! How puny and contemptible my word and all that pertaineth unto me appear unless they be related to Thy great glory. Grant that through the assistance of Thy grace whatsoever pertaineth unto me may be acceptable in Thy sight.*"[6]

12. In the Qayyúmu'l-Asmá'—the Báb's commentary on the Súrih of Joseph—characterised by the Author of the Íqán as "*the first, the greatest and mightiest*" of the books revealed by the Báb, we read the

---

1 Statement (a)
2 Statement (b)
3 Statement (c)
4 Statement (d)
5 Statement (e)
6 Statement (f)

following references to Bahá'u'lláh: "*Out of utter nothingness, O great and omnipotent Master, Thou hast, through the celestial potency of Thy might, brought me forth and raised me up to proclaim this Revelation. I have made none other but Thee my trust; I have clung to no will but Thy will ... O Thou Remnant of God! I have sacrificed myself wholly for Thee: I have accepted curses for Thy sake, and have yearned for naught but martyrdom in the path of Thy love. Sufficient witness unto me is God, the Exalted, the Protector, the Ancient of Days.*"[1] "*And when the appointed hour hath struck,*" He again addresses Bahá'u'lláh in that same commentary, "*do Thou, by the leave of God, the All-Wise, reveal from the heights of the Most Lofty and Mystic Mount a faint, an infinitesimal glimmer of Thy impenetrable Mystery, that they who have recognised the radiance of the Sinaic Splendour may faint away and die as they catch a lightening glimpse of the fierce and crimson Light that envelops Thy Revelation.*"[2]

4.3 Greatness of the Revelation of the Báb

In paragraph 9, Shoghi Effendi briefly outlines the greatness of the Revelation of the Báb, before referring to the testimonies of the Báb on the eminence of the Revelation of Bahá'u'lláh. He cites a ḥadíth from Islám about the promised Qá'im, cited by Bahá'u'lláh in *The Kitáb-i-Íqán* (*The Book of Certitude*).[3] According to this ḥadíth, the Qá'im would reveal the remaining twenty–five out of the twenty–seven letters of knowledge that all the prophets were destined to reveal. In the following sections, the background to various issues associated with this ḥadíth will be studied.

4.3.1 Promised Qá'im

In all the Holy books there are prophecies regarding the advent of two great Manifestations of God. In Islám, the majority of the followers believe that the two expected Manifestations are the "Imám Mihdí" and the "Messiah". In the Qur'án, the advent of the Promised One is referred to as the "Great Announcement". This is a recurring theme in the Qur'án, with about five thousand of the six thousand two hundred verses of the Qur'án revolving around this issue.[4]

In the Shí'ih[5] branch of Islám, due to a series of historical events following the death of Ḥasan al-'Askarí, the eleventh Imám, they came to believe that the promised Imám Mihdí was the return of the son of Ḥasan al-'Askarí. He is known as the twelfth Imám, and is supposed to have gone into occultation in childhood. According to Shí'ih Muslims, the Imams are the hereditary

---

1 Statement (g)

2 Statement (h)

3 Bahá'u'lláh, *The Kitáb-i-Íqán*, p. 243.

4 M. Mustafa, *Bahá'u'lláh the Great Announcement of the Qur'án*, p. 6.

5 Transliteration adopted is the same as *The World Order of Bahá'u'lláh.*

successors of Muḥammad. There were twelve Imams after the passing of Muḥammad.

There are different accounts regarding the story of the twelfth Imám. According to the most popular version,[1] the mother of the twelfth Imám was a Byzantine slave-girl named Narjis Khátún. The twelfth Imám was born in AD 868 and was named 'Abu'l-Qásim Muḥammad. Apparently, none of the Shí'ih Muslim notables were aware that Muḥammad had been born. In AD 874, when the eleventh Imám died, his brother Ja'far was assumed to be the twelfth Imám. When he entered the house of his brother as the new Imám to lead the prayer for the dead, a young boy came forward and said: "Uncle, stand back! For it is more fitting for me to lead the prayers for my father than for you."

According to the Shí'ih Muslim traditions, the boy was not seen after that incident and was said to have gone into occultation in a well. The well is located in a cave under the mosque next to the gold-domed Shrine of the Imám 'Alí al-Hádí and Ḥasan al-'Askarí at Sámarrá.

After the death of the eleventh Imám, Shí'ih Islám fragmented into a few groups. One group believed that Ja'far was the true successor of his brother. Another group asserted that it was the eleventh Imám who had gone into occultation. Others believed that the twelfth Imám was not born yet and would be born on the Day of Judgement. One individual, 'Uthmán al-'Amrí, claimed that Muḥammad, the son of the eleventh Imám, did exist but he was in occultation. 'Uthmán also claimed that he was the intermediary between the Hidden Imám and Shí'ih Islám. This became the belief of the Orthodox Twelver Shí'ih Muslims.

Initially, the claim of 'Uthmán was acceptable to people as it was common at that time that Imams would go into hiding to protect themselves from their enemies. There were agents who would communicate between the Imám and the people, and they would collect money for the Imám. However, after seventy years, the situation had changed and thereafter the concept of occultation became a Shí'ih Muslim doctrine.

'Uthmán nominated Abú Ja'far, his son, as his successor to be the agent of the Hidden Imám. The third person nominated as agent was 'Abu'l-Qásim Ḥusayn ibn Rúḥ an-Nawbakhtí. The fourth and last agent was 'Abu'l-Ḥusayn 'Alí ibn Muḥammad as-Sámarrí. He was only in this position for three years before dying in AD 941.

Each of these four agents was called the Báb ("Gate"), the Safír ("Ambassador") or the Ná'ib ("Deputy") by Shí'ih Muslims.

The last agent, as-Sámarrí brought the following message to the people prior to the time of his death:

> "In the name of God the Merciful, the Compassionate! O Alī ibn Muhammad as-Samarrī, may God magnify the reward of your

[1] Moojan Momen, *An Introduction to Shi'i Islam*, p. 161.

> brethren upon you! There are but six days separating you from death. So therefore arrange your affairs but do not appoint anyone to your position after you. For the second occultation has come and there will not now be a manifestation except by the permission of God and that after a long time has passed, and hearts have hardened and the earth become filled with tyranny. And there will come to my Shí'ih [believers] those who claim to have seen me, but he who claims to have seen me before the emergence of the Sufyānī and the Cry (from the heavens) is assuredly a lying imposter. And there is no power nor strength save in God the Almighty, the All-High."[1]

Hence, the Hidden Imám went from the Lesser Occultation into the Greater Occultation in AD 941. Momen suggests that it was probably around the end of the Lesser Occultation that the Hidden Imám came to be identified with the figure of the Mihdí or the Promised One.

The Hidden Imám has been given many different titles, including: Sáhibu'z-Zamán ("the Lord of the Age"), Ṣáḥíb al-Amr ("the Lord of Command"), al-Mihdí ("the Rightly-Guided One"), al-Qá'im ("He who will arise"), al-Imám al-Munṭaẓar ("the Awaited Imám") and the Baqíyyatu'lláh ("Remnant of God").[2]

4.3.2 The Báb and the Qá'im

Due to the complex historical background mentioned above, the station of the Báb was misunderstood right from the time of His declaration. In AD 1844, when the Báb declared His Mission as the Gate to one who would come after Him, people initially thought that He was another agent or gate to the promised Qá'im. Apparently, as a token of His mercy towards the people, the Báb did not make an attempt at that stage to clarify His station. However, Shoghi Effendi mentions in a letter written on his behalf that the Báb's actual claim was the station of the Qá'im and the "Báb", namely the Gate or Forerunner of "*Him Whom God will make manifest*".[3]

In the *Dalá'il-i-Sab'ih* ("*The Seven Proofs*"), the Báb explains the nature of that misunderstanding and the wisdom of not correcting it. He asks the followers of Islám to "*Consider the manifold favours vouchsafed by the Promised One, and the effusions of His bounty which have pervaded the concourse of the followers of Islám to enable them to attain unto salvation.*" While highlighting His high station, He states: "*Indeed observe how He Who representeth the origin of creation, He Who is the Exponent of the verse, 'I, in very truth, am God', identified Himself as the Gate [Báb] for the advent of the promised Qá'im, a descendant of Muḥammad, and in His first Book enjoined the observance of the laws of the Qur'án, so that the people might not be seized with perturbation by reason of a new Book and a new Revelation and might*

---

1 Moojan Momen, *An Introduction to Shi'i Islam*, p. 163.
2 Moojan Momen, *An Introduction to Shi'i Islam*, p. 165.
3 Shoghi Effendi, *Unfolding Destiny*, p. 426.

regard His Faith as similar to their own, perchance they would not turn away from the Truth and ignore the thing for which they had been called into being."[1]

In *God Passes By*, Shoghi Effendi indicates that during the captivity of the Báb in Á<u>dh</u>arbáyján "... the full implications of the station of the Báb were disclosed to His disciples, and formally announced by Him in the capital of Á<u>dh</u>arbáyján, in the presence of the Heir to the Throne."[2]

The Báb was not only the Promised One of <u>Sh</u>í'ih Islám, He "... at once fulfilled the promise of all ages and ushered in the consummation of all Revelations."[3] According to Shoghi Effendi, the Báb was "the 'Mihdí' ("One Who is guided") awaited by the Sunní Muslims; the 'Return of John the Baptist' expected by the Christians; the 'Ú<u>sh</u>ídar-Máh'[4] in the Zoroastrian Scriptures; the 'Return of Elijah' anticipated by the Jews, Whose Revelation was to show forth 'the signs and tokens of all the Prophets', Who was to 'manifest the perfection of Moses, the radiance of Jesus and the patience of Job'".[5]

4.4 Ḥadí<u>th</u>

The hadiths or holy traditions in Islám are the words of Muḥammad or stories of His deeds that have been passed orally from one generation to the next before they were finally written down. In <u>Sh</u>í'ih Islám, the hadiths also include the sayings of the Imams. The words or stories have either been narrated by a companion of Muḥammad or by someone who has met Muḥammad (these are known in Islám as Ṣaḥába, meaning "Companions") or by one who has met a Ṣáḥíb (singular of Ṣaḥába). The latter are called "Tábi'ún" or "Followers".

According to Islamic theology, there are two types of hadiths: Divine and Nabawí. A Divine ḥadí<u>th</u> is the Word of God revealed by Muḥammad—similar to the revelation of the Qur'án, whereas a Nabawí ("Prophetic") ḥadí<u>th</u> is the understanding and sayings of Muḥammad.

This distinction highlights the perception of the Muslim clergy of the different stations of Muḥammad as both a Messenger of God and as an ordinary human being. As a Messenger, His words are God's Words and He simply acts as a medium for their Revelation. As a human being, He applies the power of the intellect and the human spirit to analyse and describe concepts. However, there are other Muslim clergy who argue that there is a difference between the revelation of the Qur'án and the Divine hadiths.

---

1 The Báb, *Selections from the Writings of the Báb*, p. 119.
2 Shoghi Effendi, *God Passes By*, p. 17.
3 Shoghi Effendi, *God Passes By*, p. 57.
4 "The Promised One"
5 Shoghi Effendi, *God Passes By*, p. 57.

A full study of hadiths is a vast subject as it covers a wide range of topics including: the analysis of their nature, their authenticity, their significance and their different types.

4.5 Twenty–five out of twenty–seven letters

The ḥadíth cited by Shoghi Effendi in paragraph 9, has been recorded in three reliable Islamic books, including "Biḥáru'l-Anvár", the "'Avalím" and the "Yanbú'". The first book, Biḥáru'l-Anvár, is the encyclopaedia of Shí'ih theology written by 'Allámiy-i-Majlisí in twenty–six volumes. The "Yanbú'" is a book by Ṣádiq, son of Muḥammad-Báqir, a third century Islamic era, Shí'ih Muslim scholar.

According to this ḥadíth: "Knowledge is twenty and seven letters. All that the Prophets have revealed are two letters thereof. No man thus far hath known more than these two letters. But when the Qá'im shall arise, He will cause the remaining twenty and five letters to be made manifest."

The term "Prophet" refers to all the Manifestations of God who have appeared during the prophetic cycle, i.e. from Adam up to the Báb. If all knowledge is assumed to be equivalent to twenty–seven letters, the Prophets before the Qá'im revealed knowledge equivalent to only two letters. The promised Qá'im would reveal the remaining knowledge and mysteries of the universe, equivalent to twenty–five letters. This demonstrates the intensity of the Revelation of the Qá'im (the Báb) and consequently its significance as well as its impact on the world of creation. This ḥadíth is also cited in paragraph 60 and further discussed in section 16.6.

4.6 Persian Bayán

In paragraph 9, Shoghi Effendi refers to the *Persian Bayán* (meaning "exposition") as the "Mother Book" of the Bábí Dispensation. "The term 'Mother Book' is generally used to designate the central Book of a religious Dispensation."[1]

The Báb revealed the *Persian Bayán* during His imprisonment in the Fortress of Máh-Kú. Shoghi Effendi has referred to the Bayán as "that monumental repository of the laws and precepts of the new Dispensation and the treasury enshrining most of the Báb's references and tributes to, as well as His warning regarding, '*Him Whom God will make manifest*'".[2]

The Persian Bayán consists of eight thousand verses and is divided into nine sections, called Vaḥíds. Each Vaḥíd has nineteen chapters except for the last Vaḥíd that has only ten chapters.

The *Arabic Bayán* is a "smaller and less weighty"[3] book, which was revealed by the Báb in Chihríq towards the end of His early life.

---

1 *The Kitáb-i-Aqdas*, Notes, pp. 220–221.
2 Shoghi Effendi, *God Passes By*, pp. 24–25.
3 Shoghi Effendi, *God Passes By*, pp. 24–25.

In this section of "The Dispensation of Bahá'u'lláh", Shoghi Effendi quotes a number of testimonies from the *Persian Bayán* on the greatness of the Revelation of "*Him Whom God shall make manifest*" (Bahá'u'lláh).

4.7 Address to Vaḥíd

In paragraph 10, Shoghi Effendi cites a statement made by the Báb to Siyyid Yaḥyáy-i-Dárábí, surnamed Vaḥíd. Shoghi Effendi refers to Vaḥíd as "the most learned, the most eloquent and influential" among the followers of the Báb.

When the message of the Báb spread to every part of the country, the disturbance reached such a degree that the Sháh of Írán decided to send a representative to the Báb to disprove His claim. This delegate was Vaḥíd. Shoghi Effendi, in *God Passes By*, briefly describes this episode of the history of the Bábí Dispensation:

> "The commotion had assumed such proportions that the Sháh, unable any longer to ignore the situation, delegated the trusted Siyyid Yaḥyáy-i-Dárábí, surnamed Vaḥíd, one of the most erudite, eloquent and influential of his subjects—a man who had committed to memory no less than thirty thousand traditions—to investigate and report to him the true situation. Broad-minded, highly imaginative, zealous by nature, intimately associated with the court, he, in the course of three interviews, was completely won over by the arguments and personality of the Báb. Their first interview centred around the metaphysical teachings of Islám, the most obscure passages of the Qur'án, and the traditions and prophecies of the Imams. In the course of the second interview Vaḥíd was astounded to find that the questions, which he had intended to submit for elucidation had been effaced from his retentive memory, and yet, to his utter amazement, he discovered that the Báb was answering the very questions he had forgotten. During the third interview the circumstances attending the revelation of the Báb's commentary on the Súrih of Kawthar, comprising no less than two thousand verses, so overpowered the delegate of the Sháh that he, contenting himself with a mere written report to the Court Chamberlain, arose forthwith to dedicate his entire life and resources to the service of a Faith that was to requite him with the crown of martyrdom during the Nayríz upheaval. He who had firmly resolved to confute the arguments of an obscure siyyid of Shíráz, to induce Him to abandon His ideas, and to conduct Him to Ṭihrán as an evidence of the ascendancy he had achieved over Him, was made to feel, as he himself later acknowledged, as 'lowly as the dust beneath His feet.' Even Ḥusayn Khán, who had been Vaḥíd's host during his stay in Shíráz, was

compelled to write to the Sháh and express the conviction that his Majesty's illustrious delegate had become a Bábí."[1]

4.8 Testimonies from Qayyúmu'l-Asmá'

The Qayyúmu'l-Asmá' is the commentary of the Báb on the Súrih[2] of Joseph from the Qur'án. According to Shí'ih Islamic prophecies, the promised Qá'im was expected to reveal a commentary on this Súrih. On the night of His declaration to Mullá Ḥusayn, 22 May 1844, the Báb revealed the first chapter of this commentary.

The Qayyúmu'l-Asmá' is written in Arabic and consists of nine thousand three hundred verses divided into one hundred eleven chapters. Each chapter is a commentary on one of the verses of the Súrih.

According to Shoghi Effendi, the main purpose of this commentary "was to forecast what the true Joseph [Bahá'u'lláh] would, in a succeeding Dispensation, endure at the hands of one who was at once His arch-enemy and blood brother."[3]

The commentary "... opens with the Báb's clarion-call and dire warnings addressed to the '*concourse of kings and of the sons of kings*;' forecasts the doom of Muḥammad Sháh; commands his Grand Vizír, Ḥájí Mírzá Áqásí, to abdicate his authority; admonishes the entire Muslim ecclesiastical order; cautions more specifically the members of the Shí'ah[4] community; extols the virtues, and anticipates the coming, of Bahá'u'lláh, the 'Remnant of God,' the 'Most Great Master;' and proclaims, in unequivocal language, the independence and universality of the Bábí Revelation, unveils its import, and affirms the inevitable triumph of its Author. It, moreover, directs the '*people of the West*' to '*issue forth from your cities and aid the Cause of God;*' warns the peoples of the earth of the '*terrible, the most grievous vengeance of God;*' threatens the whole Islamic world with '*the Most Great Fire*' were they to turn aside from the newly-revealed Law; foreshadows the Author's martyrdom; eulogizes the high station ordained for the people of Bahá, the '*Companions of the crimson-coloured ruby Ark;*' prophesies the fading out and utter obliteration of some of the greatest luminaries in the firmament of the Bábí Dispensation; and even predicts '*afflictive torment,*' in both the '*Day of Our Return*' and in '*the world which is to come,*' for the usurpers of the Imamate, who '*waged war against Ḥusayn (Imám Ḥusayn) in the Land of the Euphrates.*'"[5]

---

1 Shoghi Effendi, *God Passes By*, pp. 11–12.
2 Transliteration adopted is the same as *The World Order of Bahá'u'lláh.*
3 Shoghi Effendi, *God Passes By,* pp. 22.
4 Persian transliteration as used in *God Passes By*.
5 Shoghi Effendi, *God Passes By,* p. 23.

4.9 Activities

1. Reflect on the following statements from the Báb, cited by Shoghi Effendi in paragraph 9. Briefly write down your understanding:

   a) "*The germ that holds within itself the potentialities of the Revelation that is to come is endowed with a potency superior to the combined forces of all those who follow me.*"

   b) "*Of all the tributes I have paid to Him Who is to come after Me, the greatest is this, My written confession, that no words of Mine can adequately describe Him, nor can any reference to Him in My Book, the Bayán, do justice to His Cause.*"

   c) "*The Bayán, and whosoever is therein revolve round the saying of 'Him Whom God shall make manifest,' even as the Alif (the Gospel) and whosoever was therein revolved round the saying of Muḥammad, the Apostle of God.*"

   d) "*A thousand perusals of the Bayán cannot equal the perusal of a single verse to be revealed by 'Him Whom God shall make manifest.'... Today the Bayán is in the stage of seed; at the beginning of the manifestation of 'Him Whom God shall make manifest' its ultimate perfection will become apparent .... The Bayán and such as are believers therein yearn more ardently after Him than the yearning of any lover after his beloved .... The Bayán deriveth all its glory from 'Him Whom God shall make manifest.' All blessing be upon him who believeth in Him and woe betide him that rejecteth His truth.*"

2. Considering the station of Vaḥíd, what is the significance of the Báb's address to him cited in paragraph 10?

3. Consider the following statement of the Báb cited in paragraph 12:

   "Out of utter nothingness, O great and omnipotent Master, Thou hast, through the celestial potency of Thy might, brought me forth and raised me up to proclaim this Revelation. I have made none other but Thee my trust; I have clung to no will but Thy will … O Thou Remnant of God! I have sacrificed myself wholly for Thee: I have accepted curses for Thy sake, and have yearned for naught but martyrdom in the path of Thy love. Sufficient witness unto me is God, the Exalted, the Protector, the Ancient of Days."

   a) What is your understanding of the term "*brought me forth and raised me up*"?

   b) What is the Báb referring to in the statement: "*I have sacrificed myself wholly for Thee*"?

4. Consider the following statement from paragraph 12:

   "*And when the appointed hour hath struck, do Thou, by the leave of God, the All-Wise, reveal from the heights of the Most Lofty and Mystic Mount a faint, an infinitesimal glimmer of Thy impenetrable*

Mystery, that they who have recognised the radiance of the Sinaic Splendour may faint away and die as they catch a lightening glimpse of the fierce and crimson Light that envelops Thy Revelation."

a) What is your understanding of the term "*Sinaic Splendour"*?

b) What is your understanding of the term "*the Most Lofty and Mystic Mount*"?

c) What is your overall understanding of this statement?

4.10 Glossary

Term	Meaning
Allegiance	Loyalty, faith, and dutiful support to a leader, country, idea
Assert	To state positively, declare, affirm
Categorically	Made without any doubt in the mind of the speaker or writer
Celestial	Of the sky or heaven
Commotion	Noisy and excited movement or activity
Contempt	A total lack of respect; the feeling that someone or something is completely worthless, unimportant, or undesirable
Contemptible	Deserving to be treated with contempt
Crimson	A deep red colour
Curse	A calling on God to send evil down on a person; profanity or vulgarity used in swearing to express anger, hatred or contempt.
Erudite	Full of learning, scholarly
Faint	Weak, vague, indistinct
Glimmer	Weak, faint or unsteady light
Impenetrable	Extremely difficult or impossible to understand
Pertain	To have a connection with; concern
Perusal	A careful reading
Precursor	Something that comes before another and leads to it or is developed into it
Pre-eminent	Outstanding; distinguished in some quality
Puny	Small and weak
Remnant	A part that remains
Repudiate	To refuse to accept; reject
Supersede	To take the place of, especially as an improvement
Woe betide him	He will be in trouble
Yearn (for)	To long (for), ache (for), hunger (for); to have a deep desire (for)

5. A ZOROASTRIAN PROPHECY

5.1 Introduction

This chapter covers paragraphs 13-15. Read these paragraphs and reflect on the contents before starting the lesson. In this section of his letter, Shoghi Effendi highlights the greatness of the Revelation of Bahá'u'lláh by citing the interpretation of 'Abdu'l-Bahá of an ancient Zoroastrian prophecy regarding the Manifestations of God after Zoroaster. According to this prophecy, there would be three saviours following Zoroaster. During the reign of these saviours, the sun will be still for ten days, twenty days and thirty days, respectively. 'Abdu'l-Bahá has interpreted these saviours as the Revelations of Muḥammad, the Báb and Bahá'u'lláh.

In this chapter, you need to look for and understand the following **key points**:

a) The days referred to in the Zoroastrian prophecy indicate different periods of time.
b) The Zoroastrian prophecy further recognizes and confirms the independence of the Dispensation of the Báb as a direct Revelation from God despite its short duration.
c) The followers of Bahá'u'lláh should accept the divine origin of Islám and the validity of the Imamate as the divinely appointed institution succeeding Muḥammad.
d) The Bahá'ís must strive to acquire a sound knowledge of the history and tenets of Islám.
e) According to the principle of progressive revelation, every Manifestation of God has a more intense Revelation than the previous one.

5.2 Paragraphs under study

13. As a further testimony to the greatness of the Revelation identified with Bahá'u'lláh may be cited the following extracts from a Tablet addressed by 'Abdu'l-Bahá to an eminent Zoroastrian follower of the Faith: "Thou

hadst written that in the sacred books of the followers of Zoroaster it is written that in the latter days, in three separate Dispensations, the sun must needs be brought to a standstill. In the first Dispensation, it is predicted, the sun will remain motionless for ten days; in the second for twice that time; in the third for no less than one whole month. The interpretation of this prophecy is this: the first Dispensation to which it refers is the Muhammadan Dispensation during which the Sun of Truth stood still for ten days. Each day is reckoned as one century. The Muhammadan Dispensation must have, therefore, lasted no less than one thousand years, which is precisely the period that has elapsed from the setting of the Star of the Imamate to the advent of the Dispensation proclaimed by the Báb. The second Dispensation referred to in this prophecy is the one inaugurated by the Báb Himself, which began in the year AH 1260 and was brought to a close in the year AH 1280. As to the third Dispensation—the Revelation proclaimed by Bahá'u'lláh—inasmuch as the Sun of Truth when attaining that station shineth in the plenitude of its meridian splendour its duration hath been fixed for a period of one whole month, which is the maximum time taken by the sun to pass through a sign of the Zodiac. From this thou canst imagine the magnitude of the Bahá'í cycle—a cycle that must extend over a period of at least five hundred thousand years."

14. From the text of this explicit and authoritative interpretation of so ancient a prophecy it is evident how necessary it is for every faithful follower of the Faith to accept the divine origin and uphold the independent status of the Muhammadan Dispensation. The validity of the Imamate is, moreover, implicitly recognised in these same passages—that divinely-appointed institution of whose most distinguished member the Báb Himself was a lineal descendant, and which continued for a period of no less than two hundred and sixty years to be the chosen recipient of the guidance of the Almighty and the repository of one of the two most precious legacies of Islám.

15. This same prophecy, we must furthermore recognise, attests the independent character of the Bábí Dispensation and corroborates indirectly the truth that in accordance with the principle of progressive revelation every Manifestation of God must needs vouchsafe to the peoples of His day a measure of divine guidance ampler than any which a preceding and less receptive age could have received or appreciated. For this reason, and not for any superior merit which the Bahá'í Faith may be said to inherently possess, does this prophecy bear witness to the unrivalled power and glory with which the Dispensation of Bahá'u'lláh has been invested—a Dispensation the potentialities of which we are but beginning to perceive and the full range of which we can never determine.

5.3 Prophecy to Manifestations after Zoroaster

In paragraph 13, Shoghi Effendi refers to the interpretation of 'Abdu'l-Bahá of a Zoroastrian prophecy regarding the Manifestations of God after Zoroaster. According to this prophecy, there would be three saviours following Zoroaster. During the reign of the first saviour, the sun would be still for ten days. After three years of prosperity, many would perish in a bitter winter. Then the second saviour would appear and the sun would stand still for twenty days. Once again, the creation would prosper for six years before the evil became dominant. The final saviour would bring the complete and final victory of good over evil. This time, the sun would stand still for thirty days.[1]

The origin of this prophecy is unknown, though in the Gathas that was composed by Zoroaster, there is a reference to a man who would come after Zoroaster. He "*is better than a good man—the one who will teach us for the physical existence and for that of the mind, the straight paths of salvation to the true things with which Ahura Mazda dwells—who is faithful and resembles You, O Mazda.*"[2]

'Abdu'l-Bahá provides the following interpretation of the prophecy:

a) In the first instance, the sun will stay motionless for ten days. 'Abdu'l-Bahá interprets this instance as the Dispensation of Muḥammad. Each day is counted as one century, which estimates this period as one thousand years. The last Imám of Shí'ih Islám died in AH 260 (AD 844), which signalled the end of divine guidance in the Islamic Dispensation. The Báb declared His mission in AH 1260 (AD 1844), which is exactly one thousand years later. Hence the Sun of truth was renewed and a new spiritual springtime was brought about.

b) 'Abdu'l-Bahá has interpreted the second instance as the Dispensation of the Báb which started in AH 1260 and ended in AH 1280 (AD 1864) when Bahá'u'lláh declared His mission to His followers in the Garden of Riḍván. In this interpretation each day is counted as one year.

c) The third instance refers to the Dispensation of Bahá'u'lláh, which has one month's duration; the longest time the sun takes to go through one sign of the zodiac. The zodiac is an imaginary belt through space along which the sun, the moon, and the nearest planets appear to travel. The zodiac is divided into twelve equal parts (signs), each named after a group of stars, which were once located in those signs.

In a letter written on his behalf, Shoghi Effendi explains that the days referred to in this prophecy indicate different periods of time. He states, "… in the Scripture of various religions there are to be found frequent references to days, but these have been considered as indicating different period[s] of

---

1 Susan Maneck, "Time and the Containment of Evil in Zoroastrianism", cited at http://bahailibrary.com/?file=maneck_time_containment_evil&language=

2 Susan Maneck, "Time and the Containment of Evil in Zoroastrianism", cited at http://bahailibrary.com/?file=maneck_time_containment_evil&language=

time, as for instance in the Qur'án a day is reckoned as one thousand years. The first ten days in the above-mentioned prophecy represent each a century, making thus a total of one thousand lunar years. As to the twenty days referring to the Bábí Dispensation each of them represents only one lunar year, the total of twenty years marking the duration of the Revelation of the Báb. The thirty days in the last Dispensation should not be reckoned numerically, but should be considered as symbolizing the incomparable greatness of the Bahá'í Revelation which, though not final is none-the-less thus far the fullest revelation of God to man. From a physical point of view, the thirty days represent the maximum time taken by the sun to pass through a sign of the zodiac. They thus represent a culminating point in the evolution of this star. So also from a spiritual standpoint these thirty days should be viewed as indicating the highest, though not the final stage in the spiritual evolution of mankind."[1]

5.4 Divine origin of Islám

In paragraph 14, Shoghi Effendi states that the followers of Bahá'u'lláh should accept the divine origin of Islám. In fact, the "whole-hearted and unqualified acceptance" of "the Divine origin of both Islám and Christianity, of the prophetic functions of both Muḥammad and Jesus Christ, of the legitimacy of the institution of the Imamate, and of the primacy of St. Peter, the Prince of the Apostles" are described by Shoghi Effendi as "the central, the solid, the incontrovertible principles that constitute the bedrock of Bahá'í belief."[2]

From a Bahá'í perspective, another significance of Islám is its close association with the Bahá'í Faith. Shoghi Effendi has referred to Islám as "the source and background" of the Faith.[3] The Bahá'í Faith emerged in an Islamic environment, the early believers in the Báb and Bahá'u'lláh were Muslims, and a significant proportion of the arguments and proofs in the Sacred Bahá'í Writings are elucidations and interpretations of the content of the Qur'án and the Islamic traditions.

Accordingly, Bahá'ís must strive to acquire "a sound knowledge of the history and tenets of Islám."[4] The study of Islám and the Qur'án, equips the believers with "a background against which to study the Bahá'í Writings."[5]

Over the centuries, there has been a great deal of misrepresentation of Islám and misunderstanding of its teachings. This is confirmed by Shoghi Effendi:

---

1 Shoghi Effendi, a letter written on his behalf to the National Spiritual Assembly of the United States and Canada, 7 August 1934, *Bahá'í News*. Also in *Lights of Guidance*, p. 472.

2 Shoghi Effendi, *The Promised Day is Come*, p. 114.

3 Shoghi Effendi, *The Advent of Divine Justice*, p. 49.

4 Shoghi Effendi, *The Advent of Divine Justice*, p. 49.

5 Shoghi Effendi, *Lights of Guidance*, p. 558.

"Western historians have for many centuries distorted the facts to suit their religious and ancestral prejudices."[1]

According to Troxel,[2] "... for hundreds of years our knowledge of Muḥammad, the Holy Qur'án, and Islám in general, has come to us through biased intermediaries. Literary geniuses such as Dante, Shakespeare, Gibbon, Sale, Thomas Carlyle, and Washington Irving, have transmitted to us opinions of the Arabian Prophet which at best can be described as 'damning with faint praise' and at worst to believing Him worthy of Hell's greatest torments."

Hence, Shoghi Effendi emphasizes in his writings that the Bahá'ís should deepen their knowledge of Islám based on "unbiased and reliable sources."[3] They "... should try to study history anew, and to base all their investigations first and foremost on the written Scriptures of Islám and Christianity."[4]

In this connection, Marzieh Gail suggests: " ... to study Islám we need new books. We need a re-evaluation by future Bahá'í scholars, of all the available data, in the light of Bahá'u'lláh's Teachings. The Guardian told a pilgrim that the Bahá'ís must vindicate Islám in the West; we must convert people, not to its institutions, now abrogated by the Báb and Bahá'u'lláh, but to its truth as a further step in Divine Revelation, following Christianity."[5]

5.5 Succession to Muḥammad

Immediately after the ascension of Muḥammad, the issue of His successor became a major cause of disunity and division among the Muslims. A group of prominent Muslims gathered and elected Abú-Bakr as the Caliph or successor to Muḥammad. At this meeting 'Alí, the son-in-law of Muḥammad was absent. At the same time, a group of Muslims believed that 'Alí should have been chosen as the successor to Muḥammad, in light of the close relationship between 'Alí and Muḥammad and also based on a number of statements made by Muḥammad during His lifetime.[6]

Abú-Bakr's Caliphate lasted only two years and ended with his death. On his deathbed, Abú-Bakr appointed Umar as his successor and hence the leadership of 'Alí was again denied. Umar, in turn appointed a council of six to decide the leadership after him. The council was composed in such a way that 'Alí did not have the support to be elected as the successor. This time U<u>th</u>mán was elected as the next Caliph.

U<u>th</u>mán's Caliphate proved a disgrace to Islám and caused a great deal of dissatisfaction. Eventually, U<u>th</u>mán was murdered by forces rebelling against his rule. Immediately a group of Muslims surrounded 'Alí and urged him to

---

1 Shoghi Effendi, *Lights of Guidance*, p. 496.
2 Duane, K. Troxel, *Islám and the Bahá'í Faith: A brief guide*, cited at http://bahai-library.com/articles/islam.guide.html
3 Shoghi Effendi, *The Advent of Divine Justice*, p. 49.
4 Shoghi Effendi, in *Lights of Guidance*, p. 496.
5 Marzieh Gail, *Six Lessons on Islám*, p. 1.
6 Moojan Momen, *An Introduction to Shi'i Islam*, p. 11.

accept the Caliphate. 'Alí became the fourth Caliph and finally achieved his rightful position twenty-four years after the death of Muḥammad.

Though initially accepted by all the Muslims as the fourth Caliph, 'Alí received a great deal of opposition from different directions and was forced into war with them. He was finally assassinated in January AD 661.

After 'Alí, a group of Muslims accepted Ḥasan, his son, as his successor and the second rightful Imám. They are known as Shí'ih Muslims, whereas the majority who did not follow Ḥasan are known as Sunní Muslims.

The hereditary succession in Shí'ih Islám continued until the eleventh Imám, Ḥasan al-'Askarí, who had no son to succeed him. After his death, the Shí'ih Muslims were thrown into confusion and broke up into twenty different sects. The Imamate ended, as there was no successor.

Based on the authoritative interpretation made by 'Abdu'l-Bahá of the Zoroastrian prophecy (section 5.4), Shoghi Effendi concludes that the Imamate was the divinely appointed institution after the death of Muḥammad.

5.6 Independence of Dispensation of the Báb

In paragraph 15, Shoghi Effendi explains that the Zoroastrian prophecy further recognizes and confirms the independence of the Dispensation of the Báb as a direct Revelation from God despite its short duration.

The Dispensation of the Báb was ordained to be very brief and was to be succeeded by the Revelation of Bahá'u'lláh. Accordingly, the Báb devised only the laws and teachings that were meant to undermine the established religious doctrines and to prepare the followers for the Revelation of Bahá'u'lláh.

Shoghi Effendi explains that the Revelation of the Báb "... was essentially in the nature of a religious and indeed social revolution, and its duration had therefore to be short, but full of tragic events, of sweeping and drastic reforms. These drastic measures enforced by the Báb and His followers were taken with the view of undermining the very foundations of Shí'ah[1] orthodoxy, and thus paving the way for the coming of Bahá'u'lláh. To assert the independence of the new Dispensation, and to prepare also the ground for the approaching Revelation of Bahá'u'lláh the Báb had therefore to reveal very severe laws, even though most of them, were never enforced. But the mere fact that He revealed them was in itself a proof of the independent character of His Dispensation and was sufficient to create such widespread agitation, and excite such opposition on the part of the clergy that led them to cause His eventual martyrdom."[2]

---

1 Shoghi Effendi has used the Persian form of the word.

2 Shoghi Effendi, *Dawn of a New Day*, p. 77.

5.7 Principle of progressive revelation

In paragraph 15, the Guardian also states that the Zoroastrian prophecy affirms the principle of progressive revelation according to which every Manifestation of God "… must needs vouchsafe to the peoples of His day a divine guidance ampler than any which a preceding and less receptive age could have received or appreciated."

The concept of progressive revelation is one of the core principles of the Bahá'í philosophy of religion. This principle answers some of the fundamental questions on the source of different religions, the concept of unity in diversity of religions and the relationship between them.

There is a detailed discussion on the concept of progressive revelation in section 14.3.

5.8 Activities

1. Briefly describe your understanding of the Zoroastrian prophecy cited in paragraph 13.

2. Why has Shoghi Effendi referred to Islám as "the source and background" of the Bahá'í Faith?

3. Describe your understanding of the Imamate in Shí'ih Islám.

4. Describe your understanding of the nature and purpose of the Dispensation of the Báb.

5. Describe your understanding of the principle of progressive revelation.

6. What was the nature of disunity that occurred among the Muslims after the ascension of Muḥammad?

7. What are the "two most precious legacies of Islám"?

8. What are the main obstacles to the study of Islám?

5.9 Glossary

Term	Meaning
Attest	To be proof of
Corroborate	To support or strengthen (a statement, opinion, idea, etc.) by fresh information or proof
Explicit	Clear and fully explained
Implicit	Implied or understood though not directly expressed
Inaugurate	To be the beginning of (something, esp. an important period of time)
Legacy	Something passed on or left behind by someone or something
Lineal	In direct line of descent; (of people) following each other directly in time, esp. from parent to child.
Meridian	The highest point in the daily course of any celestial body; zenith or apex of prosperity or success
Plenitude	Completeness; fullness
Repository	A place where things are stored or found in large quantity.
Zodiac	An imaginary belt through space along which the sun, the moon, and the nearest planets appear to travel and which is divided into 12 equal parts (signs), each named after a group of stars, which were once in them.

6. THE DAY OF DAYS

6.1 Introduction

This chapter covers paragraphs 16–18. Read these paragraphs and reflect on the contents before starting the lesson. In this section of his letter, Shoghi Effendi initially identifies the Revelation of Bahá'u'lláh as the culmination of a cycle that began with Adam and ended with the Báb. Bahá'u'lláh is the supreme Manifestation of God in a universal cycle that began with Adam around 6,000 years ago. Shoghi Effendi then highlights the uniqueness of this age as the Day of Days by citing a number of statements by Bahá'u'lláh.

In this chapter, you need to look for and understand the following **key points**:

a) The period before the Revelation of Bahá'u'lláh is called the Prophetic Cycle as all the Manifestations of God in that cycle made prophecies concerning the coming of Bahá'u'lláh.
b) The cycle initiated by Bahá'u'lláh is called the Cycle of Fulfilment as He has fulfilled all the prophecies made during the Prophetic Cycle.
c) We should direct our attention to the claims made by Bahá'u'lláh in His Writings if we wish to acquire a better understanding of the nature and power of His Revelation.

6.2 Paragraphs under study

16. The Faith of Bahá'u'lláh should indeed be regarded, if we wish to be faithful to the tremendous implications of its message, as the culmination of a cycle, the final stage in a series of successive, of preliminary and progressive revelations. These, beginning with Adam and ending with the Báb, have paved the way and anticipated with an ever-increasing emphasis the advent of that Day of Days in which He Who is the Promise of All Ages should be made manifest.

17. To this truth the utterances of Bahá'u'lláh abundantly testify. A mere reference to the claims, which, in vehement language and with compelling power, He Himself has repeatedly advanced, cannot but

fully demonstrate the character of the Revelation of which He was the chosen bearer. To the words that have streamed from His pen—the fountainhead of so impetuous a Revelation—we should, therefore, direct our attention if we wish to obtain a clearer understanding of its importance and meaning. Whether in His assertion of the unprecedented claim He has advanced, or in His allusions to the mysterious forces He has released, whether in such passages as extol the glories of His long-awaited Day, or magnify the station which they who have recognised its hidden virtues will attain, Bahá'u'lláh and, to an almost equal extent, the Báb and 'Abdu'l-Bahá, have bequeathed to posterity mines of such inestimable wealth as none of us who belong to this generation can befittingly estimate. Such testimonies bearing on this theme are impregnated with such power and reveal such beauty as only those who are versed in the languages in which they were originally revealed can claim to have sufficiently appreciated. So numerous are these testimonies that a whole volume would be required to be written in order to compile the most outstanding among them. All I can venture to attempt at present is to share with you only such passages, as I have been able to glean from His voluminous writings.

18. "*I testify before God,*" proclaims Bahá'u'lláh, "*to the greatness, the inconceivable greatness of this Revelation. Again and again have We in most of Our Tablets borne witness to this truth, that mankind may be roused from its heedlessness.*"[1] "*In this most mighty Revelation,*" He unequivocally announces, "*all the Dispensations of the past have attained their highest, their final consummation.*"[2] "*That which hath been made manifest in this preeminent, this most exalted Revelation, stands unparalleled in the annals of the past, nor will future ages witness its like.*"[3] "*He it is,*" referring to Himself He further proclaims, "*Who in the Old Testament hath been named Jehovah, Who in the Gospel hath been designated as the Spirit of Truth, and in the Qur'án acclaimed as the Great Announcement.*"[4] "*But for Him no Divine Messenger would have been invested with the robe of prophethood, nor would any of the sacred scriptures have been revealed. To this bear witness all created things.*"[5] "*The word which the one true God uttereth in this day, though that word be the most familiar and commonplace of terms, is invested with supreme, with unique distinction.*"[6] "*The generality of mankind is still immature. Had it acquired sufficient capacity We would have bestowed upon it so great a measure of Our knowledge that all who dwell on earth and in heaven would have found themselves, by virtue of*

1 Statement (a)
2 Statement (b)
3 Statement (c)
4 Statement (d)
5 Statement (e)
6 Statement (f)

the grace streaming from Our pen, completely independent of all knowledge save the knowledge of God, and would have been securely established upon the throne of abiding tranquillity."[1] "*The Pen of Holiness, I solemnly affirm before God, hath writ upon My snow-white brow and in characters of effulgent glory these glowing, these musk-scented and holy words: 'Behold ye that dwell on earth, and ye denizens of heaven, bear witness, He in truth is your Well-Beloved. He it is Whose like the world of creation hath not seen, He Whose ravishing beauty hath delighted the eye of God, the Ordainer, the All-Powerful, the Incomparable!'*"[2]

6.3 Bahá'í Dispensation

In paragraph 16, Shoghi Effendi explains that the Bahá'í Faith is the culmination of a cycle that started with Adam around six thousand years ago, continued through to the appearance of Muḥammad, and ended with the Báb. This is a reference to the Cycle of Prophecy (or Adamic Cycle), which has, with the Coming of Bahá'u'lláh, given way to the Cycle of Fulfillment as illustrated in Figure 6.1.

In *Some Answered Questions,*[3] 'Abdu'l-Bahá describes two types of cycles. The first cycle represents the Dispensation of a Manifestation of God through which the laws and ordinances revealed by Him prevail. "*Each of the Divine Manifestations has ... a cycle, and during the cycle His laws and commandments prevail and are performed. When His cycle is completed by the appearance of a new Manifestation, a new cycle begins.*"[4]

The second cycle defined by 'Abdu'l-Bahá is the universal cycle: " ... *a universal cycle in the world of existence signifies a long duration of time, and innumerable and incalculable periods and epochs. In such a cycle the Manifestations appear with splendour in the realm of the visible until a great and supreme Manifestation makes the world the center of His radiance. His appearance causes the world to attain to maturity, and the extension of His cycle is very great.*"[5]

'Abdu'l-Bahá also describes the relationship between the two defined cycles: "*In this way cycles begin, end and are renewed, until a universal cycle is completed in the world, when important events and great occurrences will take place which entirely efface every trace and every record of the past; then a new universal cycle begins in the world ....*"[6]

All the Manifestations of God appearing before Bahá'u'lláh made prophecies to a "*Day of Days*" when "*the Promise of All Ages should be made*

1 Statement (g)
2 Statement (h)
3 'Abdu'l-Bahá, *Some Answered Questions*, p. 160
4 'Abdu'l-Bahá, *Some Answered Questions*, p. 160.
5 'Abdu'l-Bahá, *Some Answered Questions*, p. 160.
6 'Abdu'l-Bahá, *Some Answered Questions*, pp. 160-161.

*A-62+#3P1*Q?$:!4(! ?;! :?*!8*94=&4%! ?4I?!:?*(*!5 $%4>*(:$:4=$88*$9*&4(! M%=%$(!:?*!Kb;I0 *!=>!h9=8?*I; P7

Q?* I;I0 *!:?$: I=)) *%I*&!4?!:?*!$88*$$%I*=>^ $?3/./ 00?!4(!M%=%$(! :?*!b;I0 * =>!O.0>40) *%:(4%I*T *!?$(!>.0>400$&0!?*!89=8?*I4*() $&*&.94%H! :?*!b;I0 *!=>!h9=8?*I;7

Q?*! W4(8*%($:4=%>!:?*! ^ 3-! 89=E4&*&*! 04%M!' **%!?*! b ;I0*(! =>! h9=8?*I;! $%&O.0>40) *%:! $%&89*8$9*&!:?*! 8*=80! >=9. :?*! I=) 4%H!=> ^ $?3/./ 00?<!:?*! K`0=9,! =>!` =&P!Kp !:?*! B%$.H.9$:=9. =>! :?*! 0=%H$' $4*&!) 400*%%4 P!$%&Kp !:?*!V94H4%$:=9=>!$!%*!! +L%4E*9($0b;I0 *</!p 7P

Q?*!I=%:*S:4%! ?4I? :?*!b ;I0*(!=>h9=8?*I;! $%&C.0>400%:$9*&*>4%4&! &4>*9*%!>9=) ! :?*! I=%*S:! => KI;I0 *(P!9*>*94%H!=! :?*! &48*%$:4=%!=> $%! 4%&E4&.$05 $%4*(:$:4=%=>` =&!4%9*0$4=%:= :?*!. %E*9($0I ;I0 *7 Q?*!b ;I0*(! =>!h9=8?*I;! $%&O.0>40) *%:!894) $94! &4:4%H.(?! :?*!%$.9 *!$%&&4>*9*%I*(! =>:' =!8*94=&(4%?.) $%!4(:=9,! -*>=9*!$%&$!>*9.^ $?3/./ 00?7

, :!:?*!4%I*8:4=%=!$!.%4E*9($0I ;I0 *<?.) $%4! 4(!%=!) $:.9 *!*%=.H?!=! 9*I*4E*!:?*!@89*) *!5 $%4*(:$:4=%=>` =&!7 T *%I*!<?*9*!$9*!) $%;!&4E4%*! Y*E*0$:4=%(! 89*8$9! ?.) $%4:;!) *%$00;!$%&(!84%.$00;! :=! 9*I*4E*!:?*! @89*) *!5 $%4*(:$:4=%7

! '#$%&*'+',- ./&0'123 %145&.678'! $/2"/9 &7:"'7:5"0$7";&06/'. - . /&'

^ $?3/./003?!4(!:?*!@.89*)*!5 $%4>*(:$:4=%! =&4%!?*!I.99*%:!%4E*9($0!

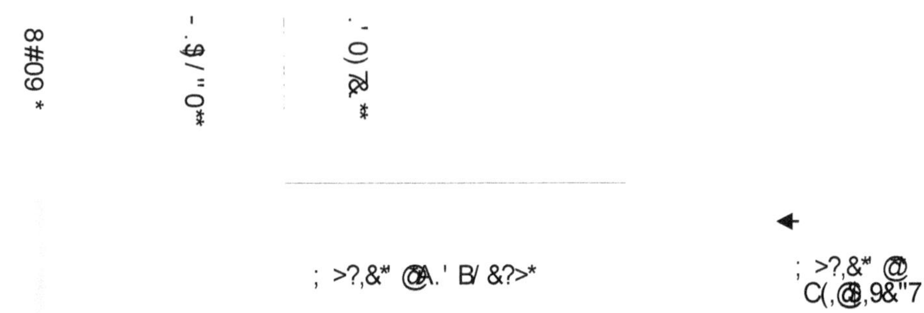

I;I0 *! :?$:! -*H$%! 4?! , &$) /! !, 0:?=.H?! ^ $?3/./003?! 4(! %=:!:?*! >49(:! 5 $%4*(:$:4=%=> ` =&! >=9.:?4(!. %E*9($0I ;I0 *<T *!4(!:?*!.0:4) $:*!8.98=(*!>=9. $00:?*!Y*E*0$:4=%($88*$9*&!*>=9*!T 4)7 !!T *%I*!4:I$%!*!($4&:?$: T *!4(!4%! >$I:!:?*!B%$.H.9$:=9$%&?*!V94H4%$:=9=>:?4(!%*'!.%4E*9($0I ;I0 * $(!T 4(G 400! ?$(!-**%&9E4%H!?*!I=.9 (*!=>*E*%(:&.94%H!?*!b ;I0 *!=>!h9=8?*I; 7!

! 8#'F#$!R44. 6/$$!/"# %&'()$* ')#' &$ -"./ 0/((." $+DCBLD

" 8#'F#$!R44. 6/$$@&)$-66#6$ 8$!-D!ND

6.4 Testimonies to His Revelation

In paragraph 17, Shoghi Effendi highlights the significance of the statements made by Bahá'u'lláh on the character of His Revelation. He makes the following points:

a) We should direct our attention to the claims made by Bahá'u'lláh in His Writings if we wish to acquire a better understanding of the nature and power of His Revelation.

b) Bahá'u'lláh, as well as the Báb and 'Abdu'l-Bahá, have left fathomless oceans of Sacred Writings on the greatness of the Revelation of Bahá'u'lláh. In these Writings we find:
   - Bahá'u'lláh's assertion of the unparalleled claims advanced by Him
   - Bahá'u'lláh's references to the mysterious forces released through His Revelation
   - Statements exalting the "glories of His long-awaited Day"
   - Passages extolling the station that "they who have recognised its hidden virtues will attain"

In paragraph 18, Shoghi Effendi cites some of such statements made by Bahá'u'lláh on the potency of His Revelation. You need to reflect on each quotation and assimilate the concepts enshrined in them. The key concept of each statement is provided in Table 6.1 to assist you in your reflections.

6.5 The Spirit of Truth

In statement (d), cited in paragraph 18, Bahá'u'lláh refers to Himself as the "Spirit of Truth" mentioned in the Gospels. The coming of the Spirit of Truth is one of the prophecies of the Gospel of Jesus Christ. 'Abdu'l-Bahá explains in Some Answered Questions that the Spirit of Truth is different from the Holy Spirit. In "*... some passages in the Holy Books the Spirit is spoken of, signifying a certain person, as it is currently said in speech and conversation that such a person is an embodied spirit, or he is a personification of mercy and generosity. In this case, it is the light we look at, and not the glass.*"[1]

As an example, 'Abdu'l-Bahá refers to the statement "*I have yet many things to say unto you, but ye cannot bear them now. Howbeit when He, the Spirit of truth, is come, He will guide you unto all truth: for He shall not speak of Himself; but whatsoever He shall bear, that shall be speak: and He will show you things to come.*"[2]

---

1 'Abdu'l-Bahá, *Some Answered* Questions, p. 108.

2 John 16:12–14

'Abdu'l-Bahá further explains that the words "*... for He shall not speak of Himself; but whatsoever He shall hear, that shall He speak,*" indicates that "*... the Spirit of truth is embodied in a Man Who has individuality, Who has ears to hear and a tongue to speak.*"

Table 6.1 – The key concepts of statements cited in paragraph 18

Statement	Key Concept
(a)	The testimony of Bahá'u'lláh on the greatness of His Revelation.
(b)	All the past Dispensations have achieved their ultimate perfection through the Revelation of Bahá'u'lláh.
(c)	That which is made manifest in the Revelation of Bahá'u'lláh is unique among all the past and future revelations.
(d)	Bahá'u'lláh is the *Jehovah* mentioned in the Bible, *the Spirit of Truth* named in the Gospel and the *Great Announcement* referred to in the Qur'án.
(e)	If not for Bahá'u'lláh, none of the earlier Divine Messengers would have been invested with the station of prophethood and none of the sacred scriptures would have been revealed.
(f)	Every word uttered by Bahá'u'lláh is invested with a unique distinction.
(g)	If the human race were mature enough, Bahá'u'lláh would have revealed a measure of divine knowledge that would have made humanity independent of all knowledge save the knowledge of God.
(h)	The world of creation has not previously seen anyone the like of Bahá'u'lláh.

Below are the other prophecies in the Gospel referring to the coming of the "Spirit of Truth":

- *"But when the Comforter is come, Whom I will send unto you from the Father, even the Spirit of Truth, which proceedeth from the Father, He shall testify of me."*[1]
- *"And I will pray the Father, and He shall give you another Comforter that he may abide with you for ever: Even the Spirit of Truth ....*"[2]

6.6 Jehovah

In statement (d) cited in paragraph 18, Bahá'u'lláh refers to Himself as Jehovah mentioned in the Old Testament. Jehovah is the promised Name of

1 John 15:26
2 John 14:16–17

God and was originally spelled as YHWH, coming from Hebrew letters: Yud, Hay, Wav and Hay.

In every Dispensation, the Manifestation of God reveals a specific Name with infinite power and potency for the believers to draw on for Divine assistance. In Judaism, this Name was Jehovah. In the *Old Testament* "Jehovah" is mentioned six thousand five hundred and nineteen times, which is more than any other references to God. Although Jehovah is first used in Genesis 2:4, God does not reveal Himself as Jehovah until Exodus 3.

6.7 The Most Great Announcement

In statement (d) cited in paragraph 18, Bahá'u'lláh refers to Himself as "the Most Great Announcement" mentioned in the Qur'án. There are prophecies regarding the Advent of two great Manifestations of God in all the Holy books. In Islám, the majority of the followers believe that the two expected Manifestations are the "Imám Mihdí" and the "Messiah". In the Qur'án, the advent of the two Promised Ones is referred to as the "Great Announcement". This is a recurring theme in the Qur'án as about five thousand out of the six thousand two hundred verses of the Qur'án revolve around this issue.[1]

Bahá'u'lláh, in *Epistle to the Son of the Wolf*, refers to this prophecy and indicates that His Revelation is the Great Announcement:

> *"Likewise, in the Qur'án He saith: 'Of what ask they of one another? Of the Great Announcement.' This is the Announcement, the greatness of which hath been mentioned in most of the Books of old and of more recent times. This is the Announcement that hath caused the limbs of mankind to quake, except such as God, the Protector, the Helper, the Succourer, hath willed to exempt. Men have indeed with their own eyes witnessed how all men and all things have been thrown into confusion and been sore perplexed, save those whom God hath chosen to exempt."*[2]

There is a more detailed discussion on the concept of "the Great Announcement" in section 17.3.2.

[1] M. Mustafa, *Bahá'u'lláh the Great Announcement of the Qur'án*, p. 6.

[2] Bahá'u'lláh, *Epistle to the Son of the Wolf*, pp. 143–144.

6.8 Activities

1. Describe your understanding of the concepts of universal cycle and the Supreme Manifestation of God.

2. Describe the relationship between the Dispensation of the Báb and the cycles of Prophecy and Fulfilment.

3. How have the past Dispensations achieved their ultimate perfection through the Revelation of Bahá'u'lláh (statement (b))?

4. What are the implications of the claim that future generations will not witness the like of what has been made manifest in the Revelation of Bahá'u'lláh, as mentioned in statement (c)?

5. What is the meaning of Bahá'u'lláh being the Jehovah in the Bible (statement (d))?

6. What is your understanding of statement (e)?

7. What is the meaning of "distinction" mentioned in statement (f)?

8. What is your understanding of statement (g)?

9. In your understanding, how can the beauty of Bahá'u'lláh delight the eye of God (statement h)?

6.9 Glossary

Term	Meaning
Allusion	An indirect or casual reference
Annals	A record of events or activities that is arranged in yearly parts
Assertion	A forceful statement or claim
Bequeath	To give to others after death
Compelling	Forceful, convincing, persuasive, undeniable
Consummation	The point at which something is made complete or perfect
Culmination	The last and highest point, when this is reached after a long period of effort or development, climax
Effulgent	Shining brightly; brilliant
Glean	To gather (facts or information) in small amounts
Impetuous	Moving forcefully or rapidly
Impregnate	To cause something to enter and spread completely through something else
Inconceivable	Impossible to imagine
Posterity	Future generations
Ravishing	Very beautiful; causing great delight
Unequivocally	Completely clear; allowing no possibility of doubt
Vehement	Showing strong feelings; forceful
Venture	Dare, undertake, especially where risk is involved

7. PROPHECIES FULFILLED—I

7.1 Introduction

This chapter covers paragraph 19 and the first statement of paragraph 20. Read these paragraphs and reflect on the contents before starting the lesson. In this section of his letter, Shoghi Effendi cites some statements from Bahá'u'lláh asserting the fulfilment of the Bible's prophecies on the advent of the Promised One through the Revelation of Bahá'u'lláh.

In this chapter, you need to look for and understand the following **key concepts**:

a) Bahá'u'lláh is the return of Christ from heaven (statement a).
b) Bahá'u'lláh is the Son of Man and the Desire of the world (statement b)
c) Bahá'u'lláh, in reference to His own Revelation, proclaims that the heavenly Father has come (statement c).
d) Bahá'u'lláh has announced the Word, which Christ told His followers they could not bear at the time (statement d).
e) Bahá'u'lláh refers in statement (e) to His Revelation as the coming of the Comforter.
f) Shoghi Effendi confirms in *God Passes By* that the City of God is the Divine Revelation, renewed at fixed intervals (statement f).
g) Shoghi Effendi has interpreted the Shrine of the Báb, as the "celestial Kaaba" (statement f).

7.2 Paragraphs under study

19. "*Followers of the Gospel,*" Bahá'u'lláh addressing the whole of Christendom exclaims, "*behold the gates of heaven are flung open. He that had ascended unto it is now come. Give ear to His voice calling aloud over land and sea, announcing to all mankind the advent of this Revelation—a Revelation through the agency of which the Tongue of Grandeur is now proclaiming: 'Lo, the sacred Pledge hath been*

fulfilled, for He, the Promised One, is come!'"[1] *"The voice of the Son of Man is calling aloud from the sacred vale: 'Here am I, here am I, O God my God!' ... whilst from the Burning Bush breaketh forth the cry: 'Lo, the Desire of the world is made manifest in His transcendent glory!'*[2] *The Father hath come. That which ye were promised in the Kingdom of God is fulfilled.*[3] *This is the Word, which the Son veiled when He said to those around Him that at that time they could not bear it ... Verily the Spirit of Truth is come to guide you unto all truth ... He is the One Who glorified the Son and exalted His Cause ..."*[4] *"The Comforter Whose advent all the scriptures have promised is now come that He may reveal unto you all knowledge and wisdom. Seek Him over the entire surface of the earth, haply ye may find Him."*[5]

20. "*Call out to Zion, O Carmel,*" writes Bahá'u'lláh, "*and announce the joyful tidings: 'He that was hidden from mortal eyes is come! His all-conquering sovereignty is manifest; His all-encompassing splendour is revealed ... Hasten forth and circumambulate the City of God that hath descended from heaven—the celestial Kaaba round which have circled in adoration the favoured of God, the pure in heart and the company of the most exalted angels.'"*[6]

7.3 Advent of the Promised One

In the statements cited in paragraph 19, Bahá'u'lláh asserts that the prophecies made in the Christian sacred Scriptures to the advent of the Promised One have been fulfilled through His Revelation.

Although prophecy is defined literally as "prediction", it has a deeper meaning in the context of religion. A religious prophecy is a vision of the future purpose of God for humanity as seen by an inspired Prophet.

There are many prophecies in the Bible referring to future spiritual events the climax of which is the establishment of the Kingdom of God on earth. In fact, the story of the coming of the Kingdom is a recurring theme throughout the Bible.

In the statements cited in this paragraph, Bahá'u'lláh makes many allusions to His Revelation in connection with the Biblical prophecy. The background information on some of the statements is provided in the following sections.

7.3.1 He that had ascended to heaven is now come

The statement "*He that had ascended to heaven in now come*" in paragraph 19 is a reference to the resurrection and ascension of Jesus Christ to heaven. A fundamental belief in Christian theology is that Christ physically ascended

---

1 Statement (a)
2 Statement (b)
3 Statement (c)
4 Statement (d)
5 Statement (e)
6 Statement (f)

to heaven three days after His crucifixion. 'Abdu'l-Bahá states that the resurrection of Christ *"... from the interior of the earth is also symbolical; it is a spiritual and divine fact, and not material; and likewise His ascension to heaven is a spiritual and not material ascension."*[1] This reflects the assertion that the coming of Christ from heaven was spiritual.

The following prophecies can be found it the Bible regarding the coming of the Promised One from heaven.

a) *"No one has ascended into heaven but he who descended from heaven, the Son of man."*[2]

b) *"For the Lord himself shall descend from heaven with a shout, with the voice of the archangel, and with the trump of God; and the dead in Christ shall rise first."*[3]

7.3.2 Sacred Vale and Burning Bush

In the first part of statement (b), Bahá'u'lláh refers to the "sacred vale". In the context of His statement describing this call raised by Christ, the "sacred vale" is different from the Holy Vale of Towa or Sacred Vale, referred to in the Qur'án[4] as "*the sacred spot where Moses put off His shoes*."[5]

In the second part of statement (b), Bahá'u'lláh states, "*... the Burning Bush breaketh forth the cry: 'Lo, the Desire of the world is made manifest.'*" Due to the mystical nature of the sacred Scriptures, abstract concepts such as "religious truth", "divine knowledge" and "spiritual reality" are often described in terms of physical experiences. For example, Moses "communicated" with God through the burning bush on Mount Sinai.[6]

In explaining the Christian concept of the Holy Trinity, 'Abdu'l-Bahá states that in every Dispensation there has been an intermediary between God and His Manifestation.[7] The burning bush was the intermediary in the Mosaic cycle, the Holy Spirit in the Dispensation of Christ, and the Angel Gabriel in the Dispensation of Muḥammad.

7.3.3 Father

In the Bible, God is referred to as "Father", "Heavenly Father" and "Everlasting Father", and the Jesus Christ as the "Son". According to a prophecy in the Bible, *"... the Son of man shall come in the Glory of his Father."*[8] In statement (c), Bahá'u'lláh, referring to His own Revelation, proclaims that the Father has come.

---

1 'Abdu'l-Bahá: *Some Answered Questions*, p. 104.
2 John 3:13
3 Thessalonians 4:16
4 *Qur'án* 20:12
5 'Abdu'l-Bahá, *Selection from the Writings of 'Abdu'l-Bahá*, p. 235.
6 Act 7:30
7 'Abdu'l-Bahá, *Tablets of Abdu'l-Baha Abbas*, vol. 1, p. 117.
8 Matthew 16:27

This reference of Bahá'u'lláh to Himself as the Father is similar in nature to the claim of Christ to be the Son. They both reflect the Divine Oneness. For example, it is mentioned in the Bible, *"The Father is in the Son and the Son is in the Father."*[1] 'Abdu'l-Bahá explains that through this statement *"Divine Oneness is proven and He revealeth Himself in the Holy Essences. The sun is one sun but manifesteth itself in different mirrors."*[2]

In another Tablet, 'Abdu'l-Bahá further elucidates the purpose of such statements in the Bible: *"... the reality of that eternal Sun had become reflected in its glory in Christ Himself. It does not signify that the Sun of Reality had descended from its place in heaven or that its essential being had effected an entrance into the mirror, for there is neither entrance nor exit for the reality of Divinity; there is no ingress or egress; it is sanctified above all things and ever occupies its own holy station. Changes and transformations are not applicable to that eternal reality. Transformation from condition to condition is the attribute of contingent realities."*[3]

According to the Bahá'í Writings, all the Manifestations of God are perfect mirrors that reflect the divine splendours. 'Abdu'l-Bahá explains: "... *these holy Manifestations or Prophets of God are as mirrors which have acquired illumination from the Sun of Truth, but the Sun does not descend from its high zenith and does not effect entrance within the mirror. In truth, this mirror has attained complete polish and purity until the utmost capacity of reflection has been developed in it; therefore, the Sun of Reality with its fullest effulgence and splendour is revealed therein. These mirrors are earthly, whereas the reality of Divinity is in its highest apogee. Although its lights are shining and its heat is manifest in them, although these mirrors are telling their story of its effulgence, the Sun, nevertheless, remains in its own lofty station; it does not descend; it does not effect entrance, because it is holy and sanctified."*[4]

Hence, the assertion of Bahá'u'lláh that He is the Father does not imply that Bahá'u'lláh is superior to Christ nor any other Manifestation of God. Bahá'u'lláh ("Father") and Jesus Christ ("Son") are both perfect mirrors reflecting the purpose of God for Their age according to the receptivity of the people.

7.3.4 Word veiled by the Son

Statement (d) is a reference to the limited understanding of Christ's followers, and His promise: *"I have yet many things to say unto you, but ye cannot bear them now. Howbeit when He, the Spirit of Truth, is come, He will guide you into all truth for he shall not speak of himself; but whatsoever he shall hear, that shall he speak: and he will shew you things to come. He shall*

---

1 John 14:11
2 'Abdu'l-Bahá, *Tablets of Abdu'l-Baha Abbas*, vol. 3, p. 513.
3 'Abdu'l-Bahá, *The Promulgation of Universal Peace*, p. 173.
4 'Abdu'l-Bahá, *The Promulgation of Universal Peace*, p. 114.

glorify me: for he shall receive of mine, and shall shew it unto you."[1] Bahá'u'lláh states that His Revelation is the Word that Christ could not have told His followers at that time.

In reference to the above promise from Christ, Shoghi Effendi asserts that from "... the words of Christ, as attested by the Gospel, every unprejudiced observer will readily apprehend the magnitude of the Faith which Bahá'u'lláh has revealed, and recognize the staggering weight of the claim He has advanced."[2]

The meaning of "*the Spirit of Truth*" is explored in section 6.6.

7.3.5 Comforter

Bahá'u'lláh refers in statement (e) to His Revelation as the coming of the Comforter. There are many prophecies in the Bible to a person called the Paraclete[3] or Pharaclete that translates to "Comforter", "Advocate" or "Redeemer". Here are some examples:

a) *"But when the Comforter comes, whom I shall send you from the Father, even the Spirit of Truth, who proceeds from the Father, he will bear witness to me."*[4]

b) *"Nevertheless I tell you the truth: it is to your advantage that I go away, for if I do not go away, the Comforter will not come to you; but if I go, I will send him to you."*[5]

c) *"And I will pray the Father, and he shall give you another Comforter, that he may abide with you for ever."*[6]

d) *"But the Comforter, which is the Holy Spirit, whom the Father will send in my name, he shall teach you all things, and bring all things to your remembrance, whatsoever I have said unto you."*[7]

Studies of the early history of Christianity reveal that the followers of Christ expected the coming of the Paraclete after Christ. A number of Christians in the second and the third centuries claimed to be that promised Paraclete.[8]

The Bahá'í Writings have interpreted prophecies of the coming of the Comforter as both the Revelation appearing immediately after Christ as His Greater Covenant and also to the Supreme Manifestation of God that has been fulfilled in the Revelation of Bahá'u'lláh.

In the context of the Revelation after Christ, 'Abdu'l-Bahá mentions that the name "Paraclete" refers to Muḥammad: "*His Holiness Christ made a*

---

1 John 16: 12–14

2 Shoghi Effendi, *The World Order of Bahá'u'lláh*, p. 25.

3 Paracletos is a corruption of the Greek word Periclytos ("Advocate").

4 John 15:26

5 John 16:7

6 John 14:16

7 John 14:26

8 A. Ishráq Khávarí, Muhádirát, p. 496 (in Fársí).

covenant concerning the Paraclete and gave the tidings of His coming."[1] A letter written on behalf of Shoghi Effendi also confirms that "References in the Bible to 'Mt. Párán' and 'Paraclete' refer to Muḥammad's Revelation."[2]

7.4 City of God and celestial Kaaba

In statement (f), Bahá'u'lláh calls on humanity to "... *circumambulate the City of God that hath descended from heaven—the celestial Kaaba round which have circled in adoration the favoured of God.*"

St. John, when recounting his vision of the second coming of the Glory of God, observes, "*And I saw a new heaven and a new earth: for the first heaven and the first earth were passed away; and there was no more sea. And I John saw the holy city, new Jerusalem, coming down from God out of heaven, prepared as a bride adorned for her husband."*[3]

'Abdu'l-Bahá states in one of His Tablets, that the new heaven and the new earth have come. "*The holy City, new Jerusalem, hath come down from on high in the form of a maid of heaven, veiled, beauteous, and unique, and prepared for reunion with her lovers on earth. The angelic company of the Celestial Concourse hath joined in a call that hath run throughout the universe, all loudly and mightily acclaiming: 'This is the City of God and His abode ....*'"[4] The Revelation of Bahá'u'lláh has fulfilled such prophecies.

'Abdu'l-Bahá also explains: *"what is most frequently meant by the Holy City, the Jerusalem of God, which is mentioned in the Holy Book, is the Law of God.*"[5] Bahá'u'lláh states in *The Kitáb-i-Íqán*[6] that Ṣáliḥ, one of the early Manifestations of God summoned people to the "City of God". Shoghi Effendi confirms in *God Passes By* that the City of God is the Divine Revelation, renewed at fixed intervals.[7]

The term "City of God" has been used in other contexts. In one of His Tablets, 'Abdu'l-Bahá exclaims, *"Jerusalem, the Holy of Holies, is a revered Temple, a sublime name, for it is the City of God.*"[8]

Bahá'u'lláh describes the City of God as "*the realm of the spirit*" to which the true seeker enters after sacrificing all things, "*That is, whatever he hath seen, and heard, and understood.*"[9]

Describing the condition of the true seeker, Bahá'u'lláh states: "*Only when the lamp of search, of earnest striving, of longing desire, of passionate devotion, of fervid love, of rapture, and ecstasy, is kindled within the seeker's*

---

1 'Abdu'l-Bahá, *Bahá'í World Faith*, p. 358.
2 Shoghi Effendi, *Letters from the Guardian to Australia and New Zealand*, p. 41.
3 Revelation 21:2–3
4 'Abdu'l-Bahá, *Selections from the Writings of 'Abdu'l-Bahá*, p. 12.
5 'Abdu'l-Bahá, *Some Answered Questions*, p. 65.
6 Bahá'u'lláh, *The Kitáb-i-Íqán*, p. 9.
7 Shoghi Effendi, *God Passes By*, p. 139.
8 'Abdu'l-Bahá, *Lights of Guidance*, p. 499.
9 Bahá'u'lláh, *Seven Valleys and Four Valleys*, p. 7.

heart, and the breeze of His loving-kindness is wafted upon his soul, will the darkness of error be dispelled, the mists of doubts and misgivings be dissipated, and the lights of knowledge and certitude envelop his being. At that hour will the mystic Herald, bearing the joyful tidings of the Spirit, shine forth from the City of God resplendent as the morn, and, through the trumpet-blast of knowledge, will awaken the heart, the soul, and the spirit from the slumber of negligence."[1]

Bahá'u'lláh designated Baghdád as the "City of God".[2]

Shoghi Effendi has referred to the Shrine of the Báb, as the "celestial Kaaba", the spiritual Centre of the Faith of Bahá'u'lláh on Mount Carmel.[3]

1 Bahá'u'lláh, *The Kitáb-i-Íqán*, p. 196.
2 Shoghi Effendi, *God Passes By*, pp. 109–110.
3 The Hands of the Cause of God, *The Ministry of Custodians*, p. 385.

7.5 Activities

1. What does Bahá'u'lláh mean by *"the gates of heaven are flung open"* in statement (a)?

2. What does Bahá'u'lláh mean by *"the sacred Pledge"* in statement (a)?

3. Describe your understanding of statement (b).

4. Describe your understanding of statement (c).

5. Describe your understanding of statement (d).

6. What is the meaning of the "City of God"?

7. What is the meaning of the "Celestial Kaaba"?

7.6 Glossary

Term	Meaning
Adoration	Deep love and respect
Adorn	To make more beautiful, attractive, or interesting
Advent	The arrival or coming of
Agency (of)	The power or force which causes a result
Agony	Very great pain or suffering of mind or body
Celestial	Of the sky or heaven
Christendom	All Christian people in general
Countenance	The face; the appearance or expression of a person's face
Fling	To throw violently or with force, esp. with lack of care for the object that is thrown
Pledge	A solemn promise or agreement
Prostrate	Lying on one's front, face downwards, esp. in obedience or worship
Redolent	Strongly reminiscent of or suggestive of; strongly smelling of, fragrant
Vale	A broad low valley
Waft	To (cause to) move or go lightly (as if) on wind or waves

8. PROPHECIES FULFILLED—II

8.1 Introduction

This chapter covers the remainder of paragraph 20. Read this paragraph and reflect on the contents before starting the lesson. In this section of his letter, Shoghi Effendi cites further statements from Bahá'u'lláh on the majesty and greatness of the Revelation of Bahá'u'lláh. In these statements, Bahá'u'lláh asserts the adoration of the Hebrew Prophets for Him, the joy of the Holy Land witnessing the coming of His Revelation and the Praise of the past Manifestations of God for Him.

In this chapter, you need to look for and understand the following **key concepts:**

a) Bahá'u'lláh is the One who was extolled by Isaiah, Whose "throne of glory" was circumambulated by Elijah, and Who was adored by Solomon (statement a, d, and e).
b) Bahá'u'lláh is the One "*with Whose name both the Torah and the Evangel were adorned.*" (statement a)
c) Sinai, Carmel, Zion, Ḥijáz and Jerusalem are joyous of the coming of Bahá'u'lláh (statements b, c and g).
d) Abraham, Moses and Muḥammad would praise Bahá'u'lláh and submit to His Will if they could attain this Day (statement f).

8.2 Paragraphs under study

20. "*I am the One,*" He in another connection affirms, "*Whom the tongue of Isaiah hath extolled, the One with Whose name both the Torah and the Evangel were adorned.*"[1] "*The glory of Sinai hath hastened to circle round the Day-Spring of this Revelation, while from the heights of the Kingdom the voice of the Son of God is heard proclaiming: 'Bestir yourselves, ye proud ones of the earth, and hasten ye towards Him.'*

[1] Statement (a)

Carmel hath in this day hastened in longing adoration to attain His court, whilst from the heart of Zion there cometh the cry: 'The promise of all ages is now fulfilled. That which had been announced in the holy writ of God, the Beloved, the Most High, is made manifest.' "[1] "*Ḥijáz is astir by the breeze announcing the tidings of joyous reunion. 'Praise be to Thee,' We hear her exclaim, 'O my Lord, the Most High. I was dead through my separation from Thee; the breeze laden with the fragrance of Thy presence hath brought me back to life. Happy is he that turneth unto Thee, and woe betide the erring.'* "[2] "*By the one true God, Elijah hath hastened unto My court and hath circumambulated in the day-time and in the night-season My throne of glory.*"[3] "*Solomon in all his majesty circles in adoration around Me in this day, uttering this most exalted word: 'I have turned my face towards Thy face, O Thou omnipotent Ruler of the world! I am wholly detached from all things pertaining unto me, and yearn for that which Thou dost possess.'* "[4] "*Had Muḥammad, the Apostle of God, attained this Day,*" Bahá'u'lláh writes in a Tablet revealed on the eve of His banishment to the penal colony of 'Akká, "*He would have exclaimed: 'I have truly recognised Thee, O Thou the Desire of the Divine Messengers!' Had Abraham attained it, He too, falling prostrate upon the ground, and in the utmost lowliness before the Lord thy God, would have cried: 'Mine heart is filled with peace, O Thou Lord of all that is in heaven and on earth! I testify that Thou hast unveiled before mine eyes all the glory of Thy power and the full majesty of Thy law!' ... Had Moses Himself attained it, He, likewise, would have raised His voice saying: 'All praise be to Thee for having lifted upon me the light of Thy countenance and enrolled me among them that have been privileged to behold Thy face!'* "[5] "*North and South both vibrate to the call announcing the advent of our Revelation. We can hear the voice of Mecca acclaiming: 'All praise be to Thee, O Lord my God, the All-Glorious, for having wafted over me the breath redolent with the fragrance of Thy presence!' Jerusalem, likewise, is calling aloud: 'Lauded and magnified art Thou, O Beloved of earth and heaven, for having turned the agony of my separation from Thee into the joy of a life-giving reunion!'* "[6]

8.3 The holy places

In paragraph 20, Shoghi Effendi cites some of the statements of Bahá'u'lláh in which He refers to Sinai, Carmel, Zion, Ḥijáz and Jerusalem. These

---

1 Statement (b)
2 Statement (c)
3 Statement (d)
4 Statement (e)
5 Statement (f)
6 Statement (g)

locations have spiritual significance to Judaism, Christianity and Islám and there are prophecies associated with them in the sacred writings.

8.3.1 Zion

Literally, the word Zion means "fortification". The word occurs one hundred and fifty times in the Bible and refers to both the city of David and the City of God. The context in which Zion is used in the Bible evolves from a physical entity to a more spiritual concept.

The first mention of the word "Zion" in the Bible is: "*Nevertheless, David captured the fortress of Zion, the City of David.*"[1] When Solomon built the Temple in Jerusalem, the word Zion was also used in reference to the Temple and the area surrounding it. Over time, the word Zion has variously represented the city of Jerusalem, the land of Judah, and the people of Israel as a whole.

After the fall of Judea (AD 70), Zion became the symbol of hope for the Jews that their homeland in Palestine would eventually be restored.

Zion is also used in the New Testament in a spiritual context, referring to the Kingdom of God and the heavenly Jerusalem. An example is: "*Therefore thus saith the Lord God, Behold, I lay in Zion for a foundation a stone, a tried stone, a precious corner stone, a sure foundation: he that believeth shall not make haste.*"[2]

8.3.2 Mount Carmel

Mount Carmel is a short mountain ridge in the north west of Israel famous for its connections with Biblical figures and events. From early times Mount Carmel was deemed a holy place.

There are prophecies that refer to the glory of Carmel on the Day of Days. At that time, the Bible tells us "*The wilderness and the dry land shall be glad, the desert shall rejoice and blossom; like the crocus it shall blossom abundantly, and rejoice with joy and signing. The glory of Lebanon shall be given to it, the majesty of Carmel and Sharon. They shall see the glory of the Lord, the majesty of our God.*"[3] And "*it shall come to pass in the last days, that the mountain of the Lord's house shall be established in the top of the mountains, and shall be exalted above the hills; and all nations shall flow unto it.*"[4]

In the Revelation of Bahá'u'lláh, both the spiritual and administrative centres of the Faith are located on Mount Carmel. As mentioned before, the "celestial Kaaba" referring to the Shrine of the Báb, was built on Mount Carmel at a location designated by Bahá'u'lláh.

---

1 Samuel 2:5:7

2 Isaiah 28:16

3 Isaiah 2:1–2

4 Isaiah 2:2

In "The Tablet of Carmel", Bahá'u'lláh refers to the sailing of "His Ark" upon the mountain. The Guardian has defined this Ark as the Laws of God. This is a reference to the establishment of the Seat of the Universal House of Justice on this holy mountain.[1]

Bahá'u'lláh designated the location of the Shrine of the Báb in 1891 and 'Abdu'l-Bahá commenced construction of the Shrine in 1909. Shoghi Effendi completed the superstructure of the Báb's holy sepulchre in 1953. The remains of the Greatest Holy Leaf were laid to rest in close proximity to the Shrine of the Báb on Mount Carmel in 1932. Later, in 1939 the remains of the Purest Branch, Bahá'u'lláh's beloved youngest son, and Navváb, His wife, were transferred to that same spot. Eighteen terraces above and below the Shrine of the Báb were completed in 1999.

The International Archives building was the first Bahá'í administrative structure constructed on Mount Carmel. It was completed in 1957. The seat of the Universal House of Justice was the next administrative building on Mount Carmel the construction of which was finished in 1982. This was followed by the completion of the Centre for the Study of the Holy Texts in 1999, and the International Teaching Centre in 2001.

8.3.3 Sinai

According to the Bible and the Qur'án, Sinai (Mount Sinai) was the place where God talked to Moses and gave Him the station of a Manifestation of God. Moses also received the Ten Commandments from Jehovah on Mount Sinai.[2] It is located in southern Sinai and is known as Jabal Mosá in Arabic.

There are many symbolic references in the Bahá'í Writings to Sinai and the Burning Bush as the dawning place of revelation. Here are two examples:

- *"Oh, how I long to announce unto every spot on the surface of the earth, and to carry to each one of its cities, the glad-tidings of this Revelation—a Revelation to which the heart of Sinai hath been attracted, and in whose name the Burning Bush is calling: 'Unto God, the Lord of Lords, belong the kingdoms of earth and heaven.'"*[3]
- *"Deliver yourselves from your evil and corrupt affections, and hasten to embrace the light of the undying Fire that gloweth on the Sinai of this mysterious and transcendent Revelation."*[4]

8.3.4 Ḥijáz

Ḥijáz is a desert in the Arabian Peninsula where the Prophet Muḥammad appeared. Mecca and Medina, the cities closely associated with Muḥammad are located in the Ḥijáz. Mecca, the birthplace of Muḥammad, is the most

---

1 Shoghi Effendi, Letter written on his behalf to the Bahá'ís of the East, in *Compilation of Compilations*, vol.1 pp. 342.

2 In Arabic it is known as Ṭúr Síná or Jabal Músá (Mountain of Moses).

3 Bahá'u'lláh, *Gleanings from the Writings of Bahá'u'lláh,* p. 16.

4 Bahá'u'lláh, *Gleanings from the Writings of Bahá'u'lláh,* p. 325.

sacred of the Muslim holy cities. Muslims around the world face Mecca during their daily prayers. Every year, during the last month of the Islamic calendar, several million Muslims make the pilgrimage, or Ḥajj, to Mecca.

Mecca was a religious centre before the time of Muḥammad, and several holy sites within the sacred precincts of its great mosque, called al-Ḥaram, had religious significance in pre-Islamic times. Abraham built the Kaaba, a windowless cube-shaped building, now situated in the courtyard of the mosque. In the south-eastern corner of the Kaaba is the Black Stone, given to Abraham by the angel Gabriel. Also within the precincts of the mosque is the sacred well, called the Zamzam, used by Hagar, the wife of Abraham and the mother of Ishmael, the son of Abraham.

8.3.5 Jerusalem

Jerusalem is the capital (this is not recognized internationally) and the largest city of Israel, situated between the Mediterranean Sea and the Dead Sea, about ninety three kilometres east of Tel Aviv, the financial centre of Israel. Jerusalem dominates the intersection of Israel and the Palestinian West Bank. Jews, Christians, and Muslims all consider Jerusalem to be a holy city since it contains sites sacred to all three religions.

According to the Old Testament, David brought the sacred Ark of the Covenant to Jerusalem and installed it in a new tabernacle. He built a royal palace and other buildings, and strengthened the city's fortifications. Although David greatly expanded the Kingdom of Israel and made Jerusalem its capital, the city and the temple he built were quite modest. Solomon, his son and successor, improved the temple and enlarged the city. He built a city wall and many buildings on a scale of magnificence previously unknown in Israel.

Solomon's temple was destroyed and the Jews exiled by the Babylonians in the year 586 BC. In 539 BC, the Persians conquered Babylonia and allowed the Jews to return to Jerusalem the following year. The construction of a new temple, the Second Jewish Temple, was then undertaken on the ruins of the old. Alexander the Great captured Jerusalem in 333 BC. After his death, Jerusalem was ruled by the Egyptians and later, the Syrians.

In 165 BC Judas Maccabeus liberated Jerusalem from the Syrians and Jerusalem became a major Jewish pilgrimage site.

In a letter to the chairman of the United Nation Special committee on Palestine, dated 14 July 1947, Shoghi Effendi highlights the significance of Jerusalem for the Jews. He states, "... whereas Jerusalem is the spiritual centre of Christendom it is not the administrative centre of either the Church of Rome or any other Christian denomination. Likewise although it is regarded by Moslems as the spot where one of its most sacred shrines is situated, the Holy Sites of the Muhammadan Faith, and the centre of its pilgrimages, are to be found in Arabia, not in Palestine. The Jews alone offer somewhat of parallel to the attachment which the Bahá'ís have for this country inasmuch as

Jerusalem holds the remains of their Holy Temple and was the seat of both the religious and political institutions associated with their past history."[1]

8.4 Hebrew Prophets

In paragraph 20, Bahá'u'lláh makes reference to three Hebrew Prophets, Isaiah, Elijah and Solomon.

8.4.1 Exaltation by Isaiah

In statement (a) Bahá'u'lláh confirms that He is the One "*Whom the tongue of Isaiah hath extolled.*"

Amongst Christians, Isaiah who lived during the 8th century BC, is considered as one of the major prophets of the Old Testament. The Book of Isaiah is the first of the three books of prophecy in the Hebrew Bible. The book has sixty–six chapters. The first thirty–nine chapters prophesize the destruction of Judah, the most powerful of the twelve tribes of Israel. The other twenty–seven chapters prophesize the coming of the Day of Days, the establishment of the Kingdom of God on earth and the restoration of the nation of Israel.

In his prophecies about the second coming of Christ, Isaiah mentions that "*... the glory of the LORD will be revealed, and all mankind together will see it. For the mouth of the LORD has spoken.*"[2]

In exaltation of the Glory of God, Isaiah states: "*And the Gentiles shall see thy righteousness, and all kings thy glory: and thou shalt be called by a new name, which the mouth of the LORD shall name. Thou shalt also be a crown of glory in the hand of the LORD, and a royal diadem in the hand of thy God.*"[3]

With the coming of the Glory of God, Isaiah calls on Zion, Jerusalem and the Daughter of Zion: "*Awake, awake, O Zion, clothe yourself with strength. Put on your garments of splendour, O Jerusalem, the holy city. The uncircumcised and defiled will not enter you again. Shake off your dust; rise up, sit enthroned, O Jerusalem. Free yourself from the chains on your neck, O captive Daughter of Zion.*"[4] The Biblical scholars have interpreted the Daughter of Zion in different terms that include the Jewish people and the Temple Mount.

8.4.2 Hastening of Elijah

In statement (d), Bahá'u'lláh announces, "*Elijah hath hastened unto My court and hath circumambulated in the day-time and in the night-season My throne of glory.*" Elijah was one of the prophets in the Kingdom of Israel in the 8th century BC. According to 'Abdu'l-Bahá, after the departure of Moses and "*... following the decline of the glory of Solomon's era ... God sent Elijah,*

---

1 Shoghi Effendi, in *Lights of Guidance*, p. 498.
2 Isaiah 40:5
3 Isaiah 62:2–3
4 Isaiah 52: 1–3

the prophet, who redeemed the people, renewed the law of God and established an era of new life for Israel."[1]

In the Bible there is a prophecy that Elijah will return "... *before the coming of the great and terrible day of the Lord.*"[2] 'Abdu'l-Bahá explains: "*in the Gospel the return of Christ and Elijah is promised.*"[3]

8.4.3 Solomon

In statement (e), Bahá'u'lláh states, "*Solomon in all his majesty circles in adoration around Me in this day.*" Solomon was a minor prophet and one of the Kings of Israel. According to the Hebrew Bible, he built the First Jewish Temple in Jerusalem. He was great in wisdom, wealth and power. According to 'Abdu'l-Bahá, during the reign of Solomon "... *science and art were made known to mankind. Even Greek philosophers became students of Solomon's teaching.*"[4] Numerous historical records also indicate "... *the Philosophers of Greece such as Pythagoras, acquired the major part of their philosophy, both divine and material, from the disciples of Solomon.*"[5]

1 'Abdu'l-Bahá, *The Promulgation of Universal Peace*, p. 406.
2 Malachi 3:23
3 'Abdu'l-Bahá, *Some Answered Questions*, p. 39.
4 'Abdu'l-Bahá, *'Abdu'l-Bahá in London*, p. 42.
5 'Abdu'l-Bahá, *The Secret of Divine Civilization*, p. 77.

8.5 Activities

1. What is the significance of statement (a)?

2. Describe your understanding of statement (b). What is the significance of Carmel and Zion mentioned in this statement?

3. What is your understanding of statement (c)?

4. What is the significance of statement (d)?

5. What is the significance of statement alluding to Solomon in statement (e)?

6. What is your understanding of statement (f)?

7. What is the meaning of the claim made by "the voice of Mecca" in statement (g)?

8. What is the "separation" suffered by Jerusalem, as mentioned in statement (g)?

8.6 Glossary

Term	Meaning
Adore	Love and respect (someone) deeply
Agony	Extreme physical or mental suffering
Astir	In a state of exited movement
Bestir	Exert or rouse oneself
Circumambulate	To circle around something out of love and worship
Countenance	A person's face or facial expression
Extol	Praise enthusiastically
Hasten	Move or travel hurriedly
Laden	Heavily loaded
Prostrate	Lying stretched out on the ground with one's face downward.
Redolent	Strongly reminiscent or suggestive of (something); strongly smelling of; fragrant
Waft	Pass or cause to pass easily or gently through or as if through the air
Writ	An official legal paper telling someone to do or not to do a particular thing

9. POTENCY OF HIS REVELATION

9.1 Introduction

This chapter covers paragraphs 21–24. Read these paragraphs and reflect on the contents before starting the lesson. In this section of his letter, Shoghi Effendi highlights further the potency and the power of the Revelation of Bahá'u'lláh by citing more statements from His Writings.

In this chapter, you need to look for and understand the following **key concepts**:

a) Bahá'u'lláh is "*... invested with so invincible an authority that all the powers of the earth are unable to withstand Him.*"[1]
b) The followers of Bahá'u'lláh can draw on His invincible power to attain victory when facing crises and challenges.
c) This Day is referred to by Bahá'u'lláh as "King of Days".
d) The past Manifestations of God have longed to attain the presence of Bahá'u'lláh.
e) The title of Muḥammad, the "Seal of the Prophets", fully demonstrates the station of this Day.
f) Every letter uttered by Bahá'u'lláh is invested with creative and regenerative power.

9.2 Paragraphs under study

21. "*By the righteousness of God,*" Bahá'u'lláh wishing to reveal the full potency of His invincible power asserts, "*should a man, all alone, arise in the name of Bahá and put on the armour of His love, him will the Almighty cause to be victorious, though the forces of earth and heaven be arrayed against him.*"[2] "*By God besides Whom is none other God! Should any one arise for the triumph of our Cause, him will God render*

---

1 Bahá'u'lláh, *Tablets of Bahá'u'lláh*, p. 48.
2 Statement (a)

victorious though tens of thousands of enemies be leagued against him. And if his love for Me wax stronger, God will establish his ascendancy over all the powers of earth and heaven. Thus have We breathed the spirit of power into all regions."[1]

22. "*This is the King of Days,*" He thus extols the age that has witnessed the advent of His Revelation, "*the Day that hath seen the coming of the Best-beloved, Him Who through all eternity hath been acclaimed the Desire of the World.*"[2] "*The world of being shineth in this Day with the resplendency of this Divine Revelation. All created things extol its saving grace and sing its praises. The universe is wrapt in an ecstasy of joy and gladness. The Scriptures of past Dispensations celebrate the great jubilee that must needs greet this most great Day of God. Well is it with him that hath lived to see this Day and hath recognised its station.*"[3] "*Were mankind to give heed in a befitting manner to no more than one word of such a praise it would be so filled with delight as to be overpowered and lost in wonder. Entranced, it would then shine forth resplendent above the horizon of true understanding.*"[4]

23. "*Be fair, ye peoples of the world;*" He thus appeals to mankind, "*is it meet and seemly for you to question the authority of one Whose presence 'He Who conversed with God' (Moses) hath longed to attain, the beauty of Whose countenance 'God's Well-beloved' (Muḥammad) had yearned to behold, through the potency of Whose love the 'Spirit of God' (Jesus) ascended to heaven, for Whose sake the 'Primal Point' (the Báb) offered up His life?*"[5] "*Seize your chance,*" He admonishes His followers, "*inasmuch as a fleeting moment in this Day excelleth centuries of a bygone age … Neither sun nor moon hath witnessed a day such as this … It is evident that every age in which a Manifestation of God hath lived is divinely ordained and may, in a sense, be characterised as God's appointed Day. This Day, however, is unique and is to be distinguished from those that have preceded it. The designation 'Seal of the Prophets' fully reveals and demonstrates its high station.*"[6]

24. Expatiating on the forces latent in His Revelation Bahá'u'lláh reveals the following: "*Through the movement of Our Pen of glory We have, at the bidding of the omnipotent Ordainer, breathed a new life into every human frame and instilled into every word a fresh potency. All created things proclaim the evidences of this world-wide regeneration.*"[7] "*This is,*" He adds, "*the most great, the most joyful tidings imparted by the pen*

---

[1] Statement (b)
[2] Statement (c)
[3] Statement (d)
[4] Statement (e)
[5] Statement (f)
[6] Statement (g)
[7] Statement (h)

of this wronged One to mankind."[1] "*How great,*" He in another passage exclaims, "*is the Cause! How staggering the weight of its message! This is the Day of which it hath been said: 'O my son! verily God will bring everything to light though it were but the weight of a grain of mustard seed, and hidden in a rock, or in the heavens or in the earth; for God is subtile, informed of all.'*"[2] "*By the righteousness of the one true God! If one speck of a jewel be lost and buried beneath a mountain of stones, and lie hidden beyond the seven seas, the Hand of Omnipotence will assuredly reveal it in this day, pure and cleansed from dross.*"[3] "*He that partaketh of the waters of My Revelation will taste all the incorruptible delights ordained by God from the beginning that hath no beginning to the end that hath no end.*"[4] "*Every single letter proceeding from Our mouth is endowed with such regenerative power as to enable it to bring into existence a new creation—a creation the magnitude of which is inscrutable to all save God. He verily hath knowledge of all things.*"[5] "*It is in Our power, should We wish it, to enable a speck of floating dust to generate, in less than the twinkling of an eye, suns of infinite, of unimaginable splendour, to cause a dewdrop to develop into vast and numberless oceans, to infuse into every letter such a force as to empower it to unfold all the knowledge of past and future ages.*"[6] "*We are possessed of such power which, if brought to light, will transmute the most deadly of poisons into a panacea of unfailing efficacy.*"[7]

9.3 Drawing on invincible power

The statements cited in paragraph 21 indicate that Bahá'u'lláh is "*... invested with so invincible an authority that all the powers of the earth are unable to withstand Him.*"[8] The spirit of this power is wafted over all the regions. The followers of Bahá'u'lláh can draw on this power to attain victory when faced with crises and challenges.

Bahá'u'lláh promises His assistance and blessings for those who arise to aid His Cause: "*We behold you from Our realm of glory, and shall aid whosoever will arise for the triumph of Our Cause with the hosts of the Concourse on high and a company of Our favoured angels.*"[9] In *The Kitáb-i-Aqdas*, He counsels, "*Arise ye, under all conditions, to render service to the*

---

1 Statement (i)
2 Statement (j)
3 Statement (k)
4 Statement (l)
5 Statement (m)
6 Statement (n)
7 Statement (o)
8 Bahá'u'lláh, *Tablets of Bahá'u'lláh*, p. 48.
9 Bahá'u'lláh *Gleanings from the Writings of Bahá'u'lláh*, p. 92.

Cause, for God will assuredly assist you through the power of His sovereignty which overshadoweth the worlds."[1]

'Abdu'l-Bahá confirms: "*Your Lord hath assuredly promised His servants who are firm and steadfast to render them victorious at all times, to exalt their word, propagate their power, diffuse their lights, strengthen their hearts, elevate their banners, assist their hosts, brighten their stars, increase the abundance of the showers of mercy upon them, and enable the brave lions to conquer.*"[2] Shoghi Effendi also reiterates the Promise of Bahá'u'lláh: "At all times we must look at the greatness of the Cause, and remember that Bahá'u'lláh will assist all who arise in His service."[3]

9.4 King of Days

In paragraph 22, Bahá'u'lláh refers to this Day as the "King of Days". The greatness and significance of this age is one of the cardinal features of the Revelation of Bahá'u'lláh. He, in many of His Writings, indicates that this is the Day of God, a Day, which all the previous Manifestations of God longed to attain. The Revelation of Bahá'u'lláh has been the "*… purpose underlying all creation*".[4] He counsels the people of the earth: "*Scatter the idols of your vain imaginings in the name of your Lord, the All-Glorious, the All-Knowing, and turn ye unto Him in this Day which God hath made the King of days.*"[5]

Bahá'u'lláh also warns us: "*Were the virtues of this Day to be recounted, all would be thunderstruck, except those whom thy Lord hath exempted.*"[6] He also provides some glimpses of the greatness of this Day and its distinction from the previous ages in His Writings. There are other similar statements by Bahá'u'lláh cited in *The Advent of Divine Justice*. In this Day, as Bahá'u'lláh asserts in these passages:[7]

a) "*The highest essence and most perfect expression of whatsoever the peoples of old have either said or written hath … been sent down from the heaven of the Will of the All-Possessing.*"
b) "*God's most excellent favours have been poured out upon men.*"
c) "*His most mighty grace hath been infused into all created things.*"
d) "*… the Ocean of God's mercy hath been manifested unto men.*"
e) "*The Daystar of His loving-kindness hath shed its radiance upon them (men).*"
f) "*The clouds of His bountiful favour have overshadowed the whole of mankind.*"
g) "*A door is open wider than both heaven and earth.*"

---

1 Bahá'u'lláh, *The Kitáb-i-Aqdas,* p. 46.
2 'Abdu'l-Bahá, *Bahá'í World Faith*, p. 357.
3 Shoghi Effendi, *The Compilations of Compilations*, vol. II, p. 223.
4 Bahá'u'lláh, cited in *The Advent of Divine Justice*, p. 77.
5 Bahá'u'lláh, *The Summons of the Lord of Hosts*, p. 61.
6 Bahá'u'lláh, cited in *The Advent of Divine Justice,* p. 79.
7 Shoghi Effendi, *The Advent of Divine Justice,* pp. 77–79.

h) *"The eye of the mercy of Him Who is the Desire of the worlds is turned towards all men."*
i) *"A different Sun hath arisen."*
j) *"A different Heaven hath been adorned with its stars and its planets."*
k) *"The world is another world, and the Cause another Cause."*
l) *"An atom, in these days, is as the sun, a drop as the ocean."*
m) *"One single breath exhaled in the love of God and for His service is written down by the Pen of Glory as a princely deed."*

The significance and greatness of the Revelation of Bahá'u'lláh does not contradict the basic teaching of the Bahá'í Faith on the unity of the Manifestations of God. According to Shoghi Effendi: "No distinction can be made amongst the Prophets in the sense that They all proceed from One Source, and are of One Essence. But their stations and function in this world are different."[1]

The greatness of this Day is due mainly to the intensity and distinctive character of the Revelation of Bahá'u'lláh as well as the station of Bahá'u'lláh as the Supreme Manifestation of God. The bounties showered upon humanity in this age have potentially existed in previous Revelations. However, humanity was not mature enough to receive these bounties and the moment in time had not yet arrived for the "Glory of God" to be revealed in such intensity.

9.5 Seal of the Prophets

In paragraph 23, Bahá'u'lláh describes the longing of past Manifestations of God to attain His presence. In statement (g), He states that the title given to Muḥammad as the "Seal of the Prophets", fully demonstrates the significance of this Day. The term "Seal of the Prophets" refers to the following verse in the Qur'án: *"Muḥammad is not the father of any of your men, but He is the Messenger of God and the Seal of the Prophets."*[2]

The word "Seal" in the above verse has been interpreted by some Muslim scholars to mean the: "Last", "Final", "Ornament" (something to adorn with), "Ring", "Seal" (as in a stamp sealing closed a document), "Seal" as in a seal of authority, and officiating a document. Such interpretations imply that Muḥammad is the last Manifestation of God and there will be no more Divine Revelations in the future.

However, there are many verses in the Qur'án and also the ḥadí<u>th</u> that contradict such finality. In such verses reference is made to the return of Jesus, the coming of the Mihdí and prophecies of a new Revelation from God. Hence, Bahá'í scholars have argued that there should be more convincing interpretations for this verse. One of those arguments, which relate to the statement made by Bahá'u'lláh, is given here.

---

1 Shoghi Effendi, a letter written of behalf of Shoghi Effendi to an individual, in *Lights of Guidance*, p. 471.

2 *Qur'án* 33:40

In Islamic theology, the Manifestations of God are divided into different categories depending on the degree of Their independence and the nature of Their Revelation. In particular, there are two distinctive groups: Messengers (in Arabic, *Rasúl*) and prophets (in Arabic, *Nabí*—this is the word used in the above verse of the Qur'án). The Messengers are the independent Manifestations of God such as Muḥammad. Prophets are sometimes defined as those who receive their inspiration in the form of dreams, such as the minor prophets of Judaism. In the Qur'án, people such as Isaac, Jacob, Ismael, Idrís, David and Solomon are also referred to as prophets.

Hence, if the Seal of the Prophets indicates any finality, it is the finality of the Prophetic Cycle or the era of revelation from God through the medium of dreams and visions. Moreover this indicates that after Islám, revelation occurs through direct inspiration from God. The reference of Bahá'u'lláh to the "Seal of Prophets" in statement (g) is an indication of how different the nature of this Revelation is from the ones received during the Prophetic Cycle.

In *The Kitáb-i-Íqán*, Bahá'u'lláh provides a very detailed explanation regarding the issue of finality.

9.6 Creative power of the Word

In paragraph 24, Shoghi Effendi cites a number of statements from Bahá'u'lláh on the regenerative power embedded in every letter uttered by Bahá'u'lláh. Every Word revealed by the Manifestations of God is endowed with a creative power. The Word is the outer form of the unlimited spiritual forces released through the Revelation. These forces affect the world of creation in two ways.

On the one hand, these forces influence the hearts of the believers, nurture and enhance their spirit of Faith and result in spiritual growth and transformation. Bahá'u'lláh, in *The Kitáb-i-Íqán,* indicates that "*the object of every Revelation*" from God is "*to effect a transformation in the whole character of mankind, a transformation that shall manifest itself both outwardly and inwardly, that shall affect both its inner life and external conditions.*" [1]

The inner life is the life of the soul. It is the attitude and the frame of mind, the thoughts and motivations of an individual. The outer life, on the other hand, is the manifestation of the inner life in ones actions, behaviour, and relationship with others. It is the translation of attitudes and qualities into words and deeds.

At the same time the Word of God releases spiritual forces that set in motion various processes towards attaining the plan of God. Shoghi Effendi refers to such processes as "... the two parallel processes of integration and

---

[1] Bahá'u'lláh, *The Kitáb-i-Íqán*, p. 240.

disintegration associated respectively with the rising fortunes of God's infant Faith and the sinking fortunes of the institutions of a declining civilisation."[1]

As the result of the commitment and endeavours of the believers and the spiritual impact of the processes set in motion, the Mission destined for a Revelation from God is attained.

Adib Taherzadeh illustrates the creative power of the Word of God by observing the influence of one injunction from Bahá'u'lláh:

> "A careful study of the Faith of Bahá'u'lláh will demonstrate that the efficacy and potency of His words are unprecedented in the annals of mankind. We can already witness the creative power of the words of Bahá'u'lláh within the present society. To cite one example, Bahá'u'lláh wrote only a few lines *in The Kitáb-i-Aqdas* enjoining upon His followers to establish, in every town, a House of Justice (at present known as a Spiritual Assembly). This injunction, written just over a hundred years ago by a prisoner in Akká, exerted such an influence upon the hearts that thousands of men and women from all walks of life, of all colours and backgrounds, left their homes, scattered throughout the world, pioneered to the most inhospitable outposts of the globe, suffered many hardships and difficulties, sacrificed their substance and poured out their resources in order to establish these institutions."[2]

---

1 Shoghi Effendi, *Messages to the Bahá'í World: 1950–1957,* p. 102.
2 Adib Taherzadeh, *The Revelation of Bahá'u'lláh*, vol. 2, p. 122.

9.7 Activities

1. What is the nature of the "victory" that Bahá'u'lláh refers to in statement (a)?

2. In relationship to statement (b), provide an example from Bahá'í history.

3. What is the significance of this Day being referred to as the "*King of Days*" in statement (c)?

4. What is your understanding of statement (f)?

5. Consider statement (g). How does "*a fleeting moment in this Day ...*" excel "*... centuries of a bygone age*"?

6. How does the title of Muḥammad, "Seal of the Prophets" distinguish this Day from those that have preceded it (statement (g))?

7. What is your understanding of statement (h)?

8. What are the implications of statements (j) and (k)?

9. What does Bahá'u'lláh mean by the "waters" of His Revelation in statement (l)?

10. Reflect on statement (m) in relationship to the two processes of destruction and integration, which have been taking place since the birth of the Revelation of Bahá'u'lláh.

11. What is your understanding of statement (n)?

9.8 Glossary

Term	Meaning
Acclaim	To greet with approval; publicly recognise
Countenance	A face; the appearance or expression of a person's face
Dross	Something that is of very poor quality, refuse, rubbish, worthless matter
Ecstasy	(A state of) very strong feeling, esp. of joy and happiness:
Entrance	To fill with great wonder and delight
Excel	To be the best or better than, surpass
Expatiate	To speak or write a lot or in detail about
Extol	To praise very highly
Impart (to/upon)	To give or pass on (information, qualities, feelings, etc.)
Inscrutable	(said of a person or a person's facial expression, actions or behaviour) Very difficult to understand; unfathomable; impenetrable; enigmatic; mysterious
Invincible	Too strong to be defeated
Jubilee	(A special occasion marking) the return of the date of some important event
League against	To unite or join against
Panacea	A medicine or other treatment that is supposed to cure any illness
Partake	To eat or drink esp. something offered
Righteousness	Morally blameless; having just cause
Speck	A very small piece, spot, or coloured mark
Staggering	Almost unbelievable; very surprising and shocking
Transmute	To change from one form, nature, substance, etc., into another, esp. of a better kind
Wax	To grow gradually larger after being small or incomplete.

10. UNPARALLELED REVELATION

10.1 Introduction

This chapter covers paragraphs 25–27. Read these paragraphs and reflect on the contents before starting the lesson. The statements cited by Shoghi Effendi in this section highlight the unparalleled character of the Revelation of Bahá'u'lláh. They cover a variety of concepts including the station of the true believer, the significance of recognizing the station of Bahá'u'lláh, the copiousness of the Revelation of Bahá'u'lláh, and the unassailable nature of His Revelation.

In this chapter, you need to look for and understand the following **key concepts**:

a) In paragraph 25, Bahá'u'lláh alludes to the high station of the true believer the full measure of which is concealed in this earthly life for the protection of the followers.

b) The statements (c) and (d) highlight the significance of recognizing the station of Bahá'u'lláh and the intensity of His Revelation, respectively.

c) In the statements cited in paragraph 25, Bahá'u'lláh illustrates the unsurpassed character of His Revelation.

d) In the statements cited in paragraph 26, Bahá'u'lláh demonstrates the unassailable nature of His Revelation.

10.2 Paragraphs under study

25. Estimating the station of the true believer He remarks: *"By the sorrows, which afflict the beauty of the All-Glorious! Such is the station ordained for the true believer that if to an extent smaller than a needle's eye the glory of that station were to be unveiled to mankind, every beholder would be consumed away in his longing to attain it. For this reason it hath been decreed that in this earthly life the full measure of the glory of his own station should remain concealed from the eyes of such a believer."*[1] *"If the veil be lifted,"* He similarly affirms, *"and the full glory of the station of those who have turned wholly towards God, and in their love for Him renounced the world, be made manifest, the entire creation would be dumbfounded."*[2]

26. Stressing the superlative character of His Revelation as compared with the Dispensation preceding it, Bahá'u'lláh makes the following affirmation: *"If all the peoples of the world be invested with the powers and attributes destined for the Letters of the Living, the Báb's chosen disciples, whose station is ten thousand times more glorious than any which the apostles of old have attained, and if they, one and all, should, swift as the twinkling of an eye, hesitate to recognise the light of My Revelation, their faith shall be of no avail and they shall be accounted among the infidels."*[3] *"So tremendous is the outpouring of Divine grace in this Dispensation that if mortal hands could be swift enough to record them, within the space of a single day and night there would stream verses of such number as to be equivalent to the whole of the Persian Bayán."*[4]

27. *"Give heed to my warning, ye people of Persia,"* He thus addresses His countrymen, *"If I be slain at your hands, God will assuredly raise up one who will fill the seat made vacant through my death; for such is God's method carried into effect of old, and no change can ye find in God's mode of dealing."*[5] *"Should they attempt to conceal His light on the continent, He will assuredly rear His head in the midmost heart of the ocean and, raising His voice, proclaim: 'I am the lifegiver of the world!' ... And if they cast Him into a darksome pit, they will find Him seated on earth's loftiest heights calling aloud to all mankind: 'Lo, the Desire of the world is come in His majesty, His sovereignty, His transcendent dominion!' And if He be buried beneath the depths of the earth, His Spirit soaring to the apex of heaven shall peal the summons: 'Behold ye the coming of the Glory; witness ye the Kingdom of God, the most Holy, the Gracious, the All-Powerful!'"*[6] *"Within the throat of this Youth,"* is yet another astounding statement, *"there lie prisoned accents which, if revealed to mankind to an extent smaller than a needle's eye, would suffice to cause every mountain to crumble, the leaves of the trees to be discoloured and their fruits to fall; would compel every head to bow down in worship and every face to turn in adoration towards this omnipotent Ruler Who, at sundry times and in diverse manners, appeareth as a devouring flame, as a billowing ocean, as a radiant light, as the tree which, rooted in the soil of holiness, lifteth its branches and*

---

1 Statement (a)
2 Statement (b)
3 Statement (c)
4 Statement (d)
5 Statement (e)
6 Statement (f)

spreadeth out its limbs as far as and beyond the throne of deathless glory."[1]

10.3 Becoming a true believer

Bahá'u'lláh alludes to the high station of the true believer in the statements cited in paragraph 25. However, the full measure of this station is concealed from humanity in this earthly life for their protection. In one of His Tablets, Bahá'u'lláh states, "*We dare not, in this Day, lift the veil that concealeth the exalted station which every true believer can attain, for the joy which such a revelation must provoke might well cause a few to faint away and die.*"[2]

Becoming a true believer is a challenge and requires constant endeavour. The recognition of the station of Bahá'u'lláh is only the first step in the process. This requires obedience to His commandments and complete submission to His Will in tests and tribulations.[3]

The process is a spiritual journey through which the traveller "... *must cling to the robe of obedience to the commandments, and hold fast to the cord of shunning all forbidden things.*" When this is done then "... *he may be nourished from the cup of the Law and informed of the mysteries of Truth.*"[4]

In this process, we need "... to let the Power of God help recreate us make us true Bahá'ís in deed as well as in belief."[5] 'Abdu'l-Bahá states that the Bahá'ís "*should justify their claim to be Bahá'ís by deeds and not by name.*"[6] He then identifies the characteristics of a true Bahá'í:

"He is a true Bahá'í who[7]

a) strives by day and by night to progress and advance along the path of human endeavour,

b) whose most cherished desire is so to live and act as to enrich and illuminate the world,

c) whose source of inspiration is the essence of divine virtue, whose aim in life is so to conduct himself as to be the cause of infinite progress."[8]

He finally states that in this Dispensation, "... *true faith is no mere acknowledgement of the unity of God, but rather the living of a life that will manifest all the perfections and virtues implied in such belief.*"[9] The process of transformation in the inner and outer lives of the individual is challenging and full of tests. The tests are either in the form of physical hardships and

---

1 Statement (g)

2 Bahá'u'lláh, *Gleanings from the Writings of Bahá'u'lláh*, p. 7.

3 Bahá'u'lláh, *The Kitáb-i-Aqdas*, p. 19.

4 Bahá'u'lláh, *Seven Valleys and Four Valleys,* p. 40.

5 The Universal House of Justice, a letter written on behalf of the Universal House of Justice to a believer, in *Lights of Guidance*, p. 76.

6 'Abdu'l-Bahá, *Compilation of Compilations*, vol. 2, p. 346.

7 List form added for emphasis.

8 'Abdu'l-Bahá, *Compilation of Compilations*, vol. 2, p. 346.

9 'Abdu'l-Bahá: *Compilation of Compilations*, vol. 2, p. 347.

persecutions, similar to the sufferings of the believers in Persia, or mental tests, which are very common at this time of the development of the Bahá'í Faith. We can win these spiritual battles when we have surrendered our will to the Will of Bahá'u'lláh.

The believer can eventually attain the station of a true believer, which, according to 'Abdu'l-Bahá "... *is the same as the one ordained for such prophets of the house of Israel.*"[1]

10.4 Copiousness of His Revelation

In the statements cited in paragraph 26, Bahá'u'lláh illustrates the unsurpassed character of His Revelation. The statements (c) and (d) highlight the significance of recognizing Bahá'u'lláh and the intensity of His Revelation, respectively.

During His lifetime, Bahá'u'lláh revealed an ocean of His Utterances in the form of books, letters to individuals in reply to their questions (known as Tablets), and prayers and meditations. Many of His Writings are either in His own handwriting or dictated to His secretary and sealed by Him. It is estimated that all the Writings of Bahá'u'lláh can be compiled into more than one hundred volumes.[2]

As Bahá'u'lláh has attested in statement (d), the outpourings of His Pen and the swiftness of His Revelation have been unique in religious history. In *God Passes By*, Shoghi Effendi cites a number of statements from Bahá'u'lláh on the copiousness of His Revelation:[3]

a) *"Such are the outpourings ... from the clouds of Divine Bounty that within the space of an hour the equivalent of a thousand verses hath been revealed."*

b) *"So great is the grace vouchsafed in this day that in a single day and night, were an amanuensis capable of accomplishing it to be found, the equivalent of the Persian Bayán would be sent down from the heaven of Divine holiness."*

c) *"I swear by God! In those days the equivalent of all that hath been sent down aforetime unto the Prophets hath been revealed."*

d) *"That which hath already been revealed in this land (Adrianople), secretaries are incapable of transcribing. It has, therefore, remained for the most part untranscribed."*

According to Shoghi Effendi, the pace of revelation was particularly intense in Adrianople. An eyewitness explains: "... the Divine verses were raining down in such number that it was impossible to record them. Mírzá Áqá Ján wrote them as they were dictated, while the Most Great Branch was continually occupied in transcribing them. There was not a moment to spare."[4]

---

1 'Abdu'l-Bahá in The *World Order of Bahá'u'lláh*, p. 111.

2 Bahá'u'lláh, *Epistle to the Son of the Wolf*, p. 115.

3 Shoghi Effendi, *God Passes By*, pp. 170–171.

4 Shoghi Effendi, *God Passes By*, p. 170.

According to Nabíl, "A number of secretaries were busy day and night and yet they were unable to cope with the task. Among them was Mírzá Báqir-i-Shírází ... He alone transcribed no less than two thousand verses every day. He laboured during six or seven months. Every month the equivalent of several volumes would be transcribed by him and sent to Persia. About twenty volumes, in his fine penmanship, he left behind as a remembrance for Mírzá Áqá Ján."[1]

In a spoken chronicle, Siyyid Asadu'lláh-i-Qumí has described how Bahá'u'lláh revealed a Tablet when he was in His presence:

> "I recall that as Mírzá Áqá Ján (Bahá'u'lláh's amanuensis) was recording the words of Bahá'u'lláh at the time of revelation, the shrill sound of His pen could be heard from a distance of about twenty paces. In the history of the Faith not a great deal has been recorded about the manner in which Tablets were revealed. For this reason ... I shall describe it ...
>
> "Mírzá Áqá Ján had a large inkpot the size of a small bowl. He also had available about ten to twelve pens and large sheets of paper in stacks. In those days Mírzá Áqá Ján received all letters, which arrived for Bahá'u'lláh. He would bring these into the presence of Bahá'u'lláh and, having obtained permission, would read them. Afterwards the Blessed Beauty would direct him to take up his pen and record the Tablet, which was revealed in reply ...
>
> "Such was the speed with which he used to write the revealed Word that the ink of the first word was scarcely yet dry when the whole page was finished. It seemed as if someone had dipped a lock of hair in the ink and applied it over the whole page. None of the words was written clearly and they were illegible to all except Mírzá Áqá Ján. There were occasions when even he could not decipher the words and had to seek the help of Bahá'u'lláh. When revelation has ceased, then in accordance with Bahá'u'lláh's instruction Mírzá Áqá Ján would rewrite the Tablet in his best hand and dispatch it to its destination ..."[2]

10.5 Unassailable Revelation

In the statements cited in paragraph 27, Bahá'u'lláh illustrates the unassailable nature of His Revelation. Humanity has witnessed the dominant nature of the Revelation of Bahá'u'lláh described in statement (f) as it has evolved and grown since 1844, despite sustained and severe opposition from the Muslim clergy and the powerful rulers of His time.

Bahá'u'lláh spared the people from experiencing the "*accents*" referred to in statement (g), which He said, lay prisoned in His throat and which, if

---

1 Shoghi Effendi, *God Passes By*, p. 170.
2 Adib Taherzadeh, *The Revelation of Bahá'u'lláh*, vol. 1, pp. 35–36.

revealed could "*cause every mountain to crumble*" and "*compel every head to bow down in worship*". However, some believers who attained the presence of Bahá'u'lláh had the bounty of getting a glimpse of His hidden divine power. One example was Siyyid Ismá'íl of Zavárih surnamed Dhábíḥ (Sacrifice) by Bahá'u'lláh. Adib Taherzadeh provides an account of Dhábíḥ's story:

"He was a devout man highly esteemed for his piety and rectitude of conduct, his learning and knowledge. He was converted to the Faith in the early days of the Báb's ministry, attained His presence in the house of the Imám- Jum'ih of Iṣfáhán ... In *The Kitáb-i- Badí'*, revealed a few years later in Adrianople, Bahá'u'lláh Himself has described His meeting with Dhábíḥ on that occasion. As was customary at that time of day, their host had provided several trays of various fruits and sweetmeats. Dhábíḥ was invited by Bahá'u'lláh to partake of the food but he begged most humbly and earnestly to receive instead, through Bahá'u'lláh's bounty, a portion of spiritual food from the unseen treasury of His divine knowledge. Favourable to his plea, Bahá'u'lláh summoned Dhábíḥ to sit before Him and hearken to His words—words of incomparable power and awe which were filled with spiritual significance and which, according to Bahá'u'lláh's testimony, no one is capable of describing.

"By hearing the utterances of Bahá'u'lláh on that day, Dhábíḥ was transformed and worlds of spirit were opened before his eyes. After this meeting he remained in a state of spiritual intoxication, wholly devoted to Bahá'u'lláh, his love for Him intensifying with the passing of each day.

"In order to pay homage to his Lord and to express his inner feelings of humility and self-effacement towards Him, Dhábíḥ took upon himself the task of sweeping the approaches to the house of Bahá'u'lláh at the hour of dawn. In those days one of the duties of a servant in any household was to sweep a small portion of the path leading to the entrance of the house. As a token of humility and lowliness, however, Dhábíḥ would, instead of using a brush, unwind his green turban, the ensign of his holy lineage, and with it would sweep the approaches of the house of Bahá'u'lláh. He would then place in the fold of his cloak the dust on which the feet of his Beloved had trodden and, unwilling that others should tread on it, would carry it all the way to the river to throw it into its waters.

"The story of Dhábíḥ is that of a passionate lover. The object of his adoration was Bahá'u'lláh, Who had ignited within his breast the fire of the love of God, a fire so intense that it began to consume his whole being. Eventually he reached a state where he would neither eat nor drink. For forty days he abstained from food. Unable, at last, to check the crushing force of love that pressed upon his soul, he came one day, at the hour of dawn, to the house of Bahá'u'lláh and for the last time swept its approaches with his turban. After performing this task, he paid a visit to the home of Áqá Muḥammad-Riḍá where he met some of the friends for the last time. Later he obtained a razor, went to the bank of the Tigris and there turning his face towards the house of Bahá'u'lláh, took his life by cutting his throat."[1]

[1] Adib Taherzadeh, *The Revelation of Bahá'u'lláh*, vol. 1, pp. 101–103.

10.6 Activities

1. Describe your understanding of the station of a true believer in the Revelation of Bahá'u'lláh.

2. Why is the station of a true believer concealed in the physical life?

3. How can one attain true faith?

4. What is your understanding of statement (c)?

5. How does the intensity of the Revelation of Bahá'u'lláh compare to the past Dispensations?

6. What is your understanding of statement (e)?

7. What is your understanding of statement (f)?

10.7 Glossary

Term	Meaning
Acquiescent	Ready to agree without argument
Avail	To be of use or advantage
Compel	To make (a person or thing) do something, by force, moral persuasion, or orders that must be obeyed
Divulge	To tell or make known (what has been secret); reveal
Dumbfounded	Unable to speak because of shock, surprise, or lack of understanding
Gird (up) one's loins	To prepare for action
Sundry	Various
Superlative	Best; of the highest quality

11. HIS RESISTLESS POWER

11.1 Introduction

This chapter covers paragraphs 28–29. Read these paragraphs and reflect on the contents before starting the lesson. The statements cited in this section further demonstrate the potency of the Revelation of Bahá'u'lláh. Paragraph 28 highlights the influence and the power of the World Order of Bahá'u'lláh. All the statements in paragraph 29 are cited from the Súratu'l-Haykal (Súrih of the Temple), one of the most challenging Tablets of Bahá'u'lláh revealed during His exile in Adrianople. In this Tablet, Bahá'u'lláh addresses the Temple (Haykal) and unveils His glory and majesty. In one of His Writings, Bahá'u'lláh states that the Haykal mentioned in this Tablet is the Person of Bahá'u'lláh and the voice addressing the Haykal is His Voice.

In this chapter, you need to look for and understand the following **key concepts:**

a) The world's equilibrium has been upset through the influence of the New World Order revealed by Bahá'u'lláh.
b) The foundation of the Revelation of Bahá'u'lláh is so strong that human strife and *"men's fanciful theories"* have no effect on it.
c) The Súratu'l-Haykal (Súrih of the Temple) is one of the most challenging Tablets of Bahá'u'lláh revealed during His exile in Adrianople.
d) The Holy Spirit is generated through a single letter revealed by Bahá'u'lláh.
e) The divinity referred to by Bahá'u'lláh in His Writings represents only the incarnation of names and attributes of God in the temple of the Manifestation of God, not His Reality.
f) Bahá'u'lláh promises that through His Revelation God will create a new race of men.

11.2 Paragraphs under study

28. Anticipating the System which the irresistible power of His Law was destined to unfold in a later age, He writes: *"The world's equilibrium hath been upset through the vibrating influence of this most great, this New World Order. Mankind's ordered life hath been revolutionised through the agency of this unique, this wondrous System—the like of which mortal eyes have never witnessed."*[1] *"The Hand of Omnipotence hath established His Revelation upon an unassailable, an enduring foundation. Storms of human strife are powerless to undermine its basis, nor will men's fanciful theories succeed in damaging its structure."*[2]

29. In the Súratu'l-Haykal, one of the most challenging works of Bahá'u'lláh, the following verses, each of which testifies to the resistless power infused into the Revelation proclaimed by its Author, have been recorded: *"Naught is seen in My temple but the Temple of God, and in My beauty but His Beauty, and in My being but His Being, and in My self but His Self, and in My movement but His Movement, and in My acquiescence but His Acquiescence, and in My pen but His Pen, the Mighty, the All-Praised. There hath not been in My soul but the Truth, and in Myself naught could be seen but God."*[3] *"The Holy Spirit Itself hath been generated through the agency of a single letter revealed by this Most Great Spirit, if ye be of them that comprehend."*[4] ... *"Within the treasury of Our Wisdom there lies unrevealed a knowledge, one word of which, if we chose to divulge it to mankind, would cause every human being to recognise the Manifestation of God and to acknowledge His omniscience, would enable every one to discover the secrets of all the sciences, and to attain so high a station as to find himself wholly independent of all past and future learning. Other knowledges We do as well possess, not a single letter of which We can disclose, nor do We find humanity able to hear even the barest reference to their meaning. Thus have We informed you of the knowledge of God, the All-Knowing, the All-Wise."*[5] *"The day is approaching when God will have, by an act of His Will, raised up a race of men the nature of which is inscrutable to all save God, the All-Powerful, the Self-Subsisting."*[6] *"He will, ere long, out of the Bosom of Power draw forth the Hands of Ascendancy and Might—Hands who will arise to win victory for this Youth and who will purge mankind from the defilement of the outcast and the ungodly. These Hands will gird up their loins to champion the Faith of God, and will, in My name the self-subsistent, the mighty, subdue the peoples and kindreds of the earth. They will enter the cities and will inspire with fear the hearts of all their inhabitants. Such are the evidences of the might of God; how fearful, how vehement is His might!"*[7]

---

1 Statement (a)
2 Statement (b)
3 Statement (c)
4 Statement (d)
5 Statement (e)
6 Statement (f)
7 Statement (g)

11.3 New World Order

In statement (a) of paragraph 28, Bahá'u'lláh alludes to the influence of the New World Order unveiled through His Revelation on the world's equilibrium. Shoghi Effendi has identified the Order referred to by Bahá'u'lláh in this statement as the same Order mentioned by the Báb twenty–five years earlier in the *Persian Bayán*: *"Well is it with him, who fixeth his gaze upon the Order of Bahá'u'lláh, and rendereth thanks unto his Lord. For He will assuredly be made manifest. God hath indeed irrevocably ordained it in the Bayán."*[1]

The characteristics of the World Order of Bahá'u'lláh are described in the Writings of Bahá'u'lláh and 'Abdu'l-Bahá, as well as in the letters of Shoghi Effendi and the Universal House of Justice. Shoghi Effendi refers to *The Kitáb-i-Aqdas* as the Charter of the World Order of Bahá'u'lláh.[2] *The Will and Testament of 'Abdu'l-Bahá* is also designated by Shoghi Effendi as "the Charter of a future world civilization" and supplementary to *The Kitáb-i-Aqdas.*[3]

According to Shoghi Effendi, the Appointed and Elected Arms of the Bahá'í Faith (see chapter 23) are building the structural basis of this Order during the Formative Age. "It is the superstructure of that self-same Order, attaining its full stature through the emergence of the Bahá'í World Commonwealth—the Kingdom of God on earth—which the Golden Age of that same Dispensation must, in the fullness of time, ultimately witness."[4]

The essential elements of the constitution of the world Bahá'í Commonwealth are enshrined in the two Charters of the World Order of Bahá'u'lláh. "The Dispensation of Bahá'u'lláh, the Ark of human salvation"[5] must be modelled according to the divinely ordained administrative principles revealed in *The Kitáb-i-Aqdas* and *The Will and Testament of 'Abdu'l-Bahá.*

11.4 Unassailable foundations

In statement (b) of paragraph 28, Bahá'u'lláh asserts that the foundation of His Revelation is so strong that human strife and *"men's fanciful theories"* have no effect on it. 'Abdu'l-Bahá confirms this: *"Verily, God effecteth that which He pleaseth; naught can annul His Covenant; naught can obstruct His favour nor oppose His Cause!"*[6] He also states, *"Everything is subject to corruption; but the Covenant of thy Lord shall continue to pervade all regions."*[7]

---

1 The Báb, the *Persian Bayán*, cited by Shoghi Effendi in *God Passes By,* p. 25.
2 Shoghi Effendi, *God Passes By*, p. 213.
3 Shoghi Effendi, *God Passed By*, p. 327.
4 Shoghi Effendi, God Passes By, p. 25.
5 Shoghi Effendi, *The World Order of Bahá'u'lláh*, p. 19.
6 'Abdu'l-Bahá, *Tablets of Abdul-Baha Abbas*, vol. 3, p. 597.
7 'Abdu'l-Bahá, *Bahá'í Scriptures*, p. 320.

Shoghi Effendi states: "The bedrock on which this Administrative Order is founded is God's immutable Purpose for mankind in this day."[1] He also declares: "... this priceless gem of Divine Revelation, now still in its embryonic state, shall evolve within the shell of His law, and shall forge ahead, undivided and unimpaired, till it embraces the whole of mankind."[2]

The organic and sustained development and expansion of the Faith of Bahá'u'lláh so far, despite strong assaults from the enemies within and without, is clear evidence of its resilience and firm foundation.

Bahá'u'lláh spent forty years in prison and confinement under the most difficult conditions. He neither sought any assistance for the promotion of His cause nor received any support from the kings or governments of His time. He submitted to the will of those hostile to Him, but He did not compromise to any extent the principles He declared necessary for the establishment of His Cause. During His lifetime, He fulfilled all the prophecies given in the previous Holy books regarding His presence in the Holy Land, though He was apparently forced by His opponents into exile to that spot.

After His ascension, the evolution of the Bahá'í Faith continued and it has transformed from a community of mainly Persian believers during His lifetime to the current diverse community of six million people spread all around the world, and consisting of many different backgrounds and ethnic groups. The infrastructure of the Administrative Order that He ordained in His Writings is now well established and is evolving towards its maturity.

At present the same dynamics govern the expansion and development of the Bahá'í Faith. This is happening through the love and sacrifice of His followers who are influenced by the Creative Power of His Revelation.

11.5 Súrih of the Temple

All the statements in paragraph 29 are cited from the Súratu'l-Haykal (the Súrih of the Temple), one of the most challenging Tablets of Bahá'u'lláh that was revealed during His exile in Adrianople. On His arrival in 'Akká, Bahá'u'lláh ordered this Tablet, in conjunction with the Tablets to the Kings, to be recast in the form of a pentacle, symbolizing the human temple.[3] The Tablets were organised in the following order: the Súratu'l-Haykal, the Tablet to Pope Pius IX, the Tablet to Napoleon III, the Tablet to Czar Alexander II, the Tablet to Queen Victoria and the Tablet to Násiri'd-Dín Sháh.

In the Súratu'l-Haykal, Bahá'u'lláh addresses the Temple (Haykal) and unveils His glory and majesty (statement (c)). In response to a question He was asked, Bahá'u'lláh states that the Haykal mentioned in this Tablet is His own Person and the voice addressing the Haykal is His Voice.[4]

---

1 Shoghi Effendi, *The World Order of Bahá'u'lláh*, p. 156.
2 Shoghi Effendi, *The World Order of Bahá'u'lláh*, p. 23.
3 Shoghi Effendi, *God Passes By*, p. 212.
4 Adib Taherzadeh, *The Revelation of Bahá'u'lláh*, vol. 3, p. 133.

In one of His Tablets, addressing the Christians, Bahá'u'lláh identified the Temple referred to in the Súratu'l-Haykal with the "Temple" mentioned by the Prophet Zechariah in the Old Testament.[1]

Zechariah was one of the Prophets of Jerusalem who lived about 2,500 years ago. He made a series of prophecies during the period of Persian rule, when the exiled Jews had lost their national sovereignty and their Temple for the first time. In his prophecies, as recorded in the Torah, Zechariah anticipates that the Messiah on His return would build a final Temple in Jerusalem and restore the glory of Israel:

> *"And speak unto him, saying, Thus speaketh the* LORD *of hosts, saying, Behold the man whose name is The* BRANCH; *and he shall grow up out of his place, and he shall build the temple of the* LORD:
>
> *Even he shall build the temple of the* LORD; *and he shall bear the glory, and shall sit and rule upon his throne; and he shall be a priest upon his throne: and the counsel of peace shall be between them both."*[2]

Bahá'u'lláh concludes the Súratu'l-Haykal with these words:

> *"Thus have We built the Temple with the hands of power and might, could ye but know it. This is the Temple promised unto you in the Book. Draw ye nigh unto it. This is that which profiteth you, could ye but comprehend it. Be fair, O peoples of the earth! Which is preferable, this, or a temple which is built of clay? Set your faces towards it. Thus have ye been commanded by God, the Help in Peril, the Self-Subsisting."*[3]

In paragraph 28 Shoghi Effendi cites five statements from this Tablet:

- Statement (c): Incarnation of the names and attributes of God in Bahá'u'lláh.
- Statement (d): Generation of the Holy Spirit through a single letter revealed by Bahá'u'lláh.
- Statement (e): The unrevealed knowledge enshrined in the Wisdom of Bahá'u'lláh.
- Statement (f): God will raise a new race of men.
- Statement (g): Bahá'u'lláh would draw forth the Hands of Ascendancy and Might to win victory for His Cause.

In the remaining part of this section, our focus will be on statements (c) and (g).

11.5.1 Divinity of the Manifestations of God

In statement (c), Bahá'u'lláh identifies Himself with God. Later in the letter, Shoghi Effendi clarifies the meaning of this statement (paragraph 37),

---

1 Shoghi Effendi *God Passes By*, p. 212.

2 Zechariah 6:12–13

3 Bahá'u'lláh, *Summons of the Lord of Hosts*, p. ii.

"The divinity attributed to so great a Being and the complete incarnation of the names and attributes of God in so exalted a Person should, under no circumstances, be misconceived or misinterpreted. The human temple that has been made the vehicle of so overpowering a Revelation must, if we be faithful to the tenets of our Faith, ever remain entirely distinguished from that *'innermost Spirit of Spirits'* and *'eternal Essence of Essences'*—that invisible yet rational God Who, however much we extol the divinity of His Manifestations on earth, can in no wise incarnate His infinite, His unknowable, His incorruptible and all-embracing Reality in the concrete and limited frame of a mortal being."[1]

Hence, the divinity referred to by Bahá'u'lláh in statement (c) represents only the incarnation of names and attributes of God in the temple of the Manifestation of God, and not the Reality of God. The Reality of God is infinite and cannot manifest itself in a mortal body.

There will be further discussion of this topic in chapter 13.

11.5.2 New race of men

In statement (g), Bahá'u'lláh gives an assurance that God will create a new race of men through His Revelation. In another statement, cited by Shoghi Effendi in *The Advent of Divine Justice,* Bahá'u'lláh sheds more light on this promise:

> *"A race of men, incomparable in character, shall be raised up which, with the feet of detachment, will tread under all who are in heaven and on earth, and will cast the sleeve of holiness over all that hath been created from water and clay."*[2]

According to the Universal House of Justice, the nature of this "new race of men", and its distinguishing characteristics are "... the theme we must pursue in our efforts to deepen in the Cause. What is Bahá'u'lláh's purpose for the human race? For what ends did He submit to the appalling cruelties and indignities heaped upon Him? What does He mean by a 'new race of men'? What are the profound changes which He will bring about?"[3] The answers to such questions "... are to be found in the Sacred Writings of our Faith and in their interpretation by 'Abdu'l-Bahá and our beloved Guardian."[4]

Furthermore, Shoghi Effendi warns the Bahá'í community that "... the supreme and distinguishing function of His Revelation, which is none other than the calling into being of a new race of men, will remain wholly unrecognized and completely obscured ...", unless "a sharp distinction between that community and that people ... be made, and resolutely and fearlessly upheld ...."[5]

---

1 Shoghi Effendi, *The World Order of Bahá'u'lláh*, p. 112.

2 Bahá'u'lláh, cited in Shoghi Effendi, *The Advent of Divine Justice*, p. 31.

3 The Universal House of Justice, in *Lights of Guidance*, p. 569.

4 The Universal House of Justice, in *Lights of Guidance*, p. 569.

5 Shoghi Effendi, *The Advent of Divine Justice*, p. 16.

Shoghi Effendi also points out that "The children who are trained in the world-embracing teachings of Bahá'u'lláh cannot but grow up to be a truly new race of men."[1]

1 Shoghi Effendi, in *Bahá'í Education*, p. 306.

11.6 Activities

1. In bullet form, list the characteristics of the World Order of Bahá'u'lláh.

2. Provide at least three evidences to show that the Revelation of Bahá'u'lláh is on unassailable foundations.

3. What is the significance of the Súratu'l-Haykal?

4. Explain your understanding of statement (c) in the context of the Divine station of the Manifestations of God.

5. What is your understanding of statement (d)?

6. What is your understanding of statement (e)?

7. What are the characteristics of the new race of men promised in statement (f)?

8. What is Bahá'u'lláh referring to by the term "Hands" in statement (g)?

11.7 Glossary

Term	Meaning
Acquiescent	Ready to agree without argument
Vehement	Showing strong feelings; forceful
Agency	Action or intervention
Omnipotence	Having unlimited power
Naught	Nothing
Divulge	Make known
Inscrutable	Impossible to understand or interpret
Defilement	Damaging the purity
Outcast	A person who has been rejected by society or a social group
Gird up ones loins	Prepare and strengthen oneself for what is to come

12. TESTIMONIES OF 'ABDU'L-BAHÁ

12.1 Introduction

This chapter covers paragraphs 30–35. Read these paragraphs and reflect on the contents before starting the lesson. In this section of his letter, Shoghi Effendi cites a number of statements from 'Abdu'l-Bahá on the nature and significance of the Revelation of Bahá'u'lláh.

In this chapter, you need to look for and understand the following **key concepts:**

a) The Revelation of Bahá'u'lláh will be unique for centuries and ages to come.
b) The holy ones of past ages yearned to live in this Day.
c) The souls of those in heaven desire to return to earth to attain the Revelation of Bahá'u'lláh.
d) The Glory of the Revelation of Bahá'u'lláh and the call from the Abhá Kingdom have enveloped the whole of creation.
e) The potentialities inherent in the Revelation of Bahá'u'lláh will gradually unfold.
f) The station of the prophets of Israel is destined for the true believer in this Day.
g) Future Manifestations in the Bahá'í Cycle will be under the shadow of Bahá'u'lláh.
h) The promised Revelation of God has been delivered and we should act now, as there is no time left for hesitation and doubt.

12.2 Paragraphs under study

30. Such is, dearly beloved friends, Bahá'u'lláh's own written testimony to the nature of His Revelation. To the affirmations of the Báb, each of which reinforces the strength, and confirms the truth, of these remarkable statements, I have already referred. What remains for me to consider in this connection are such passages in the writings of 'Abdu'l-Bahá, the appointed Interpreter of these same utterances, as throw further light upon and amplify various features of this enthralling theme. The tone of His language is indeed as emphatic and His tribute no less glowing than that of either Bahá'u'lláh or the Báb.

31. *"Centuries, nay ages, must pass away,"* He affirms in one of His earliest Tablets, *"ere the Day-Star of Truth shineth again in its mid-summer splendour, or appeareth once more in the radiance of its vernal glory ... How thankful must we be for having been made in this Day the recipients of so overwhelming a favour! Would that we had ten thousand lives that we might lay them down in thanksgiving for so rare a privilege, so high an attainment, so priceless a bounty!"*[1] *"The mere contemplation,"* He adds, *"of the Dispensation inaugurated by the Blessed Beauty would have sufficed to overwhelm the saints of bygone ages—saints who longed to partake for one moment of its great glory."*[2] *"The holy ones of past ages and centuries have, each and all, yearned with tearful eyes to live, though for one moment, in the Day of God. Their longings unsatisfied, they repaired to the Great Beyond. How great, therefore, is the bounty of the Abhá Beauty Who, notwithstanding our utter unworthiness, hath through His grace and mercy breathed into us in this divinely-illumined century the spirit of life, hath gathered us beneath the standard of the Beloved of the world, and chosen to confer upon us a bounty for which the mighty ones of bygone ages had craved in vain."*[3] *"The souls of the well-favoured among the concourse on high,"* He likewise affirms, *"the sacred dwellers of the most exalted Paradise, are in this day filled with burning desire to return unto this world, that they may render such service as lieth in their power to the threshold of the Abhá Beauty."*[4]

32. *"The effulgence of God's splendrous mercy,"* He, in a passage alluding to the growth and future development of the Faith, declares, *"hath enveloped the peoples and kindreds of the earth, and the whole world is bathed in its shining glory ... The day will soon come when the light of Divine unity will have so permeated the East and the West that no man dare any longer ignore it."*[5] *"Now in the world of being the Hand of divine power hath firmly laid the foundations of this all-highest bounty and this wondrous gift. Whatsoever is latent in the innermost of this holy cycle shall gradually appear and be made manifest, for now is but the beginning of its growth and the dayspring of the revelation of its signs. Ere the close of this century and of this age, it shall be made clear and evident how wondrous was that springtide and how heavenly was that gift!"*[6]

---

1 Statement (a)
2 Statement (b)
3 Statement (c)
4 Statement (d)
5 Statement (e)
6 Statement (f)

33. In confirmation of the exalted rank of the true believer, referred to by Bahá'u'lláh, He reveals the following: *"The station which he who hath truly recognised this Revelation will attain is the same as the one ordained for such prophets of the house of Israel as are not regarded as Manifestations 'endowed with constancy.'"*[1]

34. In connection with the Manifestations destined to follow the Revelation of Bahá'u'lláh, 'Abdu'l-Bahá makes this definite and weighty declaration: *"Concerning the Manifestations that will come down in the future 'in the shadows of the clouds,' know verily that in so far as their relation to the source of their inspiration is concerned they are under the shadow of the Ancient Beauty. In their relation, however, to the age in which they appear, each and every one of them 'doeth whatsoever He willeth.'"*[2]

35. *"O my friend!"* He thus addresses in one of His Tablets a man of recognised authority and standing, *"The undying Fire which the Lord of the Kingdom hath kindled in the midst of the holy Tree is burning fiercely in the midmost heart of the world. The conflagration it will provoke will envelop the whole earth. Its blazing flames will illuminate its peoples and kindreds. All the signs have been revealed; every prophetic allusion hath been manifested. Whatever hath been enshrined in all the Scriptures of the past hath been made evident. To doubt or hesitate is no more possible... Time is pressing. The Divine Charger is impatient, and can tarry no longer. Ours is the duty to rush forward and, ere it is too late, win the victory."*[3] And finally, is this most stirring passage which He, in one of His moments of exultation, was moved to address to one of His most trusted and eminent followers in the earliest days of His ministry: *"What more shall I say? What else can my pen recount? So loud is the call that reverberates from the Abhá Kingdom that mortal ears are well-nigh deafened with its vibrations. The whole creation, methinks, is being disrupted and is bursting asunder through the shattering influence of the Divine summons issued from the throne of glory. More than this I cannot write."*[4]

12.3 Four seasons of a revelation

In statement (a), 'Abdu'l-Bahá states: *"Centuries, nay ages, must pass away, ere the Day-Star of Truth shineth again in its mid-summer splendour."* This is a reference to the summer season of a Revelation from God. A study of the past major religions shows that they have evolved and developed through the cycles of spiritual birth and decay in their lifetime. The cycles of birth and growth, maturity, and decay of a religion have similarities to the four seasons of the year.

---

1 Statement (g)
2 Statement (h)
3 Statement (i)
4 Statement (j)

This is described by 'Abdu'l-Bahá in the context of the spiritual cycle or four seasons of a religion. A new Revelation from God goes through four cycles. The first stage is the spiritual springtime. "*When the Sun of Reality returns to quicken the world of mankind, a divine bounty descends from the heaven of generosity. The realm of thoughts and ideals is set in motion and blessed with new life. Minds are developed, hopes brighten, aspirations become spiritual, the virtues of the human world appear with freshened power of growth, and the image and likeness of God become visible in man.*"[1]

The second stage is the summer of the new revelation. At this stage "*The word of God is exalted, the Law of God is promulgated; all things reach perfection. The heavenly table is spread, the holy breezes perfume the East and the West, the teachings of God conquer the world, men become educated, praiseworthy results are produced, universal progress appears in the world of humanity, and the divine bounties surround all things. The Sun of Reality rises from the horizon of the Kingdom with the greatest power and heat.*"[2]

The season of autumn follows the summer. This is "*... when growth and development are arrested. Breezes change into blighting winds, and the unwholesome season dissipates the beauty and freshness of the gardens, plains and bowers—that is to say, attraction and goodwill do not remain, divine qualities are changed, the radiance of hearts is dimmed, the spirituality of souls is altered, virtues are replaced by vices, and holiness and purity disappear. Only the name of the Religion of God remains, and the exoteric forms of the divine teachings. The foundations of the Religion of God are destroyed and annihilated, and nothing but forms and customs exist. Divisions appear, firmness is changed into instability, and spirits become dead; hearts languish, souls become inert, and winter arrives—that is to say, the coldness of ignorance envelops the world, and the darkness of human error prevails.*"[3]

Finally "*... the mantle of winter overspreads, and only faint traces of the effulgence of that divine Sun remain. Just as the surface of the material world becomes dark and dreary, the soil dormant, the trees naked and bare and no beauty or freshness remains to cheer the darkness and desolation, so the winter of the spiritual cycle witnesses the death and disappearance of divine growth and extinction of the light and love of God.*"[4]

The winter of religion is the time of "oppression" and it is an unavoidable stage before the emergence of a new Revelation from God.

12.4 Holy cycle

In statement (f) 'Abdu'l-Bahá makes a reference to the length of the Bahá'í Cycle, which is different from the Bahá'í Dispensation.

---

1 'Abdu'l-Bahá, *The Promulgation of the Universal Peace*, p. 95.
2 'Abdu'l-Bahá, *Some answered Questions*, pp. 74–75.
3 'Abdu'l-Bahá, *Some answered Questions*, p. 75.
4 'Abdu'l-Bahá, *The Promulgation of Universal Peace*, p. 95.

In one of his messages, Shoghi Effendi states: "In spite of the vast spiritual significance of what Bahá'u'lláh has brought to the world we humans have infinite progress to make in the future. Future Prophets will bring us new laws suitable to our state of development and continue to educate us on this planet, but they will be under the shadow of Bahá'u'lláh for five thousand centuries."[1] This period of five hundred thousand years is referred to in the Bahá'í Writings as the Bahá'í Cycle.

The Dispensation of Bahá'u'lláh, on the other hand, is the period during which the laws and teachings of Bahá'u'lláh will be effective and will "... *extend over a period of no less than one thousand years*".[2] This Dispensation "... *will constitute the first stage in a series of Dispensations, to be established by future Manifestations.*"

In statement (h), 'Abdu'l-Bahá mentions that the Manifestations of God who appear after Bahá'u'lláh will be under His shadow. In a letter written on his behalf, Shoghi Effendi explains:

> "After Bahá'u'lláh many Prophets will, no doubt, appear, but they will be all under His shadow. Although they may abrogate the laws of the Dispensation, in accordance with the needs and requirements of the age in which they appear, they nevertheless draw their spiritual force from this mighty Revelation. The Faith of Bahá'u'lláh constitutes, indeed, the stage of maturity in the development of mankind. His appearance has released such spiritual forces that will continue to animate, for many long years to come, the world in its development. Whatever progress may be achieved in the later ages—after the unification of the whole human race is achieved—will be but improvements in the machinery of the world. For the machinery itself has already been created by Bahá'u'lláh. The task of continually improving and perfecting this machinery is one that later Prophets will be called upon to achieve. They will move and work within the orbit of Bahá'í cycle."[3]

On the nature of the relationship between Bahá'u'lláh and the Manifestations of God who will come under His shadow, Adib Taherzadeh explains that the future Manifestations of God will build their teachings based on the fruit of the Dispensation of Bahá'u'lláh, which is the unity of mankind. He then continues, "In Dispensations to come, man, as a result of the appearance of future Manifestations of God, will continue to develop and progress. He will acquire noble qualities and will grow spiritually to such a degree that none today can visualise the heights to which he will attain; yet he will function within the framework of the oneness of mankind established by

---

1 Shoghi Effendi, *High Endeavours*, p. 71.

2 Shoghi Effendi, *Citadel of Faith*, p. 5.

3 Shoghi Effendi, A letter written on behalf of Shoghi Effendi, 14 November 1935, in *Lights of Guidance*, p. 473.

Bahá'u'lláh, and the Manifestations of God Who appear from age to age during the Bahá'í Cycle will remain under His shadow."[1]

In the Notes section of *The Kitáb-i-Aqdas,*[2] the commencement of the one thousand years is considered to start from the first intimation received by Bahá'u'lláh of His Sublime Mission in the Síyáh-Chál of Ṭihrán, in October 1852.

12.5 Urgency of our action

In statement (i) 'Abdu'l-Bahá states: "*The undying Fire which the Lord of the Kingdom hath kindled in the midst of the holy Tree is burning fiercely ... Ours is the duty to rush forward and, ere it is too late, win the victory.*"

The potentials inherent in the Revelation of Bahá'u'lláh will gradually unfold as a result of our actions and the sacrifices we make for the Bahá'í Faith. Hence it is urgent that we act to nurture the fruits of the Revelation of Bahá'u'lláh.

Shoghi Effendi explains: "If we all choose to tread faithfully His path, surely the day is not far distant when our beloved Cause will have emerged from the inevitable obscurity of a young and struggling Faith into the broad daylight of universal recognition."[3] Following the path of Bahá'u'lláh requires nothing less than full recognition of Him, love of Him, full submission to His Will, dedication and commitment to His commandments and action according to His ordinances. This is not only our duty, being critical for the advancement of the Cause but "Therein lies the hope, the salvation of mankind." Such implications clearly demonstrate "the urgency, the sacredness, the immensity, the glory"[4] of the task we are expected to embark on.

In another letter, Shoghi Effendi indicates that our sacrifices and acts of heroism in the path of our beloved Cause should intensify as "... the international situation worsens, as the fortunes of mankind sink to a still lower ebb ... As the fabric of present-day society heaves and cracks under the strain and stress of portentous events and calamities, as the fissures, accentuating the cleavage separating nation from nation, class from class, race from race, and creed from creed ...."[5]

All the signs referred to by Shoghi Effendi in his message are very obvious in our society today. The principles and beliefs that for centuries determined the pattern of behaviour of individuals, the integrity of the family and the community are either consciously ignored or unknowingly overlooked. The ideologies that for centuries have proved successful for groups of people or nations in creating wealth and improving material comfort are becoming

---

1 Adib Taherzadeh, *The Revelation of Bahá'u'lláh,* vol. 1, p. 311.
2 *The Kitáb-i-The Kitáb-i-Aqdas,* Notes, p. 195.
3 Shoghi Effendi, *Bahá'í Administration,* p. 70.
4 Shoghi Effendi, *Bahá'í Administration,* p. 70.
5 Shoghi Effendi, *Citadel of Faith,* p. 43.

ineffective. Disunity and division in communities, nations and the world on the basis of race, language, religion, colour, etc., are rampant.

Such obvious and clear signs of destruction around us are strong indications of the urgency of our time and the degree of action required of us.

12.6 Activities

1. What are the differences between the Bahá'í Dispensation and the Bahá'í Cycle?

2. What is your understanding of statement (a)?

3. What is your understanding of the statement that for five hundred thousand years, the future Manifestations of God will be under the shadow of Bahá'u'lláh?

4. What is your understanding of statements (c) and (d)?

5. What is your understanding of statement (e)?

6. What is the meaning of *"Divine Charger"* in statement (i)?

7. In your view, what does Abdu'l-Bahá mean by "*before it is too late*" in statement (i)?

8. What are the key points in statement (j)?

12.7 Glossary

Term	Meaning
Accentuate	To direct attention to, emphasize
Asunder	Apart or in separate pieces
At a low ebb	In a bad or inactive state
Charger	Warrior's battle horse
Cleavage	A break caused by splitting; division
Conflagration	A very large fire that destroys much property, esp. buildings or forests
Enthral	To hold the complete attention and interest of (someone) as if by magic; Captivate
Fissure	A deep crack
Permeate	To spread or pass through or into every part of (a thing, place).
Portentous	That warns or tells of future unpleasant events
Reverberate	(Of sound) to be thrown back again and again, echo repeatedly
Shatter	To break suddenly into very small pieces, usu. as a result of force or violence
Summoned	Ordered or called to come
Tarry	To delay or be slow in starting, going, coming, etc.
Vernal	Of, like, or appearing in the spring season

13. GOD & HIS MANIFESTATIONS

13.1 Introduction

This chapter covers paragraphs 36–41. Read these paragraphs and reflect on the contents before starting the lesson. In this section of his letter, Shoghi Effendi stresses that Bahá'u'lláh, though manifesting the Names and Attributes of God, is to be considered as clearly distinct from God, Whose infinite and unknowable Essence can in no wise be incarnated in the physical frame of a mortal Man. Despite the overwhelming splendour of Bahá'u'lláh's Revelation, He is never to be identified with that invisible Reality, the Essence of Divinity itself. His station is that of the Manifestation of God for our time Who has renewed, emphasized and expanded the spiritual truths revealed in the previous revelations.

In this chapter, you need to look for and understand the following **key concepts:**

a) It is impossible for man to know the Reality of God.
b) The knowledge of the attributes of God is achieved through the knowledge of the Manifestation of God.
c) The human temple of Bahá'u'lláh is entirely distinguished from God.
d) The Manifestations of God have two separate natures and stations.
e) Bahá'u'lláh, despite the intensity of His Revelation, is yet another Manifestation of God, with a reality completely different from the Reality of God.

13.2 Paragraphs under study

36. Dearly beloved friends! Enough has been said, and the quoted excerpts from the writings of the Báb, of Bahá'u'lláh and of 'Abdu'l-Bahá are sufficiently numerous and varied, to convince the conscientious reader of the sublimity of this unique cycle in the world's religious history. It would be utterly impossible to over-exaggerate its significance or to overrate the influence it has exerted and which it must increasingly exert as its great system unfolds itself amidst the welter of a collapsing civilisation.

37. To whoever may read these pages a word of warning seems, however, advisable before I proceed further with the development of my argument. Let no one meditating, in the light of the fore-quoted passages, on the nature of the Revelation of Bahá'u'lláh, mistake its character or misconstrue the intent of its Author. The divinity attributed to so great a Being and the complete incarnation of the names and attributes of God in so exalted a Person should, under no circumstances, be misconceived or misinterpreted. The human temple that has been made the vehicle of so overpowering a Revelation must, if we be faithful to the tenets of our Faith, ever remain entirely distinguished from that "innermost Spirit of Spirits" and "eternal Essence of Essences"—that invisible yet rational God Who, however much we extol the divinity of His Manifestations on earth, can in no wise incarnate His infinite, His unknowable, His incorruptible and all-embracing Reality in the concrete and limited frame of a mortal being. Indeed, the God Who could so incarnate His own reality would, in the light of the teachings of Bahá'u'lláh, cease immediately to be God. So crude and fantastic a theory of Divine incarnation is as removed from, and incompatible with, the essentials of Bahá'í belief as are the no less inadmissible pantheistic and anthropomorphic conceptions of God—both of which the utterances of Bahá'u'lláh emphatically repudiate and the fallacy of which they expose.

38. He Who in unnumbered passages claimed His utterance to be the *"Voice of Divinity, the Call of God Himself"* thus solemnly affirms in *The Kitáb-i-Íqán*: *"To every discerning and illumined heart it is evident that God, the unknowable Essence, the Divine Being, is immeasurably exalted beyond every human attribute such as corporeal existence, ascent and descent, egress and regress ... He is, and hath ever been, veiled in the ancient eternity of His Essence, and will remain in His Reality everlastingly hidden from the sight of men ... He standeth exalted beyond and above all separation and union, all proximity and remoteness ... 'God was alone; there was none else beside Him' is a sure testimony of this truth."*[1]

39. *"From time immemorial,"* Bahá'u'lláh, speaking of God, explains, *"He, the Divine Being, hath been veiled in the ineffable sanctity of His exalted Self, and will everlasting continue to be wrapt in the impenetrable mystery of His unknowable Essence ... Ten thousand Prophets, each a Moses, are thunderstruck upon the Sinai of their search at God's forbidding voice, 'Thou shalt never behold Me!'; whilst a myriad Messengers, each as great as Jesus, stand dismayed upon their heavenly thrones by the interdiction 'Mine Essence thou shalt never*

[1] Statement (a)

apprehend!'"[1] *"How bewildering to me, insignificant as I am,"* Bahá'u'lláh in His communion with God affirms, *"is the attempt to fathom the sacred depths of Thy knowledge! How futile my efforts to visualise the magnitude of the power inherent in Thine handiwork—the revelation of Thy creative power!"*[2] *"When I contemplate, O my God, the relationship that bindeth me to Thee,"* He, in yet another prayer revealed in His own handwriting, testifies, *"I am moved to proclaim to all created things 'verily I am God!'; and when I consider my own self, lo, I find it coarser than clay!"*[3]

40. *"The door of the knowledge of the Ancient of Days,"* Bahá'u'lláh further states in *The Kitáb-i-Íqán*, *"being thus closed in the face of all beings, He, the Source of infinite grace ... hath caused those luminous Gems of Holiness to appear out of the realm of the spirit, in the noble form of the human temple, and be made manifest unto all men, that they may impart unto the world the mysteries of the unchangeable Being and tell of the subtleties of His imperishable Essence ... All the Prophets of God, His well-favoured, His holy and chosen Messengers are, without exception, the bearers of His names and the embodiments of His attributes ... These Tabernacles of Holiness, these primal Mirrors which reflect the Light of unfading glory, are but expressions of Him Who is the Invisible of the Invisibles."*[4]

41. That Bahá'u'lláh should, notwithstanding the overwhelming intensity of His Revelation, be regarded as essentially one of these Manifestations of God, never to be identified with that invisible Reality, the Essence of Divinity itself, is one of the major beliefs of our Faith—a belief which should never be obscured and the integrity of which no one of its followers should allow to be compromised.

13.3 Station of Divinity of Manifestations of God

In paragraph 37, Shoghi Effendi indicates that despite the statements cited in the previous paragraphs on the greatness and significance of the Revelation of Bahá'u'lláh, He is entirely distinguished from God.

For example, in statement (c), paragraph 29, Bahá'u'lláh announces, *"Naught is seen in My temple but the Temple of God, and in My beauty but His Beauty, and in My being but His Being, and in My self but His Self, and in My movement but His Movement, and in My acquiescence but His Acquiescence, and in My pen but His Pen, the Mighty, the All-Praised. There hath not been in My soul but the Truth, and in Myself naught could be seen but God."*

Shoghi Effendi explains that the divinity attributed to Bahá'u'lláh represents only the incarnation of the names and attributes of God in the

---

1 Statement (b)
2 Statement (c)
3 Statement (d)
4 Statement (e)

Temple of the Manifestation of God not His Reality. The Reality of God is infinite and cannot manifest itself in a mortal body. He then cites some statements from Bahá'u'lláh in paragraphs 38–40 to illustrate the nature of this concept.

Reference to the station of divinity of the Manifestations of God is not exclusive to the Bahá'í Faith and can be observed in all the Holy books. In this connection, Bahá'u'lláh indicates that "*the attributes of Godhead, Divinity, Supreme Singleness, and Inmost Essence, have been, and are applicable*"[1] to all the Mouthpieces of God.

In the following paragraphs, different aspects of this concept will be explored.

13.3.1 Double nature and double station

Every Manifestation of God has a double nature: a human nature pertaining to "*the world of matter*"[2] and a spiritual nature "*born of the substance of God Himself*". A Manifestation of God is also endowed with a "*double station*". The first station, "*... which is related to His innermost reality, representeth Him as One Whose voice is the voice of God Himself.*" In one of His Tablets, Bahá'u'lláh provides three examples from the Revelation of Muḥammad to illustrate such a station.[3]

a) From an Islamic tradition attributed to Muḥammad: "Manifold and mysterious is My relationship with God. I am He, Himself, and He is I, Myself, except that I am that I am, and He is that He is."
b) From the Qur'án: "*And in like manner, the words: Arise, O Muḥammad, for lo, the Lover and the Beloved are joined together and made one in Thee.*"
c) From the Qur'án: "*There is no distinction whatsoever between Thee and Them, except that They are Thy Servants.*"

There are also a number of verses in the Qur'án that attribute the deeds of Muḥammad to God. On one occasion, a large group of the followers swore allegiance to Muḥammad by placing their hands over each other's, as was the customary at the time. The hand of Muḥammad was placed on top of them all. The following verse was revealed regarding this event, "*In truth, they who plighted fealty unto thee, really plighted that fealty unto God: The hand of God was over their hands.*"[4]

In another instance during the battle of Badr, Muḥammad fought with one thousand men against three thousand Meccans. The infidels were soundly defeated and consequently this verse was revealed from God: "*So it was not you who slew them; but God slew them; Those shafts were God's, not Thine!*"[5]

---

1 Bahá'u'lláh, *Gleanings from the Writings of Bahá'u'lláh*, p. 53.
2 Bahá'u'lláh, *Gleanings from the Writings of Bahá'u'lláh*, pp. 66–67.
3 Bahá'u'lláh, *Gleanings from the Writings of Bahá'u'lláh*, pp. 66–67.
4 *Qur'án* 48:10
5 *Qur'án* 8:17

The second station is the human station, exemplified by the following verses from the Qur'án:

a) *"I am but a man like you."*[1]

b) *"Say, praise be to my Lord! Am I more than a man, an apostle?"*[2]

The divinity attributed to a Manifestation of God is applicable to His spiritual nature that is the first station.

13.3.2 Nature of divinity

The nature of divinity attributed to the Manifestations of God has been further explained and clarified in the Writings of Bahá'u'lláh and 'Abdu'l-Bahá.

In *Epistle to the Son of the Wolf,* Bahá'u'lláh describes this station as "*the station in which one dieth to himself and liveth in God. Divinity, whenever I mention it, indicateth My complete and absolute self-effacement. This is the station in which I have no control over mine own weal or woe nor over my life nor over my resurrection.*"[3]

In *The Kitáb-i-Íqán*, Bahá'u'lláh explains that in the state of divinity, the human station of a Manifestation of God is obliterated in the face of God and hence there is no mention of His "self".[4] The divine attributes and names are perfectly manifested in His Temple and fully overshadow His human station. In fact, the Manifestation of God is exhibiting absolute Servitude when asserting the station of Godhood, as mentioned by the Imám Ṣadíq, the sixth Imám of Shí'ih Islám: "Servitude is a substance, the essence of which is Divinity."[5]

'Abdu'l-Bahá provides a further explanation on the condition of "self-effacement" of a Manifestation of God, when soaring in the domain of divinity. *"Of such a one—of such a Prophet and Messenger—we can say that the Light of Divinity with the heavenly Perfections dwells in him. If we claim that the sun is seen in the mirror, we do not mean that the sun itself has descended from the holy heights of his heaven and entered into the mirror! This is impossible. The Divine Nature is seen in the Manifestations and its Light and Splendour are visible in extreme glory."*[6]

13.4 Knowledge of God

In statement (e), Bahá'u'lláh declares: "*The door of the knowledge of the Ancient of Days being thus closed in the face of all beings.*" The knowledge of the Manifestations of God is equal to the knowledge of God.

---

1 *Qur'án* 19:31

2 *Qur'án* 17:93

3 Bahá'u'lláh, *Epistle to the Son of the Wolf*, p. 41.

4 Bahá'u'lláh, *The Kitáb-i-Íqán*, p. 178.

5 Bahá'u'lláh, *Epistle to the Son of the Wolf*, p. 111.

6 'Abdu'l-Bahá, *'Abdu'l-Bahá in London*, p. 24.

In *Some Answered Questions* 'Abdu'l-Bahá explains: "*... there are two kinds of knowledge: the knowledge of the essence of a thing and the knowledge of its qualities.*"[1] A human by nature cannot acquire knowledge about the essence of anything. Our knowledge is limited only to the attributes of things. "*The essence of a thing is known through its qualities; otherwise, it is unknown and hidden.*"[2]

For example, a table is known by its shape, colour, the type of the materials used in it, etc. Further information can be gleaned through the use of computer imaging, chemical analysis and electron microscopy. Otherwise, it is impossible to acquire any knowledge about the reality or the essence of the table.

An incomparably greater limitation also applies to our knowledge of God. It is impossible for us to learn about the Reality of God. 'Abdu'l-Bahá emphasizes that "*... as things can only be known by their qualities and not by their essence, it is certain that the Divine Reality is unknown with regard to its essence and is known with regard to its attributes.*"[3]

However, a direct knowledge of the attributes of God is also impossible for human beings due to major differences that exist between the nature and reality of humanity and the Reality of God. In *Some Answered Questions,*[4] 'Abdu'l-Bahá explains such variances as:

a) God is the "Pre-existent Reality" whereas the human is the "phenomenal reality." This implies that God is ancient and eternal contrary to the way God has created the human.
b) God is infinite whereas the human is finite. The finite cannot perceive the infinite. An example is the relationship between a drop of water and the ocean. A drop of water cannot understand the complexity and the nature of the ocean.
c) There is a difference of condition and degree of existence between the human and God. For example, plants and animals are at different degrees of existence in the physical world. "*The plants, the trees, whatever progress they may make, cannot conceive of the power of sight or the powers of the other senses; and the animal cannot imagine the condition of man—that is to say, his spiritual powers.*"[5]

In addition, "*This knowledge of the attributes is also proportioned to the capacity and power of man; it is not absolute ... All that man is able to understand are the attributes of Divinity, the radiance of which appears and is visible in the world and within men's souls.*"[6]

---

1 'Abdu'l-Bahá, *Some Answered Questions*, p. 220.
2 'Abdu'l-Bahá, *Some Answered Questions*, p. 220.
3 'Abdu'l-Bahá, *Some Answered Questions*, pp. 220–221.
4 'Abdu'l-Bahá, *Some Answered Questions*, p. 221.
5 'Abdu'l-Bahá, *Some Answered Questions*, p. 221.
6 'Abdu'l-Bahá, *Some Answered Questions*, p. 221.

God, in every age, manifests His attributes in a special individual so that humanity can acquire knowledge of Him as far as it is able within the limitations of its existence. In other words, the "*bounties, splendours and attributes*" of God are reflected in the Manifestations of God. In this age, the knowledge of the "*bounties, splendours and attributes*" of Bahá'u'lláh is the same as the knowledge of God. Bahá'u'lláh clearly describes this concept in one of His Tablets:

> *"These Tabernacles of Holiness, these Primal Mirrors which reflect the light of unfading glory, are but expressions of Him Who is the Invisible of the Invisibles. By the revelation of these Gems of Divine virtue all the names and attributes of God, such as knowledge and power, sovereignty and dominion, mercy and wisdom, glory, bounty, and grace, are made manifest."*[1]

---

[1] Bahá'u'lláh, *Gleanings from the Writings of Bahá'u'lláh*, p. 47.

13.5 Activities

1. What is your understanding of the term "invisible but rational God" in paragraph 37?

2. Describe your understanding of pantheistic and anthropomorphic conceptions of God referred to paragraph 37. Why are not these concepts acceptable in the Faith?

3. Describe your understanding of the terms *"corporeal existence", "ascent and descent", "egress and regress"* used in statement (a) in connection with the Reality of God.

4. What are the meaning and significance of the references made to Moses and Jesus in statement (b)?

5. How does statement (d) relate to the two stations of a Manifestation of God?

6. What is the essence or reality of an entity?

7. What is the attribute of an entity?

8. What is the difference between the "pre-existent Reality" and the "phenomenal reality"?

9. In what sense is God infinite and a human being finite?

10. What is your understanding of paragraph 41?

13.6 Glossary

Term	Meaning
Anthropomorphism	Treating gods as having the form or qualities of a human
Avow	To state openly; admit
Conscientious	Showing great care, attention
Corporeal	That can be touched; material; physical rather than spiritual
Detract	To take something of value away from; cause to be or seem less valuable
Egress	The act, power, or right of going out, esp. from a building or enclosed place
Fathom	To obtain at the true meaning of; come to understand fully
Ineffable	Too wonderful to be described
Instil	To gradually but firmly place (ideas, feelings, etc.) into someone's mind by a continuous effort
Misconstrue	To get a wrong idea of or misinterpret
Pantheism	The religious idea that God and the universe are the same thing and that God is present in all natural things
Regress	To go back to a former and usually worse or less developed condition, way of behaving, etc.
Repudiate	To refuse to accept, to reject
Self-effacing	Keeping oneself from attracting attention, modest
Subtle	Delicate; not easy to notice, understand, or explain
The incarnation of	A person or thing that is the perfect example of a quality
Weal	Prosperity, wellbeing, welfare
Welter	A disordered mixture, general confusion
Woe	Great sorrow

14. PROGRESSIVE REVELATION

14.1 Introduction

This chapter covers paragraphs 42–52. Read these paragraphs and reflect on the contents before starting the lesson. In this section of his letter, Shoghi Effendi explains the unity of the Bahá'í Faith with all the previous divine Revelations and highlights how Bahá'u'lláh's Revelation vindicates and confirms the spiritual principles taught by the former Manifestations of God. This paradigm is known in the Bahá'í Writings as "progressive revelation" and forms the core of the Bahá'í philosophy on religion. In addition, Shoghi Effendi cites some statements from Bahá'u'lláh on His Greater Covenant.

In this chapter, you need to look for and understand the following **key concepts:**

a) The Revelation of Bahá'u'lláh does not annul the religious truths revealed in previous Revelations.
b) The Revelation of Bahá'u'lláh clarifies and enhances the principles of previous religions and demonstrates their unity.
c) The oneness of the Manifestations of God is a reflection of the power, sovereignty and glory of God.
d) The Manifestations of God differ only in the intensity of their Revelations.
e) Despite the intensity of the Revelation of Bahá'u'lláh, He is not the final Manifestation of God—there will be Revelations in the future.
f) Religious truth is relative not absolute.
g) In every Dispensation the light of divine Revelation is revealed in proportion to the spiritual capacity of people.

14.2 Paragraphs under study

42. Nor does the Bahá'í Revelation, claiming as it does to be the culmination of a prophetic cycle and the fulfilment of the promise of all ages, attempt, under any circumstances, to invalidate those first and everlasting principles that animate and underlie the religions that have preceded it. The God-given authority, vested in each one of them, it admits and

establishes as its firmest and ultimate basis. It regards them in no other light except as different stages in the eternal history and constant evolution of one religion, Divine and indivisible, of which it itself forms but an integral part. It neither seeks to obscure their Divine origin, nor to dwarf the admitted magnitude of their colossal achievements. It can countenance no attempt that seeks to distort their features or to stultify the truths, which they instil. Its teachings do not deviate a hairbreadth from the verities they enshrine, nor does the weight of its message detract one jot or one tittle from the influence they exert or the loyalty they inspire. Far from aiming at the overthrow of the spiritual foundation of the world's religious systems, its avowed, its unalterable purpose is to widen their basis, to restate their fundamentals, to reconcile their aims, to reinvigorate their life, to demonstrate their oneness, to restore the pristine purity of their teachings, to co-ordinate their functions and to assist in the realisation of their highest aspirations. These divinely revealed religions, as a close observer has graphically expressed it, "are doomed not to die, but to be reborn ... 'Does not the child succumb in the youth and the youth in the man; yet neither child nor youth perishes?'"

43. *"They Who are the Luminaries of Truth and the Mirrors reflecting the light of Divine Unity,"* Bahá'u'lláh explains in *the Kitáb-i-Íqán*, *"in whatever age and cycle they are sent down from their invisible habitations of ancient glory unto this world to educate the souls of men and endue with grace all created things, are invariably endowed with an all-compelling power and invested with invincible sovereignty ... These sanctified Mirrors, these Day-Springs of ancient glory are one and all the exponents on earth of Him Who is the central Orb of the universe, its essence and ultimate purpose. From Him proceed their knowledge and power; from Him is derived their sovereignty. The beauty of their countenance is but a reflection of His image, and their revelation a sign of His deathless glory ... Through them is transmitted a grace that is infinite, and by them is revealed the light that can never fade ... Human tongue can never befittingly sing their praise, and human speech can never unfold their mystery."*[1] *"Inasmuch as these Birds of the celestial Throne,"* He adds, *"are all sent down from the heaven of the Will of God, and as they all arise to proclaim His irresistible Faith, they therefore are regarded as one soul and the same person ... They all abide in the same tabernacle, soar in the same heaven, are seated upon the same throne, utter the same speech, and proclaim the same Faith ... They only differ in the intensity of their revelation and the comparative potency of their light ... That a certain attribute of God hath not been outwardly manifested by these Essences of Detachment doth in no wise imply that they Who are the Day-Springs of God's attributes and the Treasuries of*

---

[1] Statement (a)

His holy names did not actually possess it."[1]

44. It should also be borne in mind that, great as is the power manifested by this Revelation and however vast the range of the Dispensation its Author has inaugurated, it emphatically repudiates the claim to be regarded as the final revelation of God's will and purpose for mankind. To hold such a conception of its character and functions would be tantamount to a betrayal of its cause and a denial of its truth. It must necessarily conflict with the fundamental principle, which constitutes the bedrock of Bahá'í belief, the principle that religious truth is not absolute but relative, that Divine Revelation is orderly, continuous and progressive and not spasmodic or final. Indeed, the categorical rejection by the followers of the Faith of Bahá'u'lláh of the claim to finality which any religious system inaugurated by the Prophets of the past may advance is as clear and emphatic as their own refusal to claim that same finality for the Revelation with which they stand identified. *"To believe that all revelation is ended, that the portals of Divine mercy are closed, that from the daysprings of eternal holiness no sun shall rise again, that the ocean of everlasting bounty is forever stilled, and that out of the tabernacle of ancient glory the Messengers of God have ceased to be made manifest"* must constitute in the eyes of every follower of the Faith a grave, an inexcusable departure from one of its most cherished and fundamental principles.

45. A reference to some of the already quoted utterances of Bahá'u'lláh and 'Abdu'l-Bahá will surely suffice to establish, beyond the shadow of a doubt, the truth of this cardinal principle. Might not the following passage of the Hidden Words be, likewise, construed as an allegorical allusion to the progressiveness of Divine Revelation and an admission by its Author that the Message with which He has been entrusted is not the final and ultimate expression of the will and guidance of the Almighty? *"O Son of Justice! In the night-season the beauty of the immortal Being hath repaired from the emerald height of fidelity unto the Sadratu'l-Muntahá, and wept with such a weeping that the concourse on high and the dwellers of the realms above wailed at His lamenting. Whereupon there was asked, Why the wailing and weeping? He made reply: As bidden I waited expectant upon the hill of faithfulness, yet inhaled not from them that dwell on earth the fragrance of fidelity. Then summoned to return I beheld, and lo! certain doves of holiness were sore tried within the claws of the dogs of earth. Thereupon the Maid of heaven hastened forth unveiled and resplendent from Her mystic mansion, and asked of their names, and all were told but one. And when urged, the first letter thereof was uttered, whereupon the dwellers of the celestial chambers rushed forth out of their habitation of glory. And whilst the second letter was pronounced they fell down, one and all, upon the dust. At that moment a voice was heard from the inmost shrine: 'Thus far and no farther.' Verily*

[1] Statement (b)

We bear witness to that which they have done and now are doing."[1]

46. In a more explicit language Bahá'u'lláh testifies to this truth in one of His Tablets revealed in Adrianople: *"Know verily that the veil hiding Our countenance hath not been completely lifted. We have revealed Our Self to a degree corresponding to the capacity of the people of Our age. Should the Ancient Beauty be unveiled in the fullness of His glory mortal eyes would be blinded by the dazzling intensity of His revelation."*[2]
47. In the Súriy-i-Sabr, revealed as far back as the year 1863, on the very first day of His arrival in the garden of Riḍván, He thus affirms: *"God hath sent down His Messengers to succeed to Moses and Jesus, and He will continue to do so till 'the end that hath no end'; so that His grace may, from the heaven of Divine bounty, be continually vouchsafed to mankind."*[3]
48. *"I am not apprehensive for My own self,"* Bahá'u'lláh still more explicitly declares, *"My fears are for Him Who will be sent down unto you after Me—Him Who will be invested with great sovereignty and mighty dominion."*[4] And again He writes in the Súratu'l-Haykal: *"By those words, which I have revealed, Myself is not intended, but rather He Who will come after Me. To it is witness God, the All-Knowing." "Deal not with Him,"* He adds, *"as ye have dealt with Me."*[5]
49. In a more circumstantial passage the Báb upholds the same truth in His writings. *"It is clear and evident,"* He writes in the *Persian Bayán*, *"that the object of all preceding Dispensations hath been to pave the way for the advent of Muḥammad, the Apostle of God. These, including the Muhammadan Dispensation, have had, in their turn, as their objective the Revelation proclaimed by the Qá'im. The purpose underlying this Revelation, as well as those that preceded it, has, in like manner, been to announce the advent of the Faith of Him Whom God will make manifest. And this Faith—the Faith of Him Whom God will make manifest—in its turn, together with all the Revelations gone before it, have as their object the Manifestation destined to succeed it. And the latter, no less than all the Revelations preceding it, prepare the way for the Revelation, which is yet to follow. The process of the rise and setting of the Sun of Truth will thus indefinitely continue—a process that hath had no beginning and will have no end."*[6]
50. *"Know of a certainty,"* Bahá'u'lláh explains in this connection, *"that in every Dispensation the light of Divine Revelation hath been vouchsafed to men in direct proportion to their spiritual capacity. Consider the sun. How feeble its rays the moment it appeareth above the horizon. How*

---

1 Statement (c)
2 Statement (d)
3 Statement (e)
4 Statement (f)
5 Statement (g)
6 Statement (h)

gradually its warmth and potency increase as it approacheth its zenith, enabling meanwhile all created things to adapt themselves to the growing intensity of its light. How steadily it declineth until it reacheth its setting point. Were it all of a sudden to manifest the energies latent within it, it would no doubt cause injury to all created things ... In like manner, if the Sun of Truth were suddenly to reveal, at the earliest stages of its manifestation, the full measure of the potencies which the providence of the Almighty hath bestowed upon it, the earth of human understanding would waste away and be consumed; for men's hearts would neither sustain the intensity of its revelation, nor be able to mirror forth the radiance of its light. Dismayed and overpowered, they would cease to exist."[1]

51. In the light of these clear and conclusive statements it is our clear duty to make it indubitably evident to every seeker after truth that from *"the beginning that hath no beginning"* the Prophets of the one, the unknowable God, including Bahá'u'lláh Himself, have all, as the channels of God's grace, as the exponents of His unity, as the mirrors of His light and the revealers of His purpose, been commissioned to unfold to mankind an ever-increasing measure of His truth, of His inscrutable will and Divine guidance, and will continue to *"the end that hath no end"* to vouchsafe still fuller and mightier revelations of His limitless power and glory.

52. We might well ponder in our hearts the following passages from a prayer revealed by Bahá'u'lláh which strikingly affirm, and are a further evidence of, the reality of the great and essential truth lying at the very core of His Message to mankind: *"Praise be to Thee, O Lord my God, for the wondrous revelations of Thine inscrutable decree and the manifold woes and trials Thou hast destined for myself. At one time Thou didst deliver me into the hands of Nimrod; at another Thou hast allowed Pharaoh's rod to persecute me. Thou alone canst estimate, through Thine all-encompassing knowledge and the operation of Thy Will, the incalculable afflictions I have suffered at their hands. Again Thou didst cast me into the prison-cell of the ungodly for no reason except that I was moved to whisper into the ears of the well-favoured denizens of Thy kingdom an intimation of the vision with which Thou hadst, through Thy knowledge, inspired me and revealed to me its meaning through the potency of Thy might. And again Thou didst decree that I be beheaded by the sword of the infidel. Again I was crucified for having unveiled to men's eyes the hidden gems of Thy glorious unity, for having revealed to them the wondrous signs of Thy sovereign and everlasting power. How bitter the humiliations heaped upon me, in a subsequent age, on the plain of Karbilá! How lonely did I feel amidst Thy people; to what state of helplessness I was reduced in that land! Unsatisfied with such indignities,*

---

1 Statement (i)

> *my persecutors decapitated me and carrying aloft my head from land to land paraded it before the gaze of the unbelieving multitude and deposited it on the seats of the perverse and faithless. In a later age I was suspended and my breast was made a target to the darts of the malicious cruelty of my foes. My limbs were riddled with bullets and my body was torn asunder. Finally, behold how in this day my treacherous enemies have leagued themselves against me, and are continually plotting to instil the venom of hate and malice into the souls of Thy servants. With all their might they are scheming to accomplish their purpose ... Grievous as is my plight, O God, my Well beloved, I render thanks unto Thee, and my spirit is grateful for whatsoever hath befallen me in the path of Thy good-pleasure. I am well pleased with that which Thou didst ordain for me, and welcome, however calamitous, the pains and sorrows I am made to suffer."*[1]

14.3 Concept of Progressive Revelation

In paragraph 42, Shoghi Effendi explains the unity between the Bahá'í Faith and previous divine Revelations, and highlights how the Revelation of Bahá'u'lláh vindicates and confirms the spiritual principles taught by former Manifestations of God. This paradigm is known in the Bahá'í Writings as "progressive revelation" and forms the core of the Bahá'í philosophy on religion. It answers some of the fundamental questions regarding the source of different religions, the principle of unity in diversity of religions, and the relationship between them.

This concept has its roots in the purpose of the creation of man. Bahá'u'lláh explains that God created humanity because of His love for it. Humanity was then given the ability to reflect the qualities and attributes of God. Every human being has the duty in his/her lifetime:

- to know God,
- to worship Him,
- to develop God's given qualities and attributes in order to serve others, and
- to assist in establishing the Kingdom of God on earth.

Humanity is not able to achieve these objectives on its own. Hence, God has progressively sent His Manifestations to guide and assist humanity in this process. They have helped individuals to grow spiritually and have provided the necessary teachings and laws to overcome the social and economic problems emerging in human society. As a result, humanity has collectively evolved and continues to grow from one stage of development to the next towards its final destiny.

God has given humanity the potential to reflect His attributes and qualities. However, this can only occur to the degree that the heart has been purified and "polished" in order to reflect that "light". In the case of the Manifestations of

---

1 Statement (j)

God, they are like clear mirrors that perfectly reflect the true image and attributes of God. They also have the power to assist humanity to "polish" its spiritual "mirror". Hence the Manifestations of God reflect God in the world of creation and knowledge of Them is equivalent to the knowledge of God.

Bahá'u'lláh refers to the concept of progressive revelation in a number of His Writings including statement (e). In one of those Tablets, He explains that each one of the Manifestations of God Who have appeared in "... *the chain of successive Revelations that hath linked the Manifestation of Adam with that of the Báb"*, have been *"sent down through the operation of the Divine Will and Purpose*."[1] This part of the statement highlights the unity of those Manifestations as all have been sent according to the Will of God.

Bahá'u'lláh then continues this Tablet by expanding on the distinguishing characteristics of the Revelation brought forth by each of the Manifestations of God. He states that each one of those Manifestations has been:

- *"the bearer of a specific Message"*
- *"entrusted with a divinely-revealed Book"*
- *"commissioned to unravel the mysteries of a mighty Tablet"*
- Foreordained with a Revelation with a certain measure of intensity

In statement (i), Bahá'u'lláh further explains that the intensity of every Revelation from God is proportional to the spiritual capacity of the people who receive it. Although the reality of each revelation is absolute and pre-ordained, the religious truth that it promotes is relative, i.e. dependent on the condition of the society for which the revelation is destined.

Statement (d) highlights the fact that the energy latent in a Revelation from God is also released gradually and progressively. An example is the divinely purposed delay in the revelation of *The Kitáb-i-Aqdas* and implementation of its laws and ordinances. Bahá'u'lláh states in one of His Tablets: "*For a number of years petitions reached the Most Holy Presence from various lands begging for the laws of God, but We held back the Pen ere the appointed time had come.*"[2] This is elucidated further in the Notes section of *The Kitáb-i-Aqdas*: "Not until twenty years from the birth of His Prophetic Mission in the Síyáh-C͟hál of Ṭihrán had elapsed did Bahá'u'lláh reveal *The Kitáb-i-Aqdas*, the Repository of the laws of His Dispensation. Even after its revelation the Aqdas was withheld by Him for sometime before it was sent to the friends in Persia. This divinely purposed delay in the revelation of the basic laws of God for this age, and the subsequent gradual implementation of their provisions, illustrate the principle of progressive revelation, which applies even within the ministry of each Prophet."[3]

Every Revelation from God goes through the cycles of spiritual birth, growth, maturity and death, which is similar to the four seasons of the physical

---

1 Bahá'u'lláh, *Gleanings from the Writings of Bahá'u'lláh*, pp. 74.
2 *The Kitáb-i-Aqdas*, Notes, pp. 219–220.
3 *The Kitáb-i-Aqdas,* Notes, pp. 219–220.

world. A new spiritual springtime starts after the death of a religion, and a new religion is born (see section 12.3).

14.4 Unity and diversity of Manifestations of God

Another teaching of Bahá'u'lláh, closely related to the principle of progressive revelation, is the oneness of the Manifestations of God. Bahá'u'lláh describes the meaning of this concept in statements (a) and (b) cited in this chapter.

Statement (j) cited in paragraph 52, is a prayer in which Bahá'u'lláh describes His sufferings in previous Dispensations, thus further affirming the essential unity of the Suns of Truth. In a letter written on his behalf, Shoghi Effendi explains that the names of the prophets with whom Bahá'u'lláh identifies Himself in this Tablet "… are as follows: Abraham, Moses, Joseph, John the Baptist, Jesus, Imám Ḥusayn, on whom Bahá'u'lláh has conferred an exceptionally exalted station (and) the Báb."[1]

Such oneness does not imply uniformity, since there are differences among the Manifestations of God and their revelations. This distinction can be attributed to the following factors:

a) **Three stations:** The Manifestations of God have three stations, namely that of the physical, the human and the divine.

   "*The physical station is phenomenal; it is composed of elements, and necessarily everything that is composed is subject to decomposition*".[2]

   The second station is the rational soul or the human station. "*This also is phenomenal, and the Holy Manifestations share it with all mankind.*"[3] In this station a Manifestation of God is an individual with His own unique combination of the genetic variations that characterise all other human individuals.

   "*The third station is that of the divine appearance and heavenly splendour: it is the Word of God, the Eternal Bounty, the Holy Spirit. It has neither beginning nor end, for these things are related to the world of contingencies and not to the divine world.*"[4] This is the station common among all the Manifestations of God.

b) **Relativity of religious truth:** Bahá'u'lláh states: "*... every age requireth a fresh measure of the light of God. Every Divine Revelation has been sent down in a manner that befitted the circumstances of the age in which it hath appeared.*"[5] Accordingly the teachings of the Manifestations of God are diverse since they are revealed at different ages, for people with

---

1 Shoghi Effendi, a letter written on behalf of Shoghi Effendi to the NSA of the US and Canada, 7 August 1936, in *Lights of Guidance*, p. 475.

2 'Abdu'l-Bahá, *Some Answered Questions*, p. 151.

3 'Abdu'l-Bahá, *Some Answered Questions*, p. 151.

4 'Abdu'l-Bahá, *Some Answered Questions*, p. 152.

5 Bahá'u'lláh, *Gleanings from the Writings of Bahá'u'lláh*, p. 81.

different cultures and backgrounds, and intended to address specific problems. This makes religious truth relative rather than absolute, and revealed religions different in appearance and teachings.

c) **Intensity of Revelations**: The Manifestations of God "... *differ in the intensity of their revelation, and the comparative potency of their light."*[1] This is similar to the physical sun that has different degrees of heat and light depending on the earthly season within which it appears.

d) **Corruption of teachings**: Generally the light of a religion is dimmed by man-made superstitions and ideas as it approaches its winter of despondency. Hence, the religion assumes an appearance and a form radically different from its reality when it was originally revealed by the Manifestation of God.

14.5 The Greater Covenant of Bahá'u'lláh

In this section of his letter, Shoghi Effendi cites a number of statements from Bahá'u'lláh regarding the Manifestation of God Who is to succeed Him. Similar to the prophecies made about Bahá'u'lláh in the previous Dispensations, the full meaning of such statements will remain unknown until they are fulfilled. Nevertheless it is possible to develop some understanding of the Greater Covenant of Bahá'u'lláh and particularly to be aware of the misunderstandings that might occur.

Some of the major principles highlighted in these statements can be summarised as follows:

a) The first clear principle, as pointed out in statement (e), is that Bahá'ís should not believe in the finality of the Revelation of Bahá'u'lláh, as it is contrary to the fundamental teaching of progressive revelation.

b) The Báb has indicated in statement (h) that the process of progressive revelation will continue after Bahá'u'lláh. In the same way that the object of all the revelations before Muḥammad was to pave the way for His revelation, all the Manifestations of God, including Bahá'u'lláh have been preparing humanity for the coming of the future Manifestations of God.

c) The next Manifestation of God will be invested with *"great sovereignty and mighty dominion"* as stated in statement (f).

d) The next Manifestation of God will also be persecuted, as is evident in statements (f) and (g), to such an extent that Bahá'u'lláh has expressed His fears for Him.

---

[1] Bahá'u'lláh, *The Kitáb-i-Íqán*, p. 103.

14.6 Activities

1. Paragraph 42 describes the relationship between the Bahá'í Faith and the previous revelations from God. Identify the key points of this paragraph and list them in bullet form.

2. Consider the following sentence from statement (a):

   "... Through them is transmitted a grace that is infinite, and by them is revealed the light that can never fade ..."

   How can this statement be reconciled with the fact that each Dispensation has a fixed period and is succeeded by a new revelation?

3. What is the meaning and implications of the following sentence from statement (b)?

   "They only differ in the intensity of their revelation and the comparative potency of their light ... That a certain attribute of God hath not been outwardly manifested by these Essences of Detachment doth in no wise imply that they Who are the Day-Springs of God's attributes and the Treasuries of His holy names did not actually possess it."

4. Describe your understanding of the unity of the Manifestations of God.

5. Why is the energy latent in a revelation only gradually unfolded (statement (d))?

6. Consider statement (j). What is the key concept of this statement? Can you identify the different Prophets of God referred to in this statement?

7. What are the main characteristics of the Greater Covenant of Bahá'u'lláh?

14.7 Glossary

Term	Meaning
Allegorical	(The style of) a story, poem, painting, etc., in which the characters and actions represent general truths, good and bad qualities, etc.
Allusion	The act of alluding or speaking about something indirectly
Apprehensive	Full of fear or anxiety about the future; worried
Avow	To state openly; admit
Betrayal	The act of betraying, being disloyal or unfaithful to
Cardinal	Most important; chief
Construe	To place a particular meaning on (a statement, action, etc.); understand or explain in a particular way
Dwarf	To make (someone or something) appear small by comparison
Endue	To fill (a person) with (a good quality)
Exponent	A person who expresses, supports, performs, or is an example of a stated thing
Pristine	Pure; undamaged; fresh and clean
Spasmodic	Not continuous; showing short periods of activity; irregular
Stultify	To make stupid or dull in mind or bored
Succumb	To die, stop resisting, yield
Tabernacle	A fixed or moveable structure for worship in certain Christian churches; a tent used as a sanctuary for the Ark of the Covenant by the Israelites during the Exodus.
Tantamount	Having the same value, force, or effect as (esp. something bad or unwanted)

15. TWOFOLD STATION OF THE BÁB

15.1 Introduction

This chapter covers paragraphs 53–57. Read these paragraphs and reflect on the contents before starting the lesson. In this section of his letter, Shoghi Effendi explains the twofold station of the Báb as not only the Forerunner of Bahá'u'lláh but also as an independent Manifestation of God, Whose Revelation has fulfilled "the object of all the Prophets gone before Him",[1] as attested by Him in the *Persian Bayán*.

In this chapter, you need to look for and understand the following **key concepts**:

a) The Báb is not just the Forerunner of Bahá'u'lláh but also an independent Manifestation of God.

b) The twofold station of the Báb is the most distinctive feature of His Dispensation.

c) The greatness of the Revelation of the Báb is primarily due to His role as the author of an independent religion to an extent unrivalled by the Manifestations of God before Him.

d) The divine origin and power of the Revelation of the Báb cannot be judged based on the short duration of His Dispensation.

e) The events that occurred before the declaration of the Báb and during His Ministry, the abundance of His Revelation, His influence on the learned of His time and the miraculous events accompanying His martyrdom are other evidences of the greatness of His Revelation.

15.2 Paragraphs under study

53. Dearly-beloved friends! That the Báb, the inaugurator of the Bábí Dispensation, is fully entitled to rank as one of the self-sufficient Manifestations of God, that He has been invested with sovereign power and authority, and exercises all the rights and prerogatives of

---

[1] Shoghi Effendi, *The World Order of Bahá'u'lláh*, p. 123.

independent Prophethood, is yet another fundamental verity which the Message of Bahá'u'lláh insistently proclaims and which its followers must uncompromisingly uphold. That He is not to be regarded merely as an inspired Precursor of the Bahá'í Revelation, that in His person, as He Himself bears witness in the Persian Bayán, the object of all the Prophets gone before Him has been fulfilled, is a truth which I feel it my duty to demonstrate and emphasize. We would assuredly be failing in our duty to the Faith we profess and would be violating one of its basic and sacred principles if in our words or by our conduct we hesitate to recognise the implications of this root principle of Bahá'í belief, or refuse to uphold unreservedly its integrity and demonstrate its truth. Indeed the chief motive actuating me to undertake the task of editing and translating Nabíl's immortal Narrative[1] has been to enable every follower of the Faith in the West to better understand and more readily grasp the tremendous implications of His exalted station and to more ardently admire and love Him.

54. There can be no doubt that the claim to the twofold station ordained for the Báb by the Almighty, a claim which He Himself has so boldly advanced, which Bahá'u'lláh has repeatedly affirmed, and to which *The Will and Testament of 'Abdu'l-Bahá* has finally given the sanction of its testimony, constitutes the most distinctive feature of the Bahá'í Dispensation. It is a further evidence of its uniqueness, a tremendous accession to the strength, to the mysterious power and authority with which this holy cycle has been invested. Indeed the greatness of the Báb consists primarily, not in His being the Divinely-appointed Forerunner of so transcendent a Revelation, but rather in His having been invested with the powers inherent in the inaugurator of a separate religious Dispensation, and in His wielding, to a degree unrivalled by the Messengers gone before Him, the sceptre of independent Prophethood.

55. The short duration of His Dispensation, the restricted range within which His laws and ordinances have been made to operate, supply no criterion whatever wherewith to judge its Divine origin and to evaluate the potency of its message. *"That so brief a span,"* Bahá'u'lláh Himself explains, *"should have separated this most mighty and wondrous Revelation from Mine own previous Manifestation is a secret that no man can unravel and a mystery such as no mind can fathom. Its duration had been foreordained, and no man shall ever discover its reason unless and until he be informed of the contents of My Hidden Book."*[2] *"Behold,"* Bahá'u'lláh further explains in *The Kitáb-i-Badí'*, one of His works refuting the arguments of the people of the Bayán, *"behold, how immediately upon the completion of the ninth year of this wondrous, this*

---

[1] *The Dawn Breakers: Nabíl's narrative of the early days of the Bahá'í Revelation*, originally written by Nabíl-i-Zarandí.

[2] Statement (a)

most holy and merciful Dispensation, the requisite number of pure, of wholly consecrated and sanctified souls had been most secretly consummated."[1]

56. The marvellous happenings that have heralded the advent of the Founder of the Bábí Dispensation, the dramatic circumstances of His own eventful life, the miraculous tragedy of His martyrdom, the magic of His influence exerted on the most eminent and powerful among His countrymen, to all of which every chapter of Nabíl's stirring narrative testifies, should in themselves be regarded as sufficient evidence of the validity of His claim to so exalted a station among the Prophets.

57. However graphic the record, which the eminent chronicler of His life has transmitted to posterity, so luminous a narrative must pale before the glowing tribute paid to the Báb by the pen of Bahá'u'lláh. This tribute the Báb Himself has, by the clear assertion of His claim, abundantly supported, while the written testimonies of 'Abdu'l-Bahá have powerfully reinforced its character and elucidated its meaning.

15.3 Twofold station of the Báb

In paragraph 53, Shoghi Effendi refers to the twofold station of the Báb, which is unique in religious history. He is both an independent Manifestation of God and the Forerunner of Bahá'u'lláh.

The greatness of the Báb is primarily due to His station as a Manifestation of God. In *The Kitáb-i-Asmá* (The Book of Names), the Báb explains: "*He Who hath revealed the Qur'án unto Muḥammad, the Apostle of God, ordaining in the Faith of Islám that which was pleasing unto Him, hath likewise revealed the Bayán, in the manner ye have been promised, unto Him Who is your Qá'im, your Guide, your Mihdí, your Lord, Him Whom ye acclaim as the manifestation of God's most excellent titles.*"[2]

Further on He compares His Revelation with Islám in terms of its intensity and describes the divine power and potency of His Revelation by announcing that "*I swear by the life of Him Whom God shall make manifest! My Revelation is indeed far more bewildering than that of Muḥammad, the Apostle of God, if thou dost but pause to reflect upon the days of God. Behold, how strange that a person brought up amongst the people of Persia should be empowered by God to proclaim such irrefutable utterances as to silence every man of learning, and be enabled to spontaneously reveal verses far more rapidly than anyone could possibly set down in writing. Verily, no God is there but Him, the Help in Peril, the Self-Subsisting.*"[3]

Since the Báb is the Forerunner of Bahá'u'lláh, His Dispensation can be considered "*... together with that of Bahá'u'lláh as forming one entity, the*

---

[1] Statement (b)

[2] The Báb, *Selection from the Writings of the Báb*, p. 139.

[3] The Báb, *Selection from the Writings of the Báb*, p. 139.

former being an introductory to the advent of the latter."[1] Hence the Dispensation of the Báb and the events surrounding His declaration and martyrdom can be considered as "the early days of the Bahá'í revelation."[2]

The Dispensation of the Báb lasted for only 9 years—from 1844 to 1853 when Bahá'u'lláh received the first intimation on His Mission in the Síyáh-Chál. As indicated in statement (a), the short length of the Dispensation of the Báb is not an indication of its lesser significance compared to that of previous Manifestations of God.

Shoghi Effendi explains: "As the Báb was not only a Manifestation but a Herald of this Bahá'í Faith, the interval between His revelation and that of Bahá'u'lláh was of shorter duration."[3] However, he does emphasize that in a sense, the Dispensation of the Báb "... will last as long as Bahá'u'lláh's lasts."

15.4 Object of all previous Prophets

According to Shoghi Effendi in paragraph 53, the Revelation of the Báb has fulfilled "the object of all the Prophets gone before Him", as attested by Him in the *Persian Bayán*.

However, the station of the Báb, was initially misunderstood due to its uniqueness in religious history. The common belief of the Shí'ih Muslims regarding the life and disappearance of the Twelfth Imám was a contributing factor to this misunderstanding. The Báb was later identified with the promised Mihdí of Shí'ih Islám and was given the title al-Qá'im. See section 4.3.1 for more details.

The Báb was not only the Promised One of Shí'ih Islám, but also He "... at once fulfilled the promise of all ages and ushered in the consummation of all Revelations."[4] According to Shoghi Effendi, "the Báb was 'the Mihdí' (One Who is guided) awaited by Sunní Muslims, the 'Return of John the Baptist' expected by the Christians, the 'Úshídar-Máh' referred to in the Zoroastrian Scriptures, the 'Return of Elijah' anticipated by the Jews, Whose Revelation was to show forth 'the signs and tokens of all the Prophets', Who was to 'manifest the perfection of Moses, the radiance of Jesus and the patience of Job'".[5]

The advent of the Báb also set in motion a series of events prophesied in the past Holy Books. His appearance was:

a) "'The Second Woe', spoken of in the Apocalypse of St. John the Divine"[6]
b) "The first of the two 'Messengers'[7] Whose appearance had been

---

1 Shoghi Effendi, *Unfolding Destiny*, pp. 426–427.
2 Shoghi Effendi, *Unfolding Destiny*, pp. 426–427.
3 Shoghi Effendi, in *Lights of Guidance*, p. 470.
4 Shoghi Effendi, *God Passes By*, p. 57.
5 Shoghi Effendi, *God Passes By*, p. 57.
6 Shoghi Effendi, *God Passes By*, p. 58.
7 Qur'án 39:68–9

prophesied in the Qur'án"[1]

c) "The first 'Trumpet-Blast'[2] destined to smite the earth with extermination, announced in the latter Book"[3]

d) "'The Inevitable', 'The Catastrophe', 'The Resurrection', 'The Earthquake of the Last Hour'"[4]

Apart from the above listed prophecies, Shoghi Effendi mentions the fulfilment of many other prophecies in *God Passes By,*[5] which can be referred to for more information.

15.5 Greatness of His Revelation

As described by Shoghi Effendi in paragraph 56, the events that occurred before the declaration of the Báb and during His Ministry, His influence on the learned of His time and the miraculous condition of His martyrdom are other evidences of the greatness of His Revelation. It is not difficult to appreciate this statement of Shoghi Effendi if one considers the events that occurred during the short period of the Dispensation of the Báb and the conditions under which His followers, many of them the most learned of the time, sacrificed their lives to prove their love for Him.

The chain of events that led Mullá Ḥusayn to meet the Báb, from the time of Shaykh Aḥmad Aḥsá'í, is all mysterious in nature and clearly providential. Mullá Ḥusayn-i-Bushrú'í, after his first meeting with the Báb has narrated:

> "I felt possessed of such courage and power that were the world, all its peoples and its potentates, to rise against me, I would, alone and undaunted, withstand their onslaught. The universe seemed but a handful of dust in my grasp. I seemed to be the Voice of Gabriel personified, calling unto all mankind: 'Awake, for lo! The morning Light has broken.'"[6]

Such an impact was experienced by all those who met the Báb. In addition, the episodes of Nayríz, Zanján, Shaykh Ṭabarsí, the bravery shown by the followers of the Báb, and the martyrdom of thousands of them are clear evidences of the spirit of courage and detachment that the Revelation of the Báb had infused into their souls.

The extraordinary drama of the martyrdom of the Báb clearly demonstrates the power and ability of the Báb to save Himself and to overpower those hostile towards Him. However, He accepted death when He was satisfied that His Mission was completed.[7]

---

1 Shoghi Effendi, *God Passes By*, p. 58.
2 Qur'án 39:68–9
3 Shoghi Effendi, *God Passes By*, p. 58.
4 Shoghi Effendi, *God Passes By*, p. 58.
5 Shoghi Effendi, *God Passes By,* pp. 58–59.
6 Shoghi Effendi: *The Dawn Breaker*, p. 65.
7 Douglas Martin, "The Mission of the Báb: Retrospective, 1844–1994", *The Bahá'í World*, 1994–1995, pp. 193–225.

In reference to the society in which the Báb declared His mission, Shoghi Effendi states: "... of all the peoples and nations of the civilized world, that race and nation had, as so often depicted by 'Abdu'l-Bahá, sunk to such ignominious depths, and manifested so great a perversity, as to find no parallel among its contemporaries."[1] It consisted of a superstitious and ignorant population influenced and ruled by a corrupt Muslim clergy and governed by the barbaric regime of the Qájár dynasty.

It was such a people that the Báb had summoned to integrity of conduct and purity of heart, and the outcome was astonishing. The spirit released through the Revelation of the Báb created a deep transformation in those who recognized Him. As a result, they manifested attributes and qualities radically different from those of their fellow countrymen. Edward Browne, a historian and an orientalist, has accurately portrayed this transformation:

> "To the Western observer, however, it is the complete sincerity of the Bábís, their fearless disregard of death and torture undergone for the sake of their religion, their certain conviction as to the truth of their faith, their generally admirable conduct towards mankind and especially towards their fellow-believers, which constitutes their strongest claim on his attention."[2]

According to Douglas Martin, the influence of the Báb was not limited to the Persian society but could be observed in Europe in the opinions of the educated elite of the 19th century.[3] Jules Bois, the French literary critic, describes the impact of the Báb:

> "All Europe was stirred to pity and indignation ... Among the litterateurs of my generation, in the Paris of 1890, the martyrdom of the Báb was still as fresh a topic as had been the first news of His death [in 1850]. We wrote poems about Him. Sara Bernhardt entreated Caulle Mendes for a play on the theme of this historic tragedy."[4]

Many writers as diverse as Joseph Arthur de Gobineau, Edward Granville Brown, Ernest Renan, Aleksandr Tumansky, A. L. M. Nicolas, Viktor Rosen, Clement Huart, George Curzon, Matthew Arnold, and Leo Tolstoy were affected by the spiritual impact of the life and martyrdom of the Báb and they wrote about Him.

---

1 Shoghi Effendi, *The Advent of Divine Justice*, p. 16.

2 E.G. Browne, Introduction to Myron H. Phelps, *Life and Teachings of Abbas Effendi*, 2nd rev., p. xvi, 1912.

3 Douglas Martin, "The Mission of the Báb: Retrospective, 1844–1994", *The Bahá'í World*, 1994–1995, pp. 193–225.

4 Shoghi Effendi, *God Passes By*, p. 56.

15.6 Activities

1. Describe your understanding of the following statement from paragraph 53:

   "That the Báb, the inaugurator of the Bábí Dispensation, is fully entitled to rank as one of the self-sufficient Manifestations of God, that He has been invested with sovereign power and authority, and exercises all the rights and prerogatives of independent Prophethood, is yet another fundamental verity which the Message of Bahá'u'lláh insistently proclaims and which its followers must uncompromisingly uphold."

2. What has been the main motivation of Shoghi Effendi in translating Nabíl's narrative into English?

3. In your view, why was the Dispensation of the Báb of such a short duration?

4. What is your understanding of statement (b)?

5. Briefly describe the prophecies made in the previous Dispensations referring to the Revelation of the Báb.

6. What are the major events referred to in paragraph 56?

7. What was the extent of spiritual transformation in the followers of the Báb?

15.7 Glossary

Term	Meaning
Commotion	Noisy and excited movement or activity
Consecrate	To dedicate ones life to; To declare as holy
Precursor	Something that comes before another and leads to it or is developed into it
Prerogative	A special right belonging to a particular person, esp. because of the official position they hold
Profess	To have (a religion or belief)
Requisite	Needed for a purpose; necessary
Sceptre	A short rod carried by a king or queen on ceremonial occasions as a sign of power
Smite	To strike hard
Wield	To have and/or use (power, influence, etc.)

16. CONSTANCY IN THE BÁB'S CAUSE

16.1 Introduction

This chapter covers paragraphs 58–61. Read these paragraphs and reflect on the contents before starting the lesson. In this section of his letter, Shoghi Effendi cites some of the statements made by Bahá'u'lláh in *The Kitáb-i-Íqán* on the sublimity of the Revelation of the Báb. These statements highlight the constancy of the Báb in His Cause and the abundance of His Revelation. Bahá'u'lláh also declares that no understanding can comprehend the nature of the Revelation of the Báb.

In this chapter, you need to look for and understand the following **key concepts**:

a) Bahá'u'lláh refers to the constancy of the Báb in claiming His Mission as a further proof of His Revelation. This quality is particularly awe-inspiring when we consider the Báb's youthfulness.
b) Bahá'u'lláh describes the abundance and rapidity with which the sacred verses were revealed by the Báb as another significant feature of His Revelation.
c) The degree of self-sacrifice demonstrated by the followers of the Báb is a testimony to the truth of the Revelation of the Báb.
d) It is impossible to understand the full nature of the Revelation of the Báb.
e) "Knowledge is twenty and seven letters. All that the Prophets have revealed are two letters thereof ... But when the Qá'im shall arise, He will cause the remaining twenty and five letters to be made manifest."

16.2 Paragraphs under study

58. Where else if not in *The Kitáb-i-Íqán* can the student of the Bábí Dispensation seek to find those affirmations that unmistakably attest the power and spirit which no man, except he be a Manifestation of God, can manifest? "*Could such a thing,*" exclaims Bahá'u'lláh, "*be made manifest except through the power of a Divine Revelation and the potency of God's invincible Will? By the righteousness of God! Were*

any one to entertain so great a Revelation in his heart the thought of such a declaration would alone confound him! Were the hearts of all men to be crowded into his heart, he would still hesitate to venture upon so awful an enterprise."[1] "*No eye,*" He in another passage affirms, "*hath beheld so great an outpouring of bounty, nor hath any ear heard of such a Revelation of loving-kindness ... The Prophets 'endowed with constancy,' whose loftiness and glory shine as the sun, were each honoured with a Book, which all have seen, and the verses of which have been duly ascertained. Whereas the verses, which have rained from this Cloud of divine mercy have been so abundant that none hath yet been able to estimate their number ... How can they belittle this Revelation? Hath any age witnessed such momentous happenings?*"[2]

59. Commenting on the character and influence of those heroes and martyrs whom the spirit of the Báb had so magically transformed Bahá'u'lláh reveals the following: "*If these companions be not the true strivers after God, who else could be called by this name? ... If these companions, with all their marvellous testimonies and wondrous works, be false, who then is worthy to claim for himself the truth? ... Has the world since the days of Adam witnessed such tumult, such violent commotion? ... Methinks, patience was revealed only by virtue of their fortitude, and faithfulness itself was begotten only by their deeds.*"[3]

60. Wishing to stress the sublimity of the Báb's exalted station as compared with that of the Prophets of the past, Bahá'u'lláh in that same epistle asserts: "*No understanding can grasp the nature of His Revelation, nor can any knowledge comprehend the full measure of His Faith.*"[4] He then quotes, in confirmation of His argument, these prophetic words: "*Knowledge is twenty and seven letters. All that the Prophets have revealed are two letters thereof. No man thus far hath known more than these two letters. But when the Qá'im shall arise, He will cause the remaining twenty and five letters to be made manifest.*"[5] "*Behold,*" He adds, "*how great and lofty is His station! His rank excelleth that of all the Prophets and His Revelation transcendeth the comprehension and understanding of all their chosen ones.*"[6] "*Of His Revelation,*" He further adds, "*the Prophets of God, His saints and chosen ones, have either not been informed, or, in pursuance of God's inscrutable decree, they have not disclosed.*"[7]

61. Of all the tributes, which Bahá'u'lláh's unerring pen has chosen to pay to the memory of the Báb, His "*Best-Beloved,*" the most memorable and

---

1 Statement (a)
2 Statement (b)
3 Statement (c)
4 Statement (d)
5 Statement (e)
6 Statement (f)
7 Statement (g)

touching is this brief, yet eloquent passage, which so greatly enhances the value of the concluding passages of that same epistle. "*Amidst them all,*" He writes, referring to the afflictive trials and dangers besetting Him in the city of Baghdád, "*We stand life in hand wholly resigned to His Will, that perchance through God's loving kindness and grace, this revealed and manifest Letter (Bahá'u'lláh) may lay down His life as a sacrifice in the path of the Primal Point, the most exalted Word (the Báb). By Him, at Whose bidding the Spirit hath spoken, but for this yearning of Our soul, We would not, for one moment, have tarried any longer in this city.*"[1]

16.3 Constancy in His claim

In statement (a), Bahá'u'lláh refers to the constancy of the Báb in claiming His Mission as a further proof of the Báb's Revelation. This quality is particularly awe-inspiring when we consider the Báb's youthfulness. At the age of 25, He claimed to be the promised Qá'im for whose coming Shí'ih Muslims had been praying for more than one thousand years. Even the thought of such a claim is so bewildering that a person "*would still hesitate to venture upon so awful an enterprise,*" even were "*the hearts of all men to be crowded into his heart.*"

What occurred in Tabríz during the questioning of the Báb by the Muslim clergy is a powerful evidence of the audacity of the Báb. This gathering was held in the residence and the presence of the governor of Ádhirbáyján; Násiri'd-Dín Mírzá, the heir to the throne. The ecclesiastical dignitaries of Tabríz, the leaders of the Shaykhí community, the Shaykhu'l-Islám, and the Imám-Jum'ih of Tabríz were also present. The chair of the meeting was Ḥájí Mullá Maḥmúd, the Niẓámu'l-'Ulamá, the Prince's tutor.[2]

> "Upon His arrival, the Báb observed that every seat in that hall was occupied except one which had been reserved for the Valí-'Ahd [the heir to the throne]. He greeted the assembly and, without the slightest hesitation, proceeded to occupy that vacant seat. The majesty of His gait, the expression of overpowering confidence which sat upon His brow—above all, the spirit of power which shone from His whole being, appeared to have for a moment crushed the soul out of the body of those whom He had greeted. A deep, a mysterious silence, suddenly fell upon them. Not one soul in that distinguished assembly dared breathe a single word. At last the stillness which brooded over them was broken by the Niẓámu'l-'Ulamá'. 'Whom do you claim to be,' he asked the Báb, 'and what is the message which you have brought?' '*I am,*' thrice exclaimed the Báb, '*I am, I am, the promised One! I am the One whose name you have for a thousand years invoked, at whose mention you have risen, whose advent you have*

---

1 Statement (h)

2 Shoghi Effendi, *God Passes By*, p. 21.

> *longed to witness, and the hour of whose Revelation you have prayed God to hasten. Verily I say, it is incumbent upon the peoples of both the East and the West to obey My word and to pledge allegiance to My person.'* ... Immediately after He had declared Himself to be the promised One, a feeling of awe seized those who were present. They had dropped their heads in silent confusion. The pallor of their faces betrayed the agitation of their hearts. Mullá Muḥammad, that one-eyed and white-bearded renegade, insolently reprimanded Him, saying: 'You wretched and immature lad of Shíráz! You have already convulsed and subverted 'Iráq; do you now wish to arouse a like turmoil in Ádhirbáyján?' '*Your Honour,*' replied the Báb, '*I have not come hither of My own accord. I have been summoned to this place.*' 'Hold your peace,' furiously retorted Mullá Muḥammad, 'you perverse and contemptible follower of Satan!' '*Your Honour,*' the Báb again answered, '*I maintain what I have already declared.*'"[1]

In statement (a), Bahá'u'lláh indicates that such audacity and daring cannot be manifested but through the power of divine Revelation. What else could be the source of such courage or the motivation behind such a claim? Do those hostile to the Báb "*... accuse Him of folly as they accused the Prophets of old? Or do they maintain that His motive was none other than leadership and the acquisition of earthly riches?*"[2]

16.4 Abundance of His Revelation

In statement (b) cited in paragraph 58 from *The Kitáb-i-Íqán*, Bahá'u'lláh describes the abundance and rapidity with which the sacred verses were revealed by the Báb as another significant feature of His Revelation. The volume of the Writings of the Báb, and the speed at which He composed elaborate commentaries, prayers and expositions, with no premeditation, are considered as significant proofs of His sublime station.[3] He Himself bears witness to this fact by this statement: "*Verily the equivalent of that which God revealed unto Muḥammad during twenty-three years, hath been revealed unto Me within the space of two days and two nights.*"[4] But He warns His followers: "*... no distinction is to be drawn between the two. He, in truth, hath power over all things.*"

In *the Qayyúmu'l-Asmá*[5] He announces: "*Verily We made the revelation of verses to be a testimony for Our message unto you.*" He then challenges His ecclesiastical opponents by asking them: "*Can ye produce a single letter to match these verses? Bring forth, then, your proofs, if ye be of those who can*

---

1 Shoghi Effendi, *The Dawn Breakers*, pp. 316–317.

2 Bahá'u'lláh, *The Kitáb-i-Íqán*, p. 231.

3 J. E. Esslemont, *Bahá'u'lláh and the New Era*, 5th rev. ed. (Wilmette: Bahá'í Publishing Trust, 1987), p. 19.

4 The Báb, *Selection from the Writings of the Báb*, p. 139.

5 The Báb, *Selection from the Writings of the Báb*, p. 43.

discern the one true God. I solemnly affirm before God, should all men and spirits combine to compose the like of one chapter of this Book, they would surely fail, even though they were to assist one another."

Vaḥíd (Siyyid Yaḥyá) was present when the Báb revealed the commentary on the Súrih of Kawthar for him. He has recorded his experience:

> "It was still in the afternoon when the Báb requested Ḥájí Mírzá Siyyid 'Alí to bring His pen-case and some paper. He then started to reveal His commentary on the Súrih of Kawthar. How am I to describe this scene of inexpressible majesty? Verses streamed from His pen with a rapidity that was truly astounding. The incredible swiftness of His writings, the soft and gentle murmur of His voice, and the stupendous force of His style, amazed, and bewildered me. He continued in this manner until the approach of sunset. He did not pause until the entire commentary of the Súrih was completed. He then laid down His pen and asked for tea. Soon after, He began to read it aloud in my presence. My heart leaped madly as I heard Him pour out, in accents of unutterable sweetness, those treasures enshrined in that sublime commentary."[1]

16.5 Self-sacrifice and martyrdom

In statement (c), Bahá'u'lláh states that the degree of self-sacrifice demonstrated by the followers of the Báb is a testimony to the truth of the Revelation of the Báb. For the sake of their Beloved they gave their lives when they were asked to either deny their belief or face death.

The short period of the Ministry of the Báb is rich in heroic acts manifested by His followers. In particular, these events were intensified after the death of Muḥammad Sháh. Násiri'd-Dín Mírzá, the new seventeen-year old king, left all his affairs in the hands of his Amír-Niẓám,[2] Mírzá Taqí Khán who ordered the immediate persecution and punishment of the Bábís across the country. This resulted in a systematic campaign by civil and ecclesiastical powers against the Cause of the Báb.[3]

As to the extent of the havoc caused by such an order, Shoghi Effendi writes that "... in remote and isolated centres the scattered disciples of a persecuted community were pitilessly struck down by the sword of their foes, while in centres where large numbers had congregated measures were taken in self-defence, which, misconstrued by a cunning and deceitful adversary, served in their turn to inflame still further the hostility of the authorities, and multiply the outrages perpetrated by the oppressor. In the East at Shaykh Ṭabarsí, in the south in Nayríz, in the west in Zanján, and in the capital itself, massacres, upheavals, demonstrations, engagements, sieges, acts of treachery proclaimed, in rapid succession, the violence of the storm which had broken out, and

---

1 Shoghi Effendi, *The Dawn-Breakers*, p. 175.

2 The Grand-Vizír

3 Shoghi Effendi, *God Passes By*, p. 37.

exposed the bankruptcy, and blackened the annals, of a proud yet degenerate people."[1]

It is important to note that all of these individuals were forced to choose between recanting their faith or death. Those who were killed at the hands of the enemies of the Faith accepted martyrdom in preference to denouncing their Beloved. However, this did not mean that they volunteered for martyrdom nor had suicidal tendencies.

16.6 Challenge to understand Revelation of the Báb

In paragraph 60, Shoghi Effendi quotes Bahá'u'lláh's statement that it is impossible to fully understand the nature of the Revelation of the Báb. As evidence of this, Bahá'u'lláh refers to a ḥadíth that had been recorded in three reliable Islamic books, including "Biḥáru'l-Anvár", the "Avalím", and the "Yanbú'". Shoghi Effendi refers to this ḥadíth briefly in paragraph 9 (see section 4.5). The first book, "Biḥáru'l-Anvár", is the encyclopaedia of Shí'ih theology written by 'Allámeh Majlisí in twenty–six volumes.

The Avalím is a book by Shaykh 'Abdu'lláh-ibn Shaykh Núru'lláh-i- Baḥ rání and consists of one hundred volumes, covering various traditions as well as Islamic history.[2]

The "Yanbú'" is a book by Ṣadíq, son of Muḥammad, a Shí'ih Muslim scholar who lived in the third century of the Islamic era.

According to the above-mentioned ḥadíth, "Knowledge is twenty and seven letters. All that the Prophets have revealed are two letters thereof. No man thus far hath known more than these two letters. But when the Qá'im shall arise, He will cause the remaining twenty and five letters to be made manifest."

The remaining knowledge and the mysteries of the universe that will be revealed after the appearance of the Promised Qá'im will be equivalent to twenty–five letters. These numbers indicate the intensity of the Revelation of the Qá'im (the Báb) and consequently its significance as well as impact on the world of creation.

16.7 Sacrifice for the Primal Point

In paragraph 61, Shoghi Effendi cites statement (h) from Bahá'u'lláh that is a touching tribute to the Báb. This statement, revealed in the concluding paragraphs of *The Kitáb-i-Íqán*, is part of a section in which Bahá'u'lláh recounts the condition of the Bábí community in Baghdád at the time of His return from Sulaymáníyyih and the tribulations that He experienced as a result. This is the complete paragraph:

> *"What pen can recount the things We beheld upon Our return! Two years have elapsed during which Our enemies have ceaselessly and assiduously contrived to exterminate Us, whereunto all witness.*

---

1 Shoghi Effendi, *God Passes By*, pp. 37–38.

2 A. Ishráq Khávarí, *Ghamus-i-Íqán* (in Fársí), vol. II, pp. 1133–1135.

> *Nevertheless, none amongst the faithful hath risen to render Us any assistance, nor did any one feel inclined to help in Our deliverance. Nay, instead of assisting Us, what showers of continuous sorrows, their words and deeds have caused to rain upon Our soul! Amidst them all, We stand, life in hand, wholly resigned to His will; that perchance, through God's loving kindness and His grace, this revealed and manifest Letter may lay down His life as a sacrifice in the path of the Primal Point, the most exalted Word. By Him at Whose bidding the Spirit hath spoken, but for this yearning of Our soul, We would not, for one moment, have tarried any longer in this city. 'Sufficient Witness is God unto Us.'"*[1]

According to Shoghi Effendi, Bahá'u'lláh was saddened by the demoralisation and degradation of the Bábí community to the extent that "He refused for some time to leave His house, except for His visits to Káẓimayn and for His occasional meetings with a few of His friends who resided in that town and in Baghdád."[2]

Káẓimayn is now a neighbourhood of Baghdád about five kilometres north west of the city centre. At the time of Bahá'u'lláh, mainly Persians inhabited the town. The two Káẓims, the seventh and the ninth Imams of Shí'ih Islám are buried in Káẓimayn.

---

1 Bahá'u'lláh, *The Kitáb-i-Íqán*, pp. 251–252.
2 Shoghi Effendi, *God Passes By*, pp. 125–126.

16.8 Activities

1. Describe your understanding of statement (a).

2. Describe some of the facts mentioned in this chapter regarding the abundance of the Revelation of the Báb.

3. Describe your understanding of statement (c).

4. Why is the degree of self-sacrifice demonstrated by the followers of the Báb another evidence of the truth of His Revelation?

5. Describe your understanding of the following ḥadíth cited in paragraph 60:

   "Knowledge is twenty and seven letters. All that the Prophets have revealed are two letters thereof. No man thus far hath known more than these two letters. But when the Qá'im shall arise, He will cause the remaining twenty and five letters to be made manifest."

6. What is your understanding of statement (f)?

7. What is your understanding of statement (g)?

8. What is your understanding of statement (h)?

16.9 Glossary

Term	Meaning
Ascertain	To discover (the truth about something)
Beset	Surround and harass; assail on all sides
Inscrutable	Impossible to understand or interpret
Refute	To prove that (someone or something) is mistaken or incorrect
Tarry	To delay or be slow in starting, going, coming, etc.
Tribute	An act, statement, or gift that is intended to show gratitude, respect, or admiration
Tumult	State of confusion and excitement, uproar

17. OTHER TESTIMONIES REGARDING THE BÁB

17.1 Introduction

This chapter covers paragraphs 62–67. Read these paragraphs and reflect on the contents before starting the lesson. In this section of his letter, Shoghi Effendi further illustrates the station and power of the Báb based on the statements made by the Báb Himself and 'Abdu'l-Bahá.

In this chapter, you need to look for and understand the following **key concepts**:

a) The Báb refers to Himself as "*The Mystic Fane*". A fane is defined as a temple and its equivalent word in Arabic and Hebrew is "Haykal".

b) The Báb calls Himself "*The Great Announcement*", which is a reference in the Holy Scriptures to a time of upheaval and great events —also hailed as the Day of Judgement, the Day of Gathering, the Day of Meeting God, and the Day of Resurrection.

c) The Báb refers to Himself as "*the Lamp, which the Finger of God hath lit within its niche and caused to shine with deathless splendour,*" and "*the Flame of that supernal Light that glowed upon Sinai in the gladsome Spot.*"

d) The Báb further refers to Himself as the Primal Point, (Nuqtiy-i-Úlá), which was the title He adopted for Himself in the Tablet to Muḥammad Sháh.

e) According to 'Abdu'l-Bahá, the intensity of the Revelation of Bahá'u'lláh is greater than that of the Revelation of the Báb.

17.2 Paragraphs under study

62. Dearly-beloved friends! So resounding a praise, so bold an assertion issued by the pen of Bahá'u'lláh in so weighty a work, are fully re-echoed in the language in which the Source of the Bábí Revelation has chosen to clothe the claims He Himself has advanced. "*I am the Mystic Fane,*" the Báb thus proclaims His station in the Qayyúmu'l-Asmá', "*which the Hand of Omnipotence hath reared. I am the Lamp, which*

the Finger of God hath lit within its niche and caused to shine with deathless splendour. I am the Flame of that supernal Light that glowed upon Sinai in the gladsome Spot, and lay concealed in the midst of the Burning Bush."[1] "*O Qurratu'l-'Ayn!*" He, addressing Himself in that same commentary, exclaims, "*I recognise in Thee none other except the 'Great Announcement'—the Announcement voiced by the Concourse on high. By this name, I bear witness, they that circle the Throne of Glory have ever known Thee.*"[2] "*With each and every Prophet, Whom We have sent down in the past,*" He further adds, "*We have established a separate Covenant concerning the 'Remembrance of God' and His Day. Manifest, in the realm of glory and through the power of truth, are the 'Remembrance of God' and His Day before the eyes of the angels that circle His mercy-seat.*"[3] "*Should it be Our wish,*" He again affirms, "*it is in Our power to compel, through the agency of but one letter of Our Revelation, the world and all that is therein to recognise, in less than the twinkling of an eye, the truth of Our Cause.*"[4]

63. "*I am the Primal Point,*" the Báb thus addresses Muḥammad Sháh from the prison-fortress of Máh-Kú, "*from which have been generated all created things ... I am the Countenance of God Whose splendour can never be obscured, the light of God whose radiance can never fade ... All the keys of heaven God hath chosen to place on My right hand, and all the keys of hell on My left ... I am one of the sustaining pillars of the Primal Word of God. Whosoever hath recognised Me, hath known all that is true and right, and hath attained all that is good and seemly ... The substance wherewith God hath created Me is not the clay out of which others have been formed. He hath conferred upon Me that which the worldly-wise can never comprehend, nor the faithful discover.*"[5] "*Should a tiny ant,*" the Báb, wishing to stress the limitless potentialities latent in His Dispensation, characteristically affirms, "*desire in this day to be possessed of such power as to be able to unravel the abstrusest and most bewildering passages of the Qur'án, its wish will no doubt be fulfilled, inasmuch as the mystery of eternal might vibrates within the innermost being of all created things.*"[6] "*If so helpless a creature,*" is 'Abdu'l-Bahá's comment on so startling an affirmation, "*can be endowed with so subtle a capacity, how much more efficacious must be the power released through the liberal effusions of the grace of Bahá'u'lláh!*"[7]

64. To these authoritative assertions and solemn declarations made by

---

1 Statement (a)
2 Statement (b)
3 Statement (c)
4 Statement (d)
5 Statement (e)
6 Statement (f)
7 Statement (g)

Bahá'u'lláh and the Báb must be added 'Abdu'l-Bahá's own incontrovertible testimony. He, the appointed interpreter of the utterances of both Bahá'u'lláh and the Báb, corroborates, not by implication but in clear and categorical language, both in His Tablets and in His Testament, the truth of the statements to which I have already referred.

65. In a Tablet addressed to a Bahá'í in Mázindarán, in which He unfolds the meaning of a misinterpreted statement attributed to Him regarding the rise of the Sun of Truth in this century, He sets forth, briefly but conclusively, what should remain for all time our true conception of the relationship between the two Manifestations associated with the Bahá'í Dispensation. "*In making such a statement,*" He explains, "*I had in mind no one else except the Báb and Bahá'u'lláh, the character of whose Revelations it had been my purpose to elucidate. The Revelation of the Báb may be likened to the sun, its station corresponding to the first sign of the Zodiac—the sign Aries—which the sun enters at the Vernal Equinox. The station of Bahá'u'lláh's Revelation, on the other hand, is represented by the sign Leo, the sun's mid-summer and highest station. By this is meant that this holy Dispensation is illumined with the light of the Sun of Truth shining from its most exalted station, and in the plenitude of its resplendency, its heat and glory.*"[1]

66. "*The Báb, the Exalted One,*" 'Abdu'l-Bahá more specifically affirms in another Tablet, "*is the Morn of Truth, the splendour of Whose light shineth throughout all regions. He is also the Harbinger of the Most Great Light, the Abhá Luminary. The Blessed Beauty is the One promised by the sacred books of the past, the revelation of the Source of light that shone upon Mount Sinai, Whose fire glowed in the midst of the Burning Bush. We are, one and all, servants of their threshold and stand each as a lowly keeper at their door.*"[2] "*Every proof and prophecy,*" is His still more emphatic warning, "*every manner of evidence, whether based on reason or on the text of the scriptures and traditions, are to be regarded as centred in the persons of Bahá'u'lláh and the Báb. In them is to be found their complete fulfilment.*"[3]

67. And finally, in His Will and Testament, the repository of His last wishes and parting instructions, He in the following passage, specifically designed to set forth the guiding principles of Bahá'í belief, sets the seal of His testimony on the Báb's dual and exalted station: "*The foundation of the belief of the people of Bahá (may my life be offered up for them) is this: His holiness the exalted One (the Báb) is the Manifestation of the unity and oneness of God and the Forerunner of the Ancient Beauty (Bahá'u'lláh). His holiness, the Abhá Beauty (Bahá'u'lláh) (may my*

---

1 Statement (h)
2 Statement (i)
3 Statement (j)

life be offered up as a sacrifice for His steadfast friends) is the supreme Manifestation of God and the Day-Spring of His most divine Essence." "All others," He significantly adds, *"are servants unto Him and do His bidding."*[1]

17.3 Significance of the Báb's references to Himself

In paragraphs 62 and 63, Shoghi Effendi cites a number of statements from the Báb on the greatness of His Revelation. The major points addressed in these statements are explored in this section.

17.3.1 Mystic Fane

In statement (a), the Báb refers to Himself as "*The Mystic Fane*". A fane is defined as a temple or any building dedicated to religion, and translates into the word Haykal in both Arabic and Hebrew. In Hebrew Haykal means "temple", particularly the first and second Jewish Temples in Jerusalem. In Arabic, in addition to the meaning of a Jewish or Christian temple, this word also means the body or form of something, particularly the human body. Bahá'u'lláh has written a Tablet called the Súratu'l-Haykal (The Tablet of the Temple) in which the primary sense of Haykal is the human body, particularly the body of the Manifestation of God (see section 11.5). The meaning of "temple" is also presented in this Tablet.[2]

Mysticism is defined as an attempt to gain knowledge of real truth and union with God through prayer and meditation. A mystic is defined as a person who seeks by prayer, meditation and self-surrender to attain unity with God or the Absolute, and so reach truths beyond human understanding.

The term "Mystic Fane" has been used in the Bahá'í Writings as a symbolic reference to the Manifestations of God.

17.3.2 The Great Announcement

In statement (b), the Báb calls Himself "*The Great Announcement*". The Great Announcement is a reference made in the Holy Scriptures to a time of upheaval and great events. It has also been referred to as the Day of Judgement, the Day of Gathering, the Day of Meeting God, and the Day of Resurrection. Here are two examples from the Qur'án:

a) *"And listen for the Day when the Caller will call out from a place quite near. The Day when they will hear a (mighty) Blast in (very) truth: that will be the Day of Resurrection. Who would be this caller, and where is this place that is quite near? In the past, the call came from the Messenger."*[3]

b) *"And there shall be a blast on the Trumpet, and all who are in the Heaven and all who are on the earth shall expire, save those whom God shall*

---

1 Statement (k)

2 John Walbridge, Encyclopaedia Article, *Tablet of the Temple*, cited at http://Bahá'í-library.org/encylcopedia/haykal.html

3 *Qur'án* 50:41–2

vouchsafe to live. Then shall there be another blast on it, and lo! arising they shall gaze around them: and the earth shall shine with the light of her Lord."[1]

There are also prophecies regarding the advent of two great Manifestations of God in all the Holy books. In Islám, the majority of the followers believe that the Promised Ones are the "Imám Mihdí" and the "Messiah". In the Qur'án, the advent of the Promised Ones is referred to as the "Great Announcement". This is a recurring theme in the Qur'án as about five thousand out of the six thousand two hundred verses of the Qur'án revolve around this issue.[2] See sections 4.3.1 and 6.7.

In the Bahá'í Writings, such events are all defined as the time when a Manifestation of God appears. Bahá'u'lláh describes the Resurrection as "... *the rise of the Manifestation of God to proclaim His Cause.*"[3] Furthermore, the Báb explains, "... *what is meant by the Day of* Resurrection *is this, that from the time of the appearance of Him Who is the Tree of divine Reality, at whatever period and under whatever name, until the moment of His disappearance, is the Day of Resurrection. For example, from the inception of the mission of Jesus—may peace be upon Him—till the day of His ascension was the Resurrection of Moses.*"[4]

Bahá'u'lláh has also referred to His Revelation as the "Great Announcement". In a Tablet, He announces: "*By Him Who is the Great Announcement! The All-Merciful is come invested with undoubted sovereignty. The Balance hath been appointed, and all them that dwell on earth have been gathered together.*"[5] He has also referred to His Revelation as the Day of Judgement: "*But, as a token of divine retribution upon those heedless ones, their erroneous beliefs and pursuits have, in this Day of Judgement, been made clear and evident to every man of discernment and understanding.*"[6]

17.3.3 Divine light

In statement (a), the Báb refers to Himself as the Light of God in two contexts. In the first instance, He states: "*I am the Lamp, which the Finger of God hath lit within its niche and caused to shine with deathless splendour.*" This is a reference to the following verse from the Qur'án in which the imagery of light is mentioned a number of times:

> *"God is the light of the Heavens and of the Earth. His Light is like a niche in which is a lamp—the lamp encased in glass—the glass, as it were, a glistening star. From a blessed tree it is lighted, the olive neither of the East nor of the West, whose oil would well-nigh shine*

---

1 *Qur'án* 39:68–69

2 M. Mustafa, *Bahá'u'lláh the Great Announcement of the Qur'án*, p. 6.

3 Bahá'u'lláh, *The Kitáb-i-Íqán*, p. 170.

4 The Báb, *Selection from the Writings of the Báb*, p. 106.

5 Bahá'u'lláh, *Gleanings from the Writings of Bahá'u'lláh*, p. 40.

6 Bahá'u'lláh, *The Tablets of Bahá'u'lláh*, p. 124.

out, even though fire touched it not! It is light upon light. God guideth whom He will to His light, and God setteth forth parables to men, for God knoweth all things."[1]

'Abdu'l-Bahá states that the light mentioned in this verse is the Divine Light. This is the Light by which Moses "... *was enabled to see and comprehend the Divine Appearance, and to hear the Heavenly Voice which spoke to him from the Burning Bush.*"[2]

He also mentions in *The Tablets of Divine Plan* that the propagation and teaching of the Cause of Bahá'u'lláh is the realisation of this verse of the Qur'án.[3]

In the second context, alluding to Himself, the Báb states: "*I am the Flame of that supernal Light that glowed upon Sinai in the gladsome Spot, and lay concealed in the midst of the Burning Bush.*" There are a number of references to the term "Burning Bush" in the Writings of Bahá'u'lláh and the Báb. This term symbolises the dawning place of revelation and has its roots in the Bible, in the book of Exodus. God, known as Yahweh or Jehovah in Hebrew, appeared to the 80-year-old Moses on Mount Sinai in a burning bush and commanded him to go back to Egypt and deliver his people from their bondage. The Bible describes the event as follows:

> *"And the angel of the LORD appeared unto him in a flame of fire out of the midst of a bush: and he looked, and, behold, the bush burned with fire, and the bush was not consumed.*
>
> *And Moses said, I will now turn aside, and see this great sight, why the bush is not burnt.*
>
> *And when the LORD saw that he turned aside to see, God called unto him out of the midst of the bush, and said, Moses, Moses. And he said, Here am I.*
>
> *And he said, Draw not nigh hither: put off thy shoes from off thy feet, for the place whereon thou standest is holy ground.*
>
> *Moreover he said, I am the God of thy father, the God of Abraham, the God of Isaac, and the God of Jacob. And Moses hid his face; for he was afraid to look upon God."*[4]

In this context, the Báb claims to be the Light (*flame of fire*) that appeared in the burning bush. In a similar statement, the Báb writes: "*Indeed We conversed with Moses by the leave of God from the midst of the Burning Bush in the Sinai and revealed an infinitesimal glimmer of Thy Light upon the Mystic*

---

1 *Qur'án* 24:35
2 'Abdu'l-Bahá, *Paris Talks*, p. 68.
3 'Abdu'l-Bahá, *The Tablets of Divine Plan*, p. 62.
4 Exodus 3.2–3.6

Mount and its dwellers, whereupon the Mount shook to its foundations and was crushed into dust ...."[1]

There are also numerous references to the Burning Bush in the Writings of Bahá'u'lláh. In *The Kitáb-i-Aqdas*, Bahá'u'lláh states, "*Say ... He it is Who hath caused the Rock to shout, and the Burning Bush to lift up its voice, upon the Mount rising above the Holy Land, and proclaim: 'The Kingdom is God's, the sovereign Lord of all, the All-Powerful, the Loving!'*"[2]

According to Shoghi Effendi, such statements do not imply that the Báb and Bahá'u'lláh are the Intermediaries between God and His Manifestations. In a letter to an individual, he explicitly explains: "Bahá'u'lláh is not the Intermediary between other Manifestations and God. Each has His own relation to the Primal Source. But in the sense that Bahá'u'lláh is the greatest Manifestation to yet appear, the One Who consummates the Revelation of Moses; He was the One Moses conversed with in the Burning Bush. In other words Bahá'u'lláh identifies the glory of the Godhead on that occasion with Himself."[3] He also warns: "No distinction can be made amongst the Prophets in the sense that They all proceed from One Source, and are of One Essence. But Their stations and functions in this world are different."[4]

17.3.4 Primal Point

In statement (e), the Báb further reveals His authority and power. Initially He refers to Himself as the Primal Point, (Nuqtiy-i-Úlá), which was the title He adopted for Himself in the Tablet to Muḥammad Sh͟áh. According to John Esslemont in his book *Bahá'u'lláh and the New Era*[5], this was a title given to Muḥammad (the Prophet of Islám) by His followers. Using this title, the Báb announced His station as a Manifestation of God comparable to Muḥammad. For this reason, Sh͟í'ih Muslims denounced him as an impostor.

It is interesting to note that Bahá'u'lláh addresses the Báb as "*the Primal Point, the most exalted Word*".[6] In a Tablet, 'Abdu'l-Bahá describes the relationship between the "Letter" and the "Word":

> "*It is evident that the Letter is a member of the Word, and this membership in the Word signifieth that the Letter is dependent for its value on the Word, that is, it deriveth its grace from the Word; it has a spiritual kinship with the Word, and is accounted an integral part of the Word. The Apostles were even as Letters, and Christ was the essence of the Word Itself; and the meaning of the Word, which is grace everlasting, cast a splendour on those Letters. Again, since*

---

1 The Báb, *Selection from the Writings of the Báb*, p. 72.
2 Bahá'u'lláh, *The Kitáb-i-Aqdas*, p. 57.
3 Shoghi Effendi, *Lights of Guidance*, p. 471.
4 Shoghi Effendi, *Lights of Guidance*, p. 471.
5 J. E. Esslemont, *Bahá'u'lláh and the New Era*, 5th rev. ed. (Wilmette: Bahá'í Publishing Trust, 1987), p. 16.
6 Shoghi Effendi, *The World Order of Bahá'u'lláh*, p. 125.

the Letter is a member of the Word, it therefore, in its inner meaning, is consonant with the Word."[1]

Shoghi Effendi calls our attention to the significance of the term "Primal Point" in relation to the location of the Báb's resting-place on Mount Carmel. He wrote in a letter dated 18 February 1951 to the National Spiritual Assembly of the Bahá'ís of the United States:

> "For, just as in the realm of the spirit, the reality of the Báb has been hailed by the Author of the Bahá'í Revelation as 'The Point round Whom the realities of the Prophets and Messengers revolve,' so, on this visible plane, His sacred remains constitute the heart and centre of what may be regarded as nine concentric circles, paralleling thereby, and adding further emphasis to the central position accorded by the Founder of our Faith to One 'from Whom God hath caused to proceed the knowledge of all that was and shall be,' 'the Primal Point from which have been generated all created things.'"[2]

Finally, with regard to the term "Point", it is a title given by the Báb to the Manifestations of God. He refers to Himself as the "*Point of the Bayán*", and to Muḥammad as the "*Point of the Qur'án*" and to each Manifestation as the "*Focal Point of God's Primal Will*".[3]

17.4 Relationship between the Twin Revelations

In statement (h), 'Abdu'l-Bahá describes the relationship between the Báb and Bahá'u'lláh. In order to illustrate this relationship, He uses the signs of the Zodiac, which is an imaginary belt through space along which the sun, the moon, and the nearest planets appear to travel. This belt is divided into 12 equal parts known as signs, each named after a group of stars, which were once in them.

'Abdu'l-Bahá's illustration is based on the Persian calendar in which Naw-Rúz on the 21st March is the first day of the year, corresponding to the first day of spring and the sign of Aries in the Zodiac. This is when the sun enters the Vernal Equinox. 'Abdu'l-Bahá indicates that the Revelation of the Báb is like the first appearance of the sun (in spring) in the sign of Aries, when the fresh, new sun appears in its earthly springtime.

Similarly, 'Abdu'l-Bahá states that the Revelation of Bahá'u'lláh is like the appearance of the sun at its maximum splendour and brilliance during the sign of Leo. This is the highest station of the radiance of the Sun of Truth. The sign of Leo corresponds to the period of 21st of July to 20th of August. This is mid-summer in the Northern Hemisphere when the sun reaches its maximum splendour and brilliance.

---

1 'Abdu'l-Bahá, *Selection from the Writings of 'Abdu'l-Bahá*, p. 60.
2 Shoghi Effendi, *Citadel of Faith*, p. 95.
3 The Báb, *Selections from the Writings of the Báb*, pp. 79– 83 and p. 195.

In His simple simile, 'Abdu'l-Bahá affirms a number of fundamental beliefs of the Bahá'í Faith. The first is the unity of the Manifestations of God according to which the Revelations of the Báb and Bahá'u'lláh are simply the manifestation of the same sun at different times.

The second concept addressed by 'Abdu'l-Bahá is that the differences observed between different Revelations from God are due to a variance in the intensity of those Revelations not their significance or rank (see Section 14.4).

Finally, the statement of 'Abdu'l-Bahá also highlights that the intensity of the Revelation of Bahá'u'lláh is greater than that of the Revelation of the Báb. This is logical when the Missions of the two Revelations are compared.

17.5 Activities

1. Briefly describe your understanding of the Báb's statements in references to Himself in paragraphs 62 and 63.

2. How does 'Abdu'l-Bahá's analogy of the Zodiac apply to the relationship between the Bahá'í Faith and other religions?

3. Considering the events of the Ministry of the Báb, can you give one or two examples of the power of His Revelation?

4. Whom is the Báb referring to by the term: *'the Remembrance of God'* in statement (c)?

5. What is the meaning of the statement of the Báb: "*All the keys of heaven God hath chosen to place on My right hand, and all the keys of hell on My left*" cited in paragraph 63?

6. What is the main message conveyed by 'Abdu'l-Bahá in statement (j)?

7. What is your understanding of statement (h)?

8. What are the basic Bahá'í principles specified by 'Abdu'l-Bahá in statement (k)?

17.6 Glossary

Term	Meaning
Abstruse	Difficult to understand
Assertion	A forceful statement or claim
Efficacious	Producing the desired effect
Effusion	An unrestrained expression of strong feelings in speech or writing
Elucidate	To explain or make clear (a difficulty or mystery)
Equinox	Either of the two times in the year (about March 21 and September 22) when all places in the world have day and night of equal length.
Fane	A temple, a place dedicated to religion
Gladsome	Causing joy, happiness
Harbinger	A person or thing showing that something is going to happen or is on its way
Leo the "Lion"	Zodiac sign for the period 23 July to 22 August. This is mid-summer in the northern hemisphere, and the time when the sun reaches its maximum splendour and brilliance.
Mystic	A person who seeks by prayer, meditation and self-surrender to attain unity with God or the Absolute, and so reach truths beyond human understanding.
Mysticism	Knowledge of real truth and union with God obtained through prayer and meditation
Naw-Rúz	Naw-Rúz is a thirteen day Persian national festival that celebrates the Iranian new year. The date of Naw-Rúz is determined by the solar calendar and begins on the first day of spring. In the Badí' or Bahá'í solar calendar, Naw-Rúz is celebrated on the 21 March, corresponding to the first day of spring in the northern hemisphere, and the first day of the year.
Plenitude	Completeness; fullness
Qurratu'l-'Ayn	Solace of the Eyes
Resounding	Emphatic; echoing, loud and clear
Resplendency	Brightness
Solemn	Serious
Startle	To cause a sudden shock or surprise to someone or something
Vernal	Of, like, or appearing in the spring season

18. STATION OF 'ABDU'L-BAHÁ

18.1 Introduction

This chapter covers paragraphs 68–74. Read these paragraphs and reflect on the contents before starting the lesson. In this section of his letter, Shoghi Effendi initially summarises the topics that he has so far addressed in the book. He then proffers a clarification regarding the station of 'Abdu'l-Bahá, and highlights the significance of His position in the Dispensation of Bahá'u'lláh.

In this chapter, you need to look for and understand the following **key concepts:**

a) The station of 'Abdu'l-Bahá has been a source of confusion, particularly during His own lifetime.

b) 'Abdu'l-Bahá was explicitly appointed by the Blessed Beauty as the authorized and unerring interpreter of His Words and the Centre of His Covenant.

c) In contrast to His function and station, 'Abdu'l-Bahá chose the title of "Servant of Bahá" for Himself and manifested utmost humility and purity of spirit in all His deeds and words.

d) At present only the Báb and Bahá'u'lláh can claim to be a Manifestation of God before the expiry of one thousand years from the date of the declaration of Bahá'u'lláh.

e) Although 'Abdu'l-Bahá has a rank radically different from that of the Báb and Bahá'u'lláh, He is considered to be one of the Central Figures of the Bahá'í Dispensation together with Bahá'u'lláh and the Báb.

18.2 Paragraphs under study

68. Dearly-beloved friends! I have in the foregoing pages ventured to attempt an exposition of such truths as I firmly believe are implicit in the claim of Him Who is the Fountain-Head of the Bahá'í Revelation. I have moreover endeavoured to dissipate such misapprehensions as may naturally arise in the mind of any one contemplating so superhuman a manifestation of the glory of God. I have striven to explain the meaning

of the divinity with which He Who is the vehicle of so mysterious an energy must needs be invested. That the Message which so great a Being has, in this age, been commissioned by God to deliver to mankind recognises the divine origin and upholds the first principles of every Dispensation inaugurated by the prophets of the past, and stands inextricably interwoven with each one of them, I have also to the best of my ability undertaken to demonstrate. That the Author of such a Faith, Who repudiates the claim to finality which leaders of various denominations uphold has, despite the vastness of His Revelation, disclaimed it for Himself I have, likewise, felt it necessary to prove and emphasize. That the Báb, notwithstanding the duration of His Dispensation, should be regarded primarily, not as the chosen Precursor of the Bahá'í Faith, but as One invested with the undivided authority assumed by each of the independent Prophets of the past, seemed to me yet another basic principle the elucidation of which would be extremely desirable at the present stage of the evolution of our Cause.

69. An attempt I strongly feel should now be made to clarify our minds regarding the station occupied by 'Abdu'l-Bahá and the significance of His position in this holy Dispensation. It would be indeed difficult for us, who stand so close to such a tremendous figure and are drawn by the mysterious power of so magnetic a personality, to obtain a clear and exact understanding of the role and character of One Who, not only in the Dispensation of Bahá'u'lláh but in the entire field of religious history, fulfils a unique function. Though moving in a sphere of His own and holding a rank radically different from that of the Author and the Forerunner of the Bahá'í Revelation, He, by virtue of the station ordained for Him through the Covenant of Bahá'u'lláh, forms together with them what may be termed the Three Central Figures of a Faith that stands unapproached in the world's spiritual history. He towers, in conjunction with them, above the destinies of this infant Faith of God from a level to which no individual or body ministering to its needs after Him, and for no less a period than a full thousand years, can ever hope to rise. To degrade His lofty rank by identifying His station with or by regarding it as roughly equivalent to, the position of those on whom the mantle of His authority has fallen would be an act of impiety as grave as the no less heretical belief that inclines to exalt Him to a state of absolute equality with either the central Figure or Forerunner of our Faith. For wide as is the gulf that separates 'Abdu'l-Bahá from Him Who is the Source of an independent Revelation, it can never be regarded as commensurate with the greater distance that stands between Him Who is the Centre of the Covenant and His ministers who are to carry on His work, whatever be their name, their rank, their functions or their future achievements. Let those who have known 'Abdu'l-Bahá, who through their contact with His magnetic personality have come to cherish for Him so fervent an admiration, reflect, in the light of this statement, on

the greatness of One Who is so far above Him in station.

70. That 'Abdu'l-Bahá is not a Manifestation of God, that, though the successor of His Father, He does not occupy a cognate station, that no one else except the Báb and Bahá'u'lláh can ever lay claim to such a station before the expiration of a full thousand years—are verities which lie embedded in the specific utterances of both the Founder of our Faith and the Interpreter of His teachings.

71. "*Whoso layeth claim to a Revelation direct from God,*" is the express warning uttered in *The Kitáb-i-Aqdas*, "*ere the expiration of a full thousand years, such a man is assuredly a lying imposter. We pray God that He may graciously assist him to retract and repudiate such claim. Should he repent, God will no doubt forgive him. If, however, he persists in his error, God will assuredly send down one who will deal mercilessly with him. Terrible indeed is God in punishing!*" "*Whosoever,*" He adds as a further emphasis, "*interpreteth this verse otherwise than its obvious meaning is deprived of the Spirit of God and of His mercy which encompasseth all created things.*"[1] "*Should a man appear,*" is yet another conclusive statement, "*ere the lapse of a full thousand years—each year consisting of twelve months according to the Qur'án, and of nineteen months of nineteen days each, according to the Bayán—and if such a man reveal to your eyes all the signs of God, unhesitatingly reject him!*"[2]

72. 'Abdu'l-Bahá's own statements, in confirmation of this warning, are no less emphatic and binding: "*This is,*" He declares, "*my firm, my unshakable conviction, the essence of my unconcealed and explicit belief—a conviction and belief which the denizens of the Abhá Kingdom fully share: The Blessed Beauty is the Sun of Truth, and His light the light of truth. The Báb is likewise the Sun of Truth, and His light the light of truth ... My station is the station of servitude—a servitude which is complete, pure and real, firmly established, enduring, obvious, explicitly revealed and subject to no interpretation whatever ... I am the Interpreter of the Word of God; such is my interpretation.*"[3]

73. Does not 'Abdu'l-Bahá in His own Will—in a tone and language that might well confound the most inveterate among the breakers of His Father's Covenant—rob of their chief weapon those who so long and so persistently had striven to impute to Him the charge of having tacitly claimed a station equal, if not superior, to that of Bahá'u'lláh? "*The foundation of the belief of the people of Bahá is this,*" thus proclaims one of the weightiest passages of that last document left to voice in perpetuity the directions and wishes of a departed Master, "*His Holiness the Exalted One (the Báb) is the Manifestation of the unity and oneness*

---

1 Statement (a)
2 Statement (b)
3 Statement (c)

of God and the Forerunner of the Ancient Beauty. His Holiness the Abhá Beauty (Bahá'u'lláh) (may my life be a sacrifice for His steadfast friends) is the supreme Manifestation of God and the Day-Spring of His most divine Essence. All others are servants unto Him and do His bidding."[1]

74. From such clear and formally laid down statements, incompatible as they are with any assertion of a claim to Prophethood, we should not by any means infer that 'Abdu'l-Bahá is merely one of the servants of the Blessed Beauty, or at best one whose function is to be confined to that of an authorized interpreter of His Father's teachings. Far be it from me to entertain such a notion or to wish to instil such sentiments. To regard Him in such a light is a manifest betrayal of the priceless heritage bequeathed by Bahá'u'lláh to mankind. Immeasurably exalted is the station conferred upon Him by the Supreme Pen above and beyond the implications of these, His own written statements. Whether in *The Kitáb-i-Aqdas*, the most weighty and sacred of all the works of Bahá'u'lláh, or in *The Kitáb-i-'Ahd*, the Book of His Covenant, or in the Súriy-i-Ghusn (Tablet of the Branch), such references as have been recorded by the pen of Bahá'u'lláh—references which the Tablets of His Father addressed to Him mightily reinforce—invest 'Abdu'l-Bahá with a power, and surround Him with a halo, which the present generation can never adequately appreciate.

18.3 Confusion regarding the station of 'Abdu'l-Bahá

The station of 'Abdu'l-Bahá has been a source of confusion, particularly during His own lifetime. 'Abdu'l-Bahá had a function that was unique not only in the Dispensation of Bahá'u'lláh but also in religious history. The Blessed Beauty explicitly appointed 'Abdu'l-Bahá as the authorized and unerring interpreter of His Words and the Centre of His Covenant.

This is a role, which had not been conferred upon any religious leader in the past. In previous Dispensations, the appointment of the successors was ad-hoc and the interpretation of the Words of God was open to anyone. In fact, this has been one of the major causes of division and disunity in the past.

At the same time, the titles and descriptions given to 'Abdu'l-Bahá by Bahá'u'lláh, and the charismatic and spiritually strong character of 'Abdu'l-Bahá had left no doubt in the mind of everyone coming into contact with Him of His high station and dignity.

In contrast with His function and station, 'Abdu'l-Bahá chose the title of "Servant of Bahá" for Himself and manifested utmost humility and purity of spirit in all His deeds and words.

Under these circumstances, there were many believers at the time of 'Abdu'l-Bahá who could not fully comprehend the role and function of 'Abdu'l-Bahá. This was particularly true of those whose background was

[1] Statement (d)

strongly rooted in Christianity or Islám. Some have even assumed that He was a Manifestation of God. Others have suggested that He was the return of Christ.[1] Such assumptions used to cause intense grief to the heart of 'Abdu'l-Bahá.

In response to a question asked about His station, 'Abdu'l-Bahá states: "*My name is 'Abdu'l-Bahá, my identity is 'Abdu'l-Bahá, my qualification is 'Abdu'l-Bahá, my reality is 'Abdu'l-Bahá, my praise is 'Abdu'l-Bahá.*"[2] Emphasizing His servitude to Bahá'u'lláh, He continues, "*Thraldom to the Blessed Perfection is my glorious and refulgent diadem; and servitude to all the human race is my perpetual religion.*"[3]

In the same Tablet, 'Abdu'l-Bahá illustrates His power and authority by indicating: "*Through the bounty and favour of the Blessed Perfection, 'Abdu'l-Bahá is the Ensign of the Most-Great-Peace, which is waving from the Supreme Apex; and through the gift of the Greatest name, he is the Lamp of Universal Salvation, which is shining with the light of the love of God. The Herald of the Kingdom is he, so that he may awaken the people of the East and of the West. The Voice of Friendship, Uprightness, Truth and Reconciliation is he, so as to cause acceleration throughout all regions.*"[4]

He continues that Tablet by expressing the desire of His heart: "*No name, no title, no mention, no commendation hath he nor will ever have except 'Abdu'l-Bahá. This is my longing. This is my supreme apex. This is my greatest yearning. This is my eternal life. This is my everlasting glory!*"[5]

18.4 True station of 'Abdu'l-Bahá

In paragraph 69, Shoghi Effendi proffers a clarification regarding the station occupied by 'Abdu'l-Bahá and the significance of His position in the Dispensation of Bahá'u'lláh. He highlights the following key points:

a) It is impossible for us to acquire an accurate understanding of the station and character of 'Abdu'l-Bahá due to our closeness to His time.
b) The function of 'Abdu'l-Bahá is unique not only in the Dispensation of Bahá'u'lláh but also in the entire history of religion.
c) 'Abdu'l-Bahá, together with the Báb and Bahá'u'lláh are considered as the Central Figures of the Bahá'í Faith and Their station is supreme above all others for the next one thousand years.
d) Nevertheless the rank of 'Abdu'l-Bahá is radically different from that of the Báb and Bahá'u'lláh.
e) It is wrong to assume that the station of 'Abdu'l-Bahá is equal to that of Bahá'u'lláh and the Báb. It is equally incorrect to suggest that the station

---

1 J. E. Esslemont, *Bahá'u'lláh and the New Era*, 5th rev. ed. (Wilmette: Bahá'í Publishing Trust, 1987), p. 67.
2 'Abdu'l-Bahá, *Tablets of Abdul-Baha Abbas*, vol. 2, p. 430.
3 'Abdu'l-Bahá, *Tablets of Abdul-Baha Abbas*, vol. 2, p. 430.
4 'Abdu'l-Bahá, *Tablets of Abdul-Baha Abbas*, vol. 2, p. 430.
5 'Abdu'l-Bahá, *Tablets of Abdul-Baha Abbas*, vol. 2, p. 430.

of 'Abdu'l-Bahá is the same as that of the other followers of Bahá'u'lláh.

f) The gap separating the station of 'Abdu'l-Bahá from that of other followers of Bahá'u'lláh is greater than the gap between His station and that of Bahá'u'lláh.
g) The station of 'Abdu'l-Bahá will tower over every other follower of Bahá'u'lláh for the next one thousand years.

18.5 'Abdu'l-Bahá is not a Manifestation of God

In paragraphs 70–74, Shoghi Effendi explains that 'Abdu'l-Bahá is not a Manifestation of God. In paragraph 70, he states that no one but the Báb and Bahá'u'lláh can claim to be a Manifestation of God before the expiry of one thousand years from the declaration of Bahá'u'lláh. These are verities embedded in the Writings of Bahá'u'lláh and 'Abdu'l-Bahá.

In paragraph 71, Shoghi Effendi cites statements (a) and (b) from Bahá'u'lláh in which He explicitly indicates that there will be no Manifestation of God before the expiry of one thousand years.

In paragraph 72, Shoghi Effendi cites statement (c) from 'Abdu'l-Bahá in which He describes the Báb and Bahá'u'lláh as the "Sun of Truth" and His own station as the station of servitude. This statement is perfectly explicit and clear and is not open to interpretation.

In paragraph 73, Shoghi Effendi cites a statement from *The Will and Testament of 'Abdu'l-Bahá* in which the station of the Báb is defined as the Manifestation of God and the Forerunner of Bahá'u'lláh, the station of Bahá'u'lláh as the supreme Manifestation of God, and everyone else as servants to the commandments of Bahá'u'lláh. Section 18.6 provides further information on *The Will and Testament of 'Abdu'l-Bahá.*

In paragraph 74, Shoghi Effendi sheds further light on the station of 'Abdu'l-Bahá. Despite the references made by 'Abdu'l-Bahá to Himself, we should not simply conclude that 'Abdu'l-Bahá is merely one of the servants of Bahá'u'lláh or, at best, an authorized interpreter of His teachings. The statements made by Bahá'u'lláh in *The Kitáb-i-Íqán*, *The Kitáb-i-'Ahd* (The Will and Testament of Bahá'u'lláh), The Súriy-i-Ghusn (The Tablet of the Branch) and other Tablets addressed to 'Abdu'l-Bahá, invest Him with a power and station that the present generation cannot fully appreciate.

18.6 Will and Testament of 'Abdu'l-Bahá

In paragraph 73, Shoghi Effendi cites a statement from *The Will and Testament of 'Abdu'l-Bahá* in which 'Abdu'l-Bahá rejects the accusation made by the covenant breakers that He was claiming a station equal to Bahá'u'lláh.

'Abdu'l-Bahá wrote His Will and Testament in Akká during the years 1901 and 1908 when His life was threatened by the plots of the Covenant- breakers and those hostile towards Him. It consists of three sections written at different times during that period, all addressed to Shoghi Effendi. The whole document was written by 'Abdu'l-Bahá in His own handwriting, signed and sealed by Him, and kept in His safe.

At the time of the passing of 'Abdu'l-Bahá, Shoghi Effendi was in Oxford studying at Balliol College. On the receipt of the news, he prepared to travel to the Holy Land. He sailed from England on 16 December and arrived in Haifa on the 29th, one month after the passing of 'Abdu'l-Bahá. The family were waiting for his arrival to open *The Will and Testament of 'Abdu'l-Bahá* and read it to them. This occurred a few days after Shoghi Effendi's arrival.

The contents of the Will were completely unexpected for Shoghi Effendi. In reference to this matter, Rúḥíyyih Khánum writes that Shoghi Effendi "... himself stated on more than one occasion, not only to me, but to others who were present at the table of the Western Pilgrim House, that he had had no foreknowledge of the existence of the Institution of Guardianship, least of all that he was appointed as Guardian."[1]

On 3 January 1922, *The Will and Testament of 'Abdu'l-Bahá* was formally presented to nine senior members of the family of 'Abdu'l-Bahá, in the absence of Shoghi Effendi. The Will was read aloud and its seal, signature and handwriting were shown to those present.

In *God Passes By*, Shoghi Effendi provides a summary of the content of *The Will and Testament of 'Abdu'l-Bahá*[2]:

- "The Document establishing that Order, the Charter of a future world civilization, which may be regarded in some of its features as supplementary to no less weighty a Book than *The Kitáb-i-Aqdas*, signed and sealed by 'Abdul-Bahá, entirely written by His own hand;
- its first section composed during one of the darkest periods of His incarceration in the prison-fortress of Akká, proclaims, categorically and unequivocally, the fundamental beliefs of the followers of the Faith of Bahá'u'lláh;
- reveals, in unmistakable language, the twofold character of the Mission of the Báb; discloses the full station of the Author of the Bahá'í Revelation;
- asserts that 'all others are servants unto Him and do His bidding';
- stresses the importance of *The Kitáb-i-Aqdas*;
- establishes the institution of the Guardianship as a hereditary office and outlines its essential function;
- provides the measures for the election of the International House of Justice, defines its scope and sets forth its relationship to that Institution;
- prescribes the obligations, and emphasizes the responsibilities, of the Hands of the Cause of God;
- and extols the virtues of the indestructible Covenant established by Bahá'u'lláh.
- That Document, furthermore, lauds the courage and constancy of the supporters of Bahá'u'lláh's Covenant;
- expatiates on the sufferings endured by its appointed Centre;

---

1 Rúḥíyyih Khánum, *The Priceless Pearl*, p. 42.

2 Bullets are added for emphasis.

- recalls the infamous conduct of Mírzá Yaḥyá and his failure to heed the warnings of the Báb;
- exposes, in a series of indictments, the perfidy and rebellion of Mírzá Muḥammad-'Alí, and the complicity of his son Shu'á'u'lláh and of his brother Mírzá Badí'u'lláh;
- reaffirms their excommunication, and predicts the frustration of all their hopes; summons the Afnán (the Báb's kindred), the Hands of the Cause and the entire company of the followers of Bahá'u'lláh to arise unitedly to propagate His Faith, to disperse far and wide, to labour tirelessly and to follow the heroic example of the Apostles of Jesus Christ;
- warns them against the dangers of association with the Covenant-breakers, and bids them shield the Cause from the assaults of the insincere and the hypocrite;
- and counsels them to demonstrate by their conduct the universality of the Faith they have espoused, and vindicate its high principles.
- In that same Document its Author reveals the significance and purpose of the Ḥuqúqu'lláh (Right of God), already instituted in *The Kitáb-i-Aqdas*;
- enjoins submission and fidelity towards all monarchs who are just;
- expresses His longing for martyrdom, and voices His prayers for the repentance as well as the forgiveness of His enemies."[1]

More information on *The Will and Testament of 'Abdu'l-Bahá* and its relationship with the Bahá'í administration is provided in section 21.4.

[1] Shoghi Effendi, *God Passes By*, p. 328.

18.7 Activities

1. Why was there confusion about the station of 'Abdu'l-Bahá during His Ministry?

2. Why is the station of 'Abdu'l-Bahá unique in religious history?

3. Briefly describe your understanding of the key points of paragraph 69.

4. What is the meaning of the statement "Though moving in a sphere of His own" in paragraph 69? What are the characteristics of this "sphere"?

5. Why cannot 'Abdu'l-Bahá be considered a Manifestation of God?

6. Why has Bahá'u'lláh defined so accurately what He means by the term "year" in statement (b)?

7. What is your understanding of the nature of the "station of servitude"?

8. What is your understanding of paragraph 74?

18.8 Glossary

Term	Meaning
Assertion	A forceful statement or claim
Bequeath	To leave (property) to a beneficiary by a last will and testament. To hand down; pass on
Betrayal	The act of being disloyal or unfaithful to
Cognate	Someone or something related in origin or sharing some qualities with another person or thing
Commensurate	In the right proportion; appropriate
Confound	To confuse and surprise by being unexpected
Dissipate	Disappear or scatter
Exposition	Explanation, clarification, proclamation, public statement or exhibition
Elucidate	To explain, make clear
Halo	A golden circle representing light around the heads of holy people in religious paintings
Impiety	Lack of reverence or respect, esp. for religion
Impostor	Someone who deceives by pretending to be someone else
Impute	To claim that (someone or something) possesses or has done, esp. unjustly
Inextricable	Which cannot be untied, solved or separated
Inveterate	Firmly settled in a usually bad habit; habitual
Mantle	An important role or responsibility that passes from one person to another [alluding to the passing of Elijah's cloak to Elisha (2 Kings 2:13)
Misapprehension	A mistaken belief; misunderstanding:
Thraldom	The state of being in someone's power; slavery
Venture	To risk going somewhere or doing something

19. MYSTERY OF GOD—'ABDU'L-BAHÁ

19.1 Introduction

This chapter covers paragraphs 75–82. Read these paragraphs and reflect on the contents before starting the lesson. The main focus of this section is on the station of 'Abdu'l-Bahá as the Centre of the Covenant of Bahá'u'lláh. Initially, Shoghi Effendi refers to all the appellations given to 'Abdu'l-Bahá and then cites various statements in which Bahá'u'lláh exalts the station of 'Abdu'l-Bahá and appoints Him as His successor, the Centre of His Covenant and the unerring interpreter of His Writings.

In this chapter, you need to look for and understand the following **key points:**

a) The title "Mystery of God" (Sirru'lláh), conferred on 'Abdu'l-Bahá by Bahá'u'lláh, "... indicates how in the person of 'Abdu'l-Bahá the incompatible characteristics of a human nature and superhuman knowledge and perfection have been blended and are completely harmonised."[1]
b) The Lesser Covenant is made between a Manifestation of God and His followers according to which "... they will accept His appointed successor after Him."[2]
c) As His Lesser Covenant, Bahá'u'lláh in *The Kitáb-i-'Ahd,* commands His followers to turn to 'Abdu'l-Bahá after His passing.
d) The Lesser Covenant was later extended by 'Abdu'l-Bahá when He appointed the twin crowning institutions of the Guardianship and the Universal House of Justice as His successors, and Shoghi Effendi, His grandson as the first Guardian of the Bahá'í Faith.
e) 'Abdu'l-Bahá is "... the Centre and Pivot of Bahá'u'lláh's peerless and

---

1 Shoghi Effendi, *The World Order of Bahá'u'lláh*, p. 134.
2 The Universal House of Justice in *The Compilation of Compilations*, vol. 1, p. 111, Bahá'í Publications Australia, 1991.

all-enfolding Covenant."[1]

f) In the Tablet of the Branch, 'Abdu'l-Bahá is referred to as a Branch of the Sadratu'l-Muntahá, the tree beyond which there is no passing.

19.2 Paragraphs under study

75. He is, and should for all time be regarded, first and foremost, as the Centre and Pivot of Bahá'u'lláh's peerless and all-enfolding Covenant, His most exalted handiwork, the stainless Mirror of His light, the perfect Exemplar of His teachings, the unerring Interpreter of His Word, the embodiment of every Bahá'í ideal, the incarnation of every Bahá'í virtue, the Most Mighty Branch sprung from the Ancient Root, the Limb of the Law of God, the Being "*round Whom all names revolve*," the Mainspring of the Oneness of Humanity, the Ensign of the Most Great Peace, the Moon of the Central Orb of this most holy Dispensation—styles and titles that are implicit and find their truest, their highest and fairest expression in the magic name 'Abdu'l-Bahá. He is, above and beyond these appellations, the "*Mystery of God*"—an expression by which Bahá'u'lláh Himself has chosen to designate Him, and which, while it does not by any means justify us to assign to Him the station of Prophethood, indicates how in the person of 'Abdu'l-Bahá the incompatible characteristics of a human nature and superhuman knowledge and perfection have been blended and are completely harmonised.

76. "*When the ocean of My presence hath ebbed and the Book of My Revelation is ended,*" proclaims *The Kitáb-i-Aqdas*, "*turn your faces towards Him Whom God hath purposed, Who hath branched from this Ancient Root.*"[2] And again, "*When the Mystic Dove will have winged its flight from its Sanctuary of Praise and sought its far-off goal, its hidden habitation, refer ye whatsoever ye understand not in the Book to Him Who hath branched from this mighty Stock.*"[3]

77. In The *Kitáb-i-'Ahd*, moreover, Bahá'u'lláh solemnly and explicitly declares: "*It is incumbent upon the Aghsán, the Afnán and My kindred to turn, one and all, their faces towards the Most Mighty Branch. Consider that which We have revealed in Our Most Holy Book: 'When the ocean of My presence hath ebbed and the Book of My Revelation is ended, turn your faces toward Him Whom God hath purposed, Who hath branched from this Ancient Root.' The object of this sacred verse is none other except the Most Mighty Branch ('Abdu'l-Bahá). Thus have We graciously revealed unto you our potent Will, and I am verily the Gracious, the All-Powerful.*"[4]

78. In the Súriy-i-Ghusn (Tablet of the Branch) the following verses have

---

1 Shoghi Effendi, *The World Order of Bahá'u'lláh*, p. 133.
2 Statement (a)
3 Statement (b)
4 Statement (c)

been recorded: "*There hath branched from the Sadratu'l-Muntahá this sacred and glorious Being, this Branch of Holiness; well is it with him that hath sought His shelter and abideth beneath His shadow. Verily the Limb of the Law of God hath sprung forth from this Root, which God hath firmly implanted in the Ground of His Will, and Whose Branch hath been so uplifted as to encompass the whole of creation. Magnified be He, therefore, for this sublime, this blessed, this mighty, this exalted Handiwork! ... A Word hath, as a token of Our grace, gone forth from the Most Great Tablet—a Word which God hath adorned with the ornament of His own Self, and made it sovereign over the earth and all that is therein, and a sign of His greatness and power among its people ... Render thanks unto God, O people, for His appearance; for verily He is the most great Favour unto you, the most perfect bounty upon you; and through Him every mouldering bone is quickened. Whoso turneth towards Him hath turned towards God, and whoso turneth away from Him hath turned away from My beauty, hath repudiated My Proof, and transgressed against Me. He is the Trust of God amongst you, His charge within you, His manifestation unto you and His appearance among His favoured servants ... We have sent Him down in the form of a human temple. Blest and sanctified be God Who createth whatsoever He willeth through His inviolable, His infallible decree. They who deprive themselves of the shadow of the Branch, are lost in the wilderness of error, are consumed by the heat of worldly desires, and are of those who will assuredly perish.*"[1]

79. "*O Thou Who art the apple of Mine eye!*" Bahá'u'lláh, in His own handwriting, thus addresses 'Abdu'l-Bahá, "*My glory, the ocean of My loving-kindness, the sun of My bounty, the heaven of My mercy rest upon Thee. We pray God to illumine the world through Thy knowledge and wisdom, to ordain for Thee that which will gladden Thine heart and impart consolation to Thine eyes.*"[2] "*The glory of God rest upon Thee,*" He writes in another Tablet, "*and upon whosoever serveth Thee and circleth around Thee. Woe, great woe, betide him that opposeth and injureth Thee. Well is it with him that sweareth fealty to Thee; the fire of hell torment him who is Thine enemy.*"[3] "*We have made Thee a shelter for all mankind,*" He, in yet another Tablet, affirms, "*a shield unto all who are in heaven and on earth, a stronghold for whosoever hath believed in God, the Incomparable, the All-Knowing. God grant that through Thee He may protect them, may enrich and sustain them, that He may inspire Thee with that which shall be a wellspring of wealth unto all created things, an ocean of bounty unto all men, and the*

1 Statement (d)
2 Statement (e)
3 Statement (f)

dayspring of mercy unto all peoples."[1]

80. "*Thou knowest, O my God,*" Bahá'u'lláh, in a prayer revealed in 'Abdu'l-Bahá's honour, supplicates, "*that I desire for Him naught except that which Thou didst desire, and have chosen Him for no purpose save that which Thou hadst intended for Him. Render Him victorious, therefore, through Thy hosts of earth and heaven ... Ordain, I beseech Thee, by the ardour of My love for Thee and My yearning to manifest Thy Cause, for Him, as well as for them that love Him, that which Thou hast destined for Thy Messengers and the Trustees of Thy Revelation. Verily, Thou art the Almighty, the All-Powerful.*"[2]

81. In a letter dictated by Bahá'u'lláh and addressed by Mírzá Áqá Ján, His amanuensis, to 'Abdu'l-Bahá while the latter was on a visit to Beirut, we read the following: "*Praise be to Him Who hath honoured the Land of Bá (Beirut) through the presence of Him round Whom all names revolve. All the atoms of the earth have announced unto all created things that from behind the gate of the Prison-city there hath appeared and above its horizon there hath shone forth the Orb of the beauty of the great, the Most Mighty Branch of God—His ancient and immutable Mystery—proceeding on its way to another land. Sorrow, thereby, hath enveloped this Prison-city, whilst another land rejoiceth ... Blessed, doubly blessed, is the ground which His footsteps have trodden, the eye that hath been cheered by the beauty of His countenance, the ear that hath been honoured by hearkening to His call, the heart that hath tasted the sweetness of His love, the breast that hath dilated through His remembrance, the pen that hath voiced His praise, the scroll that hath borne the testimony of His writings.*"[3]

82. 'Abdu'l-Bahá, writing in confirmation of the authority conferred upon Him by Bahá'u'lláh, makes the following statement: "*In accordance with the explicit text of the Kitáb-i-Aqdas Bahá'u'lláh hath made the Centre of the Covenant the Interpreter of His Word—a Covenant so firm and mighty that from the beginning of time until the present day no religious Dispensation hath produced its like.*"[4]

19.3 Titles of 'Abdu'l-Bahá

In paragraph 75, Shoghi Effendi portrays the complex, and the mystical station and function of 'Abdu'l-Bahá by referring to various appellations attributed to Him. They include:

- "The Centre and Pivot of Bahá'u'lláh's peerless and all-enfolding Covenant"
- "His [Bahá'u'lláh's] most exalted handiwork"
- "The stainless Mirror of His [Bahá'u'lláh's] light"

---

1 Statement (g)
2 Statement (h)
3 Statement (i)
4 Statement (j)

- "The perfect Exemplar of His [Bahá'u'lláh's] teachings"
- "The unerring Interpreter of His [Bahá'u'lláh's] Word"
- "The embodiment of every Bahá'í ideal"
- "The incarnation of every Bahá'í virtue"
- "The Most Mighty Branch sprung from the Ancient Root"
- "The Limb of the Law of God"
- "The Being '*round Whom all names revolve*'"
- "The Mainspring of the Oneness of Humanity"
- "The Ensign of the Most Great Peace"
- "The Moon of the Central Orb of this most holy Dispensation"
- "The Mystery of God"

The title "Mystery of God" (Sirru'lláh) was conferred on 'Abdu'l-Bahá by Bahá'u'lláh during the period of His residence in Baghdád. Shoghi Effendi states that while this title, "... does not by any means justify us to assign to Him the station of Prophethood, indicates how in the person of 'Abdu'l-Bahá the incompatible characteristics of a human nature and superhuman knowledge and perfection have been blended and are completely harmonised."

In *God Passes By*, Shoghi Effendi refers to some of these titles and identifies the Tablets in which they have been conferred on 'Abdu'l-Bahá.[1] This section of *God Passes By* is cited below and the titles and their sources are bolded for emphasis:

> "He alone had been accorded the privilege of being called "**the Master,**" an honour from which His Father had strictly excluded all His other sons. Upon Him that loving and unerring Father had chosen to confer the unique title of "**Sirru'lláh**" (**the Mystery of God**), a designation so appropriate to One Who, though essentially human and holding a station radically and fundamentally different from that occupied by Bahá'u'lláh and His Forerunner, could still claim to be the **perfect Exemplar of His Faith**, to be endowed with super-human knowledge, and to be regarded as the **stainless mirror reflecting His light**. To Him, whilst in Adrianople, that same Father had, in **the Súriy-i-Ghusn (Tablet of the Branch)**, referred as **"this sacred and glorious Being, this Branch of Holiness,"** as **"the Limb of the Law of God,"** as **His "most great favour"** unto men, as **His "most perfect bounty"** conferred upon them, as **One through Whom "every mouldering bone is quickened,"** declaring that **"whoso turneth towards Him hath turned towards God,"** and that **"they who deprive themselves of the shadow of the Branch are lost in the wilderness of error."** To Him He, whilst still in that city, had alluded (in a Tablet addressed to Ḥájí Muḥammad Ibráhím-i-Khalíl) as the one amongst His sons "**from Whose tongue God will**

[1] Shoghi Effendi, *God Passes By*, pp. 242–243.

cause the signs of His power to stream forth," and as the one Whom "**God hath specially chosen for His Cause.**"

19.4 Lesser Covenant of Bahá'u'lláh

There are many types of religious covenants but the source of all is the "Eternal Covenant". This is the recognition of, and response to God through whomsoever He has manifested Himself. The majority of religious covenants primarily govern our development and behaviour. There are, however, two major covenants, which are concerned with the succession in a particular religion and how it is linked to religions before and after it, in the chain of the progressive revelations from God. In the Bahá'í Writings, they are referred to as the Greater Covenant and the Lesser Covenant.

The Greater Covenant is made between every Manifestation of God and His followers, "promising that, in the fullness of time a new Manifestation will be sent, and taking from them the undertaking to accept Him when this occurs."[1]

The Lesser Covenant is made between a Manifestation of God and His followers according to which "they will accept His appointed successor after Him. If they do so, the Faith can remain united and pure. If not, the Faith becomes divided and its force spent."[2]

Bahá'u'lláh defines His Lesser Covenant in statements cited in paragraphs 76 and 77. He commands His followers to turn to 'Abdu'l-Bahá after His passing. This Covenant was later extended by 'Abdu'l-Bahá when He appointed the twin crowning institutions of the Guardianship and the Universal House of Justice as His successors, and Shoghi Effendi, His grandson as the Guardian of the Faith.

Hence, *The Kitáb-i-'Ahd* (The Book of the Covenant of Bahá'u'lláh) and *The Will and Testament of 'Abdu'l-*Bahá are the two major documents upon which the Lesser Covenant of Bahá'u'lláh is based.

Nineteen years before His ascension, Bahá'u'lláh revealed statements (a) and (b) in *The Kitáb-i-Aqdas:*

> *"When the ocean of My presence hath ebbed and the Book of My Revelation is ended, turn your faces towards Him Whom God hath purposed, Who hath branched from this Ancient Root."*[3]
>
> *"When the Mystic Dove will have winged its flight from its Sanctuary of Praise and sought its far-off goal, its hidden habitation, refer ye whatsoever ye understand not in the Book to Him Who hath branched from this mighty Stock."*[4]

---

1 Shoghi Effendi, *God Passes By*, pp. 242–243.

2 The Universal House of Justice in *The Compilation of Compilations*, vol. 1. p. 111, Bahá'í Publications Australia, 1991.

3 Bahá'u'lláh, *The Kitáb-i-Aqdas*, p. 62.

4 Bahá'u'lláh, *The Kitáb-i-Aqdas*, p. 82.

Later, in *The Kitáb-i-'Ahd*, alluding to the above statements in *The Kitáb-i-Aqdas,* Bahá'u'lláh declares that the object of the Sacred Verse "*turn your faces toward Him Whom God hath purposed, Who hath branched from this Ancient Root*" was none other than 'Abdu'l-Bahá, as described in statement (c).

According to Shoghi Effendi, in a Tablet revealed during that same period and addressed to Mírzá Muḥammad Qulíy-i-Sabzivárí, Bahá'u'lláh has referred to 'Abdu'l-Bahá as "*the Gulf that hath branched out of this Ocean that hath encompassed all created things,*"[1] and has commanded His followers to turn their faces towards it.

The Lesser Covenant of Bahá'u'lláh is unique in religious history, as it has been explicitly set out by Bahá'u'lláh and 'Abdu'l-Bahá in *The Kitáb-i-'Ahd* and *The Will and Testament of 'Abdu'l-Bahá,* respectively. 'Abdu'l-Bahá confirms the uniqueness of this Covenant: "*So firm and mighty is this Covenant that from the beginning of time until the present day no religious Dispensation has produced its like.*"[2]

19.5 Centre of the Covenant

In paragraph 75, Shoghi Effendi states that 'Abdu'l-Bahá is "the Centre and Pivot of Bahá'u'lláh's peerless and all-enfolding Covenant." As explained in section 19.4, every Manifestation of God makes a Lesser Covenant with His followers to accept His appointed successor after Him. According to Bahá'u'lláh, 'Abdu'l-Bahá is the Centre of the Covenant He has made with His followers.

The word "centre" has different meanings, the most relevant of which in this context are:

a) a pivot or axis of rotation,
b) a core,
c) a point at which an activity or a process is focused.

Based on such definitions, 'Abdu'l-Bahá as the Centre of the Covenant can be considered as:

a) The pivot around which the Lesser Covenant of Bahá'u'lláh rotates.
b) The core of the Lesser Covenant of Bahá'u'lláh.
c) The focal point of the Lesser Covenant of Bahá'u'lláh.

'Abdu'l-Bahá in His role as the Centre of the Covenant has maintained the effective flow of the forces released through the Revelation of Bahá'u'lláh towards achieving its mission. Through this Covenant, the unity of the Bahá'í community has been preserved despite fierce opposition of the enemies of the Faith from within and without. 'Abdu'l-Bahá confirms: "*Were it not for the protecting power of the Covenant to guard the impregnable fort of the Cause*

---

1 Bahá'u'lláh, cited by Shoghi Effendi in *God Passes By*, p. 243.
2 'Abdu'l-Bahá, cited by Shoghi Effendi in *God Passes By*, p. 238.

of God, there would arise among the Bahá'ís, in one day, a thousand different sects ..."[1]

19.6 The Branch of Holiness

In statement (d) from the *Tablet of the Branch*, Bahá'u'lláh describes the origin of the reality of 'Abdu'l-Bahá in a beautiful analogy. He refers to 'Abdu'l-Bahá as a Branch of the Sadratu'l-Muntahá, the tree beyond which there is no passing. This tree is equivalent to the Sacred Lote-Tree mentioned in the Qur'án,[2] and is a symbol for the Manifestation of God. Bahá'u'lláh further describes His Revelation as the Root which has been established by God in the Ground of His Will and 'Abdu'l-Bahá as the main Branch springing up from this Root.

This Branch has been sent down in the form of a *"human temple"* and is *"the most great Favour"* and *"the most perfect bounty"* from God upon His creatures. It is intended as a shelter for the whole of mankind.

1 'Abdu'l-Bahá, *The Compilation of Compilations*, vol. 1, p. 128.

2 *Qur'án* 53:14 and 53:16

19.7 Activities

1. The titles of 'Abdu'l-Bahá mentioned in paragraph 75 are listed below. Describe your understanding of each title.

   a) "The Centre and Pivot of Bahá'u'lláh's peerless and all-enfolding Covenant"

   b) "His [Bahá'u'lláh's] most exalted handiwork"

   c) "The stainless Mirror of His [Bahá'u'lláh's] light"

   d) "The perfect Exemplar of His [Bahá'u'lláh's] teachings"

   e) "The unerring Interpreter of His [Bahá'u'lláh's] Word"

   f) "The embodiment of every Bahá'í ideal"

   g) "The incarnation of every Bahá'í virtue"

   h) "The Most Mighty Branch sprung from the Ancient Root"

   i) "The Limb of the Law of God"

j) "The Being '*round Whom all names revolve*'"

k) "The Mainspring of the Oneness of Humanity"

l) "The Ensign of the Most Great Peace"

m) "The Moon of the Central Orb of this most holy Dispensation"

n) "The Mystery of God"

2. To what extent has the following statement of Bahá'u'lláh been demonstrated through the history of the Bahá'í Faith?

   "They who deprive themselves of the shadow of the Branch, are lost in the wilderness of error, are consumed by the heat of worldly desires, and are of those who will assuredly perish."

3. Who are the "A<u>gh</u>sán", and the "Afnán"?

4. What is the meaning and implication of the terms "shelter", "shield" and "stronghold" used in statement (g)?

5. What is your understanding of the Lesser Covenant of Bahá'u'lláh?

6. Describe your understanding of the function of 'Abdu'l-Bahá as "the Centre and Pivot of Bahá'u'lláh's peerless and all-enfolding Covenant."

7. 'Abdu'l-Bahá is the authoritative interpreter of the Words of Bahá'u'lláh. What is your understanding of this function?

19.8 Glossary

Term	Meaning
Appellation	A name or title, esp. one that is formal or descriptive
Consolation	(A person or thing that gives) comfort during a time of sadness or disappointment
Ebb	Of the tide—to flow away from the shore
Embodiment	Someone or something that represents, includes, or is very typical of something
Enfolding	To envelop, surround, enclose, embrace
Ensign	The Standard-bearer; a military or naval flag indicating nationality
Fealty	Loyalty to one's king or Lord
Hearken	To listen
Immutable	Unchangeable
Inviolable	Too highly respected to be attacked, changed, etc.
Limb	A (large) branch of a tree
Mainspring	Main agent of motivation: the chief force or reason that makes something happen
Mouldering	Decaying slowly
Sadratu'l-Muntahá	The Sacred Lote-Tree
Sanctuary	Any place where refuge is provided
Woe betide you/him/them, etc.	You/He/They, etc. will be in trouble

20. BAHÁ'U'LLÁH & 'ABDU'L-BAHÁ

20.1 Introduction

This chapter covers paragraphs 83–90. Read these paragraphs and reflect on the contents before starting the lesson. In this section of his letter, Shoghi Effendi identifies some of the sources of misunderstanding about the station of 'Abdu'l-Bahá and emphasizes that those who overestimate the station of 'Abdu'l-Bahá are as reprehensible as those who underestimate it. He also warns us that such misinterpretations can cause irrational and superstitious beliefs to creep into the teachings of the Bahá'í Faith as happened in the first century of Christianity.

In this chapter, you need to look for and understand the following **key concepts**:

a) There is no evidence in the Bahá'í Writings to equate the station of 'Abdu'l-Bahá with Bahá'u'lláh or any preceding Manifestation.
b) Soon after the ascension of Bahá'u'lláh, some believers made an attempt to elevate the station of 'Abdu'l-Bahá to that of Bahá'u'lláh based on their personal interpretation of the contents of the Tablet of the Branch.
c) The exaggerated interpretation of the terms and titles used in the Tablet of the Branch (Súrih-i-Ghusn) was one of the sources of misunderstanding.
d) The introduction into its English translation of the Tablet of the Branch, "certain words that are either non-existent, misleading, or ambiguous in their connotation" was another source.
e) The station of the Báb is superior to 'Abdu'l-Bahá, not vice versa.
f) Bahá'u'lláh and the Báb are one in Their realities.

20.2 Paragraphs under study

83. Exalted as is the rank of 'Abdu'l-Bahá, and however profuse the praises with which in these sacred Books and Tablets Bahá'u'lláh has glorified His son, so unique a distinction must never be construed as conferring upon its recipient a station identical with, or equivalent to, that of His Father, the Manifestation Himself. To give such an interpretation to any of these quoted passages would at once, and for obvious reasons, bring it into conflict with the no less clear and authentic assertions and

warnings to which I have already referred. Indeed, as I have already stated, those who overestimate 'Abdu'l-Bahá's station are just as reprehensible and have done just as much harm as those who underestimate it. And this for no other reason except that by insisting upon an altogether unwarranted inference from Bahá'u'lláh's writings they are inadvertently justifying and continuously furnishing the enemy with proofs for his false accusations and misleading statements.

84. I feel it necessary, therefore, to state without any equivocation or hesitation that neither in *The Kitáb-i-Aqdas* nor in the Book of Bahá'u'lláh's Covenant, nor even in the Tablet of the Branch, nor in any other Tablet, whether revealed by Bahá'u'lláh or 'Abdu'l-Bahá, is there any authority whatever for the opinion that inclines to uphold the so-called "mystic unity" of Bahá'u'lláh and 'Abdu'l-Bahá, or to establish the identity of the latter with His Father or with any preceding Manifestation. This erroneous conception may, in part, be ascribed to an altogether extravagant interpretation of certain terms and passages in the Tablet of the Branch, to the introduction into its English translation of certain words that are either non-existent, misleading, or ambiguous in their connotation. It is, no doubt, chiefly based upon an altogether unjustified inference from the opening passages of a Tablet of Bahá'u'lláh, extracts of which, as reproduced in the Bahá'í Scriptures, immediately precede, but form no part of, the said Tablet of the Branch. It should be made clear to every one reading those extracts that by the phrase "the Tongue of the Ancient" no one else is meant but God, and that the term "the Greatest Name" is an obvious reference to Bahá'u'lláh, and that "the Covenant" referred to is not the specific Covenant of which Bahá'u'lláh is the immediate Author and 'Abdu'l-Bahá the Centre but that general Covenant which, as inculcated by the Bahá'í teaching, God Himself invariably establishes with mankind when He inaugurates a new Dispensation. "The Tongue" that "gives," as stated in those extracts, the "glad-tidings" is none other than the Voice of God referring to Bahá'u'lláh, and not Bahá'u'lláh referring to 'Abdu'l-Bahá.

85. Moreover, to maintain that the assertion "He is Myself," instead of denoting the mystic unity of God and His Manifestations, as explained in *The Kitáb-i-Íqán*, establishes the identity of Bahá'u'lláh with 'Abdu'l-Bahá, would constitute a direct violation of the oft-repeated principle of the oneness of God's Manifestations—a principle which the Author of these same extracts is seeking by implication to emphasize.

86. It would also amount to a reversion to those irrational and superstitious beliefs which have insensibly crept, in the first century of the Christian era, into the teachings of Jesus Christ, and by crystallising into accepted dogmas have impaired the effectiveness and obscured the purpose of the Christian Faith.

87. "*I affirm,*" is 'Abdu'l-Bahá's own written comment on the Tablet of the

Branch, "*that the true meaning, the real significance, the innermost secret of these verses, of these very words, is my own servitude to the sacred Threshold of the Abhá Beauty, my complete self-effacement, my utter nothingness before Him. This is my resplendent crown, my most precious adorning. On this I pride myself in the kingdom of earth and heaven. Therein I glory among the company of the well-favoured!*"[1] "*No one is permitted,*" He warns us in the passage, which immediately follows, "*to give these verses any other interpretation.*" "*I am,*" He, in this same connection, affirms, "*according to the explicit texts of the Kitáb-i-Aqdas and the Kitáb-i-'Ahd the manifest Interpreter of the Word of God ... Whoso deviates from my interpretation is a victim of his own fancy.*"[2]

88. Furthermore, the inescapable inference from the belief in the identity of the Author of our Faith with Him Who is the Centre of His Covenant would be to place 'Abdu'l-Bahá in a position superior to that of the Báb, the reverse of which is the fundamental, though not as yet universally recognised, principle of this Revelation. It would also justify the charge with which, all throughout 'Abdu'l-Bahá's ministry, the Covenant-Breakers have striven to poison the minds and pervert the understanding of Bahá'u'lláh's loyal followers.

89. It would be more correct, and in consonance with the established principles of Bahá'u'lláh and the Báb, if instead of maintaining this fictitious identity with reference to 'Abdu'l-Bahá, we regard the Forerunner and the Founder of our Faith as identical in reality—a truth which the text of the Súratu'l-Haykal unmistakably affirms. "*Had the Primal Point (the Báb) been someone else beside Me as ye claim,*" is Bahá'u'lláh's explicit statement, "*and had attained My presence, verily He would have never allowed Himself to be separated from Me, but rather We would have had mutual delights with each other in My Days.*"[3] "*He Who now voiceth the Word of God,*" Bahá'u'lláh again affirms, "*is none other except the Primal Point Who hath once again been made manifest.*"[4] "*He is,*" He thus refers to Himself in a Tablet addressed to one of the Letters of the Living, "*the same as the One, Who appeared in the year sixty (AH 1260). This verily is one of His mighty signs.*"[5] "*Who,*" He pleads in the Súriy-i-Damm, "*will arise to secure the triumph of the Primal Beauty (the Báb) revealed in the countenance of His Manifestation?*"[6] Referring to the Revelation proclaimed by the Báb He conversely characterizes it as "*My own previous*

1 Statement (a)
2 Statement (b)
3 Statement (c)
4 Statement (d)
5 Statement (e)
6 Statement (f)

Manifestation."[1]

90. That 'Abdu'l-Bahá is not a Manifestation of God, that He gets His light, His inspiration and sustenance direct from the Fountain-head of the Bahá'í Revelation; that He reflects even as a clear and perfect Mirror the rays of Bahá'u'lláh's glory, and does not inherently possess that indefinable yet all-pervading reality the exclusive possession of which is the hallmark of Prophethood; that His words are not equal in rank, though they possess an equal validity with the utterances of Bahá'u'lláh; that He is not to be acclaimed as the return of Jesus Christ, the Son Who will come "*in the glory of the Father*"—these truths find added justification, and are further reinforced, by the following statement of 'Abdu'l-Bahá, addressed to some believers in America, with which I may well conclude this section: "*You have written that there is a difference among the believers concerning the 'Second Coming of Christ.' Gracious God! Time and again this question hath arisen, and its answer hath emanated in a clear and irrefutable statement from the pen of 'Abdu'l-Bahá, that what is meant in the prophecies by the 'Lord of Hosts' and the 'Promised Christ' is the Blessed Perfection (Bahá'u'lláh) and His holiness the Exalted One (the Báb). My name is 'Abdu'l-Bahá. My qualification is 'Abdu'l-Bahá. My reality is 'Abdu'l-Bahá. My praise is 'Abdu'l-Bahá. Thraldom to the Blessed Perfection is my glorious and refulgent diadem, and servitude to all the human race my perpetual religion ... No name, no title, no mention, no commendation have I, nor will ever have, except 'Abdu'l-Bahá. This is my longing. This is my greatest yearning. This is my eternal life. This is my everlasting glory.*"[2]

20.3 Sources of misunderstanding

In paragraph 83, Shoghi Effendi states that those who overestimate the station of 'Abdu'l-Bahá are as reprehensible as those who underestimate it. This statement is a reference to the confusion that existed at the time of Shoghi Effendi about the station of 'Abdu'l-Bahá.

Soon after the ascension of Bahá'u'lláh, there were differences of opinion among the believers regarding the station of 'Abdu'l-Bahá. Based on personal interpretation of the contents of the Tablet of the Branch, some believers made an attempt to elevate the station of 'Abdu'l-Bahá to that of Bahá'u'lláh.

In paragraph 84, Shoghi Effendi explicitly rejects such a possibility. He states that "neither in *The Kitáb-i-Aqdas* nor in the Book of Bahá'u'lláh's Covenant, nor even in the Tablet of the Branch, nor in any other Tablet, whether revealed by Bahá'u'lláh or 'Abdu'l-Bahá", is there any authority supporting the "mystic unity" of Bahá'u'lláh and 'Abdu'l-Bahá.

---

1 Statement (g)

2 Statement (h)

On the contrary; 'Abdu'l-Bahá in many of His Tablets has clarified His own position as the lowly servant of Bahá'u'lláh, although, He was appointed by Bahá'u'lláh as the Centre of His Covenant and the Interpreter of His Words.

Shoghi Effendi identifies two factors contributing to such a misunderstanding. The first was the exaggerated interpretation of the terms and titles used in the Tablet of the Branch (Súrih-i-Ghusn) by some Bahá'ís. Bahá'u'lláh revealed this Tablet in Arabic during His exile in Adrianople. The Tablet is addressed to Mírzá-Riḍáy-i-Mústawfí, a believer from Khurásán.[1] The main theme of the Tablet is the nature of the station of 'Abdu'l-Bahá.

The other factor was the introduction into its English translation of the Tablet of the Branch, certain words that were "either non-existent, misleading, or ambiguous in their connotation."

Shoghi Effendi also states that such interpretations were mainly the result of erroneous conclusions drawn from the opening passages of a Tablet of Bahá'u'lláh, the extracts of which had been published before the Tablet of the Branch in a compilation called *Bahá'í Scriptures*. The extracts referred to by the Guardian are:

> *"In His Name who shines forth from the Horizon of Might! Verily, the Tongue of the Ancient gives glad-tidings to those who are in the world concerning the appearance of the Greatest Name, and who takes His Covenant among the nations."*
>
> *"Verily, He [*] is Myself; the Shining-Place of My Identity; the East of My Justice; the Standard of My Love."*

In the early prints of *Bahá'í Scriptures*, the asterisk on page 255 was footnoted as "'Abdu'l-Bahá"—later changed to "Bahá'u'lláh". Shoghi Effendi emphasizes that such an interpretation was wrong. He then provides the authoritative explanation of the true meaning of the terms used in this Tablet by Bahá'u'lláh in paragraphs 84–86:

- The term "*the Tongue of the Ancient*" is a reference to God
- The term "*the Greatest Name*" is a reference to Bahá'u'lláh.
- The term "the Covenant" means the Covenant that God makes with mankind at the advent of a new Dispensation.
- The "*glad-tidings*" are the voice of God referring to Bahá'u'lláh, not Bahá'u'lláh referring to 'Abdu'l-Bahá.
- The station "*He is Myself*" refers to the mystic unity of God and Bahá'u'lláh and not Bahá'u'lláh and 'Abdu'l-Bahá. There are similar passages in *The Kitáb-i-Íqán* in which Bahá'u'lláh makes such a claim. Here are some examples:

    a) *"Were any of the all-embracing Manifestations of God to declare: 'I am God', He verily speaketh the truth, and no doubt attacheth thereto. For it hath been repeatedly demonstrated that through their*

[1] Adib Taherzadeh, *The Revelation of Bahá'u'lláh*, vol. 3, p. 388.

Revelation, their attributes and names, the Revelation of God, His name and His attributes, are made manifest in the world."[1]

b) "*Even as He hath said: 'There is no distinction whatsoever between Thee and Them; except that they are Thy servants, and are created of Thee.' This is the significance of the tradition: 'I am He, Himself, and He is I, myself'.*"[2]

At some stage, Ḥájí Mírzá Haydar-'Alí[3], one of the prominent early Bahá'ís living at the time of both Bahá'u'lláh and 'Abdu'l-Bahá, "… wrote a letter to 'Abdu'l-Bahá and asked Him to explain the significance of the Bahá'u'lláh's utterances in the Súrih-i-Ghusn [the Tablet of the Branch] and other Tablets including certain verses in the *Mathnaví*[4] concerning the exalted station of the Branch. In reply 'Abdu'l-Bahá wrote a Tablet in which He announced …"[5] His station of servitude. Shoghi Effendi quotes an extract of this Tablet in paragraph 87, statements (a) and (b).

'Abdu'l-Bahá also draws on the power of interpretation of the Words of Bahá'u'lláh endowed on Him in *The Kitáb-i-Aqdas* and *The Kitáb-i-'Ahd* to emphasize that His interpretation of the statements made about Him in the Tablet of the Branch was the correct one and that no one should deviate from it.

---

1 Bahá'u'lláh, *The Kitáb-i-Íqán*, p. 100.

2 Bahá'u'lláh, *The Kitáb-i-Íqán*, p. 100.

3 Adib Taherzadeh, in *The Revelation of Bahá'u'lláh*, vol. 1, pp. 2–29, states that Ḥájí Mírzá Haydar-'Alí "… was a native of Iṣfáhán who embraced the Faith soon after its inception. He first attained the presence of Bahá'u'lláh in Adrianople. From there he was sent by Bahá'u'lláh to Constantinople where he acted as a channel of communication between Him and the believers in Persia and 'Iráq. Later, he was sent to Egypt where he was arrested by the enemies of the Faith and dispatched as a prisoner to the Súdán. The persecution, which he suffered there for many years, served only to strengthen his faith and intensify his love for Bahá'u'lláh. After his release, he went straight to 'Akká where he was privileged to remain for some months in the presence of his Lord. Then directed by Him, he went to Persia where he served the Cause as an outstanding Bahá'í teacher for many years. Ḥájí Mírzá Haydar-'Alí played a major role in the promotion and protection of the Covenant of Bahá'u'lláh after His ascension, defending it most ably against the onslaught of the unfaithful band of Covenant-breakers who were determined to undermine the edifice of the Cause of God and to uproot its institutions. The latter part of his long and eventful life was spent in the service of 'Abdu'l-Bahá in the Holy Land. He died in Haifa and is buried in the Bahá'í Cemetery on Mount Carmel."

4 This is a 300 line Persian poem written by Bahá'u'lláh entitled *Mathnavíy-i-Mubárak*, not the *Mathnaví* written by Mawláná Jalálu'd-Dín-i-Rúmí.

5 Adib Taherzadeh, *The Revelation of Bahá'u'lláh*, vol. 2, p. 394. Chapter 2 discusses Bahá'u'lláh's poem, the *Mathnavíy-i-Mubárak*.

20.4 Irrational and superstitious beliefs

In paragraph 86, Shoghi Effendi warns us that such misinterpretations can cause irrational and superstitious beliefs to creep into the teachings of the Bahá'í Faith as happened in the first century of Christianity. Such beliefs became crystalized into dogmas that have adversely influenced the effectiveness and purpose of the Christian Faith.

The early Christian era can be divided into the apostolic and post-apostolic periods. During the apostolic stage, which includes the years following Jesus until the death of the Twelve Apostles, the Apostles led the Church. Peter, Paul and James were the most notable leaders in this period, though Paul's thinking has had the most significant influence. The first Christian church was established in Jerusalem.

The earliest Christian creeds contained in the Gospels and New Testament Epistles express belief in the resurrection of Jesus after death. For example, in Corinthians, Paul mentions, "*For I delivered to you first of all that which I also received: that Christ died for our sins according to the Scriptures, that he was buried, that he was raised on the third day according to the Scriptures. And that he was seen of Cephas, then of the twelve. After that, he was seen of above five hundred brethren at once; of whom the greater part remain unto this present, but some are fallen asleep.*"[1]

This statement and other similar writings in the Christian Scriptures reflect the core beliefs of the Christianity that were formed about a decade after the crucifixion of Jesus, originating within the Jerusalem Church. According to such beliefs, Jesus in His physical body rose from the dead three days after His crucifixion. Hence, the tomb of Jesus was found to be empty by women who had come to anoint the body with spices. Jesus appeared a number of times to different people after His resurrection.

'Abdu'l-Bahá explicitly states: "*The resurrections of the Divine Manifestations are not of the body. All Their states, Their conditions, Their acts, the things They have established, Their teachings, Their expressions, Their parables and Their instructions have a spiritual and divine signification, and have no connection with material things.*"[2]

He then explains the meaning of the resurrection of Christ: "... *the disciples were troubled and agitated after the martyrdom of Christ. The Reality of Christ, which signifies His teachings, His bounties, His perfections and His spiritual power, was hidden and concealed for two or three days after His martyrdom, and was not resplendent and manifest. No, rather it was lost, for the believers were few in number and were troubled and agitated. The Cause of Christ was like a lifeless body; and when after three days the disciples became assured and steadfast, and began to serve the Cause of Christ, and resolved to spread the divine teachings, putting His counsels into practice, and*

---

1 Corinthians 15:3–6

2 'Abdu'l-Bahá, *Some Answered Questions*, p. 102.

arising to serve Him, the Reality of Christ became resplendent and His bounty appeared; His religion found life; His teachings and His admonitions became evident and visible. In other words, the Cause of Christ was like a lifeless body until the life and the bounty of the Holy Spirit surrounded it."[1]

20.5 Bahá'u'lláh, the Báb and 'Abdu'l-Bahá

In paragraphs 88–90, Shoghi Effendi makes further comparisons between the stations associated with the Central Figures of the Bahá'í Faith. He asserts the following major concepts:

a) Identifying the station of 'Abdu'l-Bahá with that of Bahá'u'lláh would place 'Abdu'l-Bahá in a rank higher than that of the Báb. This is against the fundamental verities of the Faith.

b) It is more correct and in conformity with the principles of the Faith to accept that Bahá'u'lláh and the Báb are one in Their realities.

c) 'Abdu'l-Bahá is not a Manifestation of God and receives "*His light, His inspiration, and sustenance*" from Bahá'u'lláh.

d) As a perfect mirror, 'Abdu'l-Bahá reflects the glory of Bahá'u'lláh.

e) 'Abdu'l-Bahá does not inherently possess that reality which is exclusive to the Manifestations of God.

f) The Words of 'Abdu'l-Bahá are not equal in rank to the utterances of Bahá'u'lláh, but have the same validity.

g) 'Abdu'l-Bahá cannot be considered as the return of Jesus Christ, the Son Who will come "*in the glory of the Father*".

[1] 'Abdu'l-Bahá, *Some Answered Questions*, p. 104.

20.6 Activities

1. Why is overestimating of the station of 'Abdu'l-Bahá as harmful as underestimating it?

2. Why is the concept of the "mystic unity" of Bahá'u'lláh and 'Abdu'l-Bahá unacceptable?

3. Describe some of "those irrational and superstitious beliefs" that crept into Christianity in its first century as referred to by Shoghi Effendi in paragraph 86.

4. What was the main strategy of the Covenant-breakers to "poison the minds and pervert the understanding" of the Bahá'ís during the time of 'Abdu'l-Bahá (paragraph 88)?

5. Consider statement (e) in paragraph 89.

   a) Who is the person who appeared in the year sixty?

   b) What is your understanding of this quotation?

6. Consider statement (f) in paragraph 89.

   a) What is your understanding of this quotation?

   b) Why does Bahá'u'lláh refer to the Revelation proclaimed by the Báb as *"My own previous Manifestation"?*

7. Identify the key points of paragraph 90.

20.7 Glossary

Term	Meaning
Appellation	A name or title, esp. one that is formal or descriptive
Ascribe	To believe (something) to be the result or work of
Assertion	A forceful statement or claim
Connotation	(Any of) the feelings or ideas that are suggested by a word in addition to the primary meaning of the word
Consonance	Agreement, compatibility, harmony
Equivocal	(Of words or statements) having a double or doubtful meaning; ambiguous
Equivocation	Ambiguity
Erroneous	(Of a statement, belief, etc.) incorrect; mistaken
Extravagant	(Of ideas, behaviour, and the expression of feeling) uncontrolled; beyond what is reasonable
Impair	To weaken or make worse
Inadvertently	(Done) without paying attention or by accident
Inculcate	To fix (ideas, principles, etc.) in the mind of someone
Inference	The judgement that one forms about the meaning of something done, said, etc.
Perpetual	Continuing endlessly
Pervading	(Of smells and of ideas, feelings, etc.) to spread through every part of
Precede	To come, go, or happen (just) before
Profuse	Plentiful, abundant; Produced, flowing, or poured out freely and in great quantity
Refulgent	Very bright; brilliant
Reprehensible	(Of a person or their behaviour) deserving to be blamed; extremely bad
Reversion	A return to a former (usu. undesirable) condition or habit
Sustenance	Nourishment; means of sustaining life.
Appellation	A name or title, esp. one that is formal or descriptive

21. CHARTERS OF THE BAHÁ'Í WORLD ORDER

21.1 Introduction

This chapter covers paragraphs 91–95. Read these paragraphs and reflect on the contents before starting the lesson. In this section of his letter, the Guardian describes the Divine origin of the Bahá'í Administration and highlights its relationship with *The Will and Testament of 'Abdu'l-Bahá* and *The Kitáb-i-Aqdas.*

In this chapter, you need to look for and understand the following **key concepts**:

a) The ascension of Bahá'u'lláh ended fifty years of continuous revelation of the Dispensation of Bahá'u'lláh.

b) The passing of 'Abdu'l-Bahá ended the Heroic Age of the Faith, but opened the Formative Age that will continue until the establishment of the Golden Age of the Cause of Bahá'u'lláh.

c) The Bahá'í Administration is the result of the evolution of the energies released through the Revelation of Bahá'u'lláh in the mind of 'Abdu'l-Bahá.

d) *The Will and Testament of 'Abdu'l-Bahá* can be considered as the offspring of the "mystic intercourse" between Bahá'u'lláh and 'Abdu'l-Bahá.

e) *The Will and Testament of 'Abdu'l-Bahá* is referred to by Shoghi Effendi as the Charter of the Administrative Order of Bahá'u'lláh.

f) *The Will and Testament of 'Abdu'l-Bahá* and *The Kitáb-i-Aqdas* "... are not only complementary, but that they mutually confirm one another and are inseparable parts of one complete unit."[1]

g) *The Will and Testament of 'Abdu'l-Bahá* sets out the framework on which the Bahá'í Administration is built.

h) The Bahá'í Administration will reveal the full implications and

[1] Shoghi Effendi, *The World Order of Bahá'u'lláh*, p. 3.

potentialities of *The Will and Testament of 'Abdu'l-Bahá* as it evolves and expands.

21.2 Paragraphs under study

91. Dearly-beloved brethren in 'Abdu'l-Bahá! With the ascension of Bahá'u'lláh the Day-Star of Divine guidance which, as foretold by Shaykh Aḥmad and Siyyid Káẓim, had risen in Shíráz, and, while pursuing its westward course, had mounted its zenith in Adrianople, had finally sunk below the horizon of 'Akká, never to rise again ere the complete revolution of one thousand years. The setting of so effulgent an Orb brought to a definite termination the period of Divine Revelation—the initial and most vitalising stage in the Bahá'í era. Inaugurated by the Báb, culminating in Bahá'u'lláh, anticipated and extolled by the entire company of the Prophets of this great prophetic cycle, this period has, except for the short interval between the Báb's martyrdom and Bahá'u'lláh's shaking experiences in the Síyáh-Chál of Ṭihrán, been characterized by almost fifty years of continuous and progressive Revelation—a period which by its duration and fecundity must be regarded as unparalleled in the entire field of the world's spiritual history.

92. The passing of 'Abdu'l-Bahá, on the other hand, marks the closing of the Heroic and Apostolic Age of this same Dispensation—that primitive period of our Faith the splendours of which can never be rivalled, much less be eclipsed, by the magnificence that must needs distinguish the future victories of Bahá'u'lláh's Revelation. For neither the achievements of the champion-builders of the present-day institutions of the Faith of Bahá'u'lláh, nor the tumultuous triumphs which the heroes of its Golden Age will in the coming days succeed in winning, can measure with, or be included within the same category as, the wondrous works associated with the names of those who have generated its very life and laid its pristine foundations. That first and creative age of the Bahá'í era must, by its very nature, stand above and apart from the formative period into which we have entered and the golden age destined to succeed it.

93. 'Abdu'l-Bahá, Who incarnates an institution for which we can find no parallel whatsoever in any of the world's recognised religious systems, may be said to have closed the Age to which He Himself belonged and opened the one in which we are now labouring. His Will and Testament should thus be regarded as the perpetual, the indissoluble link which the mind of Him Who is the Mystery of God has conceived in order to insure the continuity of the three ages that constitute the component parts of the Bahá'í Dispensation. The period in which the seed of the Faith had been slowly germinating is thus intertwined both with the one, which must witness its efflorescence and the subsequent age in which that seed will have finally yielded its golden fruit.

94. The creative energies released by the Law of Bahá'u'lláh, permeating and evolving within the mind of 'Abdu'l-Bahá, have, by their very impact and close interaction, given birth to an Instrument which may be viewed as the Charter of the New World Order which is at once the glory and the promise of this most great Dispensation. The Will may thus be acclaimed as the inevitable offspring resulting from that mystic intercourse between Him Who communicated the generating influence of His divine Purpose and the One Who was its vehicle and chosen recipient. Being the Child of the Covenant—the Heir of both the Originator and the Interpreter of the Law of God—the Will and Testament of 'Abdu'l-Bahá can no more be divorced from Him Who supplied the original and motivating impulse than from the One Who ultimately conceived it. Bahá'u'lláh's inscrutable purpose, we must ever bear in mind, has been so thoroughly infused into the conduct of 'Abdu'l-Bahá, and their motives have been so closely wedded together, that the mere attempt to dissociate the teachings of the former from any system which the ideal Exemplar of those same teachings has established would amount to a repudiation of one of the most sacred and basic truths of the Faith.

95. The Administrative Order, which ever since 'Abdu'l-Bahá's ascension has evolved and is taking shape under our very eyes in no fewer than forty countries of the world, may be considered as the framework of the Will itself, the inviolable stronghold wherein this new-born child is being nurtured and developed. This Administrative Order, as it expands and consolidates itself, will no doubt manifest the potentialities and reveal the full implications of this momentous Document—this most remarkable expression of the Will of One of the most remarkable Figures of the Dispensation of Bahá'u'lláh. It will, as its component parts, its organic institutions, begin to function with efficiency and vigour, assert its claim and demonstrate its capacity to be regarded not only as the nucleus but the very pattern of the New World Order destined to embrace in the fullness of time the whole of mankind.

21.3 Progression of the Day-Star of Divine guidance

In paragraph 91, Shoghi Effendi portrays the period of revelation starting with the declaration of the Báb and ending with the ascension of Bahá'u'lláh as the rising and setting of the Day-Star of Divine guidance. In this journey, the Day-Star arose from Shíráz, was renewed in the Síyáh-Chál of Ṭihrán, took its course westward and reached its zenith in Adrianople, and finally set in 'Akká.

This period, except for the short gap between the martyrdom of the Báb and the declaration of Bahá'u'lláh in the Síyáh-Chál, represents fifty years of continuous revelation that is unprecedented in religious history.

The milestones identified by Shoghi Effendi in the course of the Day-Star of Divine guidance correspond to the significant events in the Dispensations of the Báb and Bahá'u'lláh. The Báb declared His mission on 23 May 1844 and was martyred on 9 July 1850. Bahá'u'lláh received intimation of His Revelation in the Síyáh-Chál of Ṭihrán in 1852. He was exiled first to Baghdád and then Constantinople. On His Journey to Constantinople, He publicly declared His mission as the universal Manifestation of God for this age in the Garden of Riḍván in 1863.

After four months, Bahá'u'lláh was exiled to Adrianople where He proclaimed His message to all the kings and rulers of the world, summoning them to recognize the Day of God and to acknowledge the Promised One of all the previous religious Scriptures. Bahá'u'lláh Himself confirms, "*Never since the beginning of the world, hath the Message been so openly proclaimed.*"[1]

The physical life of Bahá'u'lláh finally ended in 1892 in 'Akká, and the Day-Star of Divine Guidance set for at least one thousand years from the time of Bahá'u'lláh's intimation of His Revelation in October 1852 in the Síyáh-Chál of Ṭihrán.

21.4 Child of the Covenant

Although the Day-Star of Divine guidance set with the ascension of Bahá'u'lláh, the creative energies released through His Revelation have continued its evolution through 'Abdu'l-Bahá and the Bahá'í Administrative Order towards realizing of the World Order envisaged and ordained by Bahá'u'lláh.

As highlighted in paragraphs 92 and 93, the passing of 'Abdu'l-Bahá ended the Heroic Age of the Faith, but opened the Formative Age which will continue until the establishment of the Golden Age of the Cause of Bahá'u'lláh. According to Shoghi Effendi, these three ages are eternally linked through *The Will and Testament of 'Abdu'l-Bahá.*

Shoghi Effendi makes the following significant references to *The Will and Testament of 'Abdu'l-Bahá* in paragraph 94:

a) It is the product of permeation and evolution of the energies released through the Law of Bahá'u'lláh within the mind of 'Abdu'l-Bahá.
b) It is the offspring of the mystical intercourse between Bahá'u'lláh and the chosen recipient of His divine Purpose, 'Abdu'l-Bahá.
c) As the Child of the Covenant, the Will "... can no more be divorced from Him Who supplied the original and motivating impulse than from the One Who ultimately conceived it."
d) The mysterious purpose of Bahá'u'lláh has been so infused into the conduct of 'Abdu'l-Bahá and their motives so united that "... the mere attempt to dissociate the teachings of the former from any system which the ideal Exemplar of those same teachings has established would amount to a repudiation of one of the most sacred and basic truths of the Faith."

---

[1] Shoghi Effendi, *God Passes By*, p. 212.

21.5 Bahá'í Administrative Order Charter

In paragraph 94 *The Will and Testament of 'Abdu'l-Bahá* is referred to by Shoghi Effendi as the Charter of the Administrative Order of Bahá'u'lláh. He states in another message: "… all the authority of the administrative bodies, as well as of the Guardian himself, is mainly derived from this tremendous document."[1]

Regarding its implications and importance, Shoghi Effendi points out that "The contents of the Will of the Master is far too much for the present generation to comprehend. It needs at least a century of actual working before the treasures of wisdom hidden in it can be revealed."[2]

There are three important provisions of the Will through which 'Abdu'l-Bahá [3] has created an infallible protection for the Cause:

a) The explicit appointment of Shoghi Effendi, His grandșon, as His successor and the Guardian of the Bahá'í Faith.
b) Defending His successor from any possible challenge.
c) Providing guidance and the means for establishing the Universal House of Justice. This in itself provides a clear structure for the implementation of the Bahá'í Administration to support the establishment and functioning of the Universal House of Justice.

In paragraph 95, Shoghi Effendi highlights that the Bahá'í Administrative Order can be considered as the framework of *The Will and Testament of 'Abdu'l-Bahá,* "the inviolable stronghold wherein this new-born child is being nurtured and developed." The potentialities and full implications of the Will be manifested as the Administrative Order expands and consolidates itself.

Shoghi Effendi refers to *The Will and Testament of 'Abdu'l-Bahá* as "this supreme, this infallible Organ for the accomplishment of a Divine Purpose"[4] and the "Charter of Bahá'u'lláh's New World Order"[5] since this document together with *The Kitáb-i-Aqdas* contains the essential elements of the civilization to be established through the World Order of Bahá'u'lláh.[6]

The Will and Testament of 'Abdu'l-Bahá and *The Kitáb-i-Aqdas* "… are not only complementary, but that they mutually confirm one another, and are inseparable parts of one complete unit."[7] On the relationship between these two documents, Shoghi Effendi further makes the following statement: "A study of the provisions of these sacred documents will reveal the close relationship that exists between them, as well as the identity of purpose and method which they inculcate. Far from regarding their specific provisions as

---

1 Shoghi Effendi, *Lights of Guidance*, p. 182.
2 Shoghi Effendi, *Lights of Guidance*, p. 182.
3 Ḥasan Balyuzi, *'Abdu'l-Bahá*, p. 484.
4 Shoghi Effendi, *The World Order of Bahá'u'lláh*, p. 89.
5 Shoghi Effendi, *God Passes By*, p. 4.
6 Shoghi Effendi, *The World Order of Bahá'u'lláh*, p. 4.
7 Shoghi Effendi, *The World Order of Bahá'u'lláh*, p. 4.

incompatible and contradictory in spirit, every fair-minded inquirer will readily admit that they are not only complementary, but that they mutually confirm one another, and are inseparable parts of one complete unit."[1]

Shoghi Effendi continues: "A comparison of their contents with the rest of Bahá'í sacred Writings will similarly establish the conformity of whatever they contain with the spirit as well as the letter of the authenticated writings and sayings of Bahá'u'lláh and 'Abdu'l-Bahá. In fact, he who reads the Aqdas with care and diligence will not find it hard to discover that the Most Holy Book itself anticipates in a number of passages the institutions which 'Abdu'l-Bahá ordains in His Will. By leaving certain matters unspecified and unregulated in His Book of Laws, Bahá'u'lláh seems to have deliberately left a gap in the general scheme of the Bahá'í Dispensation, which the unequivocal provisions of the Master's Will have filled. To attempt to divorce the one from the other, to insinuate that the Teachings of Bahá'u'lláh have not been upheld, in their entirety and with absolute integrity, by what 'Abdu'l-Bahá has revealed in His Will, is an unpardonable affront to the unswerving fidelity that has characterized the life and labours of our beloved Master."

21.6 Divine origin of the Bahá'í Administrative Order

Shoghi Effendi's statements in the previous section assert that the origin of the Bahá'í Administrative Order is based on the core of the Revelation of Bahá'u'lláh and is one of its intrinsic components. Shoghi Effendi emphatically states that the Bahá'í Administration "... is not an innovation imposed arbitrarily upon the Bahá'ís of the world since the Master's passing, but derives its authority from *The Will and Testament of 'Abdu'l-Bahá*, is specifically prescribed in unnumbered Tablets, and rests in some of its essential features upon the explicit provisions of *The Kitáb-i-Aqdas*."[2]

In *The World Order of Bahá'u'lláh*, Shoghi Effendi highlights the major references to the Bahá'í Administration made by Bahá'u'lláh and 'Abdu'l-Bahá in their Writings:[3]

a) In the Tablets of Bahá'u'lláh, the institutions of the Universal House of Justice and the Local Houses of Justice are clearly established.
b) The Institution of the Hands of the Cause was established by the appointment of four members by Bahá'u'lláh. 'Abdu'l-Bahá later named four other people posthumously as members of this institution.[4]
c) The institutions of the Local Spiritual Assemblies and National Assemblies were functioning at an embryonic stage before the passing of 'Abdu'l-Bahá.
d) The nature and operation of the Administrative Order was formally proclaimed and established by 'Abdu'l-Bahá in His Will and Testament.

---

1 Shoghi Effendi, *The World Order of Bahá'u'lláh*, p. 4.
2 Shoghi Effendi, *The World Order of Bahá'u'lláh*, p. 5.
3 Shoghi Effendi, *The World Order of Bahá'u'lláh*, p. 145.
4 'Abdu'l-Bahá, *Memorials of the Faithful*, p. 5.

e) In *The Kitáb-i-Aqdas*, the institution of the Guardianship was anticipated. In paragraph 42 of *The Kitáb-i-Aqdas*, Bahá'u'lláh states: "*Endowments dedicated to charity revert to God, the Revealer of Signs. None hath the right to dispose of them without leave from Him Who is the Dawning-place of Revelation. After Him, this authority shall pass to the Aghsán, and after them to the House of Justice—should it be established in the world by then—that they may use these endowments for the benefit of the Places which have been exalted in this Cause, and for whatsoever hath been enjoined upon them by Him Who is the God of might and power. Otherwise, the endowments shall revert to the people of Bahá who speak not except by His leave and judge not save in accordance with what God hath decreed in this Tablet—lo, they are the champions of victory betwixt heaven and earth—that they may use them in the manner that hath been laid down in the Book by God, the Mighty, the Bountiful.*"[1]

In this statement, Bahá'u'lláh envisages the termination of the line of Aghsán (His male descendants) and ordains that endowments shall pass to the "people of Bahá". According the Notes section of *The Kitáb-i-Aqdas*: "The term 'people of Bahá' is used with a number of different meanings in the Bahá'í Writings. In this instance, they are described as those '*who speak not except by His leave and judge not save in accordance with what God hath decreed in this Tablet*'".[2]

Following the sudden passing of Shoghi Effendi in 1957, the Hands of the Cause of God directed the affairs of the community until 1963 when the Universal House of Justice was elected for the first time.

Overall, the Bahá'í Administrative Order is significantly different from any other institutions developed in previous Dispensations. It is also distinct from any man-made systems and institutions governing society at present or in the past.

---

1 Bahá'u'lláh, *The Kitáb-i-Aqdas*, p. 34.
2 Notes on *The Kitáb-i-Aqdas*, p. 197.

21.7 Activities

1. Briefly express your understanding of paragraph 91.

2. How is the present period of the evolution of the Bahá'í Faith (the Formative Age) different from the Heroic Age?

3. Consider the following statement from paragraph 93:

   "His Will and Testament should thus be regarded as the perpetual, the indissoluble link which the mind of Him Who is the Mystery of God has conceived in order to insure the continuity of the three ages that constitute the component parts of the Bahá'í Dispensation."

   a) What are the three ages referred to in this statement?

   b) How does *The Will and Testament of 'Abdu'l-Bahá* ensure the continuity of "the three ages"?

4. Consider the following statement from paragraph 94:

   "The creative energies released by the Law of Bahá'u'lláh, permeating and evolving within the mind of 'Abdu'l-Bahá, have, by their very impact and close interaction, given birth to an Instrument which may be viewed as the Charter of the New World Order which is at once the glory and the promise of this most great Dispensation".

a) What is the "Instrument" referred to?

b) Briefly describe your understanding of this statement.

5. What are the three provisions in *The Will and Testament of 'Abdu'l-Bahá* through which He has created an infallible protection for the Cause?

6. Describe the relationship between *The Kitáb-i-Aqdas* and *The Will and Testament* of 'Abdu'l-Bahá.

7. What are the major references to the Bahá'í Administration made by Bahá'u'lláh and 'Abdu'l-Bahá in their Writings?

21.8 Glossary

Term	Meaning
Assert	To state or declare forcefully
Culminate	To reach the highest point, degree, or stage of development in
Efflorescence	The period or action of the formation and development of flowers on a plant
Extol	To praise very highly
Germinate	To start or cause a seed to grow
Indissoluble	Impossible to separate or break up; lasting
Intertwine	To (cause) to twist together or with something else
Inviolable	Too highly respected to be attacked, changed, etc.
Permeate	To spread or pass through or into every part of (a thing, place, etc.)
Perpetual	Lasting for ever or a long time
Pristine	Pure; undamaged; fresh and clean
Repudiate	To state that (something) is untrue or unjust; to refuse to recognise or obey
Tumultuous	Very noisy and disorderly

22. SIGNIFICANCE & DISTINCTION OF THE BAHÁ'Í ADMINSTRATIVE ORDER

22.1 Introduction

This chapter covers paragraphs 96–100. Read these paragraphs and reflect on the contents before starting the lesson. In this section of his letter, Shoghi Effendi highlights the unprecedented nature and the significance of the Bahá'í Administrative Order. This order is a vital element in both the evolution of the Bahá'í Faith and of humanity on this planet. It is the Divine channel through which the Force released through the Revelations of the Báb and Bahá'u'lláh exerts its influence until the realization of the Golden Age of the Cause and the establishment of the Kingdom of God on earth.

In this chapter, you need to look for and understand the following **key concepts**:

a) The Bahá'í Administrative Order is fundamentally different from anything established by any Manifestation of God in the previous Dispensations.
b) Neither the Gospel nor the Qur'án contained explicitly written text for Peter, the "chief of the Apostles of Christ", or Imám 'Alí, the son-in-law of Muḥammad to support their claim to the primacy with which they had both been invested, and thus to silence those who usurped their authority.
c) The provisions incorporated in the Bahá'í Administrative Order safeguard the Bahá'í Faith against any schism.
d) The Bahá'í Administrative Order represents the power and majesty that the future Bahá'í Commonwealth and the World Order of Bahá'u'lláh will manifest.

22.2 Paragraphs under study

96. It should be noted in this connection that this Administrative Order is fundamentally different from anything that any Prophet has previously established, inasmuch as Bahá'u'lláh has Himself revealed its

principles, established its institutions, appointed the person to interpret His Word and conferred the necessary authority on the body designed to supplement and apply His legislative ordinances. Therein lies the secret of its strength, its fundamental distinction, and the guarantee against disintegration and schism. Nowhere in the sacred scriptures of any of the world's religious systems, nor even in the writings of the Inaugurator of the Bábí Dispensation, do we find any provisions establishing a covenant or providing for an administrative order that can compare in scope and authority with those that lie at the very basis of the Bahá'í Dispensation. Has either Christianity or Islám, to take as an instance two of the most widely diffused and outstanding among the world's recognised religions, anything to offer that can measure with, or be regarded as equivalent to, either the Book of Bahá'u'lláh's Covenant or to the Will and Testament of 'Abdu'l-Bahá? Does the text of either the Gospel or the Qur'án confer sufficient authority upon those leaders and councils that have claimed the right and assumed the function of interpreting the provisions of their sacred scriptures and of administering the affairs of their respective communities? Could Peter, the admitted chief of the Apostles, or the Imám 'Alí, the cousin and legitimate successor of the Prophet, produce in support of the primacy with which both had been invested written and explicit affirmations from Christ and Muḥammad that could have silenced those who either among their contemporaries or in a later age have repudiated their authority and, by their action, precipitated the schisms that persist until the present day? Where, we may confidently ask, in the recorded sayings of Jesus Christ, whether in the matter of succession or in the provision of a set of specific laws and clearly defined administrative ordinances, as distinguished from purely spiritual principles, can we find anything approaching the detailed injunctions, laws and warnings that abound in the authenticated utterances of both Bahá'u'lláh and 'Abdu'l-Bahá? Can any passage of the Qur'án, which in respect to its legal code, its administrative and devotional ordinances marks already a notable advance over previous and more corrupted Revelations, be construed as placing upon an unassailable basis the undoubted authority with which Muḥammad had, verbally and on several occasions, invested His successor? Can the Author of the Bábí Dispensation however much He may have succeeded through the provisions of the *Persian Bayán* in averting a schism as permanent and catastrophic as those that afflicted Christianity and Islám—can He be said to have produced instruments for the safeguarding of His Faith as definite and efficacious as those which must for all time preserve the unity of the organized followers of the Faith of Bahá'u'lláh?

97. Alone of all the Revelations gone before it this Faith has, through the explicit directions, the repeated warnings, the authenticated safeguards incorporated and elaborated in its teachings, succeeded in raising a

structure which the bewildered followers of bankrupt and broken creeds might well approach and critically examine, and seek, ere it is too late, the invulnerable security of its world-embracing shelter.

98. No wonder that He Who through the operation of His Will has inaugurated so vast and unique an Order and Who is the Centre of so mighty a Covenant should have written these words: "*So firm and mighty is this Covenant that from the beginning of time until the present day no religious Dispensation hath produced its like.*"[1] "*Whatsoever is latent in the innermost of this holy cycle,*" He wrote during the darkest and most dangerous days of His ministry, "*shall gradually appear and be made manifest, for now is but the beginning of its growth and the dayspring of the revelation of its signs.*"[2] "*Fear not,*" are His reassuring words foreshadowing the rise of the Administrative Order established by His Will, "*fear not if this Branch be severed from this material world and cast aside its leaves; nay, the leaves thereof shall flourish, for this Branch will grow after it is cut off from this world below, it shall reach the loftiest pinnacles of glory, and it shall bear such fruits as will perfume the world with their fragrance.*"[3]

99. To what else if not to the power and majesty which this Administrative Order—the rudiments of the future all-enfolding Bahá'í Commonwealth—is destined to manifest, can these utterances of Bahá'u'lláh allude: "*The world's equilibrium hath been upset through the vibrating influence of this most great, this new World Order. Mankind's ordered life hath been revolutionized through the agency of this unique, this wondrous System—the like of which mortal eyes have never witnessed.*"[4]

100. The Báb Himself, in the course of His references to "*Him Whom God will make manifest*" anticipates the System and glorifies the World Order, which the Revelation of Bahá'u'lláh is destined to unfold. "*Well is it with him,*" is His remarkable statement in the third chapter of the Persian Bayán, "*who fixeth his gaze upon the Order of Bahá'u'lláh and rendereth thanks unto his Lord! For He will assuredly be made manifest. God hath indeed irrevocably ordained it in the Bayán.*"[5]

22.3 Uniqueness of the Covenant and Administration

The Bahá'í Administrative Order is distinctively different from any administrative structure established by the previous Manifestations of God. In paragraph 96, Shoghi Effendi identifies the primary reasons for this distinction:

a) Bahá'u'lláh Himself revealed the principles of the Bahá'í Administrative Order.

---

1 Statement (a)
2 Statement (b)
3 Statement (c)
4 Statement (d)
5 Statement (e)

b) He established its institutions.
c) He appointed His successor ('Abdu'l-Bahá) and gave Him the authority to interpret His Words.
d) He designed an infallible body (the Universal House of Justice) with authority to legislate new laws and ordinances.

None of the Holy Scriptures from earlier religions, including those of the Bábí Dispensation, offer a covenant or an administrative order comparable with the Bahá'í Administration.

Shoghi Effendi refers to Christianity and Islám as examples. Neither the Gospel nor the Qur'án contained explicitly written text regarding the authority of Peter, the "chief of the Apostles of Christ" or Imám 'Alí, the son-in-law of Muḥammad to interpret the Holy Writings or to administer the affairs of their respective communities. In fact, neither of them could produce any written assertion from Jesus Christ or Muḥammad to support the supremacy with which they had been invested with.

22.3.1 Peter the Apostle

Simon Peter was a fisherman from Bethsaida, a village in the province of Galilee. Jesus Christ chose him as one of His twelve disciples and their leader. He features prominently in the New Testament Gospels and the Acts of the Apostles. Peter accompanied Jesus during events that were witnessed by only a few of the other disciples. On the night before the crucifixion of Jesus Christ, Peter's faith was shaken and he denied Jesus Christ three times. However, afterwards he remained steadfast.[1]

Jesus designated Peter as the rock on which the church would be founded[2]. He was consistently named the first in the lists of the twelve disciples of Jesus Christ and had great influence on the Church in the early days of its formation. He is known as the leader and missionary in the early Christian church, and is traditionally considered as the first Pope by the Roman Catholic Church.

Peter, accompanied by his wife, travelled extensively in his missionary activities. He finally died the death of a martyr in Rome around AD 64.

22.3.2 Imám 'Alí

'Alí ibn 'Alí Ṭálib was the cousin and son-in-law of Muḥammad, married to His daughter Fáṭimih. 'Alí was also the first person to accept Muḥammad as a Manifestation of God and he dedicated his life to the cause of Islám.

During His lifetime, Muḥammad verbally implied that 'Alí was His successor on a number of occasions. However, when Muḥammad died in AD 632, 'Alí could not prove his right of succession. He was preceded in the caliphate by Abú Bakr, Umar, and 'U<u>th</u>mán; and hence did not become a caliph until AD 656.

---

1 'Abdu'l-Bahá, *Divine Philosophy*, p. 50.
2 Matthew 16:16–19

In the first year of his reign, 'Alí had to deal with a rebellion led by 'Á'ishah, the second wife of Muḥammad. Although the rebellion was suppressed in AD 657, not all disputes over 'Alí's right to the caliphate were resolved. One of the members of 'Uthmán's family, Mu'áwíya, did not accept the authority of 'Alí and claimed himself to be the Caliph. This conflict continued until a member of the Khawárij[1] sect murdered 'Alí at Al-Kúfih, in AD 661. See section 5.5 for more details.

22.4 Significance of the Bahá'í Administration

At present, world events and the progress of the Bahá'í Faith are under the influence of the two processes of disintegration and integration. On one hand, the elements of the old world order are progressively crumbling and perishing. On the other hand, the Bahá'í Faith is growing and its influence on the world is increasing day by day as the components of the new world order embedded within the Faith are gradually unfolded and developed.

These two processes are driven by a "God-born Force", which was released through the Revelations of the Báb and Bahá'u'lláh. This Force is "... irresistible in its sweeping power, incalculable in its potency, unpredictable in its course, mysterious in its workings, and awe-inspiring in its manifestations."[2]

During the Formative Age, this Force exerts its influence through the Bahá'í Administrative Order and will continue to drive civilization towards its ultimate goal: the Golden Age of the Cause when the Kingdom of God is established on earth. This makes the Bahá'í Administration a vital element in the evolution of both the Bahá'í Faith and humanity on this planet. In this regard, Shoghi Effendi explains: "... the Spirit breathed by Bahá'u'lláh upon the world ... can never permeate and exercise an abiding influence upon mankind unless and until it incarnates itself in a visible Order, which would bear His name, wholly identify itself with His principles, and function in conformity with His laws."[3]

The Bahá'í Administrative Order is an essential part of the Covenants of Bahá'u'lláh and 'Abdu'l-Bahá—it is designed to maintain the unity of the Bahá'í community and ensure its progress. Shoghi Effendi emphasizes that "... to dissociate the administrative principles of the Cause from the purely spiritual and humanitarian teachings would be tantamount to a mutilation of the body of the Cause, a separation that can only result in the disintegration of its component parts, and the extinction of the Faith itself."[4]

Regarding its purpose, Shoghi Effendi states: "... these administrative activities, however harmoniously and efficiently conducted, are but a means to an end, and should be regarded as direct instruments for the propagation of the

---

1 Kharijite in English

2 Shoghi Effendi, *The Advent of Divine Justice*, p. 46.

3 Shoghi Effendi, *The World Order of Bahá'u'lláh*, p. 19.

4 Shoghi Effendi, *The World Order of Bahá'u'lláh*, p. 5.

Bahá'í Faith. Let us take heed lest in our great concern for the perfection of the administrative machinery of the Cause, we lose sight of the Divine Purpose for which it has been created."[1]

22.5 Bahá'í Administration and the World Order

In paragraphs 99 and 100 Shoghi Effendi refers to the power and majesty that the Bahá'í Administrative Order—at present in its infancy—will manifest as the future all-embracing Bahá'í Commonwealth.

The Revelation of Bahá'u'lláh has given birth to a new world order that is destined, in centuries to come, to guide and govern human life on this planet. This is known as the World Order of Bahá'u'lláh. The main goal of this Order is the complete unity of the entire human race. As Bahá'u'lláh has promised, *"Soon will the present day order be rolled up, and a new one spread out in its stead."*[2]

Since its emergence, the vibrating energy of the World Order of Bahá'u'lláh, has been destabilizing the foundations of human affairs:

> *"The world's equilibrium hath been upset through the vibrating influence of this Most Great Order. Mankind's ordered life hath been revolutionised through the agency of this unique, this wondrous System, the like of which mortal eyes have never witnessed."*[3]

The Most Great Peace, which is the ultimate outcome of the spiritual unity of all nations, will be achieved only through the ordinances enshrined in the World Order of Bahá'u'lláh.

In the writings of Shoghi Effendi, the Bahá'í Administration is referred to as the "nucleus and pattern",[4] "bones and skeleton",[5] and "embryonic stage"[6] of the World Order of Bahá'u'lláh. The current Bahá'í Administration will evolve and mature to become as the instrument by which the laws and teachings of Bahá'u'lláh will be applied.

---

1 Shoghi Effendi, *Bahá'í Administration*, p. 52.
2 Shoghi Effendi, *The World Order of Bahá'u'lláh*, p. 161.
3 Shoghi Effendi, *The World Order of Bahá'u'lláh*, p. 324.
4 Shoghi Effendi, *Citadel of the Faith*, p. 5.
5 Shoghi Effendi, *Letters from the Guardian to Australia and New Zealand*, p. 76.
6 Shoghi Effendi, *Citadel of the Faith*, p. 80.

22.6 Activities

1. In paragraph 96, Shoghi Effendi states: "Therein lies the secret of its strength, its fundamental distinction, and the guarantee against disintegration and schism." What is he referring to?

2. In what ways do the administrative orders of Islám and Christianity differ from the Bahá'í Administrative order?

3. What are the distinct characteristics of the Bahá'í Administrative Order?

4. What is your understanding of the following statement of Shoghi Effendi in paragraph 96?

   " Can the Author of the Bábí Dispensation however much He may have succeeded through the provisions of the Persian Bayán in averting a schism as permanent and catastrophic as those that afflicted Christianity and Islám—can He be said to have produced instruments for the safeguarding of His Faith as definite and efficacious as those which must for all time preserve the unity of the organized followers of the Faith of Bahá'u'lláh?"

5. What is your understanding of statement (b)?

6. In what sense has the world equilibrium been upset as described in statement (d) as the result of the World Order of Bahá'u'lláh?

7. What is the relationship between the Bahá'í Administration and the World Order of Bahá'u'lláh?

22.7 Glossary

Term	Meaning
Authenticate	To prove (something) to be true or authentic
Avert	To prevent (something unpleasant) from happening
Contemporary	Of or belonging to the same (stated) time
Efficacious	Producing the desired effect, esp. in curing an illness or dealing with a problem
Enfold	Enclose
Pinnacle	The highest point or degree
Precipitate	To make (an unwanted event) happen sooner, hasten
Rudiments	The simplest parts
Schism	Separation between parts originally of the same group
Unassailable	Cannot be attacked

23. BAHÁ'Í ADMINISTRATION

23.1 Introduction

This chapter covers paragraph 101. Read this paragraph and reflect on the contents before starting the lesson. In this section of his letter, Shoghi Effendi identifies the instances in the Writings of Bahá'u'lláh and 'Abdu'l-Bahá that give us the faint glimmers of the Administrative Order that will be established in the future through *The Will and Testament of 'Abdu'l-Bahá*. An overview of the Bahá'í Administrative Order will be provided in this chapter.

In this chapter, you need to look for and understand the following **key concepts:**

a) In the Bahá'í Administrative Order, power and authority is completely taken away from the individual and transferred to the councils elected by the community through secret ballot without any electioneering or candidature.

b) Bahá'u'lláh ordained the establishment of these councils and named them the "Houses of Justice".

c) In *The Kitáb-i-Aqdas* and a number of Tablets revealed after *The Kitáb-i-Aqdas*, Bahá'u'lláh refers to two councils: the Universal House of Justice and the Local Houses of Justice.

d) In His Will and Testament, 'Abdu'l-Bahá introduced the Secondary Houses of Justice and explicitly stated: "*... in all countries a secondary House of Justice must be instituted.*"[1] This institution is currently called the National Spiritual Assembly.

e) Bahá'u'lláh established the institution of the Hands of the Cause of God during His lifetime.

f) In 1954, Shoghi Effendi established the institution of the Auxiliary Boards to provide the Hands of the Cause of God with "*adjuncts, or deputies*".[2]

---

1 'Abdu'l-Bahá, *The Will and Testament of 'Abdu'l-Bahá*, p. 14.

2 Shoghi Effendi, *Messages to the Bahá'í World: 1950–1957*, p. 44.

g) In 1968, the Universal House of Justice established the institution of the Continental Board of Counsellors since it was not authorized to appoint new Hands of the Cause.[1]

23.2 Paragraph under study

101. In the Tablets of Bahá'u'lláh where the institutions of the International and Local Houses of Justice are specifically designated and formally established; in the institution of the Hands of the Cause of God which first Bahá'u'lláh and then 'Abdu'l-Bahá brought into being; in the institution of both local and national Assemblies which in their embryonic stage were already functioning in the days preceding 'Abdu'l-Bahá's ascension; in the authority with which the Author of our Faith and the Centre of His Covenant have in their Tablets chosen to confer upon them; in the institution of the Local Fund which operated according to 'Abdu'l-Bahá's specific injunctions addressed to certain Assemblies in Persia; in the verses of *The Kitáb-i-Aqdas* the implications of which clearly anticipate the institution of the Guardianship; in the explanation which 'Abdu'l-Bahá, in one of His Tablets, has given to, and the emphasis He has placed upon, the hereditary principle and the law of primogeniture as having been upheld by the Prophets of the past—in these we can discern the faint glimmerings and discover the earliest intimation of the nature and working of the Administrative Order which the Will of 'Abdu'l-Bahá was at a later time destined to proclaim and formally establish.

23.3 First glimmers of the Bahá'í Administrative Order

In paragraph 101, Shoghi Effendi identifies the instances in the Writings of Bahá'u'lláh and 'Abdu'l-Bahá that give us the faint glimmers of the Administrative Order that will be established in the future through *The Will and Testament of 'Abdu'l-Bahá*. These references include:

- "The Tablets of Bahá'u'lláh where the institutions of the International and Local Houses of Justice are specifically designated and formally established;"
- "The institution of the Hands of the Cause of God which first Bahá'u'lláh and then 'Abdu'l-Bahá brought into being;"
- "The institution of both local and national Assemblies which in their embryonic stage were already functioning in the days preceding 'Abdu'l-Bahá's ascension;"
- "The authority with which the Author of our Faith and the Centre of His Covenant have in their Tablets chosen to confer upon them;"
- "The institution of the Local Fund which operated according to 'Abdu'l-Bahá's specific injunctions addressed to certain Assemblies in Persia;"

---

1 The Universal House of Justice, *Messages from the Universal House of Justice 1963–1986*, pp. 130–132.

- "The verses of *The Kitáb-i-Aqdas* the implications of which clearly anticipate the institution of the Guardianship;"
- "The explanation which 'Abdu'l-Bahá, in one of His Tablets, has given to, and the emphasis He has placed upon, the hereditary principle"
- "The law of primogeniture as having been upheld by the Prophets of the past."

23.4 Houses of Justice

The structure of the Bahá'í Administration is unique and unprecedented in the history of religion. In previous Dispensations, the authority and power of decision-making was left in the hands of the clergy and other religious leaders. Corrupted by ego, pride and greed, the clergy would often abuse their power.

In the Bahá'í Administration, power and authority is completely removed from the individual and transferred to the councils elected by the community through secret ballot without any electioneering or candidature.

Subsequent to the provisions regarding the Administrative Order revealed in *The Kitáb-i-Aqdas* (the Most Holy Book), Bahá'u'lláh also revealed supplementary passages in a number of other Tablets. Bahá'u'lláh has ordained the establishment of the elected councils of His future Administrative Order and referred to them as "Houses of Justice". The context of the statements made by Bahá'u'lláh clearly shows that He refers to two different entities, the Universal House of Justice and the Local Houses of Justice.

In the Tablet of Ishráqát, Bahá'u'lláh states: "*This passage, now written by the Pen of Glory, is accounted as part of the Most Holy Book: The men of God's House of Justice have been charged with the affairs of the people. They, in truth, are the Trustees of God among His servants and the daysprings of authority in His countries.*"[1] This is a reference to the Universal House of Justice.

On the other hand, in the following statement from *The Kitáb-i-Aqdas*, Bahá'u'lláh ordains the establishment of the Local Houses of Justice: "*The Lord hath ordained that in every city a House of Justice be established wherein shall gather Counsellors to the number of Bahá, and should it exceed this number it doth not matter.*"[2] The word Bahá in this statement has a numerical value of nine based on the Abjad numbering system. The Local Houses of Justice are currently called the Local Spiritual Assemblies.

'Abdu'l-Bahá provides a more explicit explanation of the Houses of Justice in His Will and Testament. In addition, 'Abdu'l-Bahá introduces the Secondary Houses of Justice and explicitly states: "... *in all countries a secondary House of Justice must be instituted.*"[3] This institution is currently called the National Spiritual Assembly.

---

1 Bahá'u'lláh, *Tablets of Bahá'u'lláh*, p. 128.

2 Bahá'u'lláh, *The Kitáb-i-Aqdas*, para. 30, p. 29.

3 'Abdu'l-Bahá, *The Will and Testament of 'Abdu'l-Bahá*, p. 14. Refer also to *The Kitáb-i-Aqdas*, Notes, No. 49, p. 188.

23.5 Institution of the Hands of the Cause

Bahá'u'lláh established the institution of the Hands of the Cause of God during His lifetime. The members of this institution consisted of devoted, learned and wise Bahá'ís who spent their lives serving the Bahá'í Faith. In order to prevent the challenges experienced in the previous Dispensations, the Hands of the Cause were primarily responsible for the protection and expansion of the Bahá'í Faith without any authority over other institutions.

Bahá'u'lláh also refers to the Hands of the Cause of God as the *"learned"* in His Book of the Covenant: "*Blessed are the rulers and learned among the people of Bahá.*"[1] In reference to this statement, Shoghi Effendi defines the learned in this holy cycle "... on the one hand, the Hands of the Cause of God, and, on the other, the teachers and diffusers of His teachings who do not rank as Hands, but who have attained an eminent position in the teaching work. As to the 'rulers' they refer to the members of the Local, National and International Houses of Justice. The duties of each of these souls will be determined in the future."[2]

Bahá'u'lláh appointed four individuals as Hands of the Cause and gave them the responsibility of protecting and propagating the Faith. They included:

a) Ḥájí Mullá 'Alí-Akbar (1842–1910), known as Ḥájí Á<u>kh</u>únd
b) Ḥájí Mírzá Muḥammad-Taqí (d. 1917), known as Ibn-i-Abhar
c) Mírzá Muḥammad-Ḥasan (1848–1919), known as Adib
d) Mírzá 'Alí -Muḥammad (d. 1928), known as Ibn-i-Aṣdaq

In *Memorials of the Faithful,* a book about the lives of a number of devoted followers of Bahá'u'lláh, 'Abdu'l-Bahá refers to another four outstanding believers, posthumously, as being Hands of the Cause of God:

a) Áqá Muḥammad-i-Qá'iní (1829–1892), known as Nabíl-i-Akbar
b) Mírzá 'Alí-Muḥammad Varqá (d. 1896), the father of Rúḥu'lláh and 'Azízu'lláh
c) Mullá Ṣadíq-i-Muqaddas, entitled Ismu'lláhu'l-Aṣdaq
d) <u>Sh</u>ay<u>kh</u> Muḥammad-Riḍáy-i-Yazdí[3]

Later, 'Abdu'l-Bahá, in His Will and Testament, formally laid down the foundations of the institution of the Hands of the Cause of God and set provisions for their nomination and appointment by the Guardian.[4] He also explicitly defined the obligations of the Hands of the Cause of God as "... *to diffuse the Divine Fragrances, to edify the souls of men, to promote learning, to improve the character of all men and to be, at all times and under all*

1 Bahá'u'lláh, *Tablets of Bahá'u'lláh*, p. 221.
2 *The Kitáb-i-Aqdas*, Notes, para. 183, p. 245.
3 'Abdu'l-Bahá, *Memorials of the Faithful,* p. 5. *The Kitáb-i-Aqdas*, Notes, para. 183, p. 245.
4 'Abdu'l-Bahá, *Will and Testament of 'Abdu'l-Bahá*, p. 12.

conditions, sanctified and detached from earthly things. They must manifest the fear of God by their conduct, their manners, their deeds and their words."[1]

On 24 December 1951, thirty years after the start of his ministry, Shoghi Effendi announced to the Bahá'ís of the world his first appointment of a group of twelve Hands of the Cause in the following cable:

> "HOUR NOW RIPE TO TAKE LONG INEVITABLY DEFERRED STEP IN CONFORMITY WITH PROVISIONS OF 'ABDU'L-BAHÁ'S TESTAMENT IN CONJUNCTION WITH SIX ABOVE-MENTIONED STEPS THROUGH APPOINTMENT OF FIRST CONTINGENT OF HANDS OF CAUSE OF GOD, TWELVE IN NUMBER, EQUALLY ALLOCATED HOLY LAND, ASIATIC, AMERICAN, EUROPEAN CONTINENTS."[2]

The twelve Hands of the Cause were: Sutherland Maxwell, Mason Remey, Amelia Collins (President and Vice-President of the International Bahá'í Council) in the Holy Land; Valíyu'lláh Varqá, Tarázu'lláh Samandarí, 'Alí-Akbar Furútan in the Cradle of the Faith; Horace Holley, Dorothy Baker, Leroy Ioas in the American continent; and George Townshend, Hermann Grossmann and Ugo Giachery in the European continent.

Shoghi Effendi appointed another seven Hands of the Cause in February 1952: Fred Schopflocher, Corinne True, Dhikru'lláh Khádim, Shu'á'u'lláh 'Alá'í, Adelbert Mühlschlegel, Músá Banání, and Clara Dunn.

The Hands of the Cause of God now numbered nineteen, with one to represent each continent.[3]

Between 1952 and 1957 five of the Hands of the Cause passed away: Sutherland Maxwell, Fred Schopflocher, Dorothy Baker, Valíyu'lláh Varqá and George Townshend. Shoghi Effendi appointed five replacements: Amatu'l-Bahá Rúḥíyyih Khánum, Jalál Kházih, Paul E. Haney, 'Alí-Muḥammad Varqá and Agnes Alexander.

Shoghi Effendi raised the membership of the Hands of the Cause to twenty–seven in his last message to the Bahá'í world. In that message he refers to the Hands of the Cause of God as the Chief Stewards of Bahá'u'lláh's embryonic World Commonwealth.[4] The new members were: Enoch Olinga, William Sears, John Robarts, Ḥasan Balyuzi, John Ferraby, Collis Featherstone, Raḥmatu'lláh Muhájir and Abu'l-Qásim Faizí.

The institution of the Hands of the Cause ended with the passing of its last surviving member, 'Alí-Muḥammad Varqá, on 22 September 2007.

---

1 'Abdu'l-Bahá, *Will and Testament of 'Abdu'l-Bahá*, p. 13.
2 Shoghi Effendi, *Messages to the Bahá'í World: 1950–1957*, p. 20.
3 Eunice Braun, *From Strength to Strength*, p. 41.
4 Shoghi Effendi, *Messages to the Bahá'í World: 1950–1957*, p. 127.

23.6 Auxiliary Board Members

In 1954, Shoghi Effendi established the institution of the Auxiliary Boards to provide the Hands of the Cause of God with *"adjuncts, or deputies."*[1] The supervision of the Auxiliary Board members was reassigned to the Counsellors after the appointment of the Continental Board of Counsellors in 1968. This released the Hands from administrative responsibilities.

The number of Auxiliary Board members has been gradually increased and their duties expanded since they were first established. They work closely with the Local Spiritual Assemblies, Bahá'í groups and individuals; and assist in the expansion and protection of the Faith. The Auxiliary Board members currently have the responsibility to advance the institute process and to facilitate the processes of expansion and consolidation of the Bahá'í Faith in clusters[2] throughout the world.

23.7 Continental Board of Counsellors

According to *The Will and Testament* of 'Abdu'l-Bahá, the Guardian was authorized to appoint new Hands of the Cause of God. Since the passing of Shoghi Effendi, no other institution, including the Universal House of Justice, is authorized to appoint new Hands of the Cause of God.

In 1968, the Universal House of Justice established the institution of the Continental Board of Counsellors and appointed eleven Counsellors.[3] This institution was given the task of the protection and propagation of the Bahá'í Faith and to extend into the future the work previously undertaken by the Hands of the Cause of God.

In June 1973 the Universal House of Justice announced the establishment of the International Teaching Centre in the Holy Land,[4] one of the institutions "ordained by Bahá'u'lláh, anticipated by 'Abdu'l-Bahá."[5] Establishment of this institution "... brings to fruition the work of the Hands of the Cause residing in the Holy Land and provides for its extension into the future, links the institution of the Boards of Counsellors even more intimately with that of the Hands of the Cause of God, and powerfully reinforces the discharge of the rapidly growing responsibilities of the Universal House of Justice."[6]

Currently, the Counsellors work closely with the National Spiritual Assemblies and the Regional Bahá'í Councils to assist with the execution of

---

1 Shoghi Effendi, *Messages to the Bahá'í World*, 1950–1957, p. 44.

2 For a definition and explanation of clusters, see the Universal House of Justice letter dated 9 January 2001.

3 The Universal House of Justice, *Messages from the Universal House of Justice, 1963–1986*, pp. 130–132.

4 The Universal House of Justice, *Messages from the Universal House of Justice, 1963–1986*, p. 246, Letter dated 8 June 1973.

5 Shoghi Effendi, *Messages to America*, p. 32.

6 The Universal House of Justice, *Messages from the Universal House of Justice 1963–1986*, para. 132.1, p. 246, Letter dated 8 June 1973.

the plans devised by the Universal House of Justice for the expansion and consolidation of the worldwide Bahá'í community.

23.8 Recent Developments

In parallel with the growth of the Bahá'í community and introduction of global plans by the Universal House of Justice, the Bahá'í Administration has evolved organically over the last two decades. The most significant developments, the establishment of the Regional Bahá'í Councils, training institutes, and cluster agencies, will be briefly reviewed in this section.

23.8.1 Regional Bahá'í Councils

The establishment of the "Regional Bahá'í Councils", announced by the Universal House of Justice in a message to the National Spiritual Assemblies on 30 May 1997, has been one of the major developments of the Bahá'í Administration in recent decades.[1] The Regional Bahá'í Councils represent a new element of Bahá'í Administration between the local and national institutions meant to reduce the complexity of the national agencies and to maintain a balance between centralization and decentralisation.

The Universal House of Justice has identified the distinguishing effects of the establishing the Regional Bahá'í Councils as:[2]

- Providing "... a level of autonomous decision-making on both teaching and administrative matters, as distinct from merely executive action, below the National Assembly and above the Local Assemblies."
- Involving "... the members of Local Spiritual Assemblies of the area in the choice of the members of the Council, thus reinforcing the bond between it and the local believers while, at the same time, bringing into public service capable believers who are known to the friends in their own region."
- Establishing "... direct consultative relationships between the Continental Counsellors and the Regional Bahá'í Councils."
- Offering "... the possibility of forming a Regional Bahá'í Council in an ethnically distinct region which covers parts of two or more countries. In such a situation the Council is designated to work directly under one of the National Assemblies involved, providing copies of its reports and minutes to the other National Assembly."[3]

A National Spiritual Assembly can establish the Regional Bahá'í Councils in the country of its jurisdiction upon the approval of the Universal House of Justice. As of December 2010, there were 170 Regional Bahá'í Councils in 45 countries.[4]

---

1 The Universal House of Justice, letter 30 May 1997 to the National Spiritual Assemblies, "Creation of the Regional Bahá'í Councils".

2 Bullets are added for emphasis.

3 The Universal House of Justice, *Messages from the Universal House of Justice 1963–1986*, para. 132.1, p. 246, letter dated 8 June 1973, p. 1.

4 The Universal House of Justice, *Five Year Plan 2011–2016*, 28 December 2010.

The duties and responsibilities of the Regional Bahá'í Councils have evolved over the last fifteen years as a result of the implementation of the global Five Year Plans and the learning acquired as a result. Currently, it is "... imperative that all Regional Councils pay close attention to the operation of the training institute and the functioning of Area Teaching Committees."[1] The nature and functions of the training institute and Area Teaching Committees will be reviewed in the next section.

23.8.2 Training Institutes and cluster agencies

In order to accelerate the dual processes of expansion and consolidation in the Bahá'í community, the Universal House of Justice has embarked on a series of global Plans, which began in 1996 and will continue for a quarter of a century until the year 2021, culminating at the centenary of the inauguration of the Faith's Formative Age. The common goal of these Plans is to foster sustained accelerated growth within the Bahá'í community.

These plans are dependent on a set of instruments and methods that have been developed, evolved and fine-tuned through a process of learning towards enhancing the capacity of the individual to engage in grassroots action.

The Universal House of Justice offers the following generic model for sustained growth and grassroots action:

> "Invariably, opportunities afforded by the personal circumstances of the believers initially involved—or perhaps a single homefront pioneer—to enter into meaningful and distinctive conversation with local residents dictate how the process of growth begins in a cluster. A study circle made up of a few friends or colleagues, a class offered for several neighbourhood children, a group formed for junior youth during after-school hours, a devotional gathering hosted for family and friends—any one of these can serve as a stimulus to growth. What happens next follows no predetermined course. Conditions may justify that one core activity be given precedence, multiplying at a rate faster than the others. It is equally possible that all four would advance at a comparable pace. Visiting teams may be called upon to provide impetus to the fledgling set of activities. But irrespective of the specifics, the outcome must be the same. Within every cluster, the level of cohesion achieved among the core activities must be such that, in their totality, a nascent programme for the sustained expansion and consolidation of the Faith can be perceived. That is to say, in whatever combination and however small in number, devotional gatherings, children's classes and junior youth groups are being maintained by those progressing through the sequence of institute courses and committed to the vision of individual and collective transformation they foster. This initial flow

[1] The Universal House of Justice, *Five Year Plan 2011–2016*, 28 December 2010.

of human resources into the field of systematic action marks the first of several milestones in a process of sustainable growth."[1]

This model identifies the elements, instruments, methods, and processes devised, developed and deployed in these Plans to stimulate sustained accelerated growth. They are described as follows:

- **Cluster**: This is a construct introduced by the Universal House of Justice in 2001 to establish geographical areas of focus for programs of growth in different parts of a region or a country.[2] The concept of the cluster has enabled the Bahá'í community to think about the accelerated growth on a manageable scale.[3] Currently, a cluster may consist of a number of villages and towns or embrace a large city and its suburbs. The characteristics of clusters and their boundaries have evolved over the last decade as a better understanding of the dynamics of growth has been acquired through the process of learning.
- **Core activities**: These are basic activities that are undertaken at grassroots in a cluster to initiate and sustain growth. In 2002, the Universal House of Justice introduced three core activities of study circles, devotional meetings, and children classes.[4] Two more core activities of junior youth groups and home visits were added in 2005.[5] The core activities provide a coherent model for lines of action within the framework of a cluster, aimed at both the Bahá'í and wider communities. The systematic multiplication of core activities within a cluster is identified as the key to ensure sustained accelerated growth.
- **Institute process:** The concept of training institutes supporting systematic growth was formally introduced in April 1998, in a document approved by the Universal House of Justice entitled "Training Institutes". In February 2000, the International Teaching Centre (ITC) provided further elucidation of the concept of training institutes and their role in promoting systematic growth. Referring to them as the institute process, the ITC defined its purpose as providing "... a sequence of courses that would create capacity and commitment on the part of the friends to carry out acts of service."[6] The core activities clearly identified the "acts of service" required for sustained accelerated growth. Hence, based on the resources offered by the Rúḥí Institute in Columbia, the curriculum of the

---

1 The Universal House of Justice, letter of 28 December 2010 to the Conference of the Continental Board of Counsellors, para. 4.

2 The Universal House of Justice, Riḍván Message BE 159, 2002.

3 The Universal House of Justice, letter of 25 December 2010 to the Conference of the Continental Board of Counsellors.

4 The Universal House of Justice, Riḍván Message BE 159, 2002.

5 The Universal House of Justice, letter of 25 December 2005 to the Conference of the Continental Board of Counsellors.

6 International Teaching Centre, *Training Institutes and Systematic Growth*, February 2000.

institute process was finalised to consist of seven books to raise the resources required to undertake the core activities and support their multiplication. According to this curriculum, Books one, two, three and five provide training to run devotional meetings, engage in home visits, teach in children's classes, and run junior youth groups, respectively. Book four is focused on the Ministries of the Báb and Bahá'u'lláh, Book six provides training for personal and collective teaching. Book seven trains those who have completed six other books to become a tutor of study circles. It is envisaged that other books will be introduced as the need arises.

- **Intensive programs of growth**: A cluster is ready to embark on an intensive program of growth when the institute process is active and adequate recourses to start multiplication of the core activities are available. The intensive programs of growth repeat every three months and consist of a steady process of expansion and strong process of human resource development.

In parallel with such developments, Bahá'í Administration has expanded to coordinate and administer the new instruments and methods. A regional Institute Board appointed jointly by the Regional Bahá'í Council and the Counsellors, supported by a Regional Coordinator oversee the institute process. In a cluster, a number of coordinators facilitate the implementation of the core activities. The number of coordinators in a cluster varies according to the size and complexity of the cluster.

An Area Teaching Committee (ATC) coordinates the teaching process during the intensive programs of growth in a cluster. The membership of the ATC consists of individuals living in the cluster. One or two Auxiliary Board members usually work closely with an ATC.

The administrative elements managing growth in a cluster including coordinators and the ATC are referred to as cluster agencies.

The overall structure of Bahá'í Administration at this juncture of its development is illustrated in Figure 23.1.

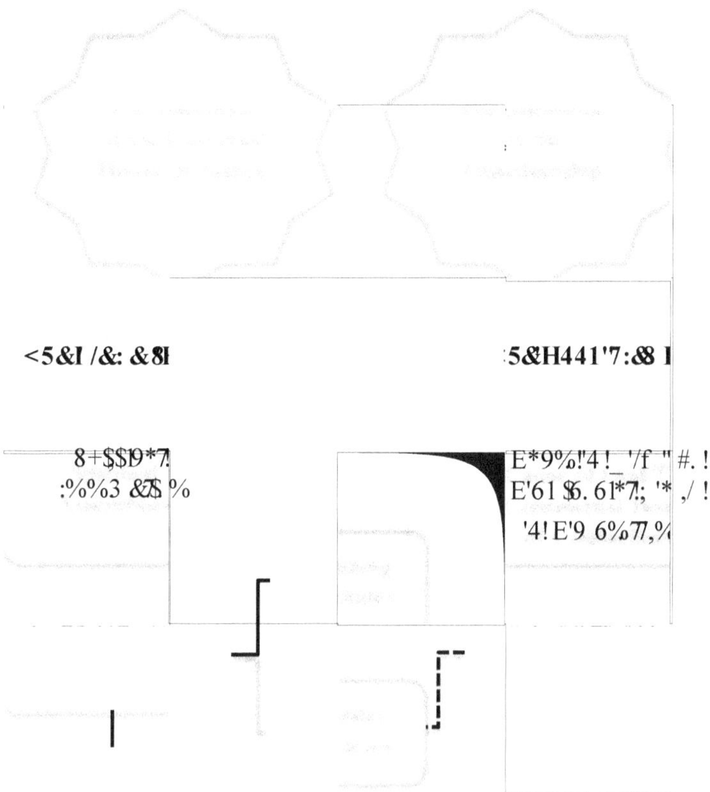

23.9 Activities

1. In paragraph 101, Shoghi Effendi refers to early signs of the nature and function of the Bahá'í Administrative Order. Identify these signs and list them.

2. Can you identify some new aspects of the Bahá'í Administrative order, which have unfolded since the passing of Shoghi Effendi?

3. Briefly describe the origin, functions and different types of the Houses of Justice?

4. What were the main functions of the Hands of the Cause?

5. What are the differences between the functions of the Houses of Justice and the institution of the Hands of the Cause?

6. What are the main differences between the nature and functions of the

institutions of the Hands of the Cause and Continental Board of Counsellors?

7. What is the origin and significance of the International Teaching Centre?

8. Describe your understanding of the pattern of growth in the Five Year Plan.

9. What are the cluster agencies?

10. What is the purpose of training institutes?

23.10 Glossary

Term	Meaning
Embryonic	In an early stage of development
Glimmering	Shining faintly, like a distant star or a light
Hereditary	Inherited or inheritable by established rules (usually legal rules) of descent
Injunction	A command or official order to do or not to do something
Intimate	To make known indirectly; suggest, imply
Primogeniture	The system according to which property owned by a father goes after his death to the eldest son

24. TWIN CROWNING INSTITUTIONS—I

24.1 Introduction

This chapter covers paragraphs 102–110. Read these paragraphs and reflect on the contents before starting the lesson. In this section of his letter, Shoghi Effendi elaborates on the striking features as well as the structure, character and the relationship of the twin institutions of the Guardianship and the Universal House of Justice as the pillars of the Bahá'í Administrative structure.

In this chapter, you need to look for and understand the following **key concepts:**

a) The twin institutions are "... divine in origin, essential in their functions and complementary in their aim and purpose."[1]
b) Without the institution of the Guardianship, the World Order of Bahá'u'lláh would have been mutilated.
c) Without the institution of the Universal House of Justice, the World Order of Bahá'u'lláh loses its ability to fill the legislative gaps intentionally left in *The Kitáb-i-Aqdas*.
d) The Guardian is the authoritative Interpreter of the Word of God.
e) The Universal House of Justice has "the function of legislating on matters not explicitly revealed in the teachings."

24.2 Paragraphs under study

102. An attempt, I feel, should at the present juncture be made to explain the character and functions of the twin pillars that support this mighty Administrative Structure—the institutions of the Guardianship and of the Universal House of Justice. To describe in their entirety the diverse elements that function in conjunction with these institutions is beyond the scope and purpose of this general exposition of the fundamental verities of the Faith. To define with accuracy and minuteness the features, and to analyze exhaustively the nature of the relationships

1 Shoghi Effendi, *The World Order of Bahá'u'lláh*, p. 148.

which, on the one hand, bind together these two fundamental organs of the Will of 'Abdu'l-Bahá and connect, on the other, each of them to the Author of the Faith and the Centre of His Covenant is a task which future generations will no doubt adequately fulfil. My present intention is to elaborate certain salient features of this scheme which, however close we may stand to its colossal structure, are already so clearly defined that we find it inexcusable to either misconceive or ignore.

103. It should be stated, at the very outset, in clear and unambiguous language, that these twin institutions of the Administrative Order of Bahá'u'lláh should be regarded as divine in origin, essential in their functions and complementary in their aim and purpose. Their common, their fundamental object is to insure the continuity of that divinely appointed authority, which flows from the Source of our Faith, to safeguard the unity of its followers and to maintain the integrity and flexibility of its teachings. Acting in conjunction with each other these two inseparable institutions administer its affairs, co-ordinate its activities, promote its interests, execute its laws and defend its subsidiary institutions. Severally, each operates within a clearly defined sphere of jurisdiction; each is equipped with its own attendant institutions—instruments designed for the effective discharge of its particular responsibilities and duties. Each exercises, within the limitations imposed upon it, its powers, its authority, its rights and prerogatives. These are neither contradictory, nor detract in the slightest degree from the position which each of these institutions occupies. Far from being incompatible or mutually destructive, they supplement each other's authority and functions, and are permanently and fundamentally united in their aims.

104. Divorced from the institution of the Guardianship the World Order of Bahá'u'lláh would be mutilated and permanently deprived of that hereditary principle which, as 'Abdu'l-Bahá has written, has been invariably upheld by the Law of God. "*In all the Divine Dispensations,*" He states, in a Tablet addressed to a follower of the Faith in Persia, "*the eldest son hath been given extraordinary distinctions. Even the station of prophethood hath been his birthright.*" Without such an institution the integrity of the Faith would be imperilled, and the stability of the entire fabric would be gravely endangered. Its prestige would suffer, the means required to enable it to take a long, an uninterrupted view over a series of generations would be completely lacking, and the necessary guidance to define the sphere of the legislative action of its elected representatives would be totally withdrawn.

105. Severed from the no less essential institution of the Universal House of Justice this same System of the Will of 'Abdu'l-Bahá would be paralyzed in its action and would be powerless to fill in those gaps which the Author of *The Kitáb-i-Aqdas* has deliberately left in the body of His legislative and administrative ordinances.

106. *"He is the Interpreter of the Word of God,"* 'Abdu'l-Bahá, referring to the functions of the Guardian of the Faith, asserts, using in His Will the very term which He Himself had chosen when refuting the argument of the Covenant-breakers who had challenged His right to interpret the utterances of Bahá'u'lláh. *"After him,"* He adds, *"will succeed the first-born of his lineal descendants."*[1] *"The mighty stronghold,"* He further explains, *"shall remain impregnable and safe through obedience to him who is the Guardian of the Cause of God."*[2] *"It is incumbent upon the members of the House of Justice, upon all the Aghsán, the Afnán, the Hands of the Cause of God, to show their obedience, submissiveness and subordination unto the Guardian of the Cause of God."*[3]

107. *"It is incumbent upon the members of the House of Justice,"* Bahá'u'lláh, on the other hand, declares in the Eighth Leaf of the Exalted Paradise, *"to take counsel together regarding those things which have not outwardly been revealed in the Book, and to enforce that, which is agreeable to them. God will verily inspire them with whatsoever He willeth, and He verily is the Provider, the Omniscient."*[4] *"Unto the Most Holy Book"* (*The Kitáb-i-Aqdas*), 'Abdu'l-Bahá states in His Will, *"every one must turn, and all that is not expressly recorded therein must be referred to the Universal House of Justice. That which this body, whether unanimously or by a majority doth carry, that is verily the truth and the purpose of God Himself. Whoso doth deviate therefrom is verily of them that love discord, hath shown forth malice, and turned away from the Lord of the Covenant."*[5]

108. Not only does 'Abdu'l-Bahá confirm in His Will Bahá'u'lláh's above-quoted statement, but invests this body with the additional right and power to abrogate, according to the exigencies of time, its own enactments, as well as those of a preceding House of Justice. *"Inasmuch as the House of Justice,"* is His explicit statement in His Will, *"hath power to enact laws that are not expressly recorded in the Book and bear upon daily transactions, so also it hath power to repeal the same ... This it can do because these laws form no part of the divine explicit text."*[6]

109. Referring to both the Guardian and the Universal House of Justice we read these emphatic words: *"The sacred and youthful Branch, the Guardian of the Cause of God, as well as the Universal House of Justice to be universally elected and established, are both under the care and protection of the Abhá Beauty, under the shelter and unerring guidance of the Exalted One (the Báb) (may my life be offered up for them both).*

---

1 Statement (a)
2 Statement (b)
3 Statement (c)
4 Statement (d)
5 Statement (e)
6 Statement (f)

Whatsoever they decide is of God."[1]

110. From these statements it is made indubitably clear and evident that the Guardian of the Faith has been made the Interpreter of the Word and that the Universal House of Justice has been invested with the function of legislating on matters not expressly revealed in the teachings. The interpretation of the Guardian, functioning within his own sphere, is as authoritative and binding as the enactments of the International House of Justice, whose exclusive right and prerogative is to pronounce upon and deliver the final judgement on such laws and ordinances, as Bahá'u'lláh has not expressly revealed. Neither can, nor will ever, infringe upon the sacred and prescribed domain of the other. Neither will seek to curtail the specific and undoubted authority with which both have been divinely invested.

24.3 Twin pillars of the Bahá'í Administration

In paragraph 102, Shoghi Effendi refers to the twin institutions of the Guardianship and the Universal House of Justice as the two fundamental organs of *The Will and Testament of 'Abdu'l-Bahá* and the twin pillars of the Bahá'í Administrative structure. The Bahá'í Administrative Order as described in chapter 23, is dependent on the two institutions of the Guardianship and the Universal House of Justice.

In paragraph 103, Shoghi Effendi highlights the common functions and distinctive authorities of each of the twin institutions. These institutions "... should be regarded as divine in origin, essential in their functions and complementary in their aim and purpose."[2] They have three common fundamental objectives:[3]

a) "to insure the continuity of that divinely-appointed authority which flows from the Source of our Faith,
b) to safeguard the unity of its followers,
c) to maintain the integrity and flexibility of its teachings."[4]

In order to achieve their common objectives, the two institutions work together for the Cause to:[5]

- "administer its affairs,
- co-ordinate its activities,
- promote its interests,
- execute its laws and
- defend its subsidiary institutions."[6]

---

1 Statement (g)
2 Shoghi Effendi, *The World Order of Bahá'u'lláh*, p. 148.
3 List form is added for emphasis.
4 Shoghi Effendi, *The World Order of Bahá'u'lláh*, p. 148.
5 Bullets are added for emphasis.
6 Shoghi Effendi, *The World Order of Bahá'u'lláh*, p. 148.

In their complimentary roles, they operate in their well-defined area of jurisdiction based on the instruments designed for their effective function. Within the limits imposed upon them, each exercises "its authority, its rights and prerogatives"— these are supplementary to each other.

At the end of paragraph 103, Shoghi Effendi emphasizes: "far from being incompatible or mutually destructive," these two institutions "supplement each other's authority and functions, and are permanently and fundamentally united in their aims."

'Abdu'l-Bahá states in His Will and Testament that:

> *"The sacred and youthful branch, the Guardian of the Cause of God, as well as the Universal House of Justice to be universally elected and established, are both under the care and protection of the Abhá Beauty, under the shelter and unerring guidance of the Exalted One (may my life be offered up for them both). Whatsoever they decide is of God."*[1]

24.4 Institution of the Guardianship

The institution of the Guardianship was established in *The Will and Testament of 'Abdu'l-Bahá* as a hereditary office. 'Abdu'l-Bahá appointed Shoghi Effendi, His grandson as the Guardian of the Bahá'í Faith. In paragraph 104, Shoghi Effendi highlights the significance of the institution of the Guardianship, without which:

a) The World Order of Bahá'u'lláh will be deprived of the hereditary principle, which "has been invariably upheld by the Law of God."
b) The "integrity of the Faith would be imperilled."
c) The "stability of the entire fabric would be gravely endangered."
d) Its "prestige would suffer."
e) The "means required to enable it to take a long, an uninterrupted view over a series of generations would be completely lacking."
f) The "necessary guidance to define the sphere of the legislative action of its elected representatives would be totally withdrawn".

Some cursory observation might indicate that "an uninterrupted view over a series of generations" mentioned in (e) is due to the fact that the Guardianship is hereditary as highlighted in (a). Ian Semple suggests an alternative understanding of this point:

> "I have not seen this point made in any of the Guardian's writings, however, and it seems to me that although, of course, there is an element of truth in the assumption [hereditary], the mere fact that each Guardian would have succeeded his father in office does not seem an adequate basis for the exercise of such an exclusive function. The function of inspired interpreter, however, does imply it. As interpreter the Guardian is able to understand not only the outward

---

[1] 'Abdu'l-Bahá, *The Will and Testament of 'Abdu'l-Bahá*, p. 11.

meaning of the Writings but their inner implications. Although others, by studying the Writings and the progress of human affairs, can gain some idea of the way society will develop, the Guardian alone could clearly see the whole panorama of Bahá'u'lláh's intention and could delineate for us the course that the Manifestation of God sees as lying before us. This, indeed, Shoghi Effendi has done in his World Order letters and also in God Passes By. The latter is not only a history book, magnificent though it may be in that respect, it is also an inspired commentary on the events it recounts, illuminates the minnows in the shallows of a vast ocean. He it was, following in the footsteps of the Master, who drew together those aspects of the Cause that require our immediate attention, showed their relationship to the vast implications of the entire Revelation, the riches of which we are only beginning to taste, and gave us a vision of our work far into the future, even to the end and beyond the end of this Dispensation."[1]

24.5 Principles of institution of the Guardianship

In paragraph 106, Shoghi Effendi cites extracts from the following section of *The Will and Testament of 'Abdu'l-Bahá* on the institution of the Guardianship:

"After the passing away of this wronged one, it is incumbent upon the Aghsán (Branches), the Afnán (Twigs) of the Sacred Lote-Tree, the Hands (pillars) of the Cause of God and the loved ones of the Abhá Beauty to turn unto Shoghi Effendi—the youthful branch branched from the two hallowed and sacred Lote-Trees and the fruit grown from the union of the two offshoots of the Tree of Holiness,—as he is the sign of God, the chosen branch, the Guardian of the Cause of God, he unto whom all the Aghsán, the Afnán, the Hands of the Cause of God and His loved ones must turn. He is the Interpreter of the Word of God and after him will succeed the first-born of his lineal descendants.

"O ye beloved of the Lord! It is incumbent upon the Guardian of the Cause of God to appoint in his own life-time him that shall become his successor, that differences may not arise after his passing. He that is appointed must manifest in himself detachment from all worldly things, must be the essence of purity, must show in himself the fear of God, knowledge, wisdom and learning. Thus, should the first-born of the Guardian of the Cause of God not manifest in himself the truth of the words:—'The child is the secret essence of its sire,' that is, should he not inherit of the spiritual within him (the Guardian of the Cause of God) and his glorious lineage not be matched with a

1 Ian Semple, "Interpretation and the Guardianship", *Lights of 'Irfán*, vol. 6, pp. 203–216, 2005.

goodly character, then must he, (the Guardian of the Cause of God) choose another branch to succeed him.

"The Hands of the Cause of God must elect from their own number nine persons that shall at all times be occupied in the important services in the work of the Guardian of the Cause of God. The election of these nine must be carried either unanimously or by majority from the company of the Hands of the Cause of God and these, whether unanimously or by a majority vote, must give their assent to the choice of the one whom the Guardian of the Cause of God hath chosen as his successor. This assent must be given in such wise as the assenting and dissenting voices may not be distinguished (i.e., secret ballot)."[1]

'Abdu'l-Bahá established the institution of the Guardianship based on the following principles described in this part of His Will and Testament:

- Shoghi Effendi is an offshoot of the twin Manifestations of God. The two statements, "*the two hallowed and sacred Lote-Trees*" and "*the two offshoots of the Tree of Holiness*" are references to Bahá'u'lláh and the Báb. Shoghi Effendi was descended from Bahá'u'lláh through his mother, Ḍiya'íyyih Khánum, the eldest daughter of 'Abdu'l-Bahá. He was also descendent from the Báb through His father, Mírzá Hádí Shírází, who was a grandson of Ḥájí Abu'l-Qásim, a cousin of the mother of the Báb and a brother of the wife of the Báb.
- Shoghi Effendi is the Interpreter of the Word of God.
- The successor of the Guardian is the first-born of his lineal descendants.
- The Guardian should appoint his successor during his lifetime.
- If the first child does not manifest the required qualities, then the Guardian should choose another branch to succeed him.
- The Hands of the Cause must elect nine members among themselves to approve the one chosen by the Guardian as his successor.

24.6 Anticipation of the Guardianship by Bahá'u'lláh

In paragraph 101, Shoghi Effendi states that Bahá'u'lláh anticipated the institution of the Guardianship in *The Kitáb-i-Aqdas*. Also when summarising the content of *The Kitáb-i-Aqdas* in *God Passes By*, Shoghi Effendi mentions that Bahá'u'lláh "*anticipates by implication the institution of Guardianship.*"[2]

In a letter written on behalf of the Universal House of Justice, the instances of the "implication" referred to by Shoghi Effendi are clarified:

> "One such implication is in the matter of Ḥuqúqu'lláh (The Right of God), which is ordained in the Kitáb-i-Aqdas without provision being made for who is to receive it; in His Will and Testament 'Abdu'l-Bahá fills this gap by stating 'It is to be offered through the

---

1 'Abdu'l-Bahá, *The Will and Testament of 'Abdu'l-Bahá*, pp. 11–12.

2 Shoghi Effendi, *God Passes By*, p. 214.

Guardian of the Cause of God ...'. Other implications of this institution can be seen in the terms in which 'Abdu'l-Bahá is appointed as the Successor of Bahá'u'lláh and the interpreter of his Teachings. The faithful are enjoined to turn their faces towards the one whom 'God hath purposed' and who 'hath branched from this Ancient Root' and are bidden to refer whatsoever they do not understand in the Bahá'í Writings to him who 'hath branched from this mighty Stock.' Yet another can be seen in the provision of the 'Aqdas' concerning the disposition of international endowments—a passage which not only refers this matter to the Aghsán (male descendants of Bahá'u'lláh) but also provides for what should happen should the line of Aghsán end before the coming into being of the Universal House of Justice."[1] (see also section 21.6)

24.7 The institution of the Universal House of Justice

The Universal House of Justice is the other crowning institution of the Bahá'í Administrative Order. This is the supreme body of the Bahá'í Faith, established by Bahá'u'lláh in *The Kitáb-i-Aqdas*. As stated in paragraph 107, statement (d), Bahá'u'lláh has endowed the Universal House of Justice with the power to legislate the laws and ordinances not stated by Him. In *Kalímát-i-Firdawsíyyih* ("Words of Paradise"), Bahá'u'lláh sets out the functions of the House of Justice and promises that God will inspire them:

> *"It is incumbent upon the Trustees of the House of Justice to take counsel together regarding those things which have not outwardly been revealed in the Book, and to enforce that which is agreeable to them. God will verily inspire them with whatsoever He willeth, and He, verily, is the Provider, the Omniscient."*[2]

In *Ishráqát,* Bahá'u'lláh expands further on the responsibilities of the members of the Universal House of Justice:

> *"It is incumbent upon the men of God's House of Justice to fix their gaze by day and by night upon that which hath shone forth from the Pen of Glory for the training of peoples, the upbuilding of nations, the protection of man and the safeguarding of his honour."*[3]

'Abdu'l-Bahá provides a more explicit explanation on the functions of the Universal House of Justice in His Will and Testament, as cited by Shoghi Effendi in statement (e). He defines the responsibilities of the institution of the Universal House of Justice and highlights the legislative authority and infallibility of this institution. 'Abdu'l-Bahá invests the Universal House of Justice with the additional power to abrogate those laws legislated by the Universal House of Justice.

---

1 The Universal House of Justice, *Messages from the Universal House of Justice 1963-1986*, pp. 450–451.

2 Bahá'u'lláh, *Tablets of Bahá'u'lláh*, p. 68.

3 Bahá'u'lláh, *Tablets of Bahá'u'lláh*, p. 125.

Since the beginning of his ministry, Shoghi Effendi rigorously endeavoured to develop the administrative structure required to support the Universal House of Justice. Every newly elected National Spiritual Assembly was another pillar in the foundation on which the future Universal House of Justice was to be erected. He assured Bahá'ís that:

> "... God's Supreme House of Justice shall be erected and firmly established in the days to come. When this most great edifice shall be reared on such an immovable foundation, God's purpose, wisdom, universal truths, mysteries and realities of the Kingdom, which the mystic Revelation of Bahá'u'lláh has deposited within the Will and Testament of 'Abdu'l-Bahá, shall gradually be revealed and made manifest."[1]

Shoghi Effendi has referred to the Universal House of Justice as the "supreme legislative body of the future Bahá'í Commonwealth"[2] and "the exponent and guardian of that Divine Justice which can alone insure the security of, and establish the reign of law and order in, a strangely disordered world."[3] The Future generations will regard the Universal House of Justice "as the last refuge of a tottering civilization."[4]

24.8 Election of the first Universal House of Justice

In addition to expanding on the functions and authorities of the Universal House of Justice in His Will and Testament, 'Abdu'l-Bahá defines how this institution should be elected. The Universal House of Justice "... *must be elected by universal suffrage, that is, by the believers ... in all countries a secondary House of Justice must be instituted, and these secondary Houses of Justice must elect the members of the Universal one.*"

In connection with the above statement of 'Abdu'l-Bahá, Shoghi Effendi explains: "... these words clearly indicate that a three-stage election has been provided by 'Abdu'l-Bahá for the formation of the International House of Justice."[5] This implies that "... the members of the National Spiritual Assemblies will have to be indirectly elected by the body of the believers in their respective provinces."[6]

Finally, Shoghi Effendi summarises the procedure for the election of the Universal House of Justice. The believers in every country will "... elect a certain number of delegates who, in turn, will elect their national representatives (Secondary House of Justice or National Spiritual Assembly)

---

1 Shoghi Effendi, *The Compilation of Compilations*, vol. 1, p. 328.
2 Shoghi Effendi, *Messages to the Bahá'í World*: 1950–1957, p. 149.
3 Shoghi Effendi, *The Advent of Divine Justice*, p. 22.
4 Shoghi Effendi, *The World Order of Bahá'u'lláh*, p. 89.
5 Shoghi Effendi, *Bahá'í Administration*, p. 84.
6 Shoghi Effendi, *Bahá'í Administration*, p. 84.

whose sacred obligation and privilege will be to elect in time God's Universal House of Justice."[1]

'Abdu'l-Bahá considered electing the first members of the Universal House of Justice when His life was in danger under the Turkish regime.[2] At that time those opposing Him were threatening to deport Him to North Africa. He instructed Ḥájí Mírzá Taqí Afnán, the cousin of the Báb, to arrange for the election of the Universal House of Justice if the threats were executed.[3] However, 'Abdu'l-Bahá was not deported and the election of the Universal House of Justice did not proceed at that time.

From the beginning of his ministry, Shoghi Effendi was determined to achieve the wish of 'Abdu'l-Bahá in His Will and Testament and to call for the election of the members of the first Universal House of Justice. However, this required a much greater development of the Bahá'í Administration at the local and national levels for a three-tier election of the Universal House of Justice to proceed. Hence, Shoghi Effendi embarked on the diffusion of the Bahá'í Faith throughout the world and the establishment of Local and National Spiritual Assemblies.

In a message to the National Spiritual Assembly of the Bahá'ís of India in 1941, Shoghi Effendi described the reasons preventing him from establishing the Universal House of Justice: "At this time when the National Assemblies in the Cause are not yet functioning sufficiently or fully representative of all the various important elements within it, and when some of the Bahá'ís are not even free to practice their faith, despite their numbers, it is quite impracticable to seek to establish the Universal House of Justice. Whenever conditions permit, it will be established."

As the first step towards the first election of the Universal House of Justice, Shoghi Effendi announced on 9 January 1951 the appointment of the International Bahá'í Council, which he referred to *as* "this first embryonic International Institution". Shoghi Effendi also mentioned that in the future, the Council would be an elected body that would evolve into the Universal House of Justice.

Shoghi Effendi suddenly passed away in London on 4 November 1957. Immediately the Hands of the Cause gathered in Haifa and issued an announcement on 25 November that the Guardian had left no children and hence no Guardian could be appointed to succeed him. The Hands of the Cause guided and protected the Bahá'í Community while preparing the way for the election of the first members of the Universal House of Justice.

---

1 Shoghi Effendi, *Bahá'í Administration*, p. 84.

2 Shoghi Effendi, *The World Order of Bahá'u'lláh*, p. 7.

3 The Universal House of Justice, *Messages from the Universal House of Justice: 1963-1986*, p. 53.

At Riḍván 1961, the Hands of the Cause called for the election of the International Bahá'í Council, as promised by Shoghi Effendi, as the next step towards the election of the first members of the Universal House of Justice.

In 1963 the Hands of the Cause decided the time had arrived for the members of the National Spiritual Assemblies to elect the first members of the Universal House of Justice. Five hundred and four delegates from fifty–six National and Regional Spiritual Assemblies participated in the election, which was held in Haifa.[1]

1 Eunice Braun, *From Strength to Strength*, p. 50.

24.9 Activities

1. In bullet form, list the main features of the institution of the Guardianship.

2. In bullet form, list the main features of the institution of the Universal House of Justice.

3. What are the original references to the institution of the Guardianship in the authoritative writings of the Faith?

4. What is the procedure for appointing the successor the Guardian according to *The Will and Testament of 'Abdu'l-Bahá*?

5. What are the functions, authorities and rights of the institution of the Guardianship?

6. What are the functions, authorities and rights of the institution of the Universal House of Justice?

7. What are the processes defined by 'Abdu'l-Bahá for the election of the Universal House of Justice?

8. Why did 'Abdu'l-Bahá consider calling for the election of the Universal House of Justice during His lifetime?

9. Why did Shoghi Effendi delay calling for the election of the Universal House of Justice?

24.10 Glossary

Term	Meaning
Colossal	Extremely large
Debar	To officially prevent from, exclude from
Enact	To make into law
Exposition	A comprehensive description or clarification
Infringe	To go against (a law, etc.) or take over (the right of another person)
Juncture	A particular point in time or in a course of event
Mutilate	To seriously damage (esp. a person's body) by removing a part
Outset	The beginning
Prerogative	A special right belonging to a particular person
Repeal	To officially end to (a law)
Salient	Standing out most noticeably or importantly
Severally	Differently, separately

25. TWIN CROWNING INSTITUTIONS—II

25.1 Introduction

This chapter covers paragraphs 111–116. Read these paragraphs and reflect on the contents before starting the lesson. In this section of his letter, Shoghi Effendi further highlights the rights and rank of the Guardian of the Faith, particularly in comparison with 'Abdu'l-Bahá and Bahá'u'lláh. He also defines the relationship between the institutions of the Guardianship and the Universal House of Justice.

In this chapter, you need to look for and understand the following **key concepts:**

a) The Guardian, though the head of the Universal House of Justice, has no right of exclusive legislation or of changing the decisions of the Universal House of Justice.
b) The institution of the Guardianship was anticipated by 'Abdu'l-Bahá long before His ascension.
c) Despite his power and responsibilities, the Guardian is infinitely inferior to both Bahá'u'lláh and 'Abdu'l-Bahá, and completely different in nature.
d) The Guardian does not have "the rights, the privileges and prerogatives" bestowed by Bahá'u'lláh on 'Abdu'l-Bahá.
e) It is not acceptable to "... pray to the Guardian of the Faith, to address him as lord and master, to designate him as his holiness, to seek his benediction, to celebrate his birthday, or to commemorate any event associated with his life."
f) The Guardian and the Universal House of Justice are both under the care and protection of Bahá'u'lláh and have conferred infallibility.

25.2 Paragraphs under study

111. Though the Guardian of the Faith has been made the permanent head of so august a body he can never, even temporarily, assume the right of exclusive legislation. He cannot override the decision of the majority of his fellow-members, but is bound to insist upon reconsideration by them

of any enactment he conscientiously believes to conflict with the meaning and to depart from the spirit of Bahá'u'lláh's revealed utterances. He interprets what has been specifically revealed, and cannot legislate except in his capacity as member of the Universal House of Justice. He is debarred from laying down independently the constitution that must govern the organized activities of his fellow-members, and from exercising his influence in a manner that would encroach upon the liberty of those whose sacred right is to elect the body of his collaborators.

112. It should be borne in mind that the institution of the Guardianship has been anticipated by 'Abdu'l-Bahá in an allusion He made in a Tablet addressed, long before His own ascension, to three of His friends in Persia. To their question as to whether there would be any person to whom all the Bahá'ís would be called upon to turn after His ascension He made the following reply: "*As to the question ye have asked me, know verily that this is a well-guarded secret. It is even as a gem concealed within its shell. That it will be revealed is predestined. The time will come when its light will appear, when its evidences will be made manifest, and its secrets unravelled.*"

113. Dearly beloved friends! Exalted as is the position and vital as is the function of the institution of the Guardianship in the Administrative Order of Bahá'u'lláh, and staggering as must be the weight of responsibility which it carries, its importance must, whatever be the language of the Will, be in no wise over-emphasized. The Guardian of the Faith must not under any circumstances, and whatever his merits or his achievements, be exalted to the rank that will make him a co-sharer with 'Abdu'l-Bahá in the unique position which the Centre of the Covenant occupies—much less to the station exclusively ordained for the Manifestation of God. So grave a departure from the established tenets of our Faith is nothing short of open blasphemy. As I have already stated, in the course of my references to 'Abdu'l-Bahá's station, however great the gulf that separates Him from the Author of a Divine Revelation it can never measure with the distance that stands between Him Who is the Centre of Bahá'u'lláh's Covenant and the Guardians who are its chosen ministers. There is a far, far greater distance separating the Guardian from the Centre of the Covenant than there is between the Centre of the Covenant and its Author.

114. No Guardian of the Faith, I feel it my solemn duty to place on record, can ever claim to be the perfect exemplar of the teachings of Bahá'u'lláh or the stainless mirror that reflects His light. Though overshadowed by the unfailing, the unerring protection of Bahá'u'lláh and of the Báb, and however much he may share with 'Abdu'l-Bahá the right and obligation to interpret the Bahá'í teachings, he remains essentially human and cannot, if he wishes to remain faithful to his trust, arrogate to himself, under any pretence whatsoever, the rights, the privileges and

prerogatives which Bahá'u'lláh has chosen to confer upon His Son. In the light of this truth to pray to the Guardian of the Faith, to address him as lord and master, to designate him as his holiness, to seek his benediction, to celebrate his birthday, or to commemorate any event associated with his life would be tantamount to a departure from those established truths that are enshrined within our beloved Faith. The fact that the Guardian has been specifically endowed with such power as he may need to reveal the purport and disclose the implications of the utterances of Bahá'u'lláh and of 'Abdu'l-Bahá does not necessarily confer upon him a station co-equal with those Whose words he is called upon to interpret. He can exercise that right and discharge this obligation and yet remain infinitely inferior to both of them in rank and different in nature.

115. To the integrity of this cardinal principle of our Faith the words, the deeds of its present and future Guardians must abundantly testify. By their conduct and example they must needs establish its truth upon an unassailable foundation and transmit to future generations unimpeachable evidences of its reality.

116. For my own part to hesitate in recognising so vital a truth or to vacillate in proclaiming so firm a conviction must constitute a shameless betrayal of the confidence reposed in me by 'Abdu'l-Bahá and an unpardonable usurpation of the authority with which He Himself has been invested.

25.3 Relationship between Twin Institutions

In paragraph 111, Shoghi Effendi identifies the boundaries of the Guardian's authority in relationship to the Universal House of Justice. According to 'Abdu'l-Bahá, the "*Guardian of the Cause of God*" is "*the sacred head and the distinguished member for life*" of the Universal House of Justice.[1] The life membership of the Guardian on the Universal House of Justice as well as being its permanent chair would have created a special interface between the two separate divinely guided authorities of the Bahá'í Faith, each with distinctive responsibilities and functions.

In clarifying these functions, the Universal House of Justice explains that the "Guardian reveals what the Scripture means; his interpretation is a statement of truth which cannot be varied. Upon the Universal House of Justice, in the words of the Guardian, 'has been conferred the exclusive right of legislating on matters not expressly revealed in the Bahá'í writings.' Its pronouncements, which are susceptible of amendment or abrogation by the House of Justice itself, serve to supplement and apply the Law of God."[2]

'Abdu'l-Bahá asserts: "*The sacred and youthful branch, the Guardian of the Cause of God, as well as the Universal House of Justice ... are both under*

1 'Abdu'l-Bahá, *The Will and Testament of 'Abdu'l-Bahá*, p. 14.

2 The Universal House of Justice, *Messages from the Universal House of Justice: 1963-1986*, p. 56.

the care and protection of the Abhá Beauty, under the shelter and unerring guidance of the Exalted One ...."[1] In other words both of the crowning institutions have conferred infallibility and are under the protection of Bahá'u'lláh.

Ian Semple identifies a hierarchical relationship between the function of the interpretation of the Guardian and the legislation assigned to the Universal House of Justice.[2] The Word of God as revealed by Bahá'u'lláh has the ultimate authority in the Faith. The Guardian, as the authoritative interpreter of the Word of God represents the living mouthpiece of that Word and the expounder of its true meaning. The Universal House of Justice should legislate on matters not explicitly revealed by Bahá'u'lláh. The Guardian naturally has the authority to define the legislative scope of the Universal House of Justice. He can effectively enforce this authority as the head of the Universal House of Justice.

In paragraph 111, Shoghi Effendi defines the constraints that govern the relationship between the Guardian and the Universal House of Justice. Since the Universal House of Justice is infallible in its legislation, the Guardian cannot use his authority to override a decision made by the Universal House of Justice. The separation of the functions of the Guardian and the Universal House of Justice also implies that the Guardian cannot legislate independently, but only as a member of the Universal House of Justice.

Developing the constitution of the Universal House of Justice is a legislative act and beyond the functions of the Guardian. Hence the Universal House of Justice should lay down its constitution not the Guardian.

Finally, the Guardian should not use his authority to encroach on the liberty of the members of the Universal House of Justice nor influence their judgement and decisions. He cannot override the decision of the majority of his fellow-members, but is bound to insist upon reconsideration by them of any enactment he conscientiously believes to conflict with the meaning and to depart from the spirit of Bahá'u'lláh's revealed utterances.

25.4 Rank and station of the Guardian

In paragraphs 113–114, and other letters that will be briefly studied in this section, Shoghi Effendi clarifies the nature and limitations of the rank and station of the Guardian of the Faith as defined by 'Abdu'l-Bahá in His Will and Testament.

After confirming the protection and infallibility of the twin crowning institutions in His will and testament, as cited in the previous section, 'Abdu'l-Bahá states:

---

1 'Abdu'l-Bahá, *The Will and Testament of 'Abdu'l-Bahá*, p. 11.

2 Ian Semple, "Interpretation and the Guardianship," in *Lights of 'Irfán*, vol. 6, pp. 203–215, 2005.

> *"Whatsoever they decide is of God. Whoso obeyeth him not, neither obeyeth them, hath not obeyed God; whoso rebelleth against him and against them hath rebelled against God; whoso opposeth him hath opposed God; whoso contendeth with them hath contended with God; whoso disputeth with him hath disputed with God; whoso denieth him hath denied God; whoso disbelieveth in him hath disbelieved in God; whoso deviateth, separateth himself and turneth aside from him hath in truth deviated, separated himself and turned aside from God. May the wrath, the fierce indignation, the vengeance of God rest upon him! The mighty stronghold shall remain impregnable and safe through obedience to him who is the Guardian of the Cause of God."*[1]

In light of such vehement statements, some believers at the time of Shoghi Effendi assumed a super-human station for the Guardian of the Cause, similar to that of 'Abdu'l-Bahá. As discussed in Chapter 19, Bahá'u'lláh confirmed the title "Mystery of God" (Sirru'lláh) on 'Abdu'l-Bahá, which "... indicates how in the person of 'Abdu'l-Bahá the incompatible characteristics of a human nature and superhuman knowledge and perfection have been blended and are completely harmonised."[2]

In paragraph 113, Shoghi Effendi states that exalting the Guardian "to the rank that will make him a co-sharer with 'Abdu'l-Bahá ... much less to the station exclusively ordained for the Manifestation of God" is "open blasphemy". He then compares the rank of the Guardian with that of 'Abdu'l-Bahá. The difference between the ranks of the Guardian and 'Abdu'l-Bahá is "far, far greater" than that between 'Abdu'l-Bahá and Bahá'u'lláh.

In relationship to Bahá'u'lláh, Shoghi Effendi identifies 'Abdu'l-Bahá as "His most exalted handiwork, the stainless Mirror of His light, the perfect Exemplar of His teachings, ... the embodiment of every Bahá'í ideal, the incarnation of every Bahá'í virtue".[3]

In contrast, the Guardian of the Cause cannot claim to be the perfect exemplar of the teachings of Bahá'u'lláh, and does not have the rights, the privileges and prerogatives bestowed by Bahá'u'lláh on 'Abdu'l-Bahá. Regardless of his right to interpret the utterances of Bahá'u'lláh and 'Abdu'l-Bahá, the Guardian has a different nature and is infinitely inferior to both Bahá'u'lláh and 'Abdu'l-Bahá.

Finally in paragraph 114, Shoghi Effendi deems it unacceptable to "... pray to the Guardian of the Faith, to address him as lord and master, to designate him as his holiness, to seek his benediction, to celebrate his birthday, or to commemorate any event associated with his life."

---

1 'Abdu'l-Bahá, *The Will and Testament of 'Abdu'l-Bahá*, p. 11.
2 Shoghi Effendi, *The World Order of Bahá'u'lláh*, p. 134.
3 Shoghi Effendi, *The World Order of Bahá'u'lláh*, p. 134.

25.5 Infallibility of the Guardian

One of the prerogatives bestowed on ‘Abdu’l-Bahá by Bahá’u’lláh is protection from error, technically known as infallibility. ‘Abdu’l-Bahá also bestowed infallibility on both the Guardian of the Bahá’í Faith and the Universal House of Justice. Shoghi Effendi, however, identifies the infallibility of the Guardian as being different from the infallibility of ‘Abdu’l-Bahá and Bahá’u’lláh. He describes how he provides advice: “He likes to be provided with facts by the friends, when they ask his advice, for although his decisions are guided by God, he is not, like the Prophet, omniscient at will, in spite of the fact that he often senses a situation or condition without having any detailed knowledge of it ....”[1]

In a letter written on his behalf, Shoghi Effendi states: “The infallibility of the Guardian is confined to matters which are related strictly to the cause and interpretation of the teachings; he is not an infallible authority on other subjects ... when he gives advice, such as that he gave you in a previous letter about your future, it is not binding: you are free to follow it or not as you please.”[2]

In another letter he reiterates the limitations of the Guardian’s infallibility: “The infallibility of the Guardian is confined to matters which are related strictly to the Cause and interpretations of the Teachings; he is not an infallible authority on other subjects, such as economics, science, etc.”[3]

In yet another letter, Shoghi Effendi states that in addition to interpretation of the revealed Word and its application, he is infallible in the protection of the Bahá’í Faith: “The Guardian’s infallibility covers interpretation of the revealed word, and its application. Likewise any instructions he may issue having to do with the protection of the Faith, or its well-being must be closely obeyed, as he is infallible in the protection of the Faith. He is assured of the guidance of both Bahá’u’lláh and the Báb, as *The Will and Testament of ‘Abdu’l-Bahá* clearly reveals.”[4]

It is possible to obtain a glimpse of the extent of the authority of the Guardian in the protection and propagation of the Cause from a letter written on behalf of Shoghi Effendi to Australia and New Zealand: “He is the Guardian of the Cause in the very fullness of that term, and the appointed interpreter of its teachings, and is guided in his decisions to do that which protects it and fosters its growth and highest interests.”[5]

Despite such clarifications, Shoghi Effendi explicitly indicates that it is not for the individual believer to limit or judge his infallibility: “... It is not for

---

1 Shoghi Effendi, *The Unfolding Destiny of the British Bahá’í Community*, p. 449.
2 Shoghi Effendi, *Directives from the Guardian*, p. 34.
3 Letter written on behalf of Shoghi Effendi, 1944, *Directives from the Guardian*, p. 33.
4 Letter written on behalf of Shoghi Effendi, 20 August 1956, *Lights of Guidance*, p. 313.
5 Shoghi Effendi, *Letters from the Guardian to Australia and New Zealand*, p. 55.

individual believers to limit the sphere of the Guardian's authority, or to judge when they have to obey the Guardian and when they are free to reject his judgement. Such an attitude would evidently lead to confusion and to schism. The Guardian being the appointed interpreter of the Teachings, it is his responsibility to state what matters which, affecting the interests of the Faith, demand on the part of the believers, complete and unqualified obedience to his instructions."[1]

25.6 Infallibility of the Universal House of Justice

As mentioned earlier, 'Abdu'l-Bahá asserts: "*The sacred and youthful branch, the Guardian of the Cause of God, as well as the Universal House of Justice ... are both under the care and protection of the Abhá Beauty, under the shelter and unerring guidance of the Exalted One*"[2] This statement indicates that the Universal House of Justice is infallible and under the protection of Bahá'u'lláh.

There are other statements from 'Abdu'l-Bahá reiterating the infallibility of the Universal House of Justice. In a Tablet, He warns us: "*Let it not be imagined that the House of Justice will take any decision according to its own concepts and opinions. God forbid! The Supreme House of Justice will take decisions and establish laws through the inspiration and confirmation of the Holy Spirit, because it is in the safekeeping and under the shelter and protection of the Ancient Beauty, and obedience to its decisions is a bounden and essential duty and an absolute obligation, and there is no escape for anyone.*"[3]

In another Tablet He states: "*Say, O people: Verily the Supreme House of Justice is under the wings of your Lord, the Compassionate, the All- Merciful, that is, under His protection, His care, and His shelter; for He has commanded the firm believers to obey that blessed, sanctified and all-subduing body, whose sovereignty is divinely ordained and of the Kingdom of Heaven and whose laws are inspired and spiritual.*"[4]

In yet another Tablet He affirms: "*Whatever will be its decision, by majority vote, shall be the real truth, inasmuch as that House is under the protection, unerring guidance and care of the one true Lord. He shall guard it from error and will protect it under the wing of His sanctity and infallibility. He who opposes it is cast out and will eventually be of the defeated.*"[5]

In a letter written to the friends in Írán, the Universal House of Justice elucidates the nature of this infallibility: "The infallibility of the House of

---

1 Letter written on behalf of Shoghi Effendi, cited in a letter on behalf of the Universal House of Justice to an individual believer, 22 August 1997, *Lights of Guidance*, p. 311.

2 'Abdu'l-Bahá, *The Will and Testament of 'Abdu'l-Bahá*, p. 11.

3 'Abdu'l-Bahá, cited in *The Compilations of Compilations*, vol. 1, p. 323.

4 'Abdu'l-Bahá, cited in *The Compilations of Compilations*, vol. 1, p. 323.

5 'Abdu'l-Bahá, cited in *The Compilations of Compilations,* vol. 1, p. 322.

Justice, like that of the Guardian, is "conferred", as distinct from the infallibility of the Manifestation of God, which is "innate". The House of Justice, like the Guardian, is not omniscient; when called upon to make a decision, it wants to receive information and facts and at times consults experts on the subject. Like him, it may well change its decision when new facts emerge or in light of changed conditions."[1]

The question has been asked whether the decisions of the Universal House of Justice will be free from error even when the correct information is not provided. The Universal House of Justice has responded: "In the Writings of Bahá'u'lláh and 'Abdu'l-Bahá on this matter, there is no reference to the nature and extent of the information to which the House of Justice should have access when making its decisions."[2]

1 Universal House of Justice, extracts from a letter dated 20 May 2007 to friends in Írán, trans. from Persian, *Lights of 'Irfán*, vol. 11, pp. 299–300.

2 Universal House of Justice, extracts from a letter dated 20 May 2007 to friends in Írán, trans. from Persian, *Lights of 'Irfán*, vol. 11, pp. 299–300.

25.7 Activities

1. In paragraph 111, Shoghi Effendi describes the relationship between the Guardian and the Universal House of Justice when making decisions. What are the major points made by Shoghi Effendi?

2. Describe your understanding of the rank of the Guardian of the Faith compared to Bahá'u'lláh and 'Abdu'l-Bahá.

3. In paragraph 112, Shoghi Effendi states that the institution of the Guardianship was anticipated by 'Abdu'l-Bahá long before His ascension. What are the implications of this statement?

4. What is the nature of the infallibility of the Manifestations of God?

5. What is the nature of the infallibility conferred on the Guardian?

6. What is the nature of the infallibility conferred on the Universal House of Justice?

7. What is your understanding of paragraph 115?

8. What is your understanding of paragraph 116?

25.8 Glossary

Term	Meaning
Allusion	An indirect or implicit reference.
Arrogate	To take or claim (for oneself) without a proper or legal right
August	Noble and grand
Benediction	(A prayer or religious service giving) a blessing
Blasphemy	Profane, sacrilegious or irreverent talk about God or sacred things
Conferred	Granted or bestowed (a title, degree benefit or right)
Debar	To officially prevent someone from doing something; to exclude.
Encroach	To take more of (something) than is right, usual, or acceptable; intrude upon
Innate	Inborn; natural; originating in the mind
Purport	The general meaning or intention of someone's words or actions
Tantamount	Having the same value, force, or effect as (esp. something bad or unwanted
Unimpeachable	That cannot be doubted or questioned
Usurpation	To take (power or position) for oneself illegally or without having the right to do so
Vacillate	To be continually changing from one opinion or feeling to another; be uncertain of what action to take

26. FOUNDATIONS OF THE BAHÁ'Í WORD COMMONWEALTH

26.1 Introduction

This chapter covers paragraphs 117–123. In this section of his letter, Shoghi Effendi emphatically states that the foundation of the future Bahá'í world Commonwealth is the Bahá'í Administrative Order. Then he continues by proclaiming that the Bahá'í Commonwealth "... is, both in theory and practice, not only unique in the entire history of political institutions, but can find no parallel in the annals of any of the world's recognized religious systems."

In this chapter, you need to look for and understand the following **key concepts**:

a) The past and present political systems do not provide any criteria by which to measure the potency of the Bahá'í Administrative Order.
b) The future Bahá'í commonwealth is unique, in both theory and practice, in the entire history of the world's political institutions and religious systems.
c) The Bahá'í Administrative Order embraces beneficial elements of democratic, autocratic and aristocratic forms of government, but it is distinctly different from them.
d) No matter how long it lasts, the Bahá'í Administrative Order is immune to the corruption that usually affects political and religious systems.

26.2 Paragraphs under study

117. A word should now be said regarding the theory on which this Administrative Order is based and the principle that must govern the operation of its chief institutions. It would be utterly misleading to attempt a comparison between this unique, this divinely-conceived Order and any of the diverse systems which the minds of men, at various periods of their history, have contrived for the government of human institutions. Such an attempt would in itself betray a lack of complete appreciation of the excellence of the handiwork of its great Author. How could it be otherwise when we remember that this Order constitutes the very pattern of that divine civilization which the almighty Law of Bahá'u'lláh is designed to establish upon earth? The divers and ever-shifting systems of human polity, whether past or present, whether originating in the East or in the West, offer no adequate criterion wherewith to estimate the potency of its hidden virtues or to appraise the solidity of its foundations.

118. The Bahá'í Commonwealth of the future, of which this vast Administrative Order is the sole framework, is, both in theory and practice, not only unique in the entire history of political institutions, but can find no parallel in the annals of any of the world's recognized religious systems. No form of democratic government; no system of autocracy or of dictatorship, whether monarchical or republican; no intermediary scheme of a purely aristocratic order; nor even any of the recognized types of theocracy, whether it be the Hebrew Commonwealth, or the various Christian ecclesiastical organizations, or the Imamate or the Caliphate in Islám—none of these can be identified or be said to conform with the Administrative Order which the master-hand of its perfect Architect has fashioned.

119. This new-born Administrative Order incorporates within its structure certain elements which are to be found in each of the three recognized forms of secular government, without being in any sense a mere replica of any one of them, and without introducing within its machinery any of the objectionable features which they inherently possess. It blends and harmonizes, as no government fashioned by mortal hands has as yet accomplished, the salutary truths which each of these systems undoubtedly contains without vitiating the integrity of those God-given verities on which it is ultimately founded.

120. The Administrative Order of the Faith of Bahá'u'lláh must in no wise be regarded as purely democratic in character inasmuch as the basic assumption, which requires all democracies to depend fundamentally upon getting their mandate from the people is altogether lacking in this Dispensation. In the conduct of the administrative affairs of the Faith, in the enactment of the legislation necessary to supplement the laws of *The Kitáb-i-Aqdas*, the members of the Universal House of Justice, it should be borne in mind, are not, as Bahá'u'lláh's utterances clearly imply, responsible to those whom they represent, nor are they allowed to be governed by the feelings, the general opinion, and even the convictions of the mass of the faithful, or of those who directly elect them. They are to follow, in a prayerful attitude, the dictates and promptings of their conscience. They may, indeed they must, acquaint themselves with the conditions prevailing among the community, must weigh dispassionately in their minds the merits of any case presented for

their consideration, but must reserve for themselves the right of an unfettered decision. "*God will verily inspire them with whatsoever He willeth,*" is Bahá'u'lláh's incontrovertible assurance. They, and not the body of those who either directly or indirectly elects them, have thus been made the recipients of the divine guidance, which is at once the life-blood and ultimate safeguard of this Revelation. Moreover, he who symbolizes the hereditary principle in this Dispensation has been made the interpreter of the words of its Author, and ceases consequently, by virtue of the actual authority vested in him, to be the figurehead invariably associated with the prevailing systems of constitutional monarchies.

121. Nor can the Bahá'í Administrative Order be dismissed as a hard and rigid system of unmitigated autocracy or as an idle imitation of any form of absolutistic ecclesiastical government, whether it be the Papacy, the Imamate or any other similar institution, for the obvious reason that upon the international elected representatives of the followers of Bahá'u'lláh has been conferred the exclusive right of legislating on matters not expressly revealed in the Bahá'í Writings. Neither the Guardian of the Faith nor any institution apart from the International House of Justice can ever usurp this vital and essential power or encroach upon that sacred right. The abolition of professional priesthood with its accompanying sacraments of baptism, of communion and of confession of sins, the laws requiring the election by universal suffrage of all local, national, and international Houses of Justice, the total absence of Episcopal authority with its attendant privileges, corruptions and bureaucratic tendencies, are further evidences of the non-autocratic character of the Bahá'í Administrative Order and of its inclination to democratic methods in the administration of its affairs.

122. Nor is this Order identified with the name of Bahá'u'lláh to be confused with any system of purely aristocratic government in view of the fact that it upholds, on the one hand, the hereditary principle and entrusts the Guardian of the Faith with the obligation of interpreting its teachings, and provides, on the other, for the free and direct election from among the mass of the faithful of the body that constitutes its highest legislative organ.

123. Whereas this Administrative Order cannot be said to have been modelled after any of these recognised systems of government, it nevertheless embodies, reconciles and assimilates within its framework such wholesome elements as are to be found in each one of them. The hereditary authority which the Guardian is called upon to exercise, the vital and essential functions which the Universal House of Justice discharges, the specific provisions requiring its democratic election by the representatives of the faithful—these combine to demonstrate the truth that this divinely revealed Order, which can never be identified with any of the standard types of government referred to by Aristotle in

his works, embodies and blends with the spiritual verities on which it is based the beneficent elements which are to be found in each one of them. The admitted evils inherent in each of these systems being rigidly and permanently excluded, this unique Order, however long it may endure and however extensive its ramifications, cannot ever degenerate into any form of despotism, of oligarchy, or of demagogy which must sooner or later corrupt the machinery of all man-made and essentially defective political institutions.

26.3 Uniqueness of the Bahá'í Administrative Order

In paragraph 117, Shoghi Effendi states that it is misleading to compare the Bahá'í Administrative Order, a "divinely-conceived Order", with any man-made system of governance in the past or the present. Such an act is in itself indicative of a lack of understanding of the excellence of the Bahá'í system and the role it will play in establishing a future divine civilization. If the purpose of the comparison is to measure the greatness of the Bahá'í Administrative Order or the firmness of its foundation, then past or present political systems developed by man, whether in the East or in the West, do not provide an adequate measure for such an appraisal.

In paragraph 118, Shoghi Effendi emphasizes that the future Bahá'í Commonwealth, which will be erected on the foundation of the Bahá'í Administrative Order, will be unprecedented in the entire history of human political institutions and among the recognized world religious governance systems.

In *God Passes By*, Shoghi Effendi makes a comparison between the "laws and ordinances" established by Muḥammad in Islám and the Bahá'í Administration:

> "No Prophet before Bahá'u'lláh, it can be confidently asserted, not even Muḥammad Whose Book clearly lays down the laws and ordinances of the Islamic Dispensation, has established, authoritatively and in writing, anything comparable to the Administrative Order which the authorized Interpreter of Bahá'u'lláh's teachings has instituted, an Order which, by virtue of the administrative principles which its Author has formulated, the institutions He has established, and the right of interpretation with which He has invested its Guardian, must and will, in a manner unparalleled in any previous religion, safeguard from schism the Faith from which it has sprung."[1]

Shoghi Effendi continues paragraph 118 by describing the major secular and religious governance systems of the past and present, and confirms that they can neither be identified with nor conform to the Bahá'í Administrative Order. They are described in the following sections.

---

1 Shoghi Effendi, *God Passes By*, p. 236.

26.3.1 Democracy

Democracy is a form of governance that in principle offers an equal say for all citizens in the decisions that affect their lives. Although no universally accepted definition exists for a democracy; equality and freedom are identified as the two essential characteristics of a democratic system.

The term "democracy" originates from the Greek (*dēmokratía*) "rule of the people" that consists of the words (*dêmos*) "people" and (*Kratos*) "power". The term democracy first appeared as a political and philosophical concept, and as a system of governance, in Athens during the late 6th century BC.

Currently, many interpretations and implementations are used to define democracies around the world. Some believe a democracy is characterised by political pluralism, equality before the law, civil liberties and human rights. In the United States, the separation of the powers of the legislature, the executive and the judiciary is considered to be a central characteristic of a democracy. In countries such as the United Kingdom, the foundation of democracy is parliamentary sovereignty. Some of the major forms of democracy include:

a) **Representative democracy**: The people being represented select their government officials. The system is called a democratic republic if people also democratically elect the head of state.
b) **Parliamentary democracy**: Parliamentary representatives appoint the government in contrast to 'presidential rule' wherein the president as both the head of state and the head of government is elected directly by the citizens.
c) **Presidential democracy**: Citizens elect their president. As both the head of state and the head of government, the president controls most of the executive powers for a fixed term.
d) **Liberal democracy**: The rule of law and a constitution constraint the decisions made by elected representatives in order to protect the rights and freedom of individuals.
e) **Direct democracy**: The citizens participate directly in decision making through processes such as referendums, rather than being represented by intermediaries. The voters can change constitutional law, suggest initiatives such as referendums or laws, and impose binding orders on the elected officials.

26.3.2 Autocracy or dictatorship

In a dictatorship, an individual or a group of people, govern with absolute power. Either there is no legislative parliament or it has no real power. In the majority of dictatorships, power has been taken by force or been inherited.

In modern times, an autocratic form of leadership that is unrestricted by any law, and social or political factors, is known as dictatorship—a leadership without the consent of the citizens. If nearly all aspects of public and private life of its citizens are also controlled and regulated, then it is said to be a totalitarian government.

26.3.3 Aristocracy

The word aristocracy has its roots in the Greek words *aristos* ("best") and *kratos* ("power"). The supreme power of an aristocratic government is vested in a small number of privileged people who are supposed to be the best qualified to rule.

One form is a monarchy, in which a king or a queen has the sole power. The opposite would be a democracy, in which the entire body of citizens or their representatives have the ultimate power.

Aristocratic governance was developed in ancient Greece where it was accepted as the preferred form of government.

In theory, the objective of an aristocracy is to look after the welfare of the majority, although only a few have the power of governance. An aristocracy becomes an oligarchy when the interest of the people is sacrificed for the interest of the rulers.

26.3.4 Theocracy

The word theocracy has its roots in the Greek *theokratia* ("the rule of or by God"), which is derived from the Greek words *theos* ("God") and *kratein* ("to rule").

In a theocracy, God is considered as the supreme power and the laws of the country are regarded as divine laws. Hence, power and control of the citizens is usually in the hands of the clergy.

In the first century AD, Joseph Flavious described the government of Jews as a theocracy in which God and His laws were sovereign. The Hebrew Commonwealth, various Christian ecclesiastical organisations, the Imamate and the caliphate in Islám are examples of theocratic governments.

26.4 Distinction of the Bahá'í Administrative Order

In paragraphs 119–123, Shoghi Effendi explains that although the Bahá'í Administrative Order embodies in its structure certain elements of recognized forms of governance i.e., democracy, autocracy and aristocracy, it is distinctively different from any of them. While the "wholesome elements" of these systems are embedded, reconciled, and assimilated within the framework of the Bahá'í Administrative Order, "objectionable features" are not included.

The Administrative Order of the Bahá'í Faith is not purely democratic since:

- In a democracy the legislature receives its mandate from the people who have elected them and is responsible to them. However, the members of the Universal House of Justice are not responsible to those whom they represent nor should they be affected by the feelings of those they represent. Although they should be fully aware of the conditions dominating the community, they have to make decisions according to their consciences.
- The Guardian, who represents the hereditary principle in the Bahá'í

system, has only been given the authority to interpret the Words of Bahá'u'lláh. Hence, he cannot be considered like the figurehead (king or queen) usually associated with a constitutional monarchy.

The Bahá'í Administrative Order also cannot be considered an "unmitigated autocracy" or any form of "absolutistic ecclesiastical government", since:

- The right of legislation on matters not explicitly revealed in the Writings of Bahá'u'lláh is exclusively invested with the Universal House of Justice.
- There is no professional priesthood in the Bahá'í Faith.
- The sacraments of baptism, communion and confession of sins have been abolished.
- The nature of the Bahá'í electorate and the lack of an "episcopal authority" make special privileges meaningless and prevent corruption, both of which are characteristics of autocratic governments.

Finally the Bahá'í Administrative Order cannot be considered a purely aristocratic government, since despite upholding the hereditary principle by giving the right of interpretation of the Writings to the Guardian, it provides for the free and direct election of the supreme legislative body of the Faith (the Universal House of Justice) by all members of the Bahá'í community.

In paragraph 123, Shoghi Effendi states that the Bahá'í Administrative Order is different from all the standard types of government known to Aristotle including monarchy, aristocracy and democracy.

26.5 Immunity to corruption and degeneration

The man-made political systems usually degenerate into despotism, oligarchy or demagogy as they age. As a result corruption increases and they eventually fail. In paragraph 123, Shoghi Effendi indicates that the Bahá'í Administrative Order is immune to such corruption, no matter how long it lasts.

Despotism is a form of government in which an individual (a despot) or a group of people rule with absolute power. The word despot has its roots in the Greek word "depostes" ("master" or "one with power"). Colloquially, a head of state or government who abuses his power and authority to oppress his people, subjects or subordinates is often called a despot.

In an oligarchy, power effectively rests with a small number of people who belong to a "royal" family, are wealthy, or are corporate or military leaders. Such power and influence is often passed from one generation to the next. Most oligarchies have proved to be tyrannical. The word oligarchy is derived from the Greek words *olígos* ("a few") and *archo* ("to rule, to govern, to command').

In demagogy, political power is gained by leaders who appeal to the prejudices, emotions, fears, vanities and expectations of the public. It is often achieved through emotional rhetoric and propaganda, while taking advantage of nationalist, populist or religious themes. Demagogy is derived from the Greek words *Demos* ("people") and *agein* ("to lead").

26.6 Activities

1. What is your understanding of paragraph 117?

2. Identify those elements that the Bahá'í Administrative Order has in common with the following systems of government:

   a) Purely democratic

   b) Purely autocratic

   c) Purely aristocratic

3. Analyse the Bahá'í Administrative Order and identify which element(s) should be added to or taken away from it to make it

   a) Purely democratic

   b) Purely autocratic

   c) Purely aristocratic

4. What is your understanding of the following statement of Shoghi Effendi from paragraph 119?

   "It blends and harmonizes, as no government fashioned by mortal hands has as yet accomplished, the salutary truths which each of these systems undoubtedly contains without vitiating the integrity of those God-given verities on which it is ultimately founded."

5. What is your understanding of the following statement of the Guardian from paragraph 123?

   "The evils inherent in each of these systems being rigidly and permanently excluded, this unique Order, however long it may endure and however extensive its ramifications, cannot ever degenerate into any form of despotism, of oligarchy, or of demagogy which must sooner or later corrupt the machinery of all man-made and essentially defective political institutions."

26.7 Glossary

Term	Meaning
Appraise	To judge the worth, quality, or condition of; find out the value of, evaluate
Contrive	To cause (something) to happen in accordance with ones plans or despite any difficulty
Demagogy	A type of government the leader of which tries to gain, or has gained, power by exciting people's feelings rather than by reasoned argument
Despotism	Rule by a tyrant
Episcopal	Governed by Bishops
Mandate	The right and power given to a government, or any body of people chosen to represent others, to act according to the wishes of those who voted for it
Oligarchy	Government by a small group of people, often for their own interests
Polity	(A particular form of) political or governmental organization
Replica	A close copy, esp. of a painting or other work of art
Salutary	Causing or likely to cause an improvement in character, future behaviour, health, etc.
Secular	Not connected with or controlled by a church; not religious
Suffrage	The right to vote in national elections
Unfettered	Free from control; not tied by severe rules
Universal suffrage	The right of everyone to vote
Unmitigated	Complete; not lessened or excused in any way

27. CONTRASTING THE OLD ORDER WITH THE NEW

27.1 Introduction

This chapter covers paragraphs 124–130. Read these paragraphs and reflect on the contents before starting the lesson. In this section of his letter, Shoghi Effendi compares the steady growth and consolidation of the Bahá'í Administrative Order with the continuous decline and disintegration of the world's secular and religious institutions. He also refers to the fall of the mighty monarchies in Europe, the decline in the fortunes of the Shí'ih Islamic hierarchy, and the overthrow of the Sultanate and the Caliphate, the pillars of Sunní Islám.

In this chapter, you need to look for and understand the following **key concepts**:

a) The Bahá'í Administration is manifesting such signs of power and vitality that wider society cannot ignore it.
b) The old world order is manifesting signs of steady deterioration and disintegration.
c) Such deterioration could be a prerequisite for the Bahá'í Administrative Order to grow.
d) Bahá'u'lláh revealed a number of Tablets to the powerful kings and rulers of His time during His exile in Adrianople, alluding to the fall of the mighty monarchies in Europe.
e) During the present infancy of the Bahá'í Administrative Order, no one should "misconceive its character, belittle its significance or misrepresent its purpose."

27.2 Paragraphs under study

124. Dearly beloved friends! Significant as are the origins of this mighty administrative structure, and however unique its features, the happenings that may be said to have heralded its birth and signalised the initial stage of its evolution seem no less remarkable. How striking, how edifying the contrast between the process of slow and steady

consolidation that characterises the growth of its infant strength and the devastating onrush of the forces of disintegration that are assailing the outworn institutions, both religious and secular, of present-day society!

125. The vitality which the organic institutions of this great, this ever-expanding Order so strongly exhibit; the obstacles which the high courage, the undaunted resolution of its administrators have already surmounted; the fire of an unquenchable enthusiasm that glows with undiminished fervour in the hearts of its itinerant teachers; the heights of self-sacrifice which its champion-builders are now attaining; the breadth of vision, the confident hope, the creative joy, the inward peace, the uncompromising integrity, the exemplary discipline, the unyielding unity and solidarity which its stalwart defenders manifest; the degree to which its moving Spirit has shown itself capable of assimilating the diversified elements within its pale, of cleansing them of all forms of prejudice and of fusing them with its own structure—these are evidences of a power which a disillusioned and sadly shaken society can ill afford to ignore.

126. Compare these splendid manifestations of the spirit animating this vibrant body of the Faith of Bahá'u'lláh with the cries and agony, the follies and vanities, the bitterness and prejudices, the wickedness and divisions of an ailing and chaotic world. Witness the fear that torments its leaders and paralyzes the action of its blind and bewildered statesmen. How fierce the hatreds, how false the ambitions, how petty the pursuits, how deep-rooted the suspicions of its peoples! How disquieting the lawlessness, the corruption, the unbelief that are eating into the vitals of a tottering civilization!

127. Might not this process of steady deterioration, which is insidiously invading so many departments of human activity and thought, be regarded as a necessary accompaniment to the rise of this almighty Arm of Bahá'u'lláh? Might we not look upon the momentous happenings, which, in the course of the past twenty years, have so deeply agitated every continent of the earth, as ominous signs simultaneously proclaiming the agonies of a disintegrating civilization and the birth pangs of that World Order—that Ark of human salvation—that must needs arise upon its ruins?

128. The catastrophic fall of mighty monarchies and empires in the European continent, allusions to some of which may be found in the prophecies of Bahá'u'lláh; the decline that has set in, and is still continuing, in the fortunes of the Shí'ih hierarchy in His own native land; the fall of the Qájár dynasty, the traditional enemy of His Faith; the overthrow of the Sultanate and the Caliphate, the sustaining pillars of Sunní Islám, to which the destruction of Jerusalem in the latter part of the first century of the Christian era offers a striking parallel; the wave of secularization which is invading the Muhammadan ecclesiastical institutions in Egypt and sapping the loyalty of its staunchest supporters; the humiliating

blows that have afflicted some of the most powerful Churches of Christendom in Russia, in Western Europe and Central America; the dissemination of those subversive doctrines that are undermining the foundations and overthrowing the structure of seemingly impregnable strongholds in the political and social spheres of human activity; the signs of an impending catastrophe, strangely reminiscent of the Fall of the Roman Empire in the West, which threatens to engulf the whole structure of present-day civilization—all witness to the tumult which the birth of this mighty Organ of the Religion of Bahá'u'lláh has cast into the world—a tumult which will grow in scope and in intensity as the implications of this constantly evolving Scheme are more fully understood and its ramifications more widely extended over the surface of the globe.

129. A word more in conclusion. The rise and establishment of this Administrative Order—the shell that shields and enshrines so precious a gem—constitutes the hallmark of this second and formative age of the Bahá'í era. It will come to be regarded, as it recedes farther and farther from our eyes, as the chief agency empowered to usher in the concluding phase, the consummation of this glorious Dispensation.

130. Let no one, while this System is still in its infancy, misconceive its character, belittle its significance or misrepresent its purpose. The bedrock on which this Administrative Order is founded is God's immutable Purpose for mankind in this day. The Source from which it derives its inspiration is no one less than Bahá'u'lláh Himself. Its shield and defender are the embattled hosts of the Abhá Kingdom. Its seed is the blood of no less than twenty thousand martyrs who have offered up their lives that it may be born and flourish. The axis round which its institutions revolve are the authentic provisions of *The Will and Testament of 'Abdu'l-Bahá*. Its guiding principles are the truths, which He, Who is the unerring Interpreter of the teachings of our Faith, has so clearly enunciated in His public addresses throughout the West. The laws that govern its operation and limit its functions are those, which have been expressly ordained in *The Kitáb-i-Aqdas*. The seat round which its spiritual, its humanitarian and administrative activities will cluster Mashriqu'l-Adhkár and its Dependencies. The pillars that sustain its authority and buttress its structure are the twin institutions of the Guardianship and of the Universal House of Justice. The central, the underlying aim, which animates it is the establishment of the New World Order as adumbrated by Bahá'u'lláh. The methods it employs, the standard it inculcates, incline it to neither East nor West, neither Jew nor Gentile, neither rich nor poor, neither white nor coloured. Its watchword is the unification of the human race; its standard the "Most Great Peace"; its consummation the advent of that golden millennium—the Day when the kingdoms of this world shall have become the Kingdom of God Himself, the Kingdom of Bahá'u'lláh.

27.3 Power and vitality in the Bahá'í Administrative Order

In paragraph 125, Shoghi Effendi refers to the signs of the power of the Bahá'í Administrative Order:

- The vitality exhibited by its institutions.
- The obstacles overcome by its administrators.
- The enthusiasm observed in its teachers.
- The degree of self-sacrifice demonstrated by its builders.
- The vision, hope, joy, peace, integrity, discipline, unity and solidarity manifested by its defenders.
- The power that can attract and unite people from different backgrounds by purifying them from all types of prejudice.

To some extent such observations reflect the quality of the work of the believers to develop and build the Bahá'í Administrative Order in accordance with the teachings of Bahá'u'lláh. The impact of such efforts and their outcomes are fully recorded in *The Bahá'í World* series.

An example is given by Horace Holley in an article that reviewed the Bahá'í activities in 1932:

> "... how vitally the status of the Faith of Bahá'u'lláh has transformed, in its relations to the whole progress of world events, since the previous survey was undertaken for *The Bahá'í World* in 1930.
>
> "To describe this transformation in the briefest possible way, it is only necessary to remark that the course of human history during the past two years has vindicated, or rather, exemplified, beyond denial by any informed students, the force as well as the truth of the Bahá'í teachings. The major events not only correspond to the content of these teachings with respect to their statements of spiritual truth—the events actually follow the definite predictions broadcast throughout Europe and America by 'Abdu'l-Bahá before the outbreak of war in 1914."[1]

Since the passing of Shoghi Effendi, signs of the potency of the Bahá'í Faith have continued to increase. This power is reflected in the significant growth and transformation that has occurred in the Faith of Bahá'u'lláh and its Administrative Order. For example, the sacrifices made and the enthusiasm shown by the teachers of the Bahá'í Faith during the Ten-Year Crusade (1953–1963) and all subsequent plans have been quite remarkable. Hence, the statement of Shoghi Effendi in paragraph 125 can be also considered as indicating the potentialities inherent in the followers of Bahá'u'lláh that will be manifested as the Bahá'í Faith evolves during the Formative Age.

---

1 Horace Holley, "Survey of Current Bahá'í Activities in the East and West", *The Bahá'í World*, vol. IV, 1930–1932, p. 43.

In one of his letters, Shoghi Effendi states: "I consider it my duty to warn every beginner in the faith that the promised glories of the Sovereignty which the Bahá'í teachings fore-shadow, can be revealed only in the fullness of time, that the implications of the Aqdas and the Will of 'Abdu'l-Bahá, as the twin repositories or the constituent elements of that Sovereignty, are too far-reaching for this generation to grasp and fully appreciate."[1]

27.4 Decline and disintegration of society

In paragraph 126, Shoghi Effendi describes the signs of the disintegration of the old world order and invites the reader to compare them with the evidences of the increasing strength of the World Order of Bahá'u'lláh. He refers to the "... cries and agony, the follies and vanities, the bitterness and prejudices, the wickedness and divisions of an ailing and chaotic world."

Shoghi Effendi then identifies some of the dark signs that can be observed in the society of today—such as the fear and confusion of the leaders and politicians, the depth of the hatreds, the superficiality of the ambitions, and the unworthiness of the pursuits. He finally points to three alarming signs that are everywhere eating into the foundation of the human society; lawlessness, corruption and unbelief.

Shoghi Effendi observed that the 1930's fully revealed the symptoms of an ailing world community afflicted by political, economic and moral afflictions. The great depression of the 1930's combined with strong nationalism, deep hatred and prejudice of all types, paved the way for another world war.

The pace of disintegration of the old world order has been accelerating since Shoghi Effendi identified its signs in 1934. The bankruptcy of man-made ideologies and institutions has been proven. The bewilderment of the humanity to deal with the crises arising from the chaos surrounding all human affairs can be discerned in every corner. Humanity at large has ignored the healing message of Bahá'u'lláh. Pre-occupied with material pursuits, people have remained oblivious of their true spiritual nature. Unbound by moral principles, every society is dominated by corruption, dishonesty and greed.

It is not surprising that the Guardian appeals to the followers of Bahá'u'lláh "... to disregard the prevailing notions and the fleeting fashions of the day, and to realize as never before that the exploded theories and the tottering institutions of present-day civilization must needs appear in sharp contrast with those God- given institutions which are destined to arise upon their ruin."[2]

In paragraph 127, Shoghi Effendi raises the question whether such decay in human activities and thoughts is not a complementary process to the rise of the Cause of Bahá'u'lláh. The events that we have been witnessing in the affairs of the humanity since the Revelation of the Tablets of Bahá'u'lláh to the kings and rulers can be considered as signs "proclaiming the agonies of a

---

[1] Shoghi Effendi, *The World Order of Bahá'u'lláh*, p. 16.
[2] Shoghi Effendi, *The World Order of Bahá'u'lláh*, p. 16.

disintegrating civilization and the birth pangs" of the World Order of Bahá'u'lláh, arising upon its ruins.

27.5 Fall of monarchs and rulers

In paragraph 128, Shoghi Effendi refers to the fall of the mighty monarchies in Europe, the decline in the fortunes of the Shí'ih Islamic hierarchy, and the overthrow of the Sultanate and the Caliphate, the pillars of Sunní Islám. Bahá'u'lláh revealed a number of Tablets to the powerful kings and rulers of His time during His exile in Adrianople, including: the Súriy-i-Mulúk (the Tablet to the Kings), the Tablet to Násiri'd-Dín Sháh of Írán, the first Tablet to Napoleon III, and the Súriy-i-Ra'ís to 'Álí-Páshá, the Grand-Vizír of the Ottoman Empire. The revelation of such Tablets continued in Akká. There are allusions to such significant events in these Tablets.

The first Tablet of Bahá'u'lláh to Napoleon III was received with contempt by Napoleon, who violently threw the Tablet away saying: "If this man is God, I am two gods." Bahá'u'lláh wrote a second Tablet to Napoleon in 1869 after He was informed by one of the ministers of Napoleon that there had been no reply to the first Tablet. In this Tablet Bahá'u'lláh prophesied Napoleon's downfall and declared that his doom was inevitable. A few months later, in 1870, Napoleon lost the battle of Sedan and his army was broken up. He was captured and exiled.

A Tablet was revealed to Pope Pius IX at about the same time as the Tablet to Napoleon. In this Tablet Bahá'u'lláh proclaims with majesty and authority the return of Christ in the glory of the Father and asks the Pope to leave his palace and enter the presence of Bahá'u'lláh. Very soon after the revelation of this Tablet, the earthly sovereignty of the Pope, which had lasted for centuries, was severely limited when the Papal States were seized by the Italian army in September 1870, and this power and authority has never been restored.

Czar Alexander II of Russia was another powerful ruler who received a Tablet from Bahá'u'lláh. In this Tablet, Bahá'u'lláh declared His station as the Heavenly Father and called on the Czar to arise and to summon everyone to His Cause. The Czar ignored the Tablet of Bahá'u'lláh and continued to rule his empire until 1881 when he was murdered. His dynasty was extinguished in 1917 with the rise of Bolshevism.

Bahá'u'lláh also revealed a Tablet to Queen Victoria and proclaimed to her the coming of the Lord. In this Tablet Bahá'u'lláh commended the Queen for abolishing slavery and establishing a legislative parliament. Queen Victoria was one of the exceptions who did not reject Bahá'u'lláh's claim outright, and whose rule continued successfully into old age.

Bahá'u'lláh also revealed Tablets to other kings and rulers of the world, the majority of which were either rejected or ignored by the recipients. Such denials set in motion the process of disintegration and rolling up of the old world order. The spiritual powers released through such Tablets permanently changed the course of the history. Many kingdoms, particularly those in

Europe, fell and the process of rolling up of the old order has continued to accelerate since then.

In one of His Tablets, Bahá'u'lláh provides a glimmer of this process by illustrating the penetrating effects of the Súriy-i-Ra'ís:

> *"Witness how the world is being afflicted with a fresh calamity every day. Its tribulation is continually deepening. From the moment the Súriy-i-Ra'ís (Tablet to Ra'ís) was revealed until the present day, neither hath the world been tranquillised, nor have the hearts of its peoples been at rest. At one time it hath been agitated by contentions and disputes, at another it hath been convulsed by wars, and fallen a victim to inveterate diseases. Its sickness is approaching the stage of utter hopelessness, inasmuch as the true Physician is debarred from administering the remedy, whilst unskilled practitioners are regarded with favour, and are accorded full freedom to act. ... The dust of sedition hath clouded the hearts of men, and blinded their eyes. Erelong, they will perceive the consequences of what their hands have wrought in the Day of God. Thus warneth you He Who is the All-Informed, as bidden by One Who is the Most Powerful, the Almighty."*[1]

Indeed it is quite obvious that such agitation has not only continued until the present day but its force, intensity and impact have increased.

It is important to note that there is nothing in the teachings of Bahá'u'lláh against the institution of kingship. The extinction of the monarchs and dynasties during the last 150 years is just a passing phase in the process of the unfoldment of the World Order of Bahá'u'lláh. On the contrary, in the teachings of Bahá'u'lláh "... the principle of kingship is eulogized, the rank and conduct of just and fair-minded kings is extolled, the rise of monarchs, ruling with justice and even professing His Faith, is envisaged, and the solemn duty to arise and ensure the triumph of Bahá'í sovereigns is inculcated."[2]

27.6 Hallmark of Formative Age

In paragraph 129, Shoghi Effendi identifies the Bahá'í Administrative Order as the hallmark of the Formative Age of the Bahá'í era. This agency has been given the power to usher in the Golden Age of the Bahá'í Dispensation.

Finally in the last paragraph of the book, the Guardian warns us all not to misconceive the character, belittle the significance nor misrepresent the purpose of the Bahá'í Administrative Order while still in its infancy. He then summarizes the origin and characteristics of this divinely ordained system.

---

1 Bahá'u'lláh, *Gleanings from the Writings of Bahá'u'lláh*, pp. 39–40.

2 Shoghi Effendi, *The Promised Day is Come*, p. 71.

27.7 Activities

1. Briefly describe the signs of vitality that can be observed in the Bahá'í Administrative Order today.

2. Compare the steady growth and consolidation of the Bahá'í Administrative order with the state of secular and religious institutions in the world today.

3. Describe your understanding of each of the following events and processes referred to by Shoghi Effendi in paragraph 128:
   a) Decline in the fortunes of Shí'ih Islám

   b) Overthrow of the Sultanate and the Caliphate

   c) Wave of secularisation in Egypt

   d) Blows to Churches

4. What are the subversive doctrines referred to by Shoghi Effendi in paragraph 128?

5. What is your understanding of the following statement made in paragraph 130?

   "Let no one, while this System is still in its infancy, misconceive its character, belittle its significance or misrepresent its purpose."

6. In paragraph 130, the Guardian describes the characteristics of the Bahá'í Administrative Order. Identify each and list them in bullet form.

7. Describe how this tutorial has affected your understanding of the fundamental verities of the Faith and the role of the Bahá'í Administrative Order.

27.8 Glossary

Term	Meaning
Accompaniment	Something that is used or provided with something else, esp. in order to improve it
Belittle	To cause to seem small or unimportant
Buttress	To support and strengthen
Consummation	The point at which something is made complete or perfection
Disquiet	A feeling of anxiety
Edify	To improve (the mind or character of)
Embattled	Beset by problems or difficulties
Fervour	The quality of being fervent or fervid; zeal
Folly	(An act of) stupidity
Impregnable	Which cannot be entered or taken by force
Inculcate	To fix (ideas, principles, etc.) in the mind of (someone)
Insidious	Acting gradually and without being noticed, but causing serious harm; secretly harmful:
Itinerant	Habitually travelling from place to place, esp. to practise one's trade or profession
Ominous	Giving a warning of something bad that is going to happen
Reminiscent	That reminds one of; like
Sap	To gradually weaken (a person's strength or power)
Stalwart	Strong and firm in body, mind, determination, etc.; staunch
Striking	Which draws the attention, especially because of being noticeable or unusual
Subversive	(Dangerous because) trying or likely to destroy established ideas and take power away from those at present in control, esp. secretly
Surmount	To succeed in dealing with (esp. a difficulty); overcome
Totter	To shake or move unsteadily from side to side as if about to fall
Tumult	The confused noise and excitement of a big crowd, fighting, etc.; state of confusion and excitement; uproar
Undaunted	Not at all discouraged or frightened by danger or difficulty
Vanity	The quality of being vain; unreasonable pride in oneself or appearance, abilities, etc.

28. ISSUES REGARDING THE GUARDIANSHIP

28.1 Introduction

The sudden passing of Shoghi Effendi and the fact that he did not leave any lineal descendant to succeed him as the next Guardian, created some questions in the minds of the believers, particularly when *The Will and Testament of 'Abdu'l-Bahá* and the statements made by Shoghi Effendi in "The Dispensation of Bahá'u'lláh" were considered. Some of those questions relate to the rights and authorities of the institutions of the Guardianship and the Universal House of Justice, and the relationship between them. The Universal House of Justice has written a number of messages to provide answers to these questions. These messages are compiled in Appendices A-C at the end of this book.

This chapter will first explore the possible reasons why Shoghi Effendi did not leave a will nor appoint a successor. Then the questions raised and the responses provided are studied.

In this chapter, you need to look for and understand the following **key concepts**:

a) Shoghi Effendi unexpectedly passed away on 4 November 1957 in London, in the 60th year of his life after contracting Asiatic influenza.
b) On 25 November 1957, all the Hands of the Cause of God unanimously affirmed that Shoghi Effendi had passed away without having appointed his successor.
c) On 17 November, 26 of the 27 Hands of the Cause of God gathered in the Holy Land to locate the will of Shoghi Effendi and to identify his successor. However, they could not find any will from Shoghi Effendi.
d) Shoghi Effendi did not have any children and none of the Aghsán had remained faithful to the Cause. Hence, it was impossible for him to appoint a successor.
e) Shoghi Effendi could not make any statement about an alternative solution for his succession as he had the function of interpreting the Holy Writings,

not of pronouncing on matters not recorded in Them.

f) After the election of the first members, the Universal House of Justice informed the Bahá'í friends in a message that it was not possible to appointment a successor to Shoghi Effendi.

28.2 Successor to Shoghi Effendi

Shoghi Effendi unexpectedly passed away on 4 November 1957 in London, in the 60th year of his life. This was caused by a sudden heart attack in his sleep after contracting Asiatic influenza.

Following the funeral of the Guardian, the following cable was sent from Haifa to the Bahá'í communities around the world:

> "BELOVED ALL HEARTS PRECIOUS GUARDIAN CAUSE GOD PASSED PEACEFULLY AWAY YESTERDAY AFTER ASIATIC FLU. APPEAL HANDS NATIONAL ASSEMBLIES AUXILIARY BOARDS SHELTER BELIEVERS ASSIST MEET HEARTRENDING SUPREME TEST. FUNERAL OUR BELOVED GUARDIAN SATURDAY LONDON HANDS ASSEMBLY BOARD MEMBERS INVITED ATTEND ANY PRESS RELEASE SHOULD STATE MEETING HANDS SHORTLY HAIFA WILL MAKE ARRANGEMENT TO BAHÁ'Í WORLD REGARDING FUTURE PLANS. URGE HOLD MEMORIAL MEETINGS SATURDAY. RÚḤÍYYIH"[1]

The Hand of the Cause Leroy C. Ioas, who was in Haifa at the time, received the news of the passing of Shoghi Effendi through a telephone call from Rúḥíyyih Khánum.[2] During conversation, they decided that Leroy would take all necessary precautions to protect the Holy places against the attack of those hostile to the Bahá'í Faith.

Leroy ensured that the apartment and office of Shoghi Effendi remained locked. The keys were sealed in an envelope, the envelope was signed by Sylvia Ioas, Jessie Revell, Ethel Revell and Leory Ioas, and placed in the apartment safe. It was then arranged for the two trusted servants of Shoghi Effendi to sleep outside the door of the apartment and at the foot of the steps. The Shrines of Bahá'u'lláh and the Báb, and the Mansion of Bahjí were also guarded day and night.

After attending the funeral of the beloved Guardian in London, the five Hands of the Cause of God who resided in Haifa, Rúḥíyyih Khánum, Mr Remey, Mrs Collins, Dr Giachery, and Mr Ioas, returned to the Holy Land, arriving on 15 November. They entered the Guardian's apartment, secured the sealed envelope with the keys to the apartment, and sealed the safe of the Guardian where the sacred documents were kept. They then sealed and signed both the safe and drawer of the desk of the Guardian.[3]

---

1 The Hands of the Cause of God, *Ministry of the Custodians*, p. 7.

2 The Hands of the Cause of God, *Ministry of the Custodians*, p. 25.

3 The Hands of the Cause of God, *Ministry of the Custodians*, p. 26.

On 17 November, 26 out of the 27 Hands of the Cause of God gathered in the Holy Land to locate the will of Shoghi Effendi and identify his successor. Mrs Corrine True was the only Hand who could not travel to the Holy Land due to illness.

'Abdu'l-Bahá states in His Will and Testament that the "*Hands of the Cause of God must elect from their own number nine persons that shall at all times be occupied in the important services in the work of the Guardian of the Cause of God.*"[1] In obedience to this statement, the Hands designated nine among themselves to enter the Guardian's apartment and look for his will or any document he might have left. The nine selected were: Rúḥíyyih Khánum, Mr Remey, Mrs Collins, Dr Giachery, Mr Ioas, Mr Ḥasan Balyuzi, Mr Horace Holley, Mr Músá Banání, and Dr 'Alí-Muḥammad Varqá. However, they could not find any will from Shoghi Effendi.

On 25 November 1957, all the Hands of the Cause of God as the Chief Stewards of the Faith of Bahá'u'lláh, unanimously affirmed that Shoghi Effendi had passed away "without having appointed his successor."[2] They elected nine of the Hands to serve the interests of the Faith until an election could be arranged for the members of the first Universal House of Justice. All the Hands of the Cause of God signed that declaration.

28.3 Shoghi Effendi's will

A report of the first conclave of the Hands of the Cause of God in the Mansion of Bahjí, released on 25 November 1957, "... certified that Shoghi Effendi had left no Will and Testament. It was likewise certified that the beloved Guardian had left no heir. The Aghsán (branches) one and all are either dead or have been declared violators of the Covenant by the Guardian for their faithlessness to the Master's Will and Testament and their hostility to him."[3]

This announcement challenged the faith of some believers with a poor understanding of the Covenant. They were under the impression that according to statements made by Bahá'u'lláh and 'Abdu'l-Bahá, Shoghi Effendi was required to prepare a Will and appoint a successor.

In *The Kitáb-i-Aqdas*, Bahá'u'lláh has enjoined upon every Bahá'í to write a will to confess his belief in Bahá'u'lláh and to distribute his wealth among his heirs. *The Will and Testament of 'Abdu'l-Bahá* also explicitly states: "*It is incumbent upon the guardian of the Cause of God to appoint in his own life-time him that shall become his successor, that differences may not arise after his passing.*"[4]

A closer look at the circumstances surrounding the life of Shoghi Effendi and his ministry makes it clear that the perceptions of the doubting believers

---

1 'Abdu'l-Bahá, *The Will and Testament of 'Abdu'l-Bahá*, p. 12.
2 The Hands of the Cause of God, *Ministry of the Custodians*, p. 30.
3 The Hands of the Cause of God, *Ministry of the Custodians*, pp. 35–36.
4 'Abdu'l-Bahá, *The Will and Testament of 'Abdu'l-Bahá*, p. 12.

were incorrect and invalid. Adib Taherzadeh considers the letter written by the Guardian, "The Dispensation of Bahá'u'lláh", as one of the "finest declarations of faith ever written."[1] This is only one instance of the many documents in which Shoghi Effendi has confessed his unquestionable faith in the Revelation of Bahá'u'lláh. As far as the distribution of wealth is concerned, Shoghi Effendi did not have any worldly possessions to bequeath in his will.

In His Will and Testament, 'Abdu'l-Bahá states that after Shoghi Effendi "*... will succeed the first-born of his lineal descendants.*"[2] He then states that if the first-born of the Guardian does not possess a goodly character, then the Guardian should "*... choose another branch to succeed him.*"[3] In this statement "branch" is the translation of the Arabic term "Ghusn" with the plural of "Aghsán". This term has been used by Bahá'u'lláh to designate His male descendants.[4]

Shoghi Effendi did not have any children and none of the Aghsán had remained faithful to the Cause. All the descendants of 'Abdu'l-Bahá had broken the Covenant. Hence, it was impossible for Shoghi Effendi to appoint a successor.

Also, Shoghi Effendi could not make any statement regarding an alternative solution. Shoghi Effendi had the function of interpreting what was mentioned in the Writings of Bahá'u'lláh and 'Abdu'l-Bahá. However, he could not pronounce on matters not recorded in the Holy Writings. This was the duty and function of the Universal House of Justice to legislate, as stated by 'Abdu'l-Bahá in His Will and Testament. There was no provision in *The Will and Testament of 'Abdu'l-Bahá* on how to proceed if there were no suitable "Ghusn" to be appointed. Therefore, Shoghi Effendi was unable to offer a solution to this problem.

28.4 Authoritative decision on succession

After the passing of the Guardian, the question of a successor to Shoghi Effendi seriously challenged the Bahá'í community. The believers did not know whether there would be another Guardian after Shoghi Effendi. There was no infallible body that could provide an answer to this question. Neither the Hands of the Cause of God nor the International Bahá'í Council had been endowed with any authority by the Sacred Texts to make any judgement on this matter. The Universal House of Justice was the only authority that could make an infallible decision on the issue of a successor to Shoghi Effendi.

Hence, for this and other reasons the formation of the Universal House of Justice became the primary goal of the Hands of the Cause of God who were undertaking the international administration of the Bahá'í Faith. They had the

1 Adib Taherzadeh, *The Covenant of Bahá'u'lláh*, p. 378,
2 'Abdu'l-Bahá, *The Will and Testament of 'Abdu'l-Bahá*, p. 11.
3 'Abdu'l-Bahá, *The Will and Testament of 'Abdu'l-Bahá*, p. 12.
4 *The Kitáb-i-Aqdas*, Notes, p. 196.

full support of the National Spiritual Assemblies and the majority of the believers. Since they were not certain of Divine Guidance as was assured to the Guardian and the Universal House of Justice, they decided to closely follow the course set by Shoghi Effendi until the Universal House of Justice was elected.

The Ten Year Crusade, initiated by Shoghi Effendi in 1953, provided sufficient direction and guidance for the Hands of the Cause of God to advance and expand the Bahá'í Faith until 1963. It was essential to establish and strengthen the National Spiritual Assemblies to the stage where they were able to elect the members for the first Universal House of Justice.

After the completion of the Ten Year Crusade, the Hands called on the Bahá'ís around the world to elect the members of the first Universal House of Justice. They also asked to be exempted from being considered as candidates. The election was held in Haifa in April 1963. Five hundred and four delegates from fifty–six National and Regional Spiritual Assemblies participated in the election.

After the election, the newly formed Universal House of Justice informed the friends in a message that it was not possible to appointment a successor to Shoghi Effendi:

> "After prayerful and careful study of the Holy Texts bearing upon the question of the appointment of the successor to Shoghi Effendi as Guardian of the Cause of God, and after prolonged consultation which included consideration of the views of the Hands of the Cause of God residing in the Holy Land, the Universal House of Justice finds that there is no way to appoint or legislate to make it possible to appoint a second Guardian to succeed Shoghi Effendi."[1]

28.5 Questions and responses

The remainder of this lesson covers the questions asked and references to the answers given by the Universal House of Justice to those questions in the messages reproduced in Appendices A-C.

28.5.1 Infallibility of the Universal House of Justice

Question 1

> How is the statement in paragraph 111, that the Guardian "is bound to insist upon a reconsideration by them of any enactment he conscientiously believes to conflict with the meaning and to depart from the spirit of Bahá'u'lláh's revealed utterances" consonant with the infallibility of the Universal House of Justice? 'Abdu'l-Bahá affirms in His Will and Testament that the Universal House of Justice is "*freed from all error*"?

---

[1] The Universal House of Justice, "Message to all the National Spiritual Assemblies on the Guardianship", 6 October 1963. *Messages from the Universal House of Justice 1963–1986*, p. 14.

Answer

Appendix A, Part 1, paragraphs 4–9

Question 2

How can the decisions of the Universal House of Justice be infallible in the absence of a Guardian?

Answer

Appendix A, Part 3, paragraphs 4–6

Question 3

How can the Universal House of Justice be infallible without a Guardian? Considering the following statement from paragraph 104: "Without such an institution [the Guardianship] ... the necessary guidance to define the sphere of the legislative action of its elected representatives would be totally withdrawn."

Answers

a) Appendix A, Part 2, paragraphs 17–26
b) Appendix A, Part 1 paragraphs 11–18

Question 4

a) In the absence of the Guardian, is the Universal House of Justice in danger of straying outside its proper sphere and thus falling into error?

Answers

Appendix A, Part 3, paragraphs 4-6

Question 5

a) Is the infallibility of the Universal House of Justice confined to the sphere of legislation?

Answers

Appendix C, Part 3, paragraphs 1–11

28.5.2 Functions of the Universal House of Justice

Question 1

a) How can the Universal House of Justice function in the absence of the Guardian, particularly in the case of the expulsion of members of the Universal House of Justice?

Answer

Appendix A, Part 2, paragraphs 34-35

Question 2

a) How can the Universal House of Justice discharge certain functions previously performed by the Guardian be justified?

Answer

Appendix B, paragraphs 25–28

Question 3

Are the enactments of the House of Justice inspired and spiritual?

Answer

Appendix A, Part 3, paragraphs 7–11

28.5.3 Timing of Universal House of Justice election

Question 1

Was the establishment of an "officially recognized" Bahá'í Court in the Holy Land mentioned by Shoghi Effendi as an essential step preliminary step in the evolution of the Universal House of Justice?

Answer

Appendix B, paragraphs 16–24

Questions 2-4

a) Why were steps taken to elect a Universal House of Justice with the foreknowledge that there would be no Guardian?
b) Was the time ripe (1963) for the election of the Universal House of Justice?
c) Could not the International Bahá'í Council have continued its work instead of electing the Universal House of Justice?

Answers

a) Appendix A, Part 2, paragraphs 1–16
b) Appendix A, Part 3, paragraph 1

28.5.4 Successor to Shoghi Effendi

Question 1

Has certain information concerning the successor to Shoghi Effendi been withheld from the believers, for the good of the Cause?

Answer

Appendix A, Part 3, paragraph 2

Question 2

Why did Shoghi Effendi not leave a will?

Answer

Appendix A, Part 3, paragraphs 3

Question 3

Why did Shoghi Effendi not appoint a successor?

Answer

Appendix B, paragraphs 3–13

Question 4

Why is the term "Aghsán" designated as referring to the male descendants of Bahá'u'lláh?

Answer

Appendix B, paragraphs 14–15

Question 5

How can the authority, which flows from the source of our Faith, continue in the absence of a Guardian?

Answer

Appendix A, Part 3, paragraphs 12–16

Question 6

Can the Universal House of Justice legislate for a successor to Shoghi Effendi?

Answer

Appendix A, Part 3, paragraph 22

28.6 Activities

1. What was the sequence of actions carried out by the Hands of the Cause immediately after the ascension of the Guardian?

2. In your understanding, why did not Shoghi Effendi leave a will?

3. Why did the Hands of the Cause decide to call for the election of the Universal House of Justice as the way forward to address the issue of succession to Shoghi Effendi?

4. Why did the Universal House of Justice decide that there could not be another Guardian?

5. Briefly describe your understanding of the answers provided by the Universal House of Justice to questions in section 28.5.

29. COVENANT-BREAKING OF MASON REMEY

29.1 Introduction

The defection of Charles Mason Remey and his unsubstantiated claim to the Guardianship after the passing of Shoghi Effendi created a new brand of Covenant-breakers. Adib Taherzadeh calls this episode of Covenant-breaking as one of the flimsiest among all the previous incidents.[1] Many of those who followed Mason Remey either repented and returned to the community or left the Bahá'í Faith completely. Mason Remey found it difficult to attract a significant number of followers. After his death, rivalries broke out between his lieutenants as to who would succeed him. Overall, the efforts of this group did not produce any outcome, and eventually became null and void.

This chapter provides an overview of the Covenant-breaking of Mason Remey and those who followed him. The primary source of information is provided by the document titled "Mason Remey and those who followed him" that was produced under the direction of the Universal House of Justice. This document was initially released on 31 January 1997 and was later revised and updated in January 2008. The full text of the revised document is provided in Appendix D for your study and perusal.

This chapter is structured as follows:

a) An introduction to the nature of "Covenant-breaking" will be initially provided.
b) A discussion on the importance of expelling Covenant-breakers from the Faith and then of shunning them will be carried out.
c) Finally, a summary of the document "Mason Remey and those who followed him" will be presented. You should study this summary in conjunction with the main document provided in Appendix D.

In this chapter, you need to look for and understand the following **key concepts**:

---

1 Adib Taherzadeh: *The Covenant of Bahá'u'lláh*, p. 388.

a) There were serious flaws in the claim made by Charles Mason Remy to be the successor of Shoghi Effendi as the second Guardian.
b) The efforts of Remey to increase his influence and power over the Bahá'í community after expulsion from the Faith proved fruitless.
c) The rivalry among the prominent followers of Mason Remey following his death to succeed him was appalling and futile.
d) The present pitiful plight of Mason Remey's followers represents a graphical illustration of the devastating effects of Covenant-breaking.

29.2 Nature of Covenant-breaking

The term Covenant-breaking has a specific meaning in the Bahá'í Faith. According to Universal House of Justice, "when a person declares his acceptance of Bahá'u'lláh as a Manifestation of God he becomes a party to the Covenant and accepts the totality of His Revelation. If he then turns round and attacks Bahá'u'lláh or the Central Institution of the Faith he violates the Covenant."[1]

In response to this action, "... every effort is made to help that person to see the illogicality and error of his actions, but if he persists he must, in accordance with the instructions of Bahá'u'lláh Himself, be shunned as a Covenant-breaker."[2]

A study of the cases of Covenant-breakers clearly indicates that most had impressive records of service to the Cause, and a good knowledge of its teachings and history. However, when they attacked the centre of the Bahá'í Faith and broke the Covenant, they were spiritually cut off from Bahá'u'lláh since they were fully dominated by their ego and ambitions. Spiritually blinded, they opposed the Bahá'í Faith they formerly cherished and they could not see how damaging were their actions and deeds.

Such symptoms are indicative of a spiritual disease that affects the heart and soul of a Covenant-breaker. In a letter written on behalf of Shoghi Effendi, he states that "Covenant Breaking is truly a Spiritual disease, and the whole view-point and attitude of a Covenant Breaker is so poisonous that the Master likened it to leprosy ..."[3] A leper is isolated from the community in order to prevent the spread of disease. Similarly, Covenant-breakers are expelled from the Faith and the Bahá'ís are expected not to associate with them to stop the spread of the Covenant-breaking disease.

Covenant-breakers are different from those who are hostile to the Bahá'í Faith because their attacks are due to their ignorance of the station of

---

1 The Universal House of Justice, letter to an individual believer, 23 March 1975, cited in "Developing Distinctive Baha'i Communities", NSA of the US, sect. 5.13.

2 The Universal House of Justice, letter to an individual believer, 23 March 1975, cited "Developing Distinctive Baha'i Communities", NSA of the US, sect. 5.13.

3 Shoghi Effendi, Letter written on his behalf to an individual believer, 19 July 1946, cited in *Lights of Guidance*, p. 183.

Bahá'u'lláh or the Centre of the Covenant. A Covenant-breaker is fully aware of the source of truth but does not turn to it due to egotistic and selfish reasons.

It is important to understand that Covenant-breakers are different from those who recognize Bahá'u'lláh at some stage of their lives and accept His Faith, but for some reason at a later stage they resign from it. Those who lose their voting rights because they break certain Bahá'í laws or reject Bahá'u'lláh as a Manifestation of God are also not categorized as Covenant-breakers.

Illustrating the nature of the Covenant-breaking, the Universal House of Justice explains:

> "Every Bahá'í is at liberty, nay is urged, to freely express his opinion and his understanding of the Teachings, but all this is in a totally different category from that of a Bahá'í who opposes the clear Teachings of Bahá'u'lláh or who asserts his own opinion as an authoritative and correct interpretation of the teachings, and attacks or opposes the very Institutions which Bahá'u'lláh has created to protect His Covenant. When a person declares his acceptance of Bahá'u'lláh as a Manifestation of God he becomes a party to the Covenant and accepts the totality of His Revelation. If he then turns round and attacks Bahá'u'lláh or the Central Institution of the Faith he violates the Covenant. If this happens every effort is made to help that person to see the illogicality and error of his actions, but if he persists he must, in accordance with the instructions of Bahá'u'lláh Himself, be shunned as a Covenant-breaker."[1]

29.3 Expulsion of Covenant-breakers

Declaration of a person as a Covenant-breaker by the Universal House of Justice is only the first step towards preventing the spread of the spiritual disease of Covenant-breaking. For complete protection, it is essential that the Covenant-breaker is expelled from the Bahá'í Faith.

The authority to expel Covenant-breakers was vested with Bahá'u'lláh during His lifetime. This authority later devolved to 'Abdu'l-Bahá as the Centre of the Covenant, and then to Shoghi Effendi as the Guardian of the Bahá'í Faith.

After Shoghi Effendi, the authority of expulsion and reinstatement was exercised by the Hands of the Cause of God, "... subject in each instance to the approval of the Universal House of Justice".[2] In the absence of the Hands of the Cause, "... the International Teaching Centre is invested with the mandate to watch over the security and ensure the protection of the Faith of

---

[1] The Universal House of Justice, A letter to an individual believer, March 23 1975, cited in "Developing Distinctive Baha'i Communities", NSA of the US, sect. 5.13.

[2] The Universal House of Justice, Letter to the Continental Board of Counsellors, 24 June 1968, cited in *Lights of Guidance*, p. 188.

God. It must investigate all cases of incipient Covenant-breaking—employing, as necessary, the services of the Continental Counsellors and their auxiliaries and evaluating their reports—and decide whether the offender should be expelled from the Cause, submitting the decision to the Universal House of Justice for its consideration."[1]

However, this does not exempt other institutions of the Bahá'í Faith from the responsibility of protecting the Cause. The Universal House of Justice states that "... although the Hands of the Cause of God have the specific functions of protection and propagation, and are specialized for these functions, it is also the duty of the Universal House of Justice and the Spiritual Assemblies to protect and teach the Cause—indeed teaching is a sacred obligation placed upon every believer by Bahá'u'lláh."[2]

29.4 Shunning of Covenant breakers

Since Covenant-breaking is a contagious disease, Bahá'u'lláh and 'Abdu'l-Bahá have repeatedly warned the believers to shun Covenant-breakers. In response to questions asked by an individual regarding why the believers should shun Covenant-breakers, 'Abdu'l-Bahá responded: "... *that just as bodily diseases ... are contagious, likewise the spiritual diseases are also infectious. If a consumptive should associate with a thousand safe and healthy persons, the safety and health of these thousand persons would not affect the consumptive and would not cure him of his consumption. But when this consumptive associates with those thousand souls, in a short time the disease of consumption will infect a number of those healthy persons. This is a clear and self-evident question.*"

The Universal House of Justice also states: "... the believers are commanded to shun Covenant-breakers for the same reason as healthy people do not associate with a person suffering from a serious contagious illness. A contagiously sick person cannot catch health from a thousand healthy people, but, on the contrary, he can infect them with his illness."[3]

Shunning Covenant-breakers has been strongly emphasized in *The Will and Testament of 'Abdu'l-Bahá*. He states that "*One of the greatest and most fundamental principles of the Cause of God is to shun and avoid entirely the Covenant-breakers, for they will utterly destroy the Cause of God, exterminate His Law and render of no account all efforts exerted in the past.*"[4]

With regards to shunning Covenant-breakers, Shoghi Effendi states: "Bahá'u'lláh and the Master ... have also told us, however, to pray for them.

1 The Universal House of Justice, *The Institution of the Counsellors*, p. 4.
2 Universal House of Justice, letter to an individual believer, 27 May 1966, cited *Wellspring of Guidance*, p. 86.
3 The Universal House of Justice, A letter to an individual believer, 23 March 1975, cited in a document by the NSA of the US on Developing Distinctive Bahá'í Communities.
4 'Abdu'l-Bahá, *The Will and Testament of 'Abdu'l-Bahá*, p. 20.

These souls are not lost forever. In the Aqdas, Bahá'u'lláh says that God will forgive Mírzá Yaḥyá if he repents. It follows, therefore, that God will forgive any soul if he repents. Most of them do not want to repent, unfortunately."[1]

Avoiding Covenant breakers is no hindrance to the unity of the Bahá'í Faith. Shoghi Effendi explains "... if a man cuts a cancer out of his body to preserve his health and very life, no one would suggest that for the sake of 'unity' it should be reintroduced into the otherwise healthy organism!"[2]

29.5 Mason Remey's claim to Guardianship

The most notable case of Covenant-breaking after the passing of Shoghi Effendi was the pitiful attempt of Charles Mason Remey to usurp the Guardianship. 'Abdu'l-Bahá had cautioned the Bahá'ís against the false claims to the station of Guardianship in a Tablet to Mullá 'Alí-Akbar, one of the Hands of the Cause of God:

> *"My purpose is this, that ere the expiration of a thousand years, no one has the right to utter a single word, even to claim the station of Guardianship. The most Holy Book is the Book to which all peoples shall refer, and in it the Laws of God have been revealed. Laws not mentioned in the Book should be referred to the decision of the Universal House of Justice."*[3]

Mason Remey was one of the nine Hands of the Cause of God who searched the office and apartment of Shoghi Effendi for his will. He was also one of the Hands of the Cause of God who signed the 1957 declaration that Shoghi Effendi had left neither a will nor a successor.

In April 1960, encouraged and supported by some ambition individuals, Mason Remey claimed that he was the second Guardian of the Bahá'í Faith. Although initially he gathered some followers in the United States, France, and Pakistan, the majority of the Bahá'ís rejected his claim. The Hands of the Cause of God in the Holy Land tried to bring him to his senses and withdraw his claim. However, he persisted in his claim. Consequently, in a cable on 26 July 1960 to all the National Spiritual Assemblies, the Hands of the Cause announced him a Covenant breaker and expelled him from the Faith:

> "... ENTIRE BODY HANDS OBEDIENT PROVISIONS WILL TESTAMENT CENTRE COVENANT COMMUNICATIONS BELOVED GUARDIAN ENJOINING THEM PROTECT HOLY CAUSE ATTACKS ENEMIES WITHIN WITHOUT ANNOUNCE BAHÁ'Í WORLD MASON REMEY COVENANT BREAKER EXPELLED FAITH STOP ACTION FOLLOWS LONG PERIOD

---

1 Shoghi Effendi, written on his behalf to an individual believer, cited in *Principles of Bahá'í Administration*, p. 22.

2 Shoghi Effendi, written on his behalf to an individual believer, cited in *Principles of Bahá'í Administration*, p. 22.

3 'Abdu'l-Bahá, *Persian and Arabic Tablets*, vol. III, pp. 499–501, cited by the Universal House of Justice to the National Spiritual Assembly of Bahá'ís of the Netherlands, 9 March 1965, in *Wellspring of Guidance*, p. 47.

PATIENCE FORBEARANCE OPPORTUNITY GIVEN HIM WITHDRAW SHAMEFUL PRETENSION SACRED STATION GUARDIANSHIP CONSTITUTING HERETICAL CLAIM CONTRARY EXPLICIT PROVISIONS WILL MASTER STOP DESPITE UNIVERSAL REPUDIATION DENUNCIATION BY ALL HANDS INTERNATIONAL BAHÁ'Í COUNCIL ALL NATIONAL ASSEMBLIES REMEY CONTINUING AGITATE UNFOUNDED CLAIM ACTIVELY SEEKING CREATE DIVISION RANKS FAITHFUL SOW SEEDS DOUBT HEARTS BELIEVERS UNDERMINE ACTIVITIES INSTITUTION HANDS CHIEF STEWARDS DEDICATED FULFILMENT BELOVED GUARDIAN'S TEN YEAR PLAN STOP ACCORDANCE INJUNCTION WILL TESTAMENT 'ABDU'L-BAHÁ, CALL UPON FRIENDS EVERYWHERE SHUN REMEY AND ANYONE ASSOCIATING WITH HIM OR ACTIVELY SUPPORTING HIS CLAIMS STOP CONFIDENT COMMUNITY MOST GREAT NAME UNITED WHOLEHEARTED CONDEMNATION THIS LATEST ILL-FATED ATTEMPT DISRUPT GOD'S HOLY CAUSE WILL EMERGE TRIUMPHANT STRENGTHENED GALVANIZED ISSUE FORTH WIN REMAINING GOALS GLORIOUS WORLD ENCIRCLING CRUSADE STOP CABLE MESSAGE ALL NATIONAL ASSEMBLIES."[1]

In another cable on 3 August 1960 to all the National Spiritual Assemblies, the Hands of the Cause of God announced the Covenant-breaking and expulsion of a number of believers who accepted the claim of Mason Remey. They included John Carré, Donald Harvey, Joel Marangella, and Jacques Soghomnian, who played some roles in the events that followed the baseless claim of Mason Remey:

"... BELOVED GUARDIAN'S GLORIOUS EPISTLE GOD PASSES BY CLEARLY STATES HOLY CAUSE CONSTANTLY SUBJECT CRISES GIVING RISE GREATER VICTORIES STOP HISTORY DEFECTION DISTINGUISHED BELIEVERS FOLLOWING ASCENSION FORERUNNER FAITH SUPREME MANIFESTATION CENTRE COVENANT NOW REPEATED AFTER ASCENSION PRECIOUS SHOGHI EFFENDI THROUGH MASON REMEY'S DEFECTION HIS PREPOSTEROUS UTTERLY UNFOUNDED CLAIMS STOP PROTECTION BELIEVERS FROM ACTIVITIES MISGUIDED MISCHIEF MAKERS GIVEN EVERY OPPORTUNITY REPENT NOW REQUIRES EXPULSION FAITH REMEY'S HENCHMEN JOHN CARRE BERNARD FILLON, MONEER DARAKHSHAN JOEL MARANGELLA JACQUES SOGHOMONIAN DONALD HARVEY JOHN BYERS IN FRANCE AND MARY WILKIN UNITED STATES STOP HENCEFORTH ANYONE ASSOCIATING THESE PEOPLE OR SUPPORTING REMEY CLAIM LIKEWISE CONSIDERED COVENANT BREAKER STOP CONFIDENT FAITHFUL DEVOTED BODY BELIEVERS MINDFUL INFINITE BOUNTIES PRAISES SHOWERED BELOVED GUARDIAN WILL DEMONSTRATE THROUGH UNITED ACTION IMPREGNABLE

1 The Hands of the Cause of God, *Ministry of the Custodians*, p. 223.

> SOLIDARITY ARISE ACHIEVE GLORIOUS GOALS GOD INSPIRED CRUSADE STOP CABLE MESSAGE ALL NATIONAL ASSEMBLIES."[1]

29.6 Death of Mason Remey

The Universal House of Justice advised the Bahá'í world in April 1974:

> "CHARLES MASON REMEY WHOSE ARROGANT ATTEMPT USURP GUARDIANSHIP AFTER PASSING SHOGHI EFFENDI LED TO HIS EXPULSION FROM RANKS FAITHFUL HAS DIED IN FLORENCE ITALY IN HUNDREDTH YEAR OF HIS LIFE BURIED WITHOUT RELIGIOUS RITES ABANDONED BY ERSTWHILE FOLLOWERS. HISTORY THIS PITIABLE DEFECTION BY ONE WHO HAD RECEIVED GREAT HONOURS FROM BOTH MASTER AND GUARDIAN CONSTITUTES YET ANOTHER EXAMPLE FUTILITY ALL ATTEMPTS UNDERMINE IMPREGNABLE COVENANT CAUSE BAHÁ'U'LLÁH."[2]

29.7 Basis of Mason Remey's claim

Mason Remey loosely based his claim on the statement of 'Abdu'l-Bahá in His Will and Testament[3] that the "*Guardian of the Cause of God* " is "*the sacred head and the distinguished member for life*" of the Universal House of Justice.

Shoghi Effendi formed the International Bahá'í Council in 1951 as the forerunner for the Universal House of Justice and appointed Mason Remey as the President of the Council. Mason Remey argued that since he was appointed as the President of the International Bahá'í Council, it was natural for him to become the second Guardian of the Faith and eventually the head of the Universal House of Justice as stated by 'Abdu'l-Bahá.

However, he ignored another statement from *The Will and Testament of 'Abdu'l-Bahá*, that the future Guardians should be male lineage descendants of Shoghi Effendi and hence a Branch (Ghusn)—a descendent of Bahá'u'lláh.

Those who gathered around Mason Remey and have followed him in recent times have justified their position by reinterpreting the word "branch". They argue that Bahá'u'lláh has referred to human beings as "... *fruits of one tree and the leaves of one branch.*"[4] Hence, any believer is a "branch" and is entitled to succeed Shoghi Effendi, including Mason Remey. However, this argument is flawed since the Arabic word Ghusn translated as "branch" in English is completely different from the Persian word translated as "branch" in the above quotation—its meaning is "twig". In addition, there are no capital

---

1 The Hands of the Cause of God, *Ministry of the Custodians*, p. 225.

2 The Universal House of Justice, *Mason Remey and those who followed him*, Jan 31 1997 and updated January 2008— Available in Appendix D of this book. See also The Universal House of Justice, *Messages from the Universal House of Justice 1963–1986*, p. 271.

3 'Abdu'l-Bahá: *The Will and Testament of 'Abdu'l-Bahá*, p. 14.

4 Bahá'u'lláh, *Gleanings from the Writings of Bahá'u'lláh*, p. 218.

letters in Arabic and Persian scripts. Hence, the issue of the whether the English word "branch" starts with a capital letter is not relevant to the intended meaning of Ghusn.

29.8 Events after the expulsions

Chaos and division surrounded the followers of Mason Remey very soon after his claim. This proved to be firm evidence of how disunity and destruction can reigns when the power of the Covenant is not protecting a cause. The chain of events is described in the following sections.

29.8.1 Legal challenge

In April 1963, a group of the followers of Mason Remey established what they called the "National Spiritual Assembly of the Bahá'ís of the United States under the Hereditary Guardianship" in New Mexico. A similar body was created that same month in Pakistan, but it was soon dissolved.

After incorporation in March 1964, the New Mexico group claimed to be the true voice of the American Bahá'í community, and the owner of the Wilmette Temple property and all other properties owned by the National Spiritual Assembly (NSA) of the Bahá'ís of the United States. Accordingly, it brought a lawsuit against the American NSA. The legitimate National Spiritual Assembly of the Bahá'ís of the United States lodged a counter-claim against the New Mexico group for setting up a fraudulent "National Spiritual Assembly" and using Bahá'í trademarks without permission. The NSA won the counter-claim and as a result the lawsuit lodged by the New Mexico group was rejected. The group was also prohibited from using of Bahá'í terminologies.

Mason Remey suddenly instructed the New Mexico group to withdraw an appeal and ordered their "National Assembly" to be dissolved.

29.8.2 "Second International Bahá'í Council"

On 21 September 1964 Remey created a "Second International Bahá'í Council" and appointed Joel Marangella, an American believer living in France, as its president. Following the example of Mason Remey, Joel Marangella assumed the position among the followers of Mason Remey as his possible successor. On October 1966, Mason Remey suddenly aborted the "Council" and ordered Joel Marangella to "... turn over to me such records as you have of the second Council that no longer exists". This was an indication of the emerging conflict and rivalry between Mason Remey and his followers. Further evidence on discord occurred on 29 January 1967 when Mason Remey complained: "Some friends have started the report that the Guardian is loosing [sic] his mind and that someone is controlling him ..."

29.8.3 Harvey and Marangella

On 15 May 1967, Mason Remey appointed Donald Harvey, one of his American followers, as the "third Guardian of the Faith" after his death.

However, Donald Harvey did not attempt to exercise this "authority" after the death of Mason Remey nor did he appoint a successor. He died in 1991.

On 17 November 1984, Jacques Soghomonian, one of Donald Harvey's associates produced a document apparently signed by Donald Harvey stating: "[I] do appoint and designate Mr Jacques Soghomonian ... as his [sic] successor as Fourth Guardian of the Universal Faith and Revelation of Bahá'u'lláh."

On 12 November 1969, Joel Marangella suddenly announced that he was Mason Remey's true successor. He said that he had received a sealed envelope from Mason Remey in December 1961, with a note indicating that he would know when to open the envelope. He had opened it soon after being appointed as President of the "Second Bahá'í International Council". Inside was a brief note from Mason Remey asking him to "... tell the Bahá'í World that I appoint you to be the third Guardian of the Bahá'í Faith". Apparently, Joel Marangella had not taken any action at that time.

Joel Marangella claimed that the appointment of Donald Harvey by Mason Remey was due to his irrational behaviour and that he should be ignored. At that time Mason Remey had started to attack Shoghi Effendi, claiming that the Bahá'í Administrative Order was meant to organise the "Bábí Faith" and had to be dismantled. He even called himself the "first" Guardian of the Bahá'í Faith. After announcing himself as the third Guardian, Joel Marangella established what he called the "National Bureau of the Orthodox Bahá'í Faith".

29.8.4 Other contenders

John Carré was one of early followers of Mason Remey who was expelled from the Bahá'í Faith in 1961. He suddenly emerged as the spokesperson of Jamshíd Ma'ání, who was an Iranian pioneer in Indonesia claiming to be "the One Who creates the Messengers at every instant". When Jamshíd Ma'ání showed signs of mental illness and was hospitalized in Ṭihrán, John Carré lost interest in him. John Carré later emerged as the spokesman of some organizations such as the "House of Light" and the "House of Mankind" under the pseudonym "John Christofil". His writings were mainly about the "catastrophic events" that would happen before the end of the century and would prepare the way for a "Third" Manifestation of God.

Reginald ("Rex") King, the elected secretary of the New Mexico "National Spiritual Assembly", was unhappy with Mason Remey's opposition to his leadership in the United States. He went to Italy and had a bitter meeting with Mason Remey who was living there. After the meeting, Mason Remey wrote a letter on 13 September 1969 that denounced Reginald King: "... his station to be ever and eternally that of Satan for evermore". Consequently, Reginald King turned to Joel Marangella when he claimed to be the third Guardian. However, that relationship did not last long. Reginald King announced: "... neither Mason Remey nor Joel Marangella had in truth ever been guardians ... because of the lack of lineal descendancy." Reginald King died on 1 April 1977, and left all his rights of leadership to a "Council" consisting of members of his own family.

Leland Jensen was another member of the New Mexico "National Spiritual Assembly" who had a dispute with Reginald King over leadership in 1963 when both were on the "Assembly". Leland Jenson moved to Missoula, Montana in 1964 to avoid a disastrous flood predicted by Mason Remey. There he was convicted in 1969 of "lewd and lascivious" behaviour and was sentenced to a term in Montana State Prison. In prison he claimed to be "Joshua". After serving his sentence, he travelled throughout the United States to attract the remaining followers of Mason Remey to his own religious truth. He gradually made other claims including "the return of Jesus" and the "embryonic" "Universal House of Justice". He predicted that the "end of the world" would occur on 29 April 1980. He changed the date twice—to 7 May and later to 22–23 May when it did not happen. Gradually most of his follower abandoned him.

Giuseppe Pepe was a young man who served Mason Remey in Florence as his secretary/companion and was eventually legally adopted by him. Leland Jensen wrote an open letter that stated Giuseppe Pepe was the "Crown Prince", the true successor of Mason Remey as "Fourth Guardian". He suggested that Giuseppe Pepe must secure this station by being "coronated [sic] King of the Kingdom by the High Priest ...." Leland Jensen also introduced himself as the "High Priest". Giuseppe Pepe protested against this claim when the Covenant-breakers started to use this title for him.

29.9 Current situation

The current situation of the episode that started with Mason Remey's defection is summarised by the Universal House of Justice as follows:

> "By 1996 Remey's following had largely disintegrated. Death had removed five of the principal figures: Mason Remey in 1974, Reginald King in 1977, Remey's appointed successor, Donald Harvey, in 1991, Giuseppe Pepe in 1994, and Leland Jensen in 1996. Public disgrace and ridicule had reduced Jensen's influence to that of a cult figure for two or three isolated groups in the American Midwest; those left in the BUPC[1] were divided by infighting. John Carré had drifted off into esoteric religious pursuits only tangentially related to Bahá'í subjects. Jacques Soghomonian has remained a largely isolated figure. Joel Marangella's group, the so-called "Orthodox Bahá'ís", had testified in a court proceeding in July 2007 to having only about forty members in the United States. Some others are scattered in locations in Australia and India."[2]

1 BUPC stands for Bahá'ís Under the Provisions of the Covenant

2 The Universal House of Justice, *Mason Remey and those who followed him*, 31 January 1997 and updated January 2008—See in Appendix D of this book.

While trying to establish their presence on the Internet, the remnants of the Mason Remey defection have concealed their insignificance by giving the illusion of being the rightful followers of Bahá'u'lláh.

Joel Marangella and Jacques Soghomonian, now both advanced in age, have recently announced the names of two Persians living in Australia as their successors: Nosrat'u'llah Bahremand and Enayatullah (Zabih) Yazdani.

Nosrat'u'llah Bahremand was designated as a Covenant-breaker in 2003 because of his allegiance to Mason Remey. He was initially appointed by Joel Marangella as a "Hand of the Cause" and then "Vice-President" of the "Third International Bahá'í Council" established by him in 2006. In May 2007 Joel Marangella appointed him as his successor.

Enayatullah (Zabih) Yazdani was designated a Covenant-breaker in June 2005 after many years of insisting on his view that Mason Remey was the legitimate successor to Shoghi Effendi and of accepting Donald Harvey as the "Third Guardian". Recently, Jacques Soghomonian appointed Enayatullah Yazdani as the "Fifth Guardian" upon his death.

29.10 Activities

1. What is the nature of Covenant-breaking?

2. What are the characteristics of Covenant-breakers?

3. Why should we shun Covenant-breakers?

4. Why are Covenant breakers expelled from the Bahá'í Faith?

5. Why is Covenant-breaking considered a spiritual disease?

6. Why was the claim of Mason Remey to be the legitimate successor of Shoghi Effendi flawed?

7. Briefly describe the chain of events after the death of Mason Remey?

8. What is the current situation of Mason Remey's followers?

APPENDIX A

Part 1- Questions regarding the Guardianship and the Universal House of Justice

7 December 1969[1]

1. Your recent letter, in which you share with us the questions that have occurred to some of the youth in studying "The Dispensation of Bahá'u'lláh", has been carefully considered, and we feel that we should comment both on the particular passage you mention and on a related passage in the same work, because both bear on the relationship between the Guardianship and the Universal House of Justice.
2. The first passage concerns the Guardian's duty to insist upon reconsideration by his fellow-members in the Universal House of Justice of any enactment, which he believes conflicts with the meaning and departs from the spirit of the Sacred Writings. The second passage concerns the infallibility of the Universal House of Justice without the Guardian, namely Shoghi Effendi's statement that "Without such an institution [the Guardianship] ... the necessary guidance to define the sphere of the legislative action of its elected representatives would be totally withdrawn."[2]
3. Some of the youth, you indicate, were puzzled as to how to reconcile the former of these two passages with such of 'Abdu'l-Bahá which affirms that the Universal House of Justice is "*freed from all error*".[3]
4. Just as *The Will and Testament of 'Abdu'l-Bahá* does not in any way contradict *The Kitáb-i-Aqdas* but, in the Guardian's words, "confirms, supplements, and correlates the provisions of the Aqdas",[4] so the writings of the Guardian contradict neither the revealed Word nor the

[1] The Universal House of Justice, *Messages from the Universal House of Justice 1963–1986*, pp. 156–61.
[2] Shoghi Effendi, *The World Order of Bahá'u'lláh*, p. 148.
[3] 'Abdu'l-Bahá, *The Will and Testament of 'Abdu'l-Bahá*, p. 14.
[4] Shoghi Effendi, *The World Order of Bahá'u'lláh*, p. 19.

interpretations of the Master. In attempting to understand the Writings, therefore, one must first realize that there is and can be no real contradiction in them, and in the light of this we can confidently seek the unity of meaning which they contain.

5. The Guardian and the Universal House of Justice have certain duties and functions in common; each also operates within a separate and distinct sphere. As Shoghi Effendi explained, "... it is made indubitably clear and evident that the Guardian of the Faith has been made the Interpreter of the Word and that the Universal House of Justice has been invested with the function of legislating on matters not expressly revealed in the teachings. The interpretation of the Guardian, functioning within his own sphere, is as authoritative and binding as the enactments of the International House of Justice, whose exclusive right and prerogative is to pronounce upon and deliver the final judgement on such laws and ordinances as Bahá'u'lláh has not expressly revealed." He goes on to affirm, "Neither can, nor will ever, infringe upon the sacred and prescribed domain of the other. Neither will seek to curtail the specific and undoubted authority with which both have been divinely invested."[1] It is impossible to conceive that two centres of authority, which the Master has stated are both under the care and protection of the Abhá Beauty, under the shelter and unerring guidance of His Holiness, the Exalted One",[2] could conflict with one another, because both are vehicles of the same Divine Guidance.
6. The Universal House of Justice, beyond its function as the enactor of legislation, has been invested with the more general functions of protecting and administering the Cause, solving obscure questions and deciding upon matters that have caused difference. Nowhere is it stated that the infallibility of the Universal House of Justice is by virtue of the Guardian's membership or presence on that body. Indeed, 'Abdu'l-Bahá in His Will and Shoghi Effendi in his "Dispensation of Bahá'u'lláh" have both explicitly stated that the elected members of the Universal House of Justice in consultation are recipients of unfailing Divine Guidance. Furthermore the Guardian himself in *The World Order of Bahá'u'lláh* asserted that "It must be also clearly understood by every believer that the institution of Guardianship does not under any circumstances abrogate, or even in the slightest degree detract from, the powers granted to the Universal House of Justice by Bahá'u'lláh in *The Kitáb-i-Aqdas*, and repeatedly and solemnly confirmed by 'Abdu'l-Bahá in His Will. It does not constitute in any manner a contradiction to the Will and Writings of Bahá'u'lláh, nor does it nullify any of His revealed instructions."[3]
7. While the specific responsibility of the Guardian is the interpretation of the Word, he is also invested with all the powers and prerogatives

---

1 Shoghi Effendi, *The World Order of Bahá'u'lláh*, pp. 149–50.
2 'Abdu'l-Bahá, *The Will and Testament of 'Abdu'l-Bahá*, p. 11.
3 Shoghi Effendi, *The World Order of Bahá'u'lláh*, p. 8.

necessary to discharge his function as Guardian of the Cause, its Head and supreme protector. He is, furthermore, made the irremovable head and member for life of the supreme legislative body of the Faith. It is as the head of the Universal House of Justice, and as a member of that body, that the Guardian takes part in the process of legislation. If the following passage, which gave rise to your query, is considered as referring to this last relationship, you will see that there is no contradiction between it and the other texts: "Though the Guardian of the Faith has been made the permanent head of so august a body he can never, even temporarily, assume the right of exclusive legislation. He cannot override the decision of the majority of his fellow-members, but is bound to insist upon a reconsideration by them of any enactment he conscientiously believes to conflict with the meaning and to depart from the spirit of Bahá'u'lláh's revealed utterances."[1]

8. Although the Guardian, in relation to his fellow-members within the Universal House of Justice, cannot override the decision of the majority, it is inconceivable that the other members would ignore any objection he raised in the course of consultation or pass legislation contrary to what he expressed as being in harmony with the spirit of the Cause. It is, after all, the final act of judgement delivered by the Universal House of Justice that is vouchsafed infallibility, not any views expressed in the course of the process of enactment.
9. It can be seen, therefore, that there is no conflict between the Master's statements concerning the unfailing divine guidance conferred upon the Universal House of Justice and the above passage from "The Dispensation of Bahá'u'lláh".

The process of legislation

10. It may help the friends to understand this relationship if they are aware of some of the processes that the Universal House of Justice follows when legislating. First, of course, it observes the greatest care in studying the Sacred Texts and the interpretations of the Guardian as well as considering the views of all the members. After long consultation the process of drafting a pronouncement is put into effect. During this process the whole matter may well be reconsidered. As a result of such reconsideration the final judgement may be significantly different from the conclusion earlier favoured, or possibly it may be decided not to legislate at all on that subject at that time. One can understand how great would be the attention paid to the views of the Guardian during the above process were he alive.

The Universal House of Justice in the absence of the

---

1 Shoghi Effendi, *The World Order of Bahá'u'lláh*, p. 150.

Guardian

11. In considering the second passage we must once more hold fast to the principle that the teachings do not contradict themselves.
12. Future Guardians are clearly envisaged and referred to in the Writings, but there is nowhere any promise or guarantee that the line of Guardians would endure forever; on the contrary there are clear indications that the line could be broken. Yet, in spite of this, there is a repeated insistence in the Writings on the indestructibility of the Covenant and the immutability of God's Purpose for this Day. One of the most striking passages which envisage the possibility of such a break in the line of Guardians is in the Kitáb-i-Aqdas itself:
13. *"The endowments dedicated to charity revert to God, the Revealer of Signs. No one has the right to lay hold on them without leave from the Dawning-Place of Revelation.*[1] *After Him the decision rests with the Aghsán* [Branches],[2] *and after them with the House of Justice—should it be established in the world by then—so that they may use these endowments for the benefit of the Sites exalted in this Cause, and for that which they have been commanded by God, the Almighty, the All-Powerful. Otherwise the endowments should be referred to the people of Bahá, who speak not without His leave and who pass no judgement but in accordance with that which God has ordained in this Tablet, they who are the champions of victory betwixt heaven and earth, so that they may spend them on that which has been decreed in the Holy Book by God, the Mighty, the Bountiful."*[3]
14. The passing of Shoghi Effendi in 1957 precipitated the very situation provided for in this passage, in that the line of Aghsán ended before the House of Justice had been elected. Although, as is seen, the ending of the line of Aghsán at some stage was provided for, we must never underestimate the grievous loss that the Faith has suffered. God's purpose for mankind remains unchanged, however, and the mighty Covenant of Bahá'u'lláh remains impregnable. Has not Bahá'u'lláh stated categorically, "*The Hand of Omnipotence hath established His Revelation upon an unassailable, an enduring foundation*".[4] While 'Abdu'l-Bahá confirms: `*Verily, God effecteth that which He pleaseth; naught can annul His Covenant; naught can obstruct His favour nor oppose His Cause!*"[5] "*Everything is subject to corruption; but the Covenant of thy Lord shall continue to pervade all regions.*"[6] "*The tests of every dispensation are in*

---

1 "The Dawning-Place of Revelation' is a reference to the Manifestation of God; here, a specific reference to Bahá'u'lláh.

2 Aghsán (Branches) denotes the sons and male descendants of Bahá'u'lláh.

3 Bahá'u'lláh, *The Kitáb-i-Aqdas*, p. 34.

4 Bahá'u'lláh, cited by Shoghi Effendi in *The World Order of Bahá'u'lláh*, p. 109.

5 'Abdu'l-Bahá, *Tablets of Abdul-Baha Abbas*, p. 598.

6 'Abdu'l-Bahá, *Bahá'í Scriptures*, p. 320.

direct proportion to the greatness of the Cause, and as heretofore such a manifest Covenant, written by the Supreme Pen, hath not been entered upon, the tests are proportionately severe .... These agitations of the violators are no more than the foam of the ocean, ... This foam of the ocean shall not endure and shall soon disperse and vanish, while the ocean of the Covenant shall eternally surge and roar."[1] And Shoghi Effendi has clearly stated: "The bedrock on which this Administrative Order is founded is God's immutable Purpose for mankind in this day." "... this priceless gem of Divine Revelation, now still in its embryonic state, shall evolve within the shell of His law, and shall forge ahead, undivided and unimpaired, till it embraces the whole of mankind."[2]

15. In the Bahá'í Faith there are two authoritative centres appointed to which the believers must turn, for in reality the Interpreter of the Word is an extension of that centre which is the Word itself. The Book is the record of the utterance of Bahá'u'lláh, while the divinely inspired Interpreter is the living Mouth of that Book—it is he and he alone who can authoritatively state what the Book means. Thus one centre is the Book with its Interpreter, and the other is the Universal House of Justice guided by God to decide on whatever is not explicitly revealed in the Book. This pattern of centres and their relationships is apparent at every stage in the unfoldment of the Cause. In *The Kitáb-i-Aqdas* Bahá'u'lláh tells the believer to refer after His passing to the Book, and to "*Him Whom God hath purposed, Who hath branched from this Ancient Root.*"[3] In *The Kitáb-i-'Ahdí* (the Book of Bahá'u'lláh's Covenant), He makes it clear that this reference is to 'Abdu'l-Bahá.[4] In the Aqdas Bahá'u'lláh also ordains the institution of the Universal House of Justice, and confers upon it the powers necessary for it to discharge its ordained functions. The Master in His Will and Testament explicitly institutes the Guardianship, which Shoghi Effendi states was clearly anticipated in the verses of *The Kitáb-i-Aqdas*, reaffirms and elucidates the authority of the Universal House of Justice, and refers the believers once again to the Book: "*Unto the Most Holy Book every one must turn and all that is not expressly recorded therein must be referred to the Universal House of Justice,*"[5] and at the very end of the Will He says: "*All must seek guidance and turn unto the Centre of the Cause and the House of Justice. And he that turneth unto whatsoever else is indeed in grievous error.*"[6]
16. As the sphere of jurisdiction of the Universal House of Justice in matters of legislation extends to whatever is not explicitly revealed in the Sacred

---

1 'Abdu'l-Bahá, *Tablets of Abdul-Baha Abbas*, 2:598; *Star of the West*, 4:10, p. 170; *Selections from the Writings of 'Abdu'l-Bahá*, pp. 210–211.
2 Shoghi Effendi, *The World Order of Bahá'u'lláh*, p. 23.
3 Bahá'u'lláh, *The Kitáb-i-Aqdas*, p. 62.
4 Bahá'u'lláh, *Tablets of Bahá'u'lláh*, pp. 217–223.
5 'Abdu'l-Bahá, *The Will and Testament of 'Abdu'l-Bahá*, p. 19.
6 'Abdu'l-Bahá, *The Will and Testament of 'Abdu'l-Bahá*, p. 25.

Text, it is clear that the Book itself is the highest authority and delimits the sphere of action of the House of Justice. Likewise, the Interpreter of the Book must also have the authority to define the sphere of the legislative action of the elected representatives of the Cause. The writings of the Guardian and the advice given by him over the thirty–six years of his Guardianship show the way in which he exercised this function in relation to the Universal House of Justice as well as to National and Local Spiritual Assemblies.

17. The fact that the Guardian has the authority to define the sphere of the legislative action of the Universal House of Justice does not carry with it the corollary that without such guidance the Universal House of Justice might stray beyond the limits of its proper authority; such a deduction would conflict with all the other texts referring to its infallibility, and specifically with the Guardian's own clear assertion that the Universal House of Justice never can or will infringe on the sacred and prescribed domain of the Guardianship. It should be remembered, however, that although National and Local Spiritual Assemblies can receive divine guidance if they consult in the manner and spirit described by 'Abdu'l-Bahá, they do not share in the explicit guarantees of infallibility conferred upon the Universal House of Justice. Any careful student of the Cause can see with what care the Guardian, after the passing of 'Abdu'l-Bahá, guided these elected representatives of the believers in the painstaking erection of the Administrative Order and in the formulation of Local and National Bahá'í Constitutions.

18. We hope that these elucidations will assist the friends in understanding these relationships more clearly, but we must all remember that we stand too close to the beginnings of the System ordained by Bahá'u'lláh to be able fully to understand its potentialities or the inter-relationships of its component parts. As Shoghi Effendi's secretary wrote on his behalf to an individual believer on 25 March 1930, "The contents of the Will of the Master are far too much for the present generation to comprehend. It needs at least a century of actual working before the treasures of wisdom hidden in it can be revealed. ..."

With loving Bahá'í greetings,

The Universal House of Justice

Part 2—Unassailable foundation of the Cause of God

[The following letter concerning questions about the election and infallibility of the Universal House of Justice was addressed to a National Spiritual Assembly and made available for the edification of the Bahá'ís throughout the world.][1]

1. We are glad that you have brought to our attention the questions perplexing some of the believers. It is much better for these questions to be put freely and openly than to have them, unexpressed, burdening the hearts of devoted believers. Once one grasps certain basic principles of the Revelation of Bahá'u'lláh such uncertainties are easily dispelled. This is not to say that the Cause of God contains no mysteries. Mysteries there are indeed, but they are not of a kind to shake one's faith once the essential tenets of the Cause and the indisputable facts of any situation are clearly understood.
2. The questions put by the various believers fall into three groups. The first group centres upon the following queries: Why were steps taken to elect a Universal House of Justice with the foreknowledge that there would be no Guardian? Was the time ripe for such an action? Could not the International Bahá'í Council have carried on the work?

The election of the Universal House of Justice

3. At the time of our beloved Shoghi Effendi's death it was evident, from the circumstances and from the explicit requirements of the Holy Texts, that it had been impossible for him to appoint a successor in accordance with the provisions of *The Will and Testament of 'Abdu'l-Bahá.* This situation in which the Guardian died without being able to appoint a successor, presented an obscure question not covered by the explicit Holy Text, and had to be referred to the Universal House of Justice. The friends should clearly understand that before the election of the Universal House of Justice there was no knowledge that there would be no Guardian. There could not have been any such foreknowledge, whatever opinions individual believers may have held. Neither the Hands of the Cause of God, nor the International Bahá'í Council, nor any other existing body could make a decision upon this all-important matter. Only the House of Justice had authority to pronounce upon it. This was one urgent reason for calling the election of the Universal House of Justice as soon as possible.
4. Following the passing of Shoghi Effendi the international administration of the Faith was carried on by the Hands of the Cause of God with the complete agreement and loyalty of the National Spiritual Assemblies and the body of the believers. This was in accordance with the Guardian's designation of the Hands as the "Chief Stewards of Bahá'u'lláh's

[1] The Universal House of Justice, *Messages from the Universal House of Justice 1963–1986*, pp. 50–58.

embryonic World Commonwealth."[1]

5. From the very outset of their custodianship of the Cause of God the Hands realized that since they had not certainty of Divine guidance such as is controvertibly assured to the Guardian and to the Universal House of Justice, the one safe course was to follow with undeviating firmness the instructions and policies of Shoghi Effendi. The entire history of religion shows no comparable record of such strict self-discipline, such absolute loyalty, and such complete self-abnegation by the leaders of a religion finding themselves suddenly deprived of their divinely inspired guide. The debt of gratitude which mankind for generations, nay, and ages to come, owes to this handful of grief-stricken, steadfast, heroic souls is beyond estimation.
6. The Guardian had given the Bahá'í world explicit and detailed plans covering the period until Riḍván 1963, the end of the Ten Year Crusade. From that point onward, unless the Faith were to be endangered, further Divine guidance was essential. This was the second pressing reason for the calling of the election of the Universal House of Justice. The rightness of the time was further confirmed by references in Shoghi Effendi's letters to the Ten Year Crusade's being followed by other plans under the direction of the Universal House of Justice. One such reference is the following passage from a letter addressed to the National Spiritual Assembly of the British Isles on 25 February 1951, concerning its Two Year Plan which immediately preceded the Ten Year Crusade:
7. "On the success of this enterprise, unprecedented in its scope, unique in its character and immense in its spiritual potentialities, must depend the initiation, at a later period in the Formative Age of the Faith, of undertakings embracing within their range all National Assemblies functioning throughout the Bahá'í world—undertakings constituting in themselves a prelude to the launching of world-wide enterprises destined to be embarked upon, in future epochs of that same Age, by the Universal House of Justice, that will symbolize the unity and co-ordinate and unify the activities of these National Assemblies."[2]
8. Having been in charge of the Cause of God for six years, the Hands, with absolute faith in the Holy Writings, called upon the believers to elect the Universal House of Justice, and even went so far as to ask that they themselves be not voted for. The sole, sad instance of anyone succumbing to the allurements of power was the pitiful attempt of Charles Mason Remey to usurp the Guardianship.

Principles governing the election of the Universal House of Justice

9. The following excerpts from a Tablet of 'Abdu'l-Bahá state clearly and emphatically the principles with which the friends are already familiar

[1] Shoghi Effendi, *Messages to the Bahá'í World*, 1950–1957, p. 127.
[2] Shoghi Effendi, *Unfolding Destiny*, p. 261.

from the Will and Testament of the Master and the various letters of Shoghi Effendi, and explain the basis for the election of the Universal House of Justice. The beloved Guardian himself sent this Tablet to Persia, in the early years of his ministry, for circulation among the believers.

10. "*... for 'Abdu'l-Bahá is in a tempest of dangers and infinitely abhors differences of opinion ... Praise be to God, there are no grounds for differences.*
11. "*The Báb, the Exalted One, is the Morn of Truth, the splendour of Whose light shineth through all regions. He is also the Harbinger of the Most Great Light, the Abhá Luminary. The Blessed Beauty is the One promised by the sacred books of the past, the revelation of the Source of light that shone upon Mount Sinai, Whose fire glowed in the midst of the Burning Bush. We are, one and all, servants of Their threshold, and stand each as a lowly keeper at Their door.*
12. "*My purpose is this, that ere the expiration of a thousand years, no one has the right to utter a single word, even to claim the station of Guardianship. The Most Holy Book is the Book to which all peoples shall refer, and in it the Laws of God have been revealed. Laws not mentioned in the Book should be referred to the decision of the Universal House of Justice. There will be no grounds for difference ... Beware, beware lest anyone create a rift or stir up sedition. Should there be differences of opinion, the Supreme House of Justice would immediately resolve the problems. Whatever will be its decision, by majority vote, shall be the real truth, inasmuch as that House is under the protection, unerring guidance, and care of the one true Lord. He shall guard it from error and will protect it under the wing of His sanctity and infallibility. He who opposes it is cast out and will eventually be of the defeated.*
13. "*The Supreme House of Justice should be elected according to the system followed in the election of the parliaments of Europe. And when the countries would be guided the Houses of Justice of the various countries would elect the Supreme House of Justice.*
14. "*At whatever time all the beloved of God in each country appoint the delegates, and these in turn elect their representatives, and these representatives elect a body, that body shall be regarded as the Supreme House of Justice.*
15. "*The establishment of that House is not dependent upon the conversion of all the nations of the world. For example, if conditions were favourable and no disturbances would be caused, the friends in Persia would elect their representatives, and likewise the friends in America, in India, and other areas would also elect their representatives, and these would elect a House of Justice. That House of justice would be the Supreme House of Justice. That is all.*"[1]
16. The friends should realize that there is nothing in the Texts to indicate that

---

[1] 'Abdu'l-Bahá, *Persian and Arabic Tablets of 'Abdu'l-Bahá*, vol. III, pp. 499–501.

only the Guardian could call the election of the Universal House of Justice. On the contrary, 'Abdu'l-Bahá envisaged the calling of its election in His own lifetime. At a time described by the Guardian as "the darkest moments of His (the Master's) life, under 'Abdu'l-Ḥamid's regime, when He stood to be deported to the most inhospitable regions of Northern Africa,"[1] and when even His life was threatened, 'Abdu'l-Bahá wrote to Ḥájí Mírzá Afnán, the cousin of the Báb and chief builder of the 'Ishqábád Temple, commanding him to arrange for the election of the Universal House of Justice should the threats against the Master materialize. The second part of the Master's Will is also relevant to such a situation and should be studied by the friends.

The authority of the Universal House of Justice

17. The second series of problems vexing some of the friends centres on the question of the infallibility of the Universal House of Justice and its ability to function without the presence of the Guardian. Particular difficulty has been experienced in understanding the implications of the following statement by the beloved Guardian:

18. "Divorced from the institution of the Guardianship the World Order of Bahá'u'lláh would be mutilated and permanently deprived of that hereditary principle which, as 'Abdu'l-Bahá has written, has been invariably upheld by the Law of God. 'In all the Divine Dispensations,' He states, in a Tablet addressed to a follower of the Faith in Persia, 'the eldest son hath been given extraordinary distinctions. Even the station of prophethood hath been his birthright.' Without such an institution the integrity of the Faith would be imperilled, and the stability of the entire fabric would be gravely endangered. Its prestige would suffer, the means required to enable it to make a long, an uninterrupted view over a series of generations would be completely lacking, and the necessary guidance to define the sphere of the legislative action of its elected representatives would be totally withdrawn."[2]

19. Let the friends who wish for a clearer understanding of this passage at the present time consider it in the light of the many other texts which deal with the same subject, for example the following passages gleaned from the letters of Shoghi Effendi:

20. "They have also, in unequivocal and emphatic language, appointed those twin institutions of the House of Justice and of the Guardianship as their chosen successors, destined to apply the principles, promulgate the laws, protect the institutions, adapt loyally and intelligently the Faith to the requirements of progressive society, and consummate the incorruptible inheritance which the Founders of the Faith have bequeathed to the

---

[1] Shoghi Effendi, *The World Order of Bahá'u'lláh*, p. 17.

[2] Shoghi Effendi, "The Dispensation of Bahá'u'lláh", in *The World Order of Bahá'u'lláh*, p. 148.

world."[1]

21. "It must be also clearly understood by every believer that the institution of Guardianship does not under any circumstances abrogate, or even in the slightest degree detract from, the powers granted to the Universal House of Justice by Bahá'u'lláh in *The Kitáb-i-Aqdas*, and repeatedly and solemnly confirmed by 'Abdu'l-Bahá in His will. It does not constitute in any manner a contradiction to the Will and Writings of Bahá'u'lláh, nor does it nullify any of His revealed instructions. It enhances the prestige of that exalted assembly, stabilizes its supreme position, safeguards its unity, and assures the continuity of its labours, without presuming in the slightest to infringe upon the inviolability of its clearly defined sphere of jurisdiction. We stand indeed too close to so monumental a document to claim for ourselves a complete understanding of all its implications, or to presume to have grasped the manifold mysteries it undoubtedly contains"[2]
22. "From these statements it is made indubitably clear and evident that the Guardian of the Faith has been made the Interpreter of the Word and that the Universal House of Justice has been invested with the function of legislating on matters not expressly revealed in the teachings. The interpretation of the Guardian, functioning within his own sphere, is as authoritative and binding as the enactments of the International House of Justice, whose exclusive right and prerogative is to pronounce upon and deliver the final judgment on such laws and ordinances, as Bahá'u'lláh has not expressly revealed. Neither can, nor will ever, infringe upon the sacred and prescribed domain of the other. Neither will seek to curtail the specific and undoubted authority with which both have been divinely invested."[3]
23. "Each exercises, within the limitations imposed upon it, its powers, its authority, its rights and prerogatives. These are neither contradictory, nor detract in the slightest degree from the position which each of these institutions occupies."[4]
24. "Though the Guardian of the Faith has been made the permanent head of so august a body he can never, even temporarily, assume the right of exclusive legislation. He cannot override the decision of the majority of his fellow members ...."[5]
25. Above all, let the hearts of the friends be assured by these words of

---

1 Shoghi Effendi, letter dated 21 March 1930, *The World Order of Bahá'u'lláh*, p. 20.

2 Shoghi Effendi, letter dated 27 February 1929, *The World Order of Bahá'u'lláh*, p. 8.

3 Shoghi Effendi, "The Dispensation of Bahá'u'lláh", in *The World Order of Bahá'u'lláh*, p. 150.

4 Shoghi Effendi, "The Dispensation of Bahá'u'lláh", in *The World Order of Bahá'u'lláh*, p. 148.

5 Shoghi Effendi, "The Dispensation of Bahá'u'lláh", in *The World Order of Bahá'u'lláh*, p. 150.

Bahá'u'lláh: "*The Hand of Omnipotence hath established His Revelation upon an unassailable, an enduring foundation. Storms of human strife are powerless to undermine its basis, nor will men's fanciful theories succeed in damaging its structure*"[1] and these of 'Abdu'l-Bahá: "*Verily, God effecteth that which He pleaseth; naught can annul His Covenant; naught can obstruct His favour nor oppose His Cause! He doeth with His will that which pleaseth Him and He is powerful over all things!*"[2]

26. It should be understood by the friends that before legislating upon any matter the Universal House of Justice studies carefully and exhaustively both the Sacred Texts and the writings of Shoghi Effendi on the subject. The interpretations written by the beloved Guardian cover a vast range of subjects and are equally as binding as the Text itself.

Interpretations of the Guardian and elucidations of the Universal House of Justice

27. There is a profound difference between the interpretations of the Guardian and the elucidations of the House of Justice in exercise of its function to "*deliberate upon all problems which have caused difference, questions that are obscure, and matters that are not expressly recorded in the Book.*"[3] The Guardian reveals what the Scripture means; his interpretation is a statement of truth, which cannot be varied. Upon the Universal House of Justice, in the words of the Guardian, "has been conferred the exclusive right of legislating on matters not expressly revealed in the Bahá'í Writings."[4] Its pronouncements, which are susceptible of amendment or abrogation by the House of Justice itself, serve to supplement and apply the Law of God. Although not invested with the function of interpretation, the House of Justice is in a position to do everything necessary to establish the World Order of Bahá'u'lláh on this earth. Unity of doctrine is maintained by the existence of the authentic texts of Scripture and the voluminous interpretations of 'Abdu'l-Bahá and Shoghi Effendi, together with the absolute prohibition against anyone propounding "authoritative" or "inspired" interpretations or usurping the function of the Guardian. Unity of administration is assured by the authority of the Universal House of Justice.

28. "Such," in the words of Shoghi Effendi, "is the immutability of His revealed Word. Such is the elasticity, which characterizes the functions of His appointed ministers. The first preserves the identity of His Faith, and guards the integrity of His law. The second enables it, even as a living organism, to expand and adapt itself to the needs and requirements of an

---

1 Bahá'u'lláh, cite in *The World Order of Bahá'u'lláh*, p. 109.
2 'Abdu'l-Bahá, *Tablets of Abdul-Baha Abbas*, vol. III, p. 598.
3 'Abdu'l-Bahá, *The Will and Testament of 'Abdu'l-Bahá*, p. 20.
4 Shoghi Effendi, *The World Order of Bahá'u'lláh*, p. 153.

ever-changing society."[1]

29. Every true believer, if he is to deepen in his understanding of the Cause of Bahá'u'lláh, must needs combine profound faith in the unfailing efficacy of His Message and His Covenant with the humility of recognizing that no one of this generation can claim to have embraced the vastness of His Cause nor to have comprehended the manifold mysteries and potentialities it contains. The words of Shoghi Effendi bear ample testimony to this fact:
30. "How vast is the Revelation of Bahá'u'lláh! How great the magnitude of His blessings showered upon humanity in this day! And yet, how poor, how inadequate our conception of their significance and glory! This generation stands too close to so colossal a Revelation to appreciate, in their full measure, the infinite possibilities of His Faith, the unprecedented character of His Cause, and the mysterious dispensations of His Providence."[2]
31. "We are called upon by our beloved Master in His Will and Testament not only to adopt it (Bahá'u'lláh's new World Order) unreservedly, but to unveil its merit to all the world. To attempt to estimate its full value and grasp its exact significance after so short a time since its inception would be premature and presumptuous on our part. We must trust to time, and the guidance of God's Universal House of Justice, to obtain a clearer and fuller understanding of its provisions and implications...."[3]
32. "As to the order and the management of the spiritual affairs of the friends, that which is very important now is the consolidation of the spiritual assemblies in every centre, because, on these fortified and unshakable foundations, God's Supreme House of Justice shall be erected and firmly established in the days to come. When this most great Edifice shall be reared on such an immovable foundation, God's purpose, wisdom, universal truths, mysteries, and realities of the Kingdom, which the mystic Revelation of Bahá'u'lláh has deposited within *The Will and Testament of 'Abdu'l-Bahá*, shall gradually be revealed and made manifest."[4]
33. Statements such as these indicate that the full meaning of *The Will and Testament of 'Abdu'l-Bahá*, as well as an understanding of the implications of the World Order ushered in by that remarkable Document, can be revealed only gradually to men's eyes, and after the Universal House of Justice has come into being. The friends are called upon to trust to time and to await the guidance of the Universal House of Justice, which, as circumstances require, will make pronouncements that will resolve and clarify obscure matters.

---

1 Shoghi Effendi, letter dated 21 March 1930, *The World Order of Bahá'u'lláh*, p. 23.

2 Shoghi Effendi, letter dated 21 March 1930, *The World Order of Bahá'u'lláh*, p. 24.

3 Shoghi Effendi, letter dated 23 February 1924, *Bahá'í Administration*, p. 62.

4 Shoghi Effendi, letter in Persian, dated 19 December 1922.

The authority to expel members of the Universal House of Justice

34. The third group of queries raised by the friends concerns details of functioning of the Universal House of Justice in the absence of the Guardian, particularly the matter of expulsion of members of the House of Justice. Such questions will be clarified in the constitution of the House of Justice, the formulation of which is a goal of the Nine Year Plan. Meanwhile the friends are informed that any member committing a "*sin injurious to the common weal*" may be expelled from membership of the House of Justice by a majority vote of the House itself. Should any member, God forbid, be guilty of breaking the Covenant, the matter would be investigated by the Hands of the Cause of God, and the Covenant-breaker would be expelled by decision of the Hands of the Cause of God residing in the Holy Land, subject to the approval of the House of Justice, as in the case of any other believer. The Universal House of Justice would announce the decision of the Hands in such a case to the Bahá'í world.
35. We are certain that when you share this letter with the friends and they have these quotations from the Scriptures and the writings of the Guardian drawn to their attention, their doubts and misgivings will be dispelled and they will be able to devote their efforts to spreading the Message of Bahá'u'lláh, serenely confident in the power of His Covenant to overcome whatever tests an inscrutable Providence may shower upon it, thus demonstrating its ability to redeem a travailing world and to upraise the Standard of the Kingdom of God on earth.

The Universal House of Justice
9 March 1965

Part 3—The Guardianship and the Universal House of Justice

[Passages from a letter written in response to questions asked by an individual believer on the relationship between the Guardianship and the Universal House of Justice.][1]

1. … You query the timing of the election of the Universal House of Justice in view of the Guardian's statement: "… given favourable circumstances under which the Bahá'ís of Persia and the adjoining countries under Soviet rule may be enabled to elect their national representatives ... the only remaining obstacle in the way of the definite formation of the International House of Justice will have been removed." On 19 April 1947 the Guardian, in a letter written on his behalf by his secretary, replied to the inquiry of an individual believer about this passage: "At the time he referred to Russia there were Bahá'ís there. Now the community has practically ceased to exist; therefore the formation of the International House of Justice cannot depend on a Russian national spiritual assembly, but other strong national spiritual assemblies will have to be built up before it can be established."

The provisions of 'Abdu'l-Bahá's Will

2. You suggest the possibility that, for the good of the Cause, certain information concerning the successor to Shoghi Effendi is being withheld from the believers. We assure you that nothing whatsoever is being withheld from the friends for whatever reason. There is no doubt at all that in *The Will and Testament of 'Abdu'l-Bahá*, Shoghi Effendi was the authority designated to appoint his successor; but he had no children and all the surviving Aghsán had broken the Covenant. Thus, as the Hands of the Cause stated in 1957, it is clear that there was no one he could have appointed in accordance with the provisions of the Will. To have made an appointment outside the clear and specific provisions of the Master's Will and Testament would obviously have been an impossible and unthinkable course of action for the Guardian, the divinely appointed upholder and defender of the Covenant. Moreover, that same Will had provided a clear means for the confirmation of the Guardian's appointment of his successor, as you are aware. The nine Hands to be elected by the body of the Hands were to give their assent by secret ballot to the Guardian's choice. In 1957 the entire body of the Hands, after fully investigating the matter, announced that Shoghi Effendi had appointed no successor and left no will. This is documented and established.

A sign of infallible guidance

3. The fact that Shoghi Effendi did not leave a will cannot be adduced as

[1] The Universal House of Justice, *Messages from the Universal House of Justice 1963–1986*, pp. 83–90.

evidence of his failure to obey Bahá'u'lláh—rather should we acknowledge that in his very silence there is a wisdom and a sign of his infallible guidance. We should ponder deeply the writings that we have, and seek to understand the multitudinous significances that they contain. Do not forget that Shoghi Effendi said two things were necessary for a growing understanding of the World Order of Bahá'u'lláh: the passage of time and the guidance of the Universal House of Justice.

The infallibility of the Universal House of Justice

4. The infallibility of the Universal House of Justice, operating within its ordained sphere, has not been made dependent upon the presence in its membership of the Guardian of the Cause. Although in the realm of interpretation the Guardian's pronouncements are always binding, in the area of the Guardian's participation in legislation it is always the decision of the House itself, which must prevail. This is supported by the words of the Guardian: "The interpretation of the Guardian, functioning within his own sphere, is as authoritative and binding as the enactments of the International House of Justice, whose exclusive right and prerogative is to pronounce upon and deliver the final judgment on such laws and ordinances as Bahá'u'lláh has not expressly revealed. Neither can, nor will ever, infringe upon the sacred and prescribed domain of the other. Neither will seek to curtail the specific and undoubted authority with which both have been divinely invested.
5. "Though the Guardian of the Faith has been made the permanent head of so august a body he can never, even temporarily, assume the right of exclusive legislation. He cannot override the decision of the majority of his fellow members, but is bound to insist upon a reconsideration by them of any enactment he conscientiously believes to conflict with the meaning and to depart from the spirit of Bahá'u'lláh's revealed utterances."[1]
6. However, quite apart from his function as a member and sacred head for life of the Universal House of Justice, the Guardian, functioning within his own sphere, had the right and duty "to define the sphere of the legislative action" of the Universal House of Justice. In other words, he had the authority to state whether a matter was or was not already covered by the Sacred Texts and therefore whether it was within the authority of the Universal House of Justice to legislate upon it. No other person, apart from the Guardian, has the right or authority to make such definitions. The question therefore arises: In the absence of the Guardian, is the Universal House of Justice in danger of straying outside its proper sphere and thus falling into error? Here we must remember three things: First, Shoghi Effendi, during the thirty-six years of his Guardianship, has already made innumerable such definitions, supplementing those made by 'Abdu'l-Bahá and by Bahá'u'lláh Himself. As already announced to the friends, a careful study of the Writings and interpretations on any subject

[1] Shoghi Effendi, *The World Order of Bahá'u'lláh*, p. 150.

on which the House of Justice proposes to legislate always precedes its act of legislation. Second, the Universal House of Justice, itself assured of Divine guidance, is well aware of the absence of the Guardian and will approach all matters of legislation only when certain of its sphere of jurisdiction, a sphere which the Guardian has confidently described *as* "clearly defined". Third, we must not forget the Guardian's written statement about these two institutions: "Neither can, nor will ever, infringe upon the sacred and prescribed domain of the other."[1]

Enactments of Universal House of Justice

7. As regards the need to have deductions made from the Writings to help in the formulation of the enactments of the House of Justice, there is the following text from the pen of 'Abdu'l-Bahá:

8. "*Those matters of major importance which constitute the foundation of the Law of God are explicitly recorded in the Text, but subsidiary laws are left to the House of Justice. The wisdom of this is that the times never remain the same, for change is a necessary quality and an essential attribute of this world, and of time and place. Therefore the House of Justice will take action accordingly.*

9. *"Let it not be imagined that the House of Justice will take any decision according to its own concepts and opinions. God forbid! The Supreme House of Justice will take decisions and establish laws through the inspiration and confirmation of the Holy Spirit, because it is in the safekeeping and under the shelter and protection of the Ancient Beauty, and obedience to its decisions is a bounden and essential duty and an absolute obligation, and there is no escape for anyone.*

10. *"Say, O People: Verily the Supreme House of Justice is under the wings of your Lord, the Compassionate, the All-Merciful, that is under His protection, His care, and His shelter; for He has commanded the firm believers to obey that blessed, sanctified, and all-subduing body, whose sovereignty is divinely ordained and of the Kingdom of Heaven and whose laws are inspired and spiritual.*

11. *"Briefly, this is the wisdom of referring the laws of society to the House of Justice. In the religion of Islám, similarly, not every ordinance was explicitly revealed; nay not a tenth part of a tenth part was included in the Text; although all matters of major importance were specifically referred to, there were undoubtedly thousands of laws which were unspecified. These were devised by the divines of a later age according to the laws of Islamic jurisprudence, and individual divines made conflicting deductions from the original revealed ordinances. All these were enforced. Today this process of deduction is the right of the body of the House of Justice, and the deductions and conclusions of individual learned men have no authority, unless the House of Justice endorses them. The difference is precisely this, that from the conclusions and endorsements of the body of*

---

1 Shoghi Effendi, *The World Order of Bahá'u'lláh*, p. 150.

the House of Justice whose members are elected by and known to the worldwide Bahá'í community, no differences will arise; whereas the conclusions of individual divines and scholars would definitely lead to differences, and result in schism, division, and dispersion. The oneness of the Word would be destroyed, the unity of the Faith would disappear, and the edifice of the Faith of God would be shaken."[1]

Continuity of authority

12. In the Order of Bahá'u'lláh there are certain functions, which are reserved to certain institutions, and others, which are shared in common, even though they may be more in the special province of one or the other. For example, although the Hands of the Cause of God have the specific functions of protection and propagation, and are specialized for these functions, it is also the duty of the Universal House of Justice and the spiritual assemblies to protect and teach the Cause—indeed teaching is a sacred obligation placed upon every believer in Bahá'u'lláh. Similarly, although after the Master authoritative interpretation was exclusively vested in the Guardian, and although legislation is exclusively the function of the Universal House of Justice, these two institutions are, in Shoghi Effendi's words, "complementary in their aim and purpose." "Their common, their fundamental object is to ensure the continuity of that divinely appointed authority which flows from the Source of our Faith, to safeguard the unity of its followers, and to maintain the integrity and flexibility of its teachings."[2] Whereas the Universal House of Justice cannot undertake any function, which exclusively appertained to the Guardian, it must continue to pursue the object, which it shares in common with the Guardianship.

The principle of inseparability

13. As you point out with many quotations, Shoghi Effendi repeatedly stressed the inseparability of these two institutions. Whereas he obviously envisaged their functioning together, it cannot logically be deduced from this that one is unable to function in the absence of the other. During the whole thirty-six years of his Guardianship Shoghi Effendi functioned without the Universal House of Justice. Now the Universal House of Justice must function without the Guardian, but the principle of inseparability remains. The Guardianship does not lose its significance nor position in the Order of Bahá'u'lláh merely because there is no living Guardian. We must guard against two extremes: one is to argue that because there is no Guardian all that was written about the Guardianship and its position in the Bahá'í World Order is a dead letter and was

---

1 'Abdu'l-Bahá, cited in *Bahá'í News*, 426 (September 1966), p. 2; cited in *Wellspring of Guidance*, pp. 84–86, in *The Compilation of compilations* vol. I, p. 323.

2 Shoghi Effendi, *The World Order of Bahá'u'lláh*, p. 148.

unimportant; the other is to be so overwhelmed by the significance of the Guardianship as to underestimate the strength of the Covenant, or to be tempted to compromise with the clear Texts in order to find somehow, in some way, a "Guardian".

Our part—fidelity, integrity and faith

14. Service to the cause of God requires absolute fidelity and integrity and unwavering faith in Him. No good but only evil can come from taking the responsibility for the future of God's Cause into our own hands and trying to force it into ways that we wish it to go regardless of the clear texts and our own limitations. It is His Cause. He has promised that the light will not fail. Our part is to cling tenaciously to the revealed Word and to the instructions that He has created to preserve His Covenant.
15. It is precisely in this connection that the believers must recognize the importance of intellectual honesty and humility. In past dispensations many errors arose because the believers in God's Revelation were overanxious to encompass the Divine Message within the framework of their limited understanding, to define doctrines where definition was beyond their power, to explain mysteries which only the wisdom and experience of a later age would make comprehensible, to argue that something was true because it appeared desirable and necessary. Such compromises with essential truth, such intellectual pride, we must scrupulously avoid.
16. If some of the statements of the Universal House of Justice are not detailed the friends should realize that the cause of this is not secretiveness, but rather the determination of this body to refrain from interpreting the teachings and to preserve the truth of the Guardian's statement that "Leaders of religion, exponents of political theories, governors of human institutions … need have no doubt or anxiety regarding the nature, the origin, or validity of the institutions which the adherents of the Faith are building up throughout the world. For these lie embedded in the Teachings themselves, unadulterated and unobscured by unwarranted inferences or unauthorized interpretations of His Word."

Authoritative and individual understanding

17. A clear distinction is made in our Faith between authoritative interpretation and the interpretation or understanding that each individual arrives at for himself from his study of its teachings. While the former is confined to the Guardianship, the latter, according to the guidance given to us by the Guardian himself, should by no means be suppressed. In fact such individual interpretation is considered the fruit of man's rational power and conducive to a better understanding of the teachings, provided that no disputes or arguments arise among the friends and the individual himself understands and makes it clear that his views are merely his own. Individual interpretations continually change as one grows in comprehension of the teachings. As Shoghi Effendi wrote: "To deepen in

the Cause means to read the writings of Bahá'u'lláh and the Master so thoroughly as to be able to give it to others in its pure form. There are many who have some superficial idea of what the Cause stands for. They, therefore, present it together with all sorts of ideas that are their own. As the Cause is still in its early days we must be most careful lest we fall into this error and injure the Movement we so much adore. There is no limit to the study of the Cause. The more we read the Writings, the more truths we can find in them, the more we will see that our previous notions were erroneous." So, although individual insights can be enlightening and helpful, they can also be misleading. The friends must therefore learn to listen to the views of others without being overawed or allowing their faith to be shaken, and to express their own views without pressing them on their fellow Bahá'ís.

The Covenant—the cord to which all must cling

18. The Cause of God is organic, growing and developing like a living being. Time and again it has faced crises, which have perplexed the believers, but each time the Cause, impelled by the immutable purpose of God, overcame the crisis and went on to greater heights.
19. However great may be our inability to understand the mystery and the implications of the passing of Shoghi Effendi, the strong cord to which all must cling with assurance is the Covenant. The emphatic and vigorous language of 'Abdu'l-Bahá's Will and Testament is at this time, as at the time of His own passing, the safeguard of the Cause:
20. "*Unto the Most Holy Book every one must turn and all that is not expressly recorded therein must be referred to the Universal House of Justice. That which this body, whether unanimously or by a majority doth carry, that is verily the truth and the purpose of God Himself. Whoso doth deviate therefrom is verily of them that love discord, hath shown forth malice, and turned away from the Lord of the Covenant.*"[1] And again: "*All must seek guidance and turn unto the Centre of the Cause and the House of Justice. And he that turneth unto whatsoever else is indeed in grievous error.*"[2]

The Universal House of Justice: recipient of Divine guidance

21. The Universal House of Justice, which the Guardian said would be regarded by posterity as "the last refuge of a tottering civilization," is now, in the absence of the Guardian, the sole infallibly guided institution in the world to which all must turn, and on it rests the responsibility for ensuring the unity and progress of the Cause of God in accordance with the revealed Word. There are statements from the Master and the Guardian indicating that the Universal House of Justice, in addition to being the highest legislative body of the Faith, is also the body to which all must turn, and

---

1 'Abdu'l-Bahá, *The Will and Testament of 'Abdu'l-Bahá*, p. 19.
2 'Abdu'l-Bahá, *The Will and Testament of 'Abdu'l-Bahá*, p. 25.

is the "apex" of the Bahá'í Administrative Order, as well as the "supreme organ of the Bahá'í Commonwealth." The Guardian has in his writings specified for the House of Justice such fundamental functions as the formulation of future worldwide teaching plans, the conduct of the administrative affairs of the Faith, and the guidance, organization, and unification of the affairs of the Cause throughout the world. Furthermore in God Passes By the Guardian makes the following statement: "*The Kitáb-i-Aqdas* ... not only preserves for posterity the basic laws and ordinances on which the fabric of His future World Order must rest, but ordains, in addition to the function of interpretation which it confers upon His successor, the necessary institutions through which the integrity and unity of His Faith can alone be safeguarded."[1] He has also, in "The Dispensation of Bahá'u'lláh," written that the members of the Universal House of Justice "and not the body of those who either directly or indirectly elect them, have thus been made the recipients of the Divine guidance which is at once the lifeblood and ultimate safeguard of this Revelation."[2]

22. As the Universal House of Justice has already announced, it cannot legislate to make possible the appointment of a successor to Shoghi Effendi, nor can it legislate to make possible the appointment of any more Hands of the Cause, but it must do everything within its power to ensure the performance of all those functions which it shares with these two mighty institutions. It must make provision for the proper discharge in future of the functions of protection and propagation, which the administrative bodies share with the Guardianship and the Hands of the Cause; it must, in the absence of the Guardian, receive and disburse the Ḥuqúqu'lláh, in accordance with the following statement of 'Abdu'l-Bahá: "*Disposition of the Ḥuqúq, wholly or partly, is permissible, but this should be done by permission of the authority in the Cause to whom all must turn*"; it must make provision in its constitution for the removal of any of its members who commits a sin "*injurious to the common weal.*" Above all, it must, with perfect faith in Bahá'u'lláh, proclaim His Cause and enforce His law so that the Most Great Peace shall be firmly established in this world and the foundations of the Kingdom of God on earth shall be accomplished.

The Universal House of Justice
27 May 1966

---

1 Shoghi Effendi, *God Passes By*, p. 213.
2 Shoghi Effendi, *The World Order of Bahá'u'lláh*, p. 153.

APPENDIX B: GUARDIANSHIP AND THE UNIVERSAL HOUSE OF JUSTICE

From the Universal House of Justice -18 February 2008

Letter to the Friends in Írán

Dear Bahá'í Friends,

1. We have received a letter from a believer in Iran with questions about the Guardianship and the Universal House of Justice. We appreciate that firmness in the Covenant is among the distinctive characteristics of the believers in that land, who are informed of the principles and essential facts pertaining to the succession of authority in the Cause. Nevertheless, none among them should hesitate to seek clarification of matters about which they have questions, for the enemies of the Faith are tireless in their attempts to sow seeds of confusion and doubt. Moreover, it is beneficial, in view of the beloved Master's exhortations to us all to be ever-vigilant concerning matters of protection, for the friends to review the relevant essentials from time to time. We have therefore decided to provide you with the following comments. In this connection, you are also encouraged to reacquaint yourselves with the document "Mason Remey and Those Who Followed Him",[1] a statement prepared at our instruction by an ad hoc committee. A translation of the statement is enclosed.
2. Questions concerning the Guardianship and the Universal House of Justice can be resolved through careful study of the writings of Bahá'u'lláh, 'Abdu'l-Bahá and Shoghi Effendi and the elucidations of the House of Justice, which, 'Abdu'l-Bahá states, will "*deliberate upon all problems which have caused difference, questions that are obscure and*

[1] This statement is available in Appendix D.

matters that are not expressly recorded in the Book. Whatsoever they decide," He assures the friends, *"has the same effect as the Text itself."*[1]

3. Prior to the passing of 'Abdu'l-Bahá in 1921, the provisions He had put in place in His Will and Testament to safeguard the Faith and ensure its steady advancement into the future were generally unknown. The believers anticipated a day when the Universal House of Justice would be established since it had been specifically mentioned in the Sacred Texts. There was, however, no definite understanding that there would be a Guardian. Indeed, Shoghi Effendi later indicated that he had no foreknowledge of the position to which he would be called. At most, he had reportedly thought the Will and Testament might charge him, as the eldest grandson of 'Abdu'l-Bahá, with responsibility for arranging for the election of the House of Justice. Only after the reading of the Will did the institution of the Guardianship become widely known, and the Bahá'í community worldwide acknowledged Shoghi Effendi as the Head of the Faith to whom all must turn.

4. An attentive reading of 'Abdu'l-Bahá's Will makes it clear that He did not indicate a predestined outcome but did provide for a number of circumstances which, depending on future conditions, might eventually confront the Faith. The second section of the Will, for instance, which refers only to the Universal House of Justice, with no mention of the Guardianship, was written at a time when His own life was in imminent danger and Shoghi Effendi was but a small boy. During that same period, 'Abdu'l-Bahá had made arrangements for the election of the Universal House of Justice to take place immediately, should the threat on His life materialize. Through the grace of God, the crisis passed, and it was ultimately left to Shoghi Effendi many years later, as Guardian and Head of the Faith, to determine the timing of the formation of the House of Justice. Early on he considered the possibility of holding the election soon after the passing of 'Abdu'l-Bahá, in which case the House of Justice and the Guardian would have functioned simultaneously. He determined, of course, that the foundations of the Administrative Order needed first to be firmly laid at the local and national levels, and it eventually transpired that the House of Justice was established several years after his own passing. That the transition from the ministry of the Guardian to the election of the Universal House of Justice occurred with such relative ease can, itself, be attributed to the way certain provisions in the Will were formulated.

5. 'Abdu'l-Bahá's Will and Testament clearly allows for the possibility of a successor to Shoghi Effendi, and in this light, we find statements written by him or on his behalf over the course of his thirty-six-year ministry that envision future Guardians. However, there are no assurances in the Writings that the line of Guardians would continue throughout the

---

[1] 'Abdu'l-Bahá, *The Will and Testament of 'Abdu'l-Bahá*, p. 20.

Dispensation; rather, the possibility is envisaged that such a line would come to an end. In this respect, Bahá'u'lláh states in *The Kitáb-i-Aqdas*:

6. *Endowments dedicated to charity revert to God, the Revealer of Signs. None hath the right to dispose of them without leave from Him Who is the Dawning-place of Revelation. After Him, this authority shall pass to the Aghsán, and after them to the House of Justice—should it be established in the world by then—that they may use these endowments for the benefit of the Places which have been exalted in this Cause, and for whatsoever hath been enjoined upon them by Him Who is the God of might and power. Otherwise, the endowments shall revert to the people of Bahá who speak not except by His leave and judge not save in accordance with what God hath decreed in this Tablet—lo, they are the champions of victory betwixt heaven and earth—that they may use them in the manner that hath been laid down in the Book by God, the Mighty, the Bountiful.*[1]

7. The passing of Shoghi Effendi precipitated the situation described, in which the authority vested in the Aghsán—first in 'Abdu'l-Bahá and then in Shoghi Effendi—ended before the House of Justice was established.

8. In His Will and Testament, 'Abdu'l-Bahá specifies in the clearest terms the conditions according to which Shoghi Effendi was to have named his successor as Guardian:

9. *O ye beloved of the Lord! It is incumbent upon the guardian of the Cause of God to appoint in his own life-time him that shall become his successor, that differences may not arise after his passing. He that is appointed must manifest in himself detachment from all worldly things, must be the essence of purity, must show in himself the fear of God, knowledge, wisdom and learning. Thus, should the first-born of the guardian of the Cause of God not manifest in himself the truth of the words: "The child is the secret essence of its sire," that is, should he not inherit of the spiritual within him (the guardian of the Cause of God) and his glorious lineage not be matched with a goodly character, then must he, (the guardian of the Cause of God) choose another branch to succeed him.*

10. *The Hands of the Cause of God must elect from their own number nine persons that shall at all times be occupied in the important services in the work of the guardian of the Cause of God. The election of these nine must be carried either unanimously or by majority from the company of the Hands of the Cause of God and these, whether unanimously or by a majority vote, must give their assent to the choice of the one whom the guardian of the Cause of God hath chosen as his successor. This assent must be given in such wise as the assenting and dissenting voices may not be distinguished. (i.e., secret ballot)*[2]

11. The personal views of any individual regarding the above statement, no

---

1 Bahá'u'lláh, *The Kitáb-i-Aqdas*, p. 34.

2 'Abdu'l-Bahá, *The Will and Testament of 'Abdu'l-Bahá*, p. 12.

matter how learned, cannot compare with the Guardian's infallible understanding of the passage. Shoghi Effendi, who faithfully adhered to the wishes of Bahá'u'lláh and 'Abdu'l-Bahá throughout his ministry, would never have been careless in a matter so essential to the integrity of the Faith as the question of the appointment of his successor. It is unthinkable that he would appoint someone to succeed him who did not possess the qualifications laid down by 'Abdu'l-Bahá in His Will. It is equally untenable to suggest that he would do so in a manner which deviated from the explicit requirements in that same document, which included the affirmation of his choice by nine designated Hands of the Cause of God, so that "*differences*" would "*not arise after his passing.*" How perverse the suggestion of the violators of the Covenant that Shoghi Effendi would ignore the Master's instructions and make a veiled and indirect appointment of his successor! Rather should the fact that Shoghi Effendi did not name a successor be seen as a sign of his meticulous adherence to every word of 'Abdu'l-Bahá's Will and an indication of his conclusion that there was no qualified individual whom he could appoint.

12. Therefore, it should be clear to every steadfast follower of Bahá'u'lláh that the end of the line of Guardians was not the result of any decision or action taken by the Hands of the Cause of God following the sudden passing of Shoghi Effendi. The line was brought to a close when, compelled by existing circumstances and the strict provisions of the Will, Shoghi Effendi did not name a successor. To entertain the possibility that it may one day be re-established is futile. 'Abdu'l-Bahá wrote that "*ere the expiration of a thousand years, no one has the right to utter a single word, even to claim the station of Guardianship.*" And in the same passage He exhorted the friends, "*Should there be differences of opinion, the Supreme House of Justice would immediately resolve the problems.*"[1] The Universal House of Justice, soon after its formation, stated that it "finds that there is no way to appoint or to legislate to make it possible to appoint a second Guardian to succeed Shoghi Effendi."

13. While the line of Guardians has ended, the Covenant is preserved. The vast body of interpretations of Shoghi Effendi informs the decisions of the Universal House of Justice as the Faith continues its onward march. The unity of the Faith is safeguarded, and the realization of Bahá'u'lláh's great purpose for humanity assured. "*The Hand of Omnipotence hath established His Revelation upon an unassailable, an enduring foundation,*" Bahá'u'lláh has stated. "*Storms of human strife are powerless to undermine its basis, nor will men's fanciful theories succeed in damaging its structure.*"[2]

* * *

14. With reference to the specific questions raised in the letter we have

---

[1] 'Abdu'l-Bahá, cited in *Compilation of Compilations*, vol. I, p. 322.

[2] Bahá'u'lláh, cited in *The World Order of Bahá'u'lláh,* p. 322.

received, one concerns the meaning of the designation "Aghsán", as found in the Writings. While in some cases, as affirmed by the Guardian, the term applies specifically to Bahá'u'lláh's sons, at other times it is used more broadly to include His male descendants. For example, in His Will and Testament 'Abdu'l-Bahá refers to Shoghi Effendi as "*the chosen branch*" (Ghusn-i-Mumtáz). The reference to Shoghi Effendi as Ghusn here—the singular form of Aghsán—follows the usage of Bahá'u'lláh in relation to the titles He gave His sons, that is, the Most Great Branch, the Greater Branch, and the Purest Branch. A letter written on behalf of Shoghi Effendi explains that the word Aghsán "refers to Bahá'u'lláh's descendants"; another describes Ḥussein Rabbání, the Guardian's brother, as "the grandchild of the Master, an Afnán and Aghsán mentioned in the Will and Testament of the Master." It is evident, then, that the designation Aghsán, or Ghusn, includes Shoghi Effendi and the other male descendants of Bahá'u'lláh.

15. If, at any time, male descendants of Bahá'u'lláh appear who are faithful to the Covenant, it would nevertheless not be possible for any of them to occupy the office of Guardian, for, as already explained, in the absence of appointment by Shoghi Effendi, they cannot claim the station of Guardianship and there is no way for one to be named to it by an act of the House of Justice.

* * *

16. Another query concerns the establishment of the Universal House of Justice. Specifically, the question has been asked whether the functioning of an "officially recognized" International Bahá'í Court in the Holy Land, mentioned by Shoghi Effendi, was an essential preliminary step in the evolution of the Universal House of Justice.

17. As you are no doubt aware, Shoghi Effendi explained that "'Abdu'l-Bahá, Himself, in one of His earliest Tablets, contemplated the possibility of the formation of the Universal House of Justice in His own lifetime."[1] The Master described the requirements necessary for its formation, which did not include the establishment of a religious court:

18. *The Supreme House of Justice should be elected according to the system followed in the election of the parliaments of Europe. And when the countries would be guided the Houses of Justice of the various countries would elect the Supreme House of Justice.*

19. *At whatever time all the beloved of God in each country appoint their delegates, and these in turn elect their representatives, and these representatives elect a body, that body shall be regarded as the Supreme House of Justice.*

20. *The establishment of that House is not dependent upon the conversion of all the nations of the world. For example, if conditions were favourable*

[1] Shoghi Effendi, *The World Order of Bahá'u'lláh*, p. 7.

and no disturbances would be caused, the friends in Persia would elect their representatives, and likewise the friends in America, in India, and other areas would also elect their representatives, and these would elect a House of Justice. That House of Justice would be the Supreme House of Justice. That is all.[1]

21. Over the thirty–six years of his ministry, as he guided the Bahá'í world, striving to lay the foundations of the Administrative Order, Shoghi Effendi outlined specific developmental steps to be taken, which were intended to lead to the eventual establishment of the Universal House of Justice. The accomplishment of some depended largely on the exertions of the believers themselves—an increase in the number of Local and National Spiritual Assemblies, the appointment of the International Bahá'í Council and its evolution into an elected body. Others, however, were subject to the forces operating in society and, no matter what the efforts made by the Bahá'í community, could not be accomplished.

22. In 1929, for instance, the Guardian stated, "given favourable circumstances, under which the Bahá'ís of Persia and of the adjoining countries under Soviet rule may be enabled to elect their national representatives ... the only remaining obstacle in the way of the definite formation of the International House of Justice will have been removed."[2] Later, following the expulsion of Bahá'ís from Russia by the authorities, a letter written on his behalf explained, "At the time he referred to Russia there were Bahá'ís there, now the Community has practically ceased to exist; therefore the formation of the International House of Justice cannot depend on a Russian National Spiritual Assembly."[3]

23. In the same way, goals were specified by Shoghi Effendi for the establishment of Bahá'í courts, including national courts in certain countries in Asia and, as a step in the development of the International Bahá'í Council, the precursor to the Universal House of Justice, a court in the Holy Land. Recognition by the Egyptian government of the National Spiritual Assembly as an independent Bahá'í court was sought as far back as 1929. Over time, changing conditions rendered the formation of such religious courts impossible. As the Hands of the Cause of God commented in 1959 in calling for the election of the International Bahá'í Council and the eventual establishment of the House of Justice,

24. "We wish to assure the believers that every effort will be made to establish a Bahá'í Court in the Holy Land prior to the date set for this election. We should however bear in mind that the Guardian himself clearly indicated this goal, due to the strong trend towards the secularization of Religious

---

1 'Abdu'l-Bahá, cited in *The Compilation of Compilations*, vol. I, pp. 322–323.

2 Shoghi Effendi, *The World Order of Bahá'u'lláh*, p. 7.

3 Shoghi Effendi, *The Compilation of Compilations*, vol. I, pp. 352–353.

Courts in this part of the world, might not be achieved."[1]

* * *

25. Yet another question that has been raised concerns the discharge by the Universal House of Justice of certain functions previously performed by the Guardian. With regard to Ḥuqúqu'lláh, 'Abdu'l-Bahá has explained that *"Disposition of the Ḥuqúq, wholly or partly, is permissible, but this should be done by permission of the authority in the Cause to whom all must turn."*[2] Likewise, the expulsion of Covenant-breakers is an obligation exercised by the Head of the Faith in the context of the duty to protect the Cause from those who would seek to undermine its unity. Shoghi Effendi, it is well known, was obliged to expel Covenant-breakers from the Faith at different points throughout his ministry, both before and after the appointment of the Hands of the Cause of God. This responsibility now falls on the Universal House of Justice, as the centre of authority to whom all must turn. The current procedures followed in this respect are outlined in the statement "The Institution of the Counsellors".
26. In this connection it should be noted that after the passing of Shoghi Effendi, although overwhelmed with grief, the Bahá'í world maintained its unity during the tenuous period between his ministry and the election of the Universal House of Justice. The sole challenge to its integrity appeared some two years after his death when Charles Mason Remey, who was at that time one of the Hands of the Cause, laid claim to the Guardianship. As you are aware, Remey asserted that his appointment in 1951 as president of the nascent International Bahá'í Council meant that he should automatically assume the position of head of the Universal House of Justice and was, therefore, the second Guardian.
27. The absurdity of Remey's claim is obvious and requires little elaboration. In 1957, he was among the Hands of the Cause who gathered in the Holy Land to consider what course of action should be taken following the unexpected passing of the Guardian. He personally affirmed that Shoghi Effendi had appointed no successor, signing a document issued unanimously by the Hands to this effect.
28. As signatory to yet another such document, he agreed that the entire body of the Hands of the Cause would determine when and how the evolution of the International Bahá'í Council would culminate in the election of the House of Justice. For two years, as one of the nine Hands designated to serve in the Holy Land, he participated in the consultations that guided the development of the Bahá'í community. Then, without notice or discussion with his fellow Hands, he claimed the station of Guardianship, lacking explicit appointment by Shoghi Effendi as specified in the Will

---

1 The Hands of the Cause of God, *Ministry of the Custodians*, pp. 168–169.

2 'Abdu'l-Bahá, cited in *The Compilation of Compilations*, vol. I, p. 512.

and Testament and in direct violation of the command of 'Abdu'l-Bahá that no one could make such a claim. Exercising the authority conferred on them in accordance with 'Abdu'l-Bahá's Will, the Hands of the Cause expelled him from the Faith as a Covenant- breaker.

* * *

29. In matters related to the Covenant, the friends must be firm and steadfast; they should be wary, lest the arguments put forward by those who sow seeds of doubt become the cause for confusion or lead to disputation and disunity. Should questions arise that cannot be resolved, they should be placed immediately before the Universal House of Justice. The friends must be especially careful to avoid being enticed by the whisperings of the remnants of the Covenant-breakers and their supporters, who seek to shake the believers' faith. Whereas in the past the violators of the Covenant sought to undermine the authority of Bahá'u'lláh, 'Abdu'l-Bahá, and Shoghi Effendi, today they challenge the Universal House of Justice. Of particular concern are those who, as 'Abdu'l-Bahá warns, "*assert their firmness and steadfastness in the Covenant but when they come across responsive ears they secretly sow the seeds of suspicion.*"[1]

30. Remey's small band of associates, bedevilled by half a century of infighting among competing factions, have had negligible effect on the progress of the Faith. The flurry caused by their actions does nothing more than shake a few lifeless twigs and leaves from the tree of the Cause. Those who are naive, those who are not deepened in the Teachings or not firm in the Covenant, those who are controlled by their egos and lust for leadership can be misled and fall away. The friends are urged to protect themselves and their community by adhering strictly to the emphatic exhortations repeated throughout the Sacred Texts. As 'Abdu'l-Bahá states,

31. *Unto the Most Holy Book every one must turn and all that is not expressly recorded therein must be referred to the Universal House of Justice. That which this body, whether unanimously or by a majority doth carry, that is verily the Truth and the Purpose of God Himself. Whoso doth deviate therefrom is verily of them that love discord, hath shown forth malice and turned away from the Lord of the Covenant. By this House is meant that Universal House of Justice which is to be elected from all countries, that is from those parts in the East and West where the loved ones are to be found, after the manner of the customary elections in Western countries such as those of England ....*

32. *And now, one of the greatest and most fundamental principles of the Cause of God is to shun and avoid entirely the Covenant-breakers, for they will utterly destroy the Cause of God, exterminate His Law and render of no account all efforts exerted in the past. O friends! It behoveth*

---

1 'Abdu'l-Bahá, *Selection from the Writings of 'Abdu'l-Bahá*, p. 211.

you to call to mind with tenderness the trials of His Holiness, the Exalted One, and show your fidelity to the Ever-Blest Beauty. The utmost endeavour must be exerted lest all these woes, trials and afflictions, all this pure and sacred blood that hath been shed so profusely in the Path of God, may prove to be in vain ....

33. *O ye beloved of the Lord! Strive with all your heart to shield the Cause of God from the onslaught of the insincere, for souls such as these cause the straight to become crooked and all benevolent efforts to produce contrary results.*[1]

34. The believers in the Cradle of the Faith, who have withstood for more than a century the onslaught of government and clergy, who triumphed over the perils posed by the rebellions of Azal and Muḥammad 'Alí, who severed themselves from those who opposed Shoghi Effendi, will easily discount the spurious and ridiculous arguments of those few individuals who vie among themselves to exploit Remey's deviation as a pretext for attracting a handful of personal followers. Be assured of our supplications at the Holy Threshold on behalf of the beloved friends everywhere in that sacred land.

With loving Bahá'í greetings,
[signed: The Universal House of Justice]

[1] Shoghi Effendi, *The World Order of Bahá'u'lláh*, pp. 447-448.

APPENDIX C – AUTHORITY AND CENTRALITY OF THE UNIVERSAL HOUSE OF JUSTICE

The Universal House of Justice - 7 April 2008[1]

Letter to the Friends in Írán

Dear Bahá'í Friends,

1. Further to the letter to you of 18 February 2008 concerning the Guardianship and the Universal House of Justice, we have been requested to provide the comments below on a related matter. It seems that questions have arisen regarding the infallibility of the House of Justice, in light of the presentation of the topic by Dr Udo Schaefer, a well-known Bahá'í in Germany, whose publications have been translated and circulated in Iran.
2. In his book *Making the Crooked Straight* and in other publications, Dr Schaefer offers his personal views on infallibility as it pertains to the Universal House of Justice. In an effort to defend the Faith and explain the concept in a manner acceptable to a sceptical world, he suggests that the infallibility of the House of Justice is confined to the sphere of legislation. He argues further that, as far as he can discern, the House of Justice has legislated only a small number of times, in each case, according to him, on an issue of "universal relevance" through a decision-making process that did not need to draw on any information obtained from fallible sources. Unfortunately, some have taken his conclusions another step, suggesting that believers are obliged to obey the House of Justice only in matters that fall within the narrow range of such enactments.

1 Cited at http://irfancolloquia.org/pdf/lights11_authority.pdf

3. In general, the House of Justice wishes to preserve the widest possible latitude for the friends to explore the Revelation of Bahá'u'lláh and to share their individual understanding of the Teachings. Yet it must be remembered that, with regard to deductions drawn from the Texts, the Master clearly states:

4. *... the deductions and conclusions of individual learned men have no authority, unless they are endorsed by the House of Justice. The difference is precisely this, that from the conclusions and endorsements of the body of the House of Justice whose members are elected by and known to the worldwide Bahá'í community, no differences will arise; whereas the conclusions of individual divines and scholars would definitely lead to differences, and result in schism, division, and dispersion. The oneness of the Word would be destroyed, the unity of the Faith would disappear, and the edifice of the Faith of God would be shaken.*

5. The Universal House of Justice does not intend at this time to elaborate further on previous explanations given of its duties and powers. That the House of Justice itself does not find it necessary to do so should alert the friends as to the unwisdom of their attempting to define so precisely its sphere of action. Nevertheless, it should be mentioned that, while there are explicit passages in the authoritative texts that make reference to the infallibility of the House of Justice in the enactment of legislation, the argument that it is free from error only in this respect is untenable. Surely, the many emphatic statements found in the Writings, such as the following excerpt from the Will and Testament of 'Abdu'l-Bahá, should suffice to dismiss any claims of this kind:

6. *The sacred and youthful branch, the guardian of the Cause of God as well as the Universal House of Justice, to be universally elected and established, are both under the care and protection of the Abhá Beauty, under the shelter and unerring guidance of His Holiness, the Exalted One (may my life be offered up for them both). Whatsoever they decide is of God. Whoso obeyeth him not, neither obeyeth them, hath not obeyed God; whoso rebelleth against him and against them hath rebelled against God; whoso opposeth him hath opposed God; whoso contendeth with them hath contended with God ....*

7. Apart from the question of infallibility, there is the matter of authority. A letter written on behalf of Shoghi Effendi states: "It is not for individual believers to limit the sphere of the Guardian's authority, or to judge when they have to obey the Guardian and when they are free to reject his judgement. Such an attitude would evidently lead to confusion and to schism." In regard to the Universal House of Justice, the same understanding applies.

8. Infallibility is a profound spiritual concept inherent in the Bahá'í Writings. In meditating upon the relevant passages, the believers will naturally reach their own understanding of the subject. Individual

opinions, however, should not be imposed on others, nor so promoted as to crystallize into doctrines not found in the explicit Text. When exchanging views about the Universal House of Justice—the body to which all things must be referred—the friends should exercise care lest they go to extremes, by either diminishing its station or assigning to it exaggerated attributes. What better admonition to heed in a matter of this nature than that given by the beloved Master, when some believers fell into disagreement about His own station:

9. *These discussions will yield no result or benefit: we must set all such debates and controversies entirely aside—nay, we must consign them to oblivion and arise to accomplish that which is enjoined and required in this Day. These debates are mere words bereft of inner meaning; they are mere illusions and not reality.*

10. *That which is true and real is this: that we become united and agreed in our purpose and arise to flood this darksome world with light, to banish enmity and foreignness from among the children of men, to perfume and revive the world with the sanctified breezes of the character and conduct of the Abhá Beauty, to cast the light of divine guidance upon East and West, to raise the tabernacle of the love of God and gather all people under its sheltering shadow, to confer peace and composure upon every soul beneath the shade of the blessed Tree, to show forth such love as to astonish the enemy, to turn ravenous and bloodthirsty wolves into the gazelles of the meadows of the love of God, to cause the oppressor to taste the sweet savour of meekness, to teach them that kill the submission and acquiescence of those that suffer themselves to be killed, to spread abroad the verses of the one true God, to extol the virtues and perfections of the all-glorious Lord, to raise to the highest heaven the cry of "O Thou the Glory of Glories!,"*[1] *and to cause the call of "The earth will shine with the light of her Lord!" to reach the ears of the denizens of His Kingdom.*

11. The House of Justice appeals to the friends not to become embroiled in the kind of fruitless theological discussions that caused conflict and contention in past dispensations, lest they lose sight of their responsibility to promulgate the oneness of humanity and of the role of the Covenant established by Bahá'u'lláh in uniting minds, hearts, and souls.

With loving Bahá'í greetings,
Department of the Secretariat

---

1 *Qur'án* 39:69

APPENDIX D –MASON REMEY AND THOSE WHO FOLLOWED HIM

The Universal House of Justice—31 January 1997[1]

Covering letter
Bahá'í World Centre
Department of the Secretariat

To National Spiritual Assemblies
Dear Bahá'í Friends,

In recent years advertisements have occasionally appeared in newspapers in various countries, placed by the Covenant-breaker Joel Bray Marangella, seeking to revive his claim to be the "third Guardian of the Faith." This activity could provoke questions among the friends, especially those unfamiliar with the developments associated with the actions of Mason Remey, who broke the Covenant by proclaiming himself the successor to Shoghi Effendi as Guardian. The Universal House of Justice has therefore directed us to send you a copy of a document containing background information on these developments, entitled "Mason Remey and Those Who Followed Him", which was prepared for its files some years ago. You are free to use it now or in the future, in any manner circumstances may require, to provide the friends with the facts it contains.

With loving Bahá'í greetings,
For Department of the Secretariat

[1] The original letter from the Universal House of Justice introducing the letter, cited at http://bahai-library.com/uhj_mason_remey_followers

MASON REMEY AND THOSE WHO FOLLOWED HIM

Revised January 2008[1]

Introduction

1. In addition to explaining the nature and dangers of violation of the Covenant, Shoghi Effendi several times reviewed briefly the fates of individuals and groups who had surrendered to this worst of human failings. Reflection on the consequences to those who seek to undermine the unity of the Cause helps believers, he said, to appreciate more deeply the protecting power of Bahá'u'lláh's Covenant. In the perspective of the three decades that have passed since Charles Mason Remey's violation of the Covenant, it is instructive to review the consequences to those who followed him down this barren path.

I. Covenant-breaking

The nature of Covenant-breaking

2. What is Covenant-breaking? In a letter to an individual dated 23 March 1975, the Universal House of Justice wrote:
3. When a person declares his acceptance of Bahá'u'lláh as a Manifestation of God he becomes a party to the Covenant and accepts the totality of His Revelation. If he then turns round and attacks Bahá'u'lláh or the Central Institution of the Faith he violates the Covenant. If this happens every effort is made to help that person to see the illogicality and error of his actions, but if he persists he must, in accordance with the instructions of

[1] Updated document by the Universal House of Justice, cited at http://covenantstudy.org/additional-documents/mason-remey-and-those-who-followed-him/.

Bahá'u'lláh Himself, be shunned as a Covenant- breaker.[1]

4. The personal failings that lead people to violate the Covenant to which they know they have committed themselves have been described by the Guardian as "the blind hatred, the unbounded presumption, the incredible folly, the abject perfidy, the vaulting ambition"[2] which, in varying degrees, afflict the persons concerned. While some of these may have been duped by others, 'Abdu'l-Bahá has said of them:

5. *These do not doubt the validity of the Covenant, but selfish motives have dragged them to this condition. It is not that they do not know what they do—they are perfectly aware and still they exhibit opposition.*[3]

The danger it poses

6. The Master has warned that, if unchecked, Covenant-breaking would "utterly destroy the Cause of God, exterminate His Law and render of no account all efforts exerted in the past". He sets this warning in the context of the fact that the central purpose of Bahá'u'lláh's Revelation is to create unity:

7. *Were it not for the protecting power of the Covenant to guard the impregnable fort of the Cause of God, there would arise among the Bahá'ís, in one day, a thousand different sects as was the case in former ages.*[4]

8. Apart from the danger that Covenant-breaking poses to the development of the Cause, it represents a spiritual contagion threatening the well-being of the individual believer because of its subtle appeal to the human ego. 'Abdu'l-Bahá called for the complete exclusion from the Bahá'í community of anyone found to be infected with the virus of Covenant-breaking, and urged all believers to shun any contact whatever with the persons involved.

The effect on those involved

9. In reviewing the development of the Faith, the Guardian several times cited examples of how these "movements, sponsored by deluded, self-seeking adventurers, find themselves, sooner or later, enmeshed in the machinations of their authors, are buried in shame, and sink eventually into complete oblivion". He adds:

---

1 The Universal House of Justice, in *The Power of the Covenant*, Part Two (Thornhill, Ontario: National Spiritual Assembly of the Bahá'ís of Canada, 1987), pp. 7–8.

2 Shoghi Effendi, in *The Power of the Covenant*, Part Two (Thornhill, Ontario: National Spiritual Assembly of the Bahá'ís of Canada, 1987), pp. 7–8.

3 'Abdu'l-Bahá, *Star of the West*, vol. X, p. 246; as quoted in *The Power of the Covenant*, Part Two, p. 11.

4 'Abdu'l-Bahá, *Bahá'í World Faith* (Wilmette: Bahá'í Publishing Trust, 1976), pp. 357–358.

10. The extinction of the influence precariously exerted by some of these enemies, the decline that has set in in the fortunes of others, the sincere repentance expressed by still others and their subsequent reinstatement and effectual participation in the teaching and administrative activities of the Faith, constitute in themselves sufficient evidence of the unconquerable power and invincible spirit which animate those who stand identified with, and loyally carry out the provisions and injunctions of, *The Will and Testament of 'Abdu'l-Bahá.*[1]

A cleansing process

11. Regarding a group of Covenant-breakers in the United States which was later to break up and disappear following the deaths of the two individuals who had created it, Shoghi Effendi wrote:

12. The schism which their foolish leaders had contrived so sedulously to produce within the Faith, will soon, to their utter amazement, come to be regarded as a process of purification, a cleansing agency, which, far from decimating the ranks of its followers, reinforces its indestructible unity, and proclaims anew to a world, sceptical or indifferent, the cohesive strength of the institutions of that Faith, the incorruptibility of its purposes and principles, and the recuperative powers inherent in its community life.[2]

II. Mason Remey's defection

The Hands' proclamation on the Guardianship

13. When news of the Guardian's passing was received at the Bahá'í World Centre on the evening of 4 November 1957, Shoghi Effendi's apartment was immediately locked and guarded so that no one could have access until the Hands of the Cause of God would have time to gather in the Holy Land, which they did shortly after the Guardian's funeral. 'Abdu'l-Bahá's Will and Testament is explicit in stating how the Guardian was to appoint his successor:

14. *He [Shoghi Effendi] is the expounder of the words of God and after him will succeed the first-born of his lineal descendants .... O ye beloved of the Lord! It is incumbent upon the guardian of the Cause of God to appoint in his own life-time him that shall become his successor, that differences may not arise after his passing. He that is appointed must manifest in himself detachment from all worldly things, must be the essence of purity, must show in himself the fear of God, knowledge, wisdom and learning. Thus, should the first-born of the guardian of the*

---

1 Shoghi Effendi, *This Decisive Hour: Messages from Shoghi Effendi to the North American Bahá'ís, 1932–1946* (Wilmette: Bahá'í Publishing Trust), 2002, p. 65.

2 Shoghi Effendi, *This Decisive Hour: Messages from Shoghi Effendi to the North American Bahá'ís, 1932–1946* (Wilmette: Bahá'í Publishing Trust), 2002, pp. 65–66.

Cause of God not manifest in himself the truth of the words: "The child is a secret essence of its sire," that is, should he not inherit of the spiritual within him (the guardian of the Cause of God) and his glorious lineage not be matched with a goodly character, then must he, (the guardian of the Cause of God) choose another branch to succeed him.

15. *The Hands of the Cause of God must elect from their own number nine persons ... The election of these nine must be carried either unanimously or by majority from the company of the Hands of the Cause of God and these, whether unanimously or by a majority vote, must give their assent to the choice of the one whom the guardian of the Cause of God hath chosen as his successor.*[1]

16. As soon as 26 of the 27 Hands of the Cause had gathered in the Holy Land (Mrs Corinne True, whose advanced age and health had prevented her coming, subsequently signed affidavits declaring her support for the various actions her fellow Hands took), they designated nine of their number to enter the Guardian's apartment and search for any document he might have left behind. Following their report, all the Hands, including Charles Mason Remey, signed a document stating that Shoghi Effendi had passed away "without having appointed his successor ...."[2]

17. From the first conclave of the Hands, gathered in Bahjí at that time, a proclamation was issued "To the Bahá'ís of East and West" announcing that, as "The Aghsán (branches) one and all are either dead or have been declared violators of the Covenant by the Guardian", it was apparent "that no successor to Shoghi Effendi could have been appointed by him".[3] Calling on the believers to unite in completing the Guardian's Ten Year Crusade, the Hands pointed out that, in due course, the Bahá'í world would elect "the Universal House of Justice, that Supreme Body upon which infallibility, as the Master's Testament assures us, is divinely conferred":

18. "... The entire body of the Hands, assembled by the nine Hands of the World Centre, will decide when and how the International Bahá'í Council is to evolve through the successive stages outlined by the Guardian, culminating in the call to election of the Universal House of Justice by the membership of all National Spiritual Assemblies.

19. "When that divinely ordained Body comes into existence, all the conditions of the Faith can be examined anew and the measures necessary for its future operation determined in consultation with the Hands of the

---

1 'Abdu'l-Bahá, *The Will and Testament of 'Abdu'l-Bahá* (Wilmette: Bahá'í Publishing Trust, 1971), pp. 11–12.

2 The Hands of the Cause of God, *Ministry of the Custodians* (Haifa: Bahá'í World Centre, 1992), p. 29.

3 The Hands of the Cause of God, *Ministry of the Custodians* (Haifa: Bahá'í World Centre, 1992), pp. 35–36.

Cause."[1]

20. Mason Remey again joined his fellow Hands in signing this second formal statement that there was no successor to Shoghi Effendi as Guardian of the Cause of God. For two years after the passing of the Guardian, Remey was personally involved and concurred with all actions taken by the Hands of the Cause to assume responsibility for the direction of the Faith until such time as they could arrange for the election of the House of Justice.

Mason Remey is expelled

21. Despite his written affirmations in 1957 that Shoghi Effendi had appointed no successor and could not have appointed one, Remey himself laid claim to this station in a "Proclamation" of April 1960 declaring that he was the "Second Guardian". He based this spurious claim on the fact that he had been named president of the appointed International Bahá'í Council. When he refused to renounce his attempt to thus seize control of the Cause, the Hands of the Cause expelled him from the Faith as a violator of the Covenant.
22. Shortly thereafter a number of believers in Europe, the United States, and elsewhere who had accepted his claim were likewise expelled from the Faith, among them John Carré, Donald Harvey, Joel Marangella, Reginald King, and Leland Jensen. All of these would later play major roles in provoking the series of conflicts that were to hopelessly divide the remnant of Remey's followers.

Mason Remey dies

23. In April 1974 the Universal House of Justice advised the Bahá'í world:
24. CHARLES MASON REMEY WHOSE ARROGANT ATTEMPT USURP GUARDIANSHIP AFTER PASSING SHOGHI EFFENDI LED TO HIS EXPULSION FROM RANKS FAITHFUL HAS DIED IN FLORENCE ITALY IN HUNDREDTH YEAR OF HIS LIFE BURIED WITHOUT RELIGIOUS RITES ABANDONED BY ERSTWHILE FOLLOWERS. HISTORY THIS PITIABLE DEFECTION BY ONE WHO HAD RECEIVED GREAT HONOURS FROM BOTH MASTER AND GUARDIAN CONSTITUTES YET ANOTHER EXAMPLE FUTILITY ALL ATTEMPTS UNDERMINE IMPREGNABLE COVENANT CAUSE BAHÁ'U'LLÁH.[2]

III. Divisions Among Remey's followers

"National Spiritual Assembly under the Guardianship"

25. Basing themselves on Remey's defection, a group in the United States calling themselves "Bahá'ís under the Guardianship" came together in

---

1 The Hands of the Cause of God, *Ministry of the Custodians* (Haifa: Bahá'í World Centre, 1992), pp. 37–38.

2 The Universal House of Justice, *Messages from the Universal House of Justice 1963–1986* (Wilmette: Bahá'í Publishing Trust, 1996), p. 271.

New Mexico in 1961–62 and, in April 1963, formed what they called the "National Spiritual Assembly of the Bahá'ís of the United States under the Hereditary Guardianship". A similar body was created that same month by a group in Pakistan, but it soon broke up.

26. The New Mexico group incorporated itself in March 1964, and brought legal suit against the National Spiritual Assembly of the Bahá'ís of the United States, claiming to be the rightful owners of the Wilmette Temple property as well as to represent the authorized voice of the Bahá'í Faith in the United States. The legitimate National Spiritual Assembly filed a counterclaim against this group for trademark infringement and later secured an injunction prohibiting them from the use of established Bahá'í terminology or otherwise infringing the National Assembly's rights under civil law.

27. As the New Mexico group was preparing for a second trial, Remey suddenly directed them to withdraw from the proceedings "regardless of the consequences". Shortly thereafter, Remey ordered the Santa Fe group's "National Assembly to be dissolved".

Remey's "Second International Bahá'í Council"

28. In 1964 Remey created what he called a "Second International Bahá'í Council". He appointed to the presidency of this body one Joel Marangella, an American believer living in France, who had been an early supporter of Remey and had been expelled from the Faith by the Hands of the Cause on 3 August 1960. Since Remey had sought to base his own claim to the Guardianship on his position as president of the International Bahá'í Council created by Shoghi Effendi, this action on his part appeared to give Marangella the leading position among Remey's followers.

29. That serious conflicts were developing among the band of Covenant-breakers is apparent, however, from the fact that, on 18 October 1966, Remey abruptly dissolved this "Council" and ordered Marangella, as its former president, to "turn over to me such records as you have of the second Council that no longer exists". The apparent effect of this action, which deprived Marangella of his leading role, was to increase rather than subdue the differences of opinion that had appeared in the group. On 29 January 1967 Remey complained that "Some friends have started the report that the Guardian is loosing [sic] his mind and that someone is controlling him..."

The appointment of Donald Harvey

30. On 15 May 1967, Remey formally appointed one of his followers, Donald Harvey, to succeed him at his death as "third Guardian of the Faith". Harvey, an American Bahá'í also resident in France at the time of Remey's defection, had been among the first group of Covenant-breakers. During the following year Remey appointed five of an intended "twenty-four elders" who would "administer the Faith of Bahá'u'lláh" in

cooperation with Harvey. Subsequently, however, Remey dissolved the body of elders, as he had the earlier organizations, without having completed the promised appointments.

31. Harvey, who remained Remey's appointed successor, took no action either before or following Remey's death to exercise the powers thus conferred on him. He died in 1991, his various letters disclaiming any interest in organization, saying that religious faith was a matter purely for the individual.

32. One of Harvey's associates, Jacques Soghomonian, produced a document, ostensibly signed by Harvey on 17 November 1984, which includes the statement: "[I] do appoint and designate Mr Jacques Soghomonian ... as his [sic] successor as Fourth Guardian of the Universal Faith and Revelation of Bahá'u'lláh." A member of the original group supporting Remey in 1960 who had been expelled at that time with the others, Soghomonian has had little success in attracting followers.

The claim of Joel Marangella

33. Suddenly, on 12 November 1969, Marangella announced that he rather than Harvey should be regarded as Remey's legitimate successor. According to Marangella, Remey had several years earlier, in December 1961, sent him a sealed letter with a covering note indicating that Marangella would "know when to break the seal". Marangella said that shortly after his appointment as president of the "Second International Bahá'í Council" he had opened this envelope, to discover a brief note, signed by Remey, instructing him to "tell the Bahá'í World that I appoint you to be the third Guardian of the Bahá'í Faith". Marangella, however, had hitherto taken no action on this instruction.

34. Marangella's excuse for ignoring Remey's formal appointment of Harvey as his successor was that Remey was allegedly exhibiting irrational behaviour. Remey had by this time begun attacking Shoghi Effendi, declaring that the Administrative Order represented only the organizing of "the Bábí Faith" and must be "dismantled", and that Remey now considered himself to be the "first" Guardian of the Bahá'í Faith.

35. Having made his announcement, Marangella went on to create what he called a "National Bureau of the Orthodox Bahá'í Faith". Thereafter, Harvey and Marangella, each claiming to be Remey's legitimate successor, largely ignored one another's existence.

The role of John Carré

36. By this time other contenders for leadership were pressing supposed rights of their own. John Carré, a prolific writer, had been one of Remey's earliest supporters and had been expelled as a Covenant-breaker in 1961. He had originally promoted Remey's claims to the Guardianship by sending a stream of letters to Bahá'ís whose addresses he had. As the dispute over the leadership of Remey's following broke into the open,

however, Carré suddenly emerged as a spokesman for the bizarre and entirely unrelated claims of one Jamshíd Ma'ání. The latter, an Iranian pioneer in Indonesia, had announced himself to be "the One Who creates the Messengers at every instant".

37. When Ma'ání began to show signs of mental illness, requiring his hospitalization in Ṭihrán, Carré abandoned this interest, too, appearing later under the pseudonym "John Christofil" and writing as the alleged spokesman of various organizations, including "House of Light" and "House of Mankind". In this new capacity, Carré focused his attention increasingly on the subject of "catastrophic events" that would appear before the end of the century and would prepare the way for a "Third" Manifestation of God.

The intervention of Reginald King

38. Meanwhile, in the United States, two more Covenant-breaking factions had emerged and were bitterly denouncing one another. The first of these was led by Reginald ("Rex") King, who had been elected secretary of the short-lived New Mexico "National Assembly", dissolved by Remey in 1964. Unhappy about Remey's resistance to his leadership role in the United States, King eventually went to Italy where Remey was living, and had an apparently acrimonious meeting with him. Following this encounter, on 13 September 1969 Remey issued a letter denouncing King: "his station to be ever and eternally that of Satan for evermore". King switched his allegiance to Marangella when the latter advanced his own claims two months later.

39. This relationship, however, also soon broke down. King decided that Marangella had made "a number of faulty 'interpretations' of the Writings" and declared that Marangella "had ceased to fulfil the requirements of the office of guardian". He argued, indeed, that "neither Mason Remey nor Joel Marangella had in truth ever been guardians ... because of the lack of lineal descendancy" (i.e., from Bahá'u'lláh). Harvey's position in the enterprise was ignored. What Remey had actually been, King said, was "a regent", and King came to the "realization" that he himself "was in actuality the Second Regent...."

40. Harvey and Marangella paid no more attention to this claim than they had to those of one another or of Carré, and King died on 1 April 1977, leaving whatever rights he believed he had to a "Council" consisting of members of his own family.

The case of Leland Jensen

41. King's long struggle for leadership of Remey's followers in the United States had, however, paralleled that of yet another claimant, Leland Jensen. A dispute between the two men had broken out in 1963 when both of them had been members of the New Mexico "National Assembly ... under the Hereditary Guardianship". Jensen had accused King of

having "gained control" of the United States group, and King had thereupon proposed to set up a "Bahá'í court" to have Jensen "thrown out of the Bahá'í Faith". It had been Remey's resistance to this latter manoeuvre that had begun King's disaffection from him.

42. The emergence of Jensen marks a further deterioration in the moral character of the group following Remey. After taking up residence in Missoula, Montana, in 1964 to avoid a disastrous flood predicted by Remey, Jensen was convicted in 1969 of "lewd and lascivious" behaviour and was sentenced to Montana State Prison. There, Jensen had converted several fellow inmates to his claim that an angelic visitor had told him he was "Joshua". After serving his sentence, he began travelling throughout the United States in an effort to bring Remey's remaining American followers to his own peculiar interpretations of religious truth. (Jensen claimed, for example, to be not only "Joshua" and "the return of Jesus" but also the "embryonic" Universal House of Justice.)

43. After the death of Remey, Jensen created a group called "Baha'is Under the Provisions of the Covenant" (BUPC). In 1991, he set up his "Second International Bahá'í Council". Jensen's activities suffered a severe setback in May 1980 when his widely predicted "end of the world" failed to materialize despite his changing the date of this event three different times (29 April, 7 May, 22–23 May 1980). Although some of his closer associates and family members continued their support of him, the majority of Jensen's followers abandoned him. He died in August 1996.

Attempts to involve Giuseppe Pepe

44. Perhaps the strangest development in this long and confused history was one centring on a person who was neither a member of the Faith nor had taken any role in the activities of the various Covenant-breakers. On a visit to Florence, Italy, Remey had become acquainted with a young man named Giuseppe Pepe, who later served as his secretary/companion when Remey settled in Florence following his expulsion. Eventually, Pepe was legally adopted by Remey. It was he who, through the kind assistance of the American consulate in Florence, arranged for Remey's burial in 1974. To Pepe's surprise and distress, Jensen seized upon this adoptive relationship to announce, in an open letter, that he (Pepe) was "the Crown Prince", the legitimate successor of Remey as "Fourth Guardian". What Pepe must do to secure this station was to permit himself to "be coronated [sic] King of the Kingdom by the High Priest …." The strong suggestion was that the said "High Priest" was Jensen.

45. When his protests were ignored, and Jensen's faction continued to use his name in their broadsheets and correspondence, Pepe wrote to a Bahá'í institution whose address he had to set the record straight. The actions of the Covenant-breakers had been undertaken, he said, without his permission, and repeated requests on his part that they desist had been ignored. Giuseppe Pepe apparently died in 1994.

46. In 2001, five years after Jensen's death and seven years after Pepe's death, Neal Chase, a member of Jensen's "Second International Bahá'í Council", claimed to have been adopted by Pepe and appointed his successor as Guardian. The majority of the "Council" members rejected this claim, leading to additional disputes and a lawsuit.

The current situation

47. With none of the leaders of the defection able to substantiate the conflicting claims they made, divisions continued to proliferate over the years. Most represented idiosyncratic agendas conceived by various individuals and largely unrelated to one another. Embroiled in charges and countercharges, abandoned by most of those who had originally taken them seriously, and entirely ignored by the Bahá'í community, the various Remey factions today provide a graphic illustration of 'Abdu'l-Bahá's description of Covenant-breaking given over eighty years ago:

48. *These agitations of the violators are no more than the foam of the ocean, which is one of its inseparable features; but the ocean of the Covenant shall surge and shall cast ashore the bodies of the dead, for it cannot retain them.* [1]

49. By 1996 Remey's following had largely disintegrated. Death had removed five of the principal figures: Mason Remey in 1974, Reginald King in 1977, Remey's appointed successor, Donald Harvey, in 1991, Giuseppe Pepe in 1994, and Leland Jensen in 1996. Public disgrace and ridicule had reduced Jensen's influence to that of a cult figure for two or three isolated groups in the American Midwest; those left in the BUPC were divided by infighting. John Carré had drifted off into esoteric religious pursuits only tangentially related to Bahá'í subjects. Jacques Soghomonian has remained a largely isolated figure. Joel Marangella's group, the so-called "Orthodox Bahá'ís", had testified in a court proceeding in July 2007 to having only about forty members in the United States. Some others are scattered in locations in Australia and India.

50. For the past decade, those who uphold the absurd claim of Charles Mason Remey to be the successor to Shoghi Effendi have sought to revive their fading hopes by establishing a presence on the Internet. Veiling the small size of their membership, these insignificant groups attempt to create the illusion of being rightful followers of Bahá'u'lláh and legitimate alternatives to the worldwide Bahá'í community. Though lacking the capacity to arouse interest among the general public, the remnants of the Remey defection still compete among themselves to draw in loyal Bahá'ís under their corrupting influence.

51. Because of advancing age, Joel Marangella and Jacques Soghomonian have recently announced their own successors. No doubt responding to Internet postings heaping ridicule upon their claims to be infallible

---

1 'Abdu'l-Bahá, *Selections from the Writings of 'Abdu'l-Bahá*, section 185.1.

interpreters of Sacred Texts that they cannot read in the original languages, both have selected Iranians to succeed them. While the believers in the Cradle of the Faith turned their back on Remey's machinations, two Persians outside Iran, victims of their egos and desire for leadership, now have the arrogance to claim a station equal to that of the chosen branch, Shoghi Effendi.

52. Despite efforts by the institutions of the Faith to clarify his thinking, Nosrat'u'llah Bahremand of Perth, Australia, openly accepted the pretensions of Remey and Marangella and was designated a Covenant-breaker in 2003. Within a few years, Marangella appointed him a "Hand of the Cause" and "Vice-President" of the "Third International Bahá'í Council" which Marangella had established in 2006. In May 2007 Marangella appointed him as his successor.

53. Enayatullah (Zabih) Yazdani, who resides near Sydney, Australia, began surreptitiously expressing his allegiance to Mason Remey many years ago. A prolonged effort was made to dissuade him from his course of action; yet in 2004 he openly propagated his long-held view that Remey was the legitimate successor to Shoghi Effendi and, moreover, accepted Donald Harvey as the "Third Guardian" and Jacques Soghomonian as the "Fourth Guardian". In June 2005 he was designated a Covenant-breaker. Soghomonian recently appointed Yazdani to succeed him as "Fifth Guardian" upon his death.

54. That reasonably intelligent men and women should be unable—after the passage of almost half a century—to free themselves from the relentless undertow of folly and ambition that has drowned every hope and scheme they ever cherished is a cautionary tale indeed. The fate of those who followed Charles Mason Remey is a case study in the nature and paralyzing effect of the virus of Covenant-breaking.

INDEX OF ARTICLES

INDEX OF SPECIFIC NAMES, WORDS AND PHRASES

A

B

C

T

U

V

W

Y

Z

www.ingramcontent.com/pod-product-compliance
Lightning Source LLC
Chambersburg PA
CBHW060505300426
44112CB00017B/2555
* 9 7 8 0 9 0 9 9 9 1 1 6 6 *